MW00452470

New Studies
in the History of
American Slavery

New Studies in the History of American Slavery

EDITED BY

Edward E. Baptist
and Stephanie M. H. Camp

THE UNIVERSITY OF GEORGIA PRESS
Athens and London

© 2006 by the University of Georgia Press
Athens, Georgia 30602
www.ugapress.org
All rights reserved
Designed by Sandra S. Hudson and Mindy B. Hill
Set in 10 on 13 Minion by Bookcomp

Printed digitally in the United States of America

Library of Congress Cataloging-in-Publication Data
New studies in the history of American slavery / edited by
Edwarad E. Baptist and Stephanie M. H. Camp.
viii, 306 p. : ill. ; 24 cm.
Includes bibliographical references (p. 295–298) and index.
ISBN-13: 978-0-8203-2563-7 (hardcover : alk. paper)
ISBN-10: 0-8203-2563-5 (hardcover : alk. paper)
ISBN-13: 978-0-8203-2694-8 (pbk. : alk. paper)
ISBN-10: 0-8203-2694-1 (pbk. : alk. paper)
1. Slavery—United States—History. 2. Slavery—United
States—Historiography. 3. Slavery—America—History.
4. Slavery—America—Historiography. I. Baptist, Edward E.
II. Camp, Stephanie M. H.
E441 .N53 2006
306.3'62'0973—dc22   2005018759

British Library Cataloging-in-Publication Data available

Contents

Acknowledgments

This anthology has its roots in a symposium held at the University of Washington in May 2002. Organized by Stephanie Camp, "New Studies in American Slavery" was intended to be a one-day conversation about current directions in the study of slavery. But the event generated more excitement than the organizer or any of the participants probably expected, both among faculty and graduate students at the University of Washington and among a wider Seattle audience. By the end of the day, we had begun to consider publishing an anthology that would extend the discussion. We express our appreciation to those who made this first chapter in the life of this book possible: the participants, Edward Baptist, Herman Bennett, Christopher Brown, Stephanie Camp, Sharla Fett, Walter Johnson, Dylan Penningroth, and Stephanie Smallwood; the commentators, Charles Berquist, Tracy McKenzie, and Matthew Sparke; the generous funders at the University of Washington, the Harry Bridges Center for Labor Studies, the Office of the President, the College of Arts and Sciences, the Graduate School, the Department of History, American Ethnic Studies, the Curriculum Transformation Project, and especially the Walter Chapin Simpson Center for the Humanities; and the impassioned members of the audience, who made us appreciate how much slavery studies still really matter outside the academy.

The second chapter in the life of this project came one year later, in May 2003, when Herman Bennett organized a follow-up symposium at Rutgers University, "New Directions in the Study of Americas: Slavery, a Continuing Conversation," for the purpose of reading and critiquing essays, many of which have found their way to this final collection. We are deeply grateful to Herman for his generosity in organizing this round of critical feedback as well as to all those whose papers or comments made that conversation intensely rewarding and particularly for many of the issues we address in the introduction: Mia Bay, Carolyn Brown, Christopher Brown, Vincent Brown, Kim Butler, Alexander Byrd, Indrani Chatterjee, Brian Connolly, Ann Fabian, Kim Hall, Nancy Hewitt, Allen Howard, Walter Johnson, Barbara Krauthamer, Daphne LaMothe, James Livingston, Stephanie Smallwood, and Phillip Troutman. For hosting the symposium, we thank the Black Atlantic/African Diaspora Seminar of the Rutgers Center for Historical Analysis, the Dean's Office of the Faculty of Arts and Sciences, the office of the Dean for Humanities, and the Center for African Studies, American Studies, Latin American Studies, and Women's and Gender Studies.

The final chapter came when the editors simply had to take bundles of essays and all they had learned at the two symposia and think through what is happening in current scholarship in slavery. For time to think about this question, Camp thanks the Institute for Ethnic Studies in the United States at the University of Washington. For feedback on a draft of a portion of the introduction, she is indebted to Herman Bennett, Daina Raimey Berry, Vincent Brown, Brent Edwards, Leslie Harris, Jessica Milward, Jennifer Morgan, and Deborah Gray White. Ed Baptist thanks Derek Chang for comments on at least two drafts of the introduction. He also thanks Alex Byrd, Walter Johnson, and Stephanie Smallwood, who participated in a May 2003 discussion that helped to clarify some of the key issues of the introductory essay. Finally, he thanks Stephanie Baptist, Judy Burkhard, Maggie Edwards, Jennifer Evangelista, and Katie Kristof for assisting the project in numerous and diverse ways. Both editors thank the University of Georgia's two anonymous readers for their helpful comments as well as all of the authors who contributed to the volume.

New Studies in the History of American Slavery

Introduction

A History of the History
of Slavery in the Americas

STEPHANIE M. H. CAMP

AND EDWARD E. BAPTIST

*T*he chapters in this volume hardly provide the first new thoughts about the history of slavery in the Americas. Instead, this volume represents one more step in a long process of trying to understand slavery, a process that actually began aboard the slave ships: the enslaved themselves were the first people to tell themselves and others what was happening in West and Central Africa, along the Middle Passage, and in the slave markets of the Americas. From the sixteenth through the twentieth centuries, the slaves were the first to formulate histories of enslavement. At the same time, participants in the enslavement and exploitation of human beings and even outside observers also wanted to explain their changing world. Arguments about slavery and its history permeated the political culture of owners and nonowners alike. And during and after the abolition of slavery in the Americas, such interpretations remained important touchstones for political debate in many societies.[1] Discussions of slavery have always been important outside as well as inside the portals of the ivory tower.

In the United States, slavery has for centuries constituted a source of rhetoric, inspiration, and ideas for social and cultural movements. Still, while narratives of slavery shaped politics and culture throughout the nineteenth century in particular, culminating in the Civil War, emancipation, and Reconstruction, only in the late nineteenth century did slavery become a central subject of study by professionalized historians. Since that time, academic histories of the subject have greatly changed. In the young profession of American history, the consensus held that slavery was a benign institution, that enslaved people were as content with their lot as their owners were, and that emancipation and the attempt at racial equality represented by Reconstruction (1867–77) were tremendous mistakes. Here, at the nadir, or lowest point, of race relations in the United States after emancipation, Georgia-born historian U. B. Phillips proposed that slavery was a benevolent "school" that tried to civilize an inferior race. For most historians who followed in Phillips's footsteps, ideas such as black cultural creativity or slave resistance were inconceivable. After all, such ideas might suggest black humanity or even equality. Researchers such as W. E. B. Du Bois who took seriously the actions and ideas of the enslaved met either ridicule or studied inattention from the early twentieth century's white-dominated academic establishment.[2]

The stifling dominance of openly racist histories of slavery collapsed only in the 1950s and 1960s. Movements throughout the African diaspora for civil rights, decolonization, and cultural self-respect inspired new voices that insisted on reinterpreting the colonial and slave past. Scholars now insisted that far from being good for the master and good for the slave, slavery was a system of brutal exploitation.[3] The liberation movements of the mid-twentieth century insisted on the dignity of African cultural forms and found African cultural roots relevant to the movements' political programs. With the proclamation that "black is beautiful," African and African-rooted cultural and religious practices, art, language, and even hair and clothing styles became political statements in favor of dignity, equality, and autonomy.[4] Electrified by the debates about black culture and identity, many historians refuted the assumption of black cultural inferiority or absence by arguing that the essential components of black culture in the United States and elsewhere in the Americas derived from African roots.[5]

During the 1970s and 1980s, slavery studies boomed, shaped by black liberation movements and by a wider effort among historians to write a "new social history" that told the stories not of "great men"—of presidents and parliaments—but of ordinary people such as workers, servants, slaves, nonwhites, and women. The scholars called it history "from the bottom up." Out of political/cultural developments in the African diaspora and out of developments within the historical profession emerged a history of slavery that placed the slave himself (and writers in those days usually spoke of the slave as male) front and center. In this era, many slavery historians focused on the slaves' methods of survival, rebellion, and resistance and their cultural resilience. These scholars stressed, in other words, the agency rather than the victimization of the enslaved.[6]

By the 1980s, however, other scholars began to criticize what they saw as an inordinate emphasis on resistance. In this view, slavery studies that emphasized resistance and the capabilities (rather than the troubles) of slave communities were erasing everything that made the plantation evil: exploitation, the lack of autonomy, and intense suffering. Historians were misrepresenting the enslaved as superhuman heroes immune to the conditions of their lives. Indeed, some of these writers suggested that the absence of massive revolts led by the enslaved in the United States showed their willingness to live within the system rather than die fighting against it. And indeed, not only did enslaved people in the United States survive but, in contrast to the situation in most of the Caribbean plantation colonies, North America's enslaved population had by the late eighteenth century begun to grow by natural increase. Did the enslaved, the critics wondered, survive in spirit as well as in body through cultural or hidden resistance? Or did the relative lack of slave revolts prove that the enslaved ultimately accommodated themselves—surrendered—to the system?[7]

The positions in the heated accommodation/resistance debate were staked out by the early to mid-1990s. While that dialogue has continued to exert some influence, something new is afoot: many scholars working today accept that enslaved people in the United States accommodated themselves to slavery even as they resisted it. Many scholars of slavery now explicitly explore the paradoxical qualities in bondpeople's lives and dissolve dichotomous choices. Today, we believe that we cannot understand slavery in all its complexity through an either/or framework.

Yet this rejection of dichotomies is only one of the ideas emphasized by the new studies in American slavery. In fact, three major developments in the writing of history have profoundly shaped much new work in slavery studies: the influence of cultural history, the centrality of women and gender to our understanding of experience and identity, and new questions about the meaning and stability of the social category "race." These categories are devices that allow us to think about spheres of influence rather than truly separate arenas of study. The chapters in this volume have been influenced by all of these intellectual developments, showing that the three categories are interwoven, sometimes deeply connected and sometimes distinctive in their influence. Some of the authors are more explicitly interested in gender and women, others set their sights on tackling questions of identity and community, and still others focus on the politics of culture and slavery. As editors, we have organized the chapters accordingly. We will introduce them with brief descriptions of the three main currents now reshaping the study of enslavement in the Americas.

The Cultural Turn in Slavery Studies

By the 1980s, more and more historians were pursuing "history from below" with a twist. If social historians study social inequalities and the lives of ordinary people, the cultural historians who emerged during the 1980s and 1990s study simple words, daily acts, popular fads, and the quirky habits of subcultures. They interpret culture not only for what it can say about class relations and conflicts but also for the everyday stories and ideologies that people use to understand and talk about their fears, hopes, intimate lives, identities, values, and feelings. All of these phenomena, cultural historians argue, are important and legitimate points of inquiry in and of themselves, not just because they point to other, supposedly more serious, issues such as the official politics of parties and elections.[8]

Yet cultural history is not agnostic about politics. Even less so is the interdisciplinary field of cultural studies, which argues that culture is fundamentally political and which has powerfully influenced many historians. Originating in British studies of youth culture in the mid-twentieth century, cultural studies made headway in the American academy in the 1980s and 1990s.[9] This field stresses that people's day-to-day habits, dress, discussions, and purchasing patterns express their acceptance of, engagement with, and critique of corporations, governments, the mass media, and other institutions. Of course, cultural studies' attention to these details of life was not entirely new to those who had been studying the history of American slavery. Music, stories, religion, naming practices, craft making, dress, and housing patterns all testify to enslaved people's cultural expressiveness and to their insistence on doing some things their way according to their priorities and with their values in mind. And the study of the cultures of enslaved people has always waded right into whatever political struggles over race and racism were taking place, just as American cultural studies would do. So it would be inaccurate to say that a dramatic break has occurred between the social history of the 1970s and 1980s and today's cultural histories of slavery: students of slavery's social history had long appreciated the connections between culture and the social and political contexts in which cultures grew.

However, the growing importance of cultural history and cultural studies has helped to spark a shift in slavery studies. While social history uses culture as a passageway into other, more "serious" issues such as politics, the cultural history of slavery views culture as meaningful and important in and of itself. Cultural historians' emphasis on personal experience signals a fundamental change in the perception of which subjects of inquiry are legitimate. In earlier years, scholars might have shunned the study of people's distinctive, even idiosyncratic experiences of identity as overly personal and therefore superficial. Now, many cultural historians valorize personal experience as one way—perhaps the most important way—in which we experience social such categories as race, gender, nation, class, and sexuality. Moreover, questions about the idea of race as a stable category (a point to which we will return shortly) have prompted questions about how people in the past made, remade, used, and even played with their identities to achieve their personal desires and goals.

In this sense, slavery studies' increased focus on culture, identity, the personal, and the subjective represents less a break with the social history of slavery than a product of it. Writing in a context in which open apologists for slavery reigned supreme in many areas of American and Western life, the social historians of earlier decades demonstrated that slavery was wrong, that enslaved people suffered, that they resisted, and that they were human beings with hopes and dreams and culture.[10] Social historians of slavery have successfully turned our attention to the enslaved, and the values of cultural history allow current slavery studies to dive even deeper to understand how the enslaved thought about and engaged with their lifeworlds—about death, birth, health, identity, freedom, property, family, pleasure, suffering, love, strife, and community. While elaborating the political implications of these topics, new scholarship also hints at the parts of existence that transcend politics. Cultural historians' unabashed embrace of these aspects of human life has emerged not only from social history and from the cultural turn. Women's history and the feminist movement also have taught scholars much about the deep and complex connections between the personal and the political.

Women and Gender in Slavery

Women's history initially sought to add women to the picture of the past—to discover or recover pasts long forgotten, hidden from view, or actively suppressed. The first generation of women's historians, who began to emerge in significant numbers by the late 1960s, quickly learned that their work could also transform historians' understandings about what we know and even *can* know about the past. They were soon struggling not only to include women in the story of the past but to point out the ways in which ideas about the proper roles and natures of women and men have changed over time. Thus, they suggested that "nature" and "roles" might not be as innate as had previously been assumed.[11] The pioneering work of women's historians has transformed our understandings not only of women but also of politics, men, the household, science, war, and almost every field of historical study, including slavery.

Yet women's history and the history of slavery were not always a compatible pair. As African American scholars became prominent participants in the rise of a second wave of organized feminism in the 1970s and 1980s, they criticized some of the assumptions made by earlier scholars and activists. For example, by arguing that women needed to be freed from household labor to work in the public spaces of the wage economy, mainstream feminist theory revealed its solipsism. Working-class women and women of color desired fundamental changes but usually did not require emancipation from the shackles of bourgeois domesticity: nonelite and nonwhite women in the United States had always worked outside their homes. The black feminist critique ultimately undermined the widespread assumption that "all the women are white and all the blacks are men." In the 1970s and 1980s, women of color repeatedly reminded white feminists and men of color that women of color existed and that their distinctive issues were also feminist in nature. Nonwhite women's insistence on their existence attested to the fact that they were authentically women (not just inadequate versions of white women) and that they were no less racial subjects than their male counterparts, even if they insisted on paying attention to the multiple kinds of oppressions that they experienced.[12]

Research on women of color increased dramatically during the 1970s and 1980s, in no small measure as a result of this tense yet productive dialogue. Despite decades of erasure by the historical profession (and centuries of marginalization in mainstream U.S. culture), women's historians have proved that it is possible to write histories of black women: archival material is out there, and so is an audience clamoring to read the finished product.[13] Even enslaved women, whose histories had widely been presumed lost if not irrelevant, have become the subject of a growing literature.[14]

This new scholarship on black women, especially enslaved women, has prompted further rumblings. Questions about the relationship between race and gender came into their own in the 1980s and 1990s. While most scholarly authors continued to take the categories of race and gender for granted, some historians, literary critics, and philosophers began to explore the complex webs that connected the two. Race and gender look, on closer inspection, not like two separate social categories but like ideas with hopelessly entangled histories. Neither can exist or could have come to exist in the slave societies of the Americas without the other.[15] Indeed, philosopher Elizabeth Spelman called the habit of thinking about race and gender separately an "ampersand problem," a desire to think of racism and sexism in the lives and histories of women of color as "piled upon each other." In an "additive analysis," black women's identities are "black" plus "woman." The image of identities stacking on each other but remaining essentially separate presumes that people fit into a gender category that lacks race. In addition, the assumption goes, they also fall into a genderless racial category.[16] Black women and other women of color, however, live their lives as more than the sum of their parts; in addition, they represent more than that sum in the mental worlds of others. They embody the interlocking nature of race and gender—as well, of course, as sexuality, class, and nation. Perhaps, in different ways, so do other categories—"black man," "white woman," and so on. As Elsa Barkley Brown puts it, not all women "share the same gender."[17]

Even as women of color called attention to their difference and their womanhood from the 1970s through the 1990s, mainstream feminists continued to assume that the category of "woman" meant simply "white." Evelyn Brooks Higginbotham suggested in 1992 that part of the reason for the stubbornly universalizing tendency in women's studies was the equally totalizing logic of race. Race, she argued, often serves, in history and in daily life, as a "metalanguage," as a "powerful, all-encompassing effect on the construction and representation of other social and power relations, namely, gender, class, and sexuality." As such, race has chilled the intensity of class conflict among white Americans by enveloping and obscuring the importance of that kind of conflict. Consequently, race "appears to solidify people of opposing economic classes" (whites) and "precludes unity with the same gender group" (women of different racial backgrounds). Like theorists of race and gender before her, Higginbotham viewed race and gender as socially constructed.[18]

Some historians of slavery have now taken up the task of exploring how historical processes shaped by gender helped to create the social category of race. Exciting and transformative scholarship in this vein has explored the mutually constitutive relationship of race and gender in the history of the Americas. Jennifer L. Morgan's pathbreaking scholarship is at the forefront of this work. In her chapter in this volume, " 'Some Could Suckle over Their Shoulder': Male Travelers, Female Bodies, and the Gendering of Racial Ideology," Morgan shows that male travelers to the West African coast in the early centuries of the African slave trade entertained quite clear ideas about African women's bodies and especially their reproductive capacities. These conceptions, in hindsight both familiar and puzzling, joined other ideas about Africans to help justify the turn to African slavery in the New World. Europeans used enslaved Africans to supply labor to the American plantations in no small part because of their gender ideals, which clashed with African women's gender roles.

The hard work done from the 1970s onward to dissolve the lines separating analyses of gender from those of race is in dialogue with the dissolving of other misleading lines of distinction. In her chapter, "Consciousness and Calling: African American Midwives at Work in the Antebellum South," Sharla M. Fett discusses "doctor women's" work and especially their identities as liminal (in-between) figures in the Old South. They crossed many lines in the performance of their art—between the logic of chattel slavery and the cultural and spiritual value that the enslaved placed on birth, between black and white spaces and households, and between "scientific" medicine and "motherwit." Stephanie M. H. Camp's chapter, "The Pleasures of Resistance: Enslaved Women and Body Politics in the Plantation South, 1830–1861," challenges the dichotomies of the personal and the political and the material and the cultural. She discusses the mobility and pleasure that enslaved women and men enjoyed at their rare organized gatherings. Though sneaking away into the woods to wear fancy dress, dance, and sometimes eat and drink might appear to be frivolous, these escapes in fact mattered a great deal to the enslaved—and to their owners. Just as gender and plantation space have proven to be more malleable than we at first thought, race is not nearly as solid as we once believed it to be.

Race, depicted in the nineteenth and early twentieth centuries as an unchanging biological human feature that shaped behavior and culture, has since the end of World War II come under increasing scrutiny. Both the horrifying example of Nazi Germany's uses of scientific racism and growing public criticism of segregation in the United States undermined claims that blacks were inherently inferior in intelligence or moral character to whites. The same challenges that undermined the proslavery scholarship of an earlier era also discredited the public acceptability (at least for many people) of claims that race could tell anything about a person's character or talents.[19] By the 1980s, historians were challenging the category of race itself, beginning to argue that race as we know it had not always existed, that it had in fact been invented and reinvented over time.[20]

The most significant milepost in this rethinking of race (among historians) was probably Barbara Fields's 1982 essay, "Ideology and Race in American History."[21] Fields argued that Americans and American historians have made the mistake of thinking that race is a biological and "observable physical fact" when it is in fact none of these things but rather an idea that on closer inspection looks more and more incoherent. We identify people by race in ways that are illogical and unpredictable. Take, for example, the group called "Hispanic." What, Fields asked, makes Hispanics an ethnic group, "while blacks, whites and Asians are racial groups?" "Hispanics" may share a language, but they certainly do not share physical attributes. By that same logic, shouldn't black and white Americans, who share a language, form a single ethnic group? And why are Asians a "race" in the United States? They come from different countries, speak different languages, have a wide range of physical features, and do not share a single culture. Asian Americans were first identified as a single racial group in the 1960s: How could biology suddenly make that happen? And what about the fact that in Brazil and much of the Caribbean, racial mixture "whitens" (cleanses, uplifts) and leads ultimately to whiteness, while in the United States a single drop of black blood has acted as a contaminant that can make any person with the slightest amount of observable African ancestry "black" no matter how light his or her skin? Clearly, as Fields wrote, "race is a product of history, not nature."[22]

Historians following the trail blazed by Fields began to map out a story of the creation of the ideology of race. The emergence of race was a historical rather than biological process, and scholars discovered that it emerged from the same crucible in which slavery had been forged. In the colonial Americas, the Englishmen who displaced Native Americans and imported indentured servants and slaves to Virginia, Barbados, and elsewhere haltingly hewed out an idea of race to group, describe, and divide the peoples being exploited. In the first half or so of the seventeenth century, the process of ordering people and explaining differences in their statuses was only partly about differences of color; religion and forms of government were also important issues to English decision makers.

So was gender. English settlers in Virginia, the earliest North American colony to deal explicitly with slavery, used gender to draw lines of distinction between workers and settlers. They deemed African women degraded laborers, reflecting and deepening the image of African women that had emerged in white minds on the West African coast: a tough worker and fertile breeder, not someone who could claim protection. African women were "nasty wenches" rather than "good wives," a status reserved for English women. Virginia's leaders then stigmatized African men as dependents shorn of such manhood rights as the right to carry a gun, to participate in local government, or to marry any amenable woman.

As they made these decisions, Virginia's lawmakers described themselves with such words as *English* and *Christian* rather than *white*, and they spoke of "Africans," "heathens" and "negroes" rather than "blacks." The early lines of difference focused less on color or biological differences and more on differences in gender roles, in religion, and in other cultural and linguistic factors. By the mid- to late seventeenth century, Virginia's lawmakers began to focus more and more on color and on the idea of physical differences between Africans and English people. By the end of the century, whites equated *black* with *slave* and with all the dependence, degradation, and lack of respect that first the latter and then the former came to connote in the emerging plantation society. Thus, there is nothing static or natural about race: it did not exist until it was made—almost by accident—out of anxieties about gender, civility, and savagery.[23]

Race, we now see, is a powerful historical creation, not a biological fact. And while American races and racism emerged from the context of slavery, so did the ways in which Africans and their descendants would continually modify and even re-create their complex New World identities. From the earliest years of its existence, blackness has never been unified or unitary. Throughout the Americas, enslaved Africans and their descendants improvised with the mixed cultural forms available to them to forge new cultures combining Africa, Europe, and the Americas. In the cabins of Virginia, the barracks of Saint Domingue, the swept yards of Tennessee, and the *fazendas* of Brazil, the dispossessed combined and recombined elements of countless cultures, creating new ways of framing the world and its questions, of expressing their creativity, and of experiencing pleasure and holiness.[24] Afro-Atlantic cultures acquired both the diverse and the common marks of three continents, signs not of unity or essence but of difference, constant change, and conflict.

Looking at slave cultures from this perspective, many recent historians have been loath to impose the idea of a community on the diverse and complex people who lived in the New World's slave quarters. The term devotes insufficient attention to difference and conflict among the enslaved and ascribes an unchanging quality to blackness. Indeed, since the 1990s, historians have often emphasized what we might call not community but African American communion. Enslaved people in the New World ate the same meager bread and drank from the same bitter cup of violence and dispossession. But while enslaved people in the many different New World societies often lived in similar conditions, they dealt with them in very different ways, creating diverse, varied, and sometimes contradictory outcomes, products, and ideas for their lives. This volume's chapters by Herman Bennett, Barbara Krauthamer, and Dylan Penningroth offer close and thoughtful explorations of these questions of identity and community. In "Genealogies to a Past: Africa, Ethnicity, and Marriage in Seventeenth-Century Mexico," Bennett reveals the process by which Central Africans exported into Mexico became slaves and Catholics yet remained in some respects Angolan. His examinations of marriage records allow him to explore the interaction of Angolan identity with gender roles—particularly in both men's and women's choices of marriage partners.

Krauthamer's chapter, "Kinship and Freedom: Fugitive Slave Women's Incorporation into Creek Society," looks at one of the most fundamental categories in the study of slavery and American history: freedom. Her analysis of Creek communities offers a fresh interpretation of the meaning of freedom, showing how black women in Creek societies, like the Creek, had specific understandings of what it meant to be free. Krauthamer thus places American freedom within a broader context. American freedom has often meant autonomy to those who claim it, yet for the Creeks and their former slaves, freedom was not autonomy or independence but kinship. In "My People, My People: The Dynamics of Community in Southern Slavery," Penningroth tackles the question of community among enslaved African Americans living on the cotton, tobacco, and rice plantations of the U.S. South. Drawing on perspectives from African studies, he finds that when enslaved people owned property—and sometimes they did, though they too were treated as property—that ownership fundamentally shaped their understandings and experiences of family, community, and conflict within those communities.

Cultural history has helped us all to see that ordinary people comment on and interpret their worlds, think creatively, and contest the ideas and forces that shape their lives. The remaining four chapters in this volume show how enslaved people shaped their own definitions of history and culture and sometimes even the workings of power in their societies. Vincent Brown, Phillip Troutman, and Edward E. Baptist explore the ways in which enslaved people experienced terror, heartbreak, and rebirth and told their tales, all in the process of being moved, bought, and sold. Brown's chapter, "Spiritual Terror and Sacred Authority in Jamaican Slave Society," explores the spirituality of enslaved Africans in Jamaica, examining the practices they brought and how these practices were used by the enslaved and abused by slaveholders. Spirituality proved a very effective instrument of slave control in the hands of Jamaica's notorious planters. Brown's unforgettable essay forces us to think of culture as an avenue not only of connection with Africa but also of torture. In "Correspondences in Black and White: Sentiment and the Slave Market Revolution," Troutman examines letters written by enslaved people in the midst of the domestic slave trade in the antebellum United States. As the plantation South expanded after 1790, slave traders transported hundreds of thousands of people from older states such as Virginia to newer ones, including Mississippi and Louisiana. Some of those sold away from family and friends sent written messages back to their loved ones, often employing a sentimental language also used by literary white Americans to express their most dramatic feelings. Troutman helps us to envision the countless interpersonal moments of contact that resulted from and helped to give human form to American slavery.

Not all memories and messages appear in literary form, but they nevertheless may still be products of historical thinking. In "'Stol' and Fetched Here': Enslaved Migration, Ex-slave Narratives, and Vernacular History," Baptist identifies within the oft-criticized Works Progress Administration (WPA) interviews with ex-slaves the remaining evidence of a series of oral histories created by people denied the opportunity to write texts. His essay shows that the enslaved people forced to migrate west within the United States during the cotton boom of the first half of the nineteenth century developed, in their everyday retellings of their journeys, a complex historical critique of enslavement and enslavers. Baptist suggests that memories of forced migration helped sharpen and organize African Americans' opposition to white racial solidarity, reminding us that historical thinking frames the way in which we try to shape the future. Finally, Christopher Brown's chapter, "British Slavery and British Politics: A Perspective and a Prospectus," turns to political history to describe the key ways in which the enslaved—and slavery itself—shaped not just the history that they told but also the history that they lived. Carefully mapping the politicoeconomic developments of the Atlantic world, Brown explores five ways that slavery shaped the political development of the British empire: through the production of political power, the defining of political interests, its association with political conflict, the shaping of political vocabulary, and the influence on political culture. Brown compellingly demonstrates the centrality of slavery and the enslaved to the entire English Atlantic world.

Thus, three intellectual trends—the cultural turn, the dramatically increased attention to women and gender, and the historicization of race—have influenced the chapters in this volume. While this collection does not catalog all of the relevant new scholarship, it includes some important developments, including works by a few of the most exciting scholars working in the field today. The authors who appear here explore the lives of slaves, slaveholders, and slavery with eyes open to the personal, the conflictual, seeking to tell these stories from the many different perspectives of the enslaved and turning many commonplace concepts, such as freedom and culture, into avenues that lead to some surprising results. Yet these writers also link the study of enslaved humanity with the story of all humanity. The economic and political forces that shaped the Caribbean and Brazil sometimes played out differently in the interior of North America, but all of these slave societies were part of a complex whole. And the Atlantic world, in the centuries of the European enslavement of Africans, was also the birthplace—for good or for ill—of much of the world in which we live today. From those years and those shores emerged not only race and racism but also modernity, industrial capitalism, revolutions, liberalism, conservatism, and nationalism. In making these links, these scholars follow a path blazed long ago by the first historians of slavery. After all, the enslaved themselves—again, the first historians of slavery—saw in their religion, their politics, and their stories of themselves that they were part of a much wider diaspora that linked all the descendants of Africans throughout the new world that enslavement was helping to shape.

This volume will be of use to students and teachers of slavery. We have grouped the chapters to spark classroom discussion, and a list of recommended readings gives direction to those who wish to explore more deeply slavery in the Americas. We hope that undergraduates and general readers will find in these writings some answers to questions posed both in the classroom and in their lives. We also hope that discussing the history of enslavement in the Americas can help us all to understand the world that slavery made and perhaps to help redeem its pernicious legacy.

NOTES

1. Works that acknowledge the ways in which the known history of slavery shaped ideas and acts in the era of emancipation include John Hope Franklin, *Reconstruction after the Civil War* (Chicago, 1961); Thomas C. Holt, *The Problem of Freedom: Race, Labor, Politics in Jamaica and Britain, 1832–1938* (Baltimore, 1992); Eric Foner, *Reconstruction: America's Unfinished Revolution, 1863–1877* (New York, 1988); Kim D. Butler, *Freedoms*

Given, Freedoms Won: Afro-Brazilians in Post Abolition São Paulo and Salvador (New Brunswick, 1998); David Blight, *Race and Reunion: The Civil War in American Memory* (Cambridge, 2001); Steven Hahn, *A Nation under Our Feet: Black Political Struggles in the Rural South from Slavery to the Great Migration* (Cambridge, 2003).

2. William Dunning, *Reconstruction, Political and Economic, 1865–1877* (New York, 1907); Ulrich B. Phillips, *American Negro Slavery* (1918; Baton Rouge, 1966). The rise of this racist historiography has been chronicled by John David Smith, *An Old Creed for the New South: Proslavery Ideology and Historiography, 1865–1918* (Westport, 1985). Early historians to challenge this tradition included W. E. B. Du Bois, *The Suppression of the African Slave-Trade to the United States of America, 1638–1870* (1896; Baton Rouge, 1969); W. E. B. Du Bois, *The Souls of Black Folk: Essays and Sketches* (Chicago, 1903); John Cade, "Out of the Mouths of Ex-slaves," *Journal of Negro History* 20 (July 1935): 294–337; W. E. B. Du Bois, *Black Reconstruction: An Essay toward a History of the Part Which Black Folk Played in the Attempt to Reconstruct Democracy in America, 1860–1880* (New York, 1935); C. L. R. James, *The Black Jacobins: Toussaint L'Ouverture and the San Domingo Revolution* (New York, 1938); Herbert Aptheker, *American Negro Slave Revolts* (New York, 1943); John Hope Franklin, *From Slavery to Freedom: A History of American Negroes* (New York, 1956); Herbert Aptheker, ed., *A Documentary History of the Negro People in the United States* (New York, 1969–70). Carter G. Woodson's founding of the *Journal of Negro History* in 1916 also spurred challenges to the views of slavery then pervasive in the historical profession.

3. Franklin, *From Slavery to Freedom*; John Hope Franklin, *The Militant South: 1800–1861* (Cambridge, 1956); Kenneth Stampp, *The Peculiar Institution: Slavery in the Antebellum South* (New York, 1956); Stanley M. Elkins, *Slavery: A Problem in American Institutional and Intellectual Life* (Chicago, 1959).

4. Interesting perspectives on this period in the cultural history of the African diaspora include Horace Campbell, *Rasta and Resistance: From Marcus Garvey to Walter Rodney* (Trenton, 1985); Grant Farred, *What's My Name? Black Vernacular Intellectuals* (Minneapolis, 2003); William Van Deburg, *New Day in Babylon: The Black Power Movement and American Culture, 1965–1975* (Chicago, 1992); William Van Deburg, *Black Camelot: African-American Culture Heroes in their Times, 1960–1980* (Chicago, 1997); Robin D. G. Kelley, *Race Rebels: Culture, Politics, and the Black Working Class* (New York, 1996).

5. George P. Rawick, *From Sundown to Sunup: The Making of the Black Community* (Westport, 1972); Eugene D. Genovese, *Roll, Jordan, Roll: The World the Slaves Made* (New York, 1974); Herbert G. Gutman, *The Black Family in Slavery and Freedom, 1750–1925* (New York, 1976); Leslie Howard Owens, *This Species of Property: Slave Life and Culture in the Old South* (New York, 1976); John W. Blassingame, *The Slave Community: Plantation Life in the Antebellum South* (New York, 1977); Thomas L. Webber, *Deep Like the Rivers: Education in the Slave Quarter Community, 1831–1865* (New York, 1978); Albert J. Raboteau, *Slave Religion: The "Invisible Institution" in the Antebellum South* (New York, 1978); Paul D. Escott, *Slavery Remembered: A Record of Twentieth-Century Slave Narratives* (Chapel Hill, 1979); Charles Joyner, *Down by the Riverside: A South Carolina Slave Community* (Urbana, 1984); Sterling Stuckey, *Slave Culture: Nationalist Theory and the Foundations of Black America* (New York, 1987); Margaret Washington Creel,

A Peculiar People: Slave Religion and Community-Culture among the Gullahs (New York, 1988); Joseph E. Holloway, ed., Africanisms in American Culture (Bloomington, 1990); Sylvia R. Frey, Water from the Rock: Black Resistance in a Revolutionary Age (Princeton, 1991); Roger D. Abrahams, Singing the Master: The Emergence of African American Culture in the Plantation South (New York, 1992).

6. Genovese, Roll, Jordan Roll; Eugene D. Genovese, From Rebellion to Revolution: Afro-American Slave Revolts in the Making of the Modern World (Baton Rouge, 1979). On Brazil, see João José Reis, Slave Rebellion in Brazil: The Muslim Uprising of 1835 in Bahia (Baltimore, 1993); Stuart B. Schwartz, Slaves, Peasants, and Rebels: Reconsidering Brazilian Slavery (Urbana, 1992). On the Caribbean, see David Geggus's work, especially Slavery, War, and Revolution: The British Occupation of Saint Domingue, 1793–1798 (New York, 1982); Michael Craton, Testing the Chains: Resistance to Slavery in the British West Indies (Ithaca, 1982); Carolyn Fick, The Making of Haiti: The Saint Domingue Revolution from Below (Knoxville, 1990); Hilary McD. Beckles, Natural Rebels: A Social History of Enslaved Black Women in Barbados (London, 1989). The differing demographies of the New World slave societies emerged with the new social history of the Caribbean colonies: see Elsa Goveia, Slave Society in the British Leeward Islands at the End of the Eighteenth Century (New Haven, 1965); Richard S. Dunn, Sugar and Slaves: The Rise of the Planter Class in the English West Indies, 1624–1715 (New York, 1972); Richard Sheridan, Sugar and Slavery: An Economic History of the British West Indies, 1623–1775 (Bridgetown, 1974); B. W. Higman, Slave Population and Economy in Jamaica, 1807–1834 (Cambridge, 1976). On maroons, see Richard Price, First-Time: The Historical Vision of an African-American People (Baltimore, 1983); Richard Price, Alabi's World (Baltimore, 1990); Richard Price, ed., Maroon Societies: Rebel Slave Communities in America (Garden City, 1973); Mavis Campbell, The Maroons of Jamaica, 1656–1795: A History of Resistance, Collaboration, and Betrayal (South Hadley, 1988).

7. Eugene D. Genovese, The World the Slaveholders Made: Two Essays in Interpretation (New York, 1969); Genovese, Roll, Jordan, Roll; Bertram Wyatt-Brown, Southern Honor: Ethics and Behavior in the Old South (New York, 1982); James Oakes, "The Political Significance of Slave Resistance." History Workshop Journal 22 (Fall 1986): 89–107; Elizabeth Fox-Genovese, Within the Plantation Household: Black and White Women of the Old South (Chapel Hill, 1988); Bertram Wyatt-Brown, "The Mask of Obedience: Male Slave Psychology in the Old South," American Historical Review 93 (December 1988): 1228–52; Eugene D. Genovese, The Southern Tradition: The Achievements and Limitations of an American Conservatism (Cambridge, 1994); Christopher Morris, Becoming Southern: The Evolution of a Way of Life, Warren County and Vicksburg, Mississippi, 1770–1860 (New York, 1995); Peter Kolchin, American Slavery, 1619–1877 (New York, 1993); William Dusinberre, Them Dark Days: Slavery in the American Rice Swamps (New York, 1996); Christopher Morris, "Within the Slave Cabin: Violence in Mississippi Slave Families," in Over the Threshold: Intimate Violence in Early America, ed. Christine Daniels and Michael V. Kennedy (New York, 1999), 268–86; Jeffrey Young, Domesticating Slavery: The Master Class in Georgia and South Carolina, 1670–1837 (Chapel Hill, 1999).

8. Historians of France in particular were enormously influential in forging the new cultural history; see, for example, Natalie Zemon Davis, Society and Culture in Early

Modern France: Eight Essays (Stanford, 1975); Robert Darnton, *The Great Cat Massacre and Other Episodes in French Cultural History* (New York, 1984); Lynn Hunt, *Politics, Culture, and Class in the French Revolution* (Berkeley, 1984); Lynn Hunt, *The Family Romance of the French Revolution* (Berkeley, 1992); see also Carlo Ginzburg, *The Cheese and the Worms: The Cosmos of a Sixteenth-Century Miller*, trans. John and Anne Tedeschi (Baltimore, 1980); Michel Foucault, *The History of Sexuality*, trans. Robert Hurley (New York, 1978).

9. The texts most often cited as the origin points are Richard Hoggart, *The Uses of Literacy: Aspects of Working Class Life with Special Reference to Publications and Entertainments* (London, 1957); Raymond Williams, *Culture and Society, 1780–1950* (London, 1958); E. P. Thompson, *The Making of the English Working Class* (London, 1963); Stuart Hall and Paddy Whannel, *The Popular Arts* (New York, 1964). For an account of these developments, see Stuart Hall, "Cultural Studies: Two Paradigms," *Media, Culture, and Society* 2 (January 1980), 57–72. Janice Radway, *Reading the Romance: Women, Patriarchy, and Popular Literature* (Chapel Hill, 1984), was a crucial text in the translation of this approach to American academia. See also Lynn Hunt, ed., *The New Cultural History* (Berkeley, 1989); Simon During, ed., *The Cultural Studies Reader* (London, 1993).

10. Walter Johnson, "On Agency," *Journal of Social History* 37 (Fall 2003): 113–24.

11. See, among many others, Joan Scott, "Gender: A Useful Category of Historical Analysis," *American Historical Review* 91 (December 1986): 1053–75; Carroll Smith-Rosenberg, *Disorderly Conduct: Visions of Gender in Victorian America* (New York, 1985); Nancy F. Cott, *The Grounding of Modern Feminism* (New Haven, 1987); Linda Kerber, "Separate Spheres, Female Worlds, Woman's Place: The Rhetoric of Women's History," *Journal of American History* 75 (June 1988): 9–39.

12. The Combahee River Collective, *The Combahee River Collective Statement* (New York, 1986): 9. Other texts that contributed to this turning point include Toni Cade Bambara, *The Black Woman: An Anthology* (New York, 1970); Cherríe Moraga and Gloria Anzaldúa, eds., *This Bridge Called My Back: Writings by Radical Women of Color* (Watertown, 1981); Hazel V. Carby, "White Woman Listen! Black Feminism and the Boundaries of Sisterhood," in *The Empire Strikes Back: Race and Racism in 70s Britain* (Birmingham, 1982), 212–35; Gloria T. Hull, Patricia Bell Scott, and Barbara Smith, eds., *All the Women Are White, All the Blacks Are Men, but Some of Us Are Brave: Black Women's Studies* (Old Westbury, 1982); Barbara Smith, ed., *Home Girls: A Black Feminist Anthology* (New York, 1983).

13. The most influential of the works on black women from this period include Gerda Lerner, ed., *Black Women in White America: A Documentary History* (New York, 1972); Sharon Harley and Rosalyn Terborg-Penn, eds., *The Afro-American Woman: Struggles and Images* (Baltimore, 1978); Filomina Chioma Steady, ed., *The Black Woman Cross-Culturally* (Cambridge, 1981); Paula Giddings, *When and Where I Enter: The Impact of Black Women on Race and Sex in America* (New York, 1984); Darlene Clark Hine, ed., *Black Women in the Nursing Profession: A Documentary History* (New York, 1985); Jacqueline Jones, *Labor of Love, Labor of Sorrow: Black Women, Work, and the Family from Slavery to the Present* (New York, 1985); Deborah Gray White, *Ar'n't I a Woman: Female Slaves in the Plantation South* (New York, 1985); Hazel V. Carby, *Reconstructing*

Womanhood: The Emergence of the Afro-American Woman Novelist (New York, 1987); Harriet A. Jacobs, *Incidents in the Life of a Slave Girl, Written by Herself,* ed. Jean Fagan Yellin (1861; Cambridge, 1987); Elsa Barkley Brown, "Womanist Consciousness: Maggie Lena Walker and the Independent Order of Saint Luke," *Signs* 14 (Spring 1989): 610–33.

14. In addition to works already mentioned, see Angela Y. Davis, "Reflections on the Black Woman's Role in the Community of Slaves," *Black Scholar* 3 (December 1971): 2–15; Mary Ellison, "Resistance to Oppression: Black Women's Response to Slavery in the United States," *Slavery and Abolition* 4 (May 1983): 56–63; Marietta Morrissey, *Slave Women in the New World: Gender Stratification in the Caribbean* (Lawrence, 1989); Barbara Bush, *Slave Women in Caribbean Society, 1650–1838* (Kingston, 1990); Thelma Jennings, " 'Us Colored Women Had to Go through a Plenty': Sexual Exploitation of African American Slave Women," *Journal of Women's History* 1 (Winter 1990): 45–74; Nell Irvin Painter, *Sojourner Truth: A Life, a Symbol* (New York, 1996); Nell Irvin Painter, "Representing Truth: Sojourner Truth's Knowing and Becoming Known," *Journal of American History* 81 (September 1994): 461–93; David Barry Gaspar and Darlene Clark Hine, eds., *More Than Chattel: Black Women and Slavery in the Americas* (Bloomington, 1996); Patricia Morton, ed., *Discovering the Women in Slavery: Emancipating Perspectives on the American Past* (Athens, 1996); Brenda E. Stevenson, *Life in Black and White: Family and Community in the Slave South* (New York, 1996); Leslie A. Schwalm, *A Hard Fight for We: Women's Transition from Slavery to Freedom in South Carolina* (Urbana, 1997); Hilary McD. Beckles, *Centering Woman: Gender Discourses in Caribbean Slave Society* (Kingston, 1999); Stephanie M. H. Camp, *Closer to Freedom: Enslaved Women and Everyday Resistance in the Plantation South* (Chapel Hill, 2004); Jennifer L. Morgan, *Laboring Women: Reproduction and Gender in New World Slavery* (Philadelphia, 2004). Ironically, despite the outpouring of scholarship on enslaved women, to date only a handful of book-length studies have appeared. Most of the scholarship currently exists in article, anthology and chapter form. See Morgan, *Laboring Women,* 204 n.7.

15. Angela Y. Davis, *Women, Race, and Class* (New York, 1981); bell hooks, *Ain't I a Woman: Black Women and Feminism* (Boston, 1981); Carby, "White Woman, Listen!"; Hortense J. Spillers, "Mama's Baby, Papa's Maybe: An American Grammar Book," *Diacritics* 17 (Summer 1987): 65–81; Kimberlé Crenshaw, "Demarginalizing the Intersection of Race and Sex: A Black Feminist Critique of Antidiscrimination Doctrine, Feminist Theory, and Antiracist Politics," *University of Chicago Legal Forum* 139 (1989): 139–69; Evelyn Brooks Higginbotham, "Beyond the Sound of Silence: Afro-American Women in History," *Gender and History* 1 (Spring 1989): 50–67; Elsa Barkley Brown, " 'What Has Happened Here': The Politics of Difference in Women's History and Feminist Politics," *Feminist Studies* 18 (Summer 1992): 295–312; Evelyn Brooks Higginbotham, "African-American Women's History and the Metalanguage of Race," *Signs* 17 (Winter 1992): 251–75; Kimberlé Crenshaw, "Mapping the Margins: Intersectionality, Identity Politics, and Violence against Women of Color," in *Critical Race Theory: The Key Writings That Formed the Movement,* ed. Kimberlé Crenshaw, Neil Gotanda, Gary Peller, and Kendall Thomas (New York, 1995), 357–83; Valerie Smith, *Not Just Race, Not Just Gender: Black Feminist Readings* (New York, 1998).

16. Elizabeth V. Spelman, *Inessential Woman: Problems of Exclusion in Feminist Thought* (Boston, 1988), 114, 122, 123.

17. Elsa Barkley Brown, " 'What Has Happened Here,' " 298.

18. Higginbotham, "Metalanguage of Race," 255.

19. Melville J. Herskovits, *Franz Boas: The Science of Man in the Making* (New York, 1953); Stephen J. Gould, *The Mismeasure of Man* (New York, 1981).

20. The idea that race and racism had changed over time had been explored productively at least since the 1940s; see Eric Williams, *Capitalism and Slavery* (Chapel Hill, 1944); Ashley Montagu, *Man's Most Dangerous Myth: The Fallacy of Race* (New York, 1942); Frantz Fanon, *Black Skin, White Masks*, trans. Charles Lam Markmann (New York, 1967); Winthrop Jordan, *White over Black: American Attitudes toward the Negro, 1550–1812* (Chapel Hill, 1968); George M. Fredrickson, *The Black Image in the White Mind: The Debate on Afro-American Character and Destiny, 1817–1914* (New York, 1971); William Stanton, *The Leopard's Spots: Scientific Attitudes towards Race in America, 1815–1859* (Chicago, 1960); Reginald Horsman, *Race and Manifest Destiny: The Origins of American Racial Anglo-Saxonism* (Cambridge, 1981).

21. Barbara Fields, "Ideology and Race in American History," in *Region, Race, and Reconstruction: Essays in Honor of C. Vann Woodward*, ed. J. Morgan Kousser and James M. McPherson (New York, 1982): 143–77. Others who have influenced this turn include Michael Omi and Howard Winant, *Racial Formation in the United States: From the 1960s to the 1980s* (New York, 1986); David Theo Goldberg, ed., *The Anatomy of Racism* (Minneapolis, 1990); Patricia J. Williams, *The Alchemy of Race and Rights* (Cambridge, 1991); Stuart Hall, "New Ethnicities," in *"Race," Culture, and Difference*, ed. James Donald and Ali Rattansi (London, 1992); Stuart Hall, "What Is This 'Black' in Black Popular Culture?" in *Black Popular Culture: A Project by Michele Wallace*, ed. Gina Dent (Seattle, 1992), 21–36; Paul Gilroy, *The Black Atlantic: Modernity and Double Consciousness* (Cambridge, 1993); Barbara J. Fields, *"Origins of the New South* and the Negro Question," *Journal of Southern History* 67 (November 2001): 811–26.

22. Fields, "Ideology and Race in American History," 144, 152. Americans have often built their ideas about race on the fictitious black/white dichotomy and then have either ignored those who were neither black nor white or tried to force other "races" ("Latinos," "Asians," "Indians") into parallel categories of difference. The black/white binary idea is, like the idea of race itself, a socially constructed fiction, yet it has also produced a real history: of erasure of those who are neither black nor white; of heightened intensity between black and white. See Gary Y. Okihiro, *Margins and Mainstreams: Asians in American History and Culture* (Seattle, 1994); Neil Foley, *The White Scourge: Mexicans, Blacks, and Poor Whites in Texas Cotton Culture* (Berkeley, 1997); Nancy Hewitt, *Southern Discomfort: Women's Activism in Tampa, Florida, 1880s–1920s* (Urbana, 2001); Claudio Saunt, "The Paradox of Freedom: Tribal Sovereignty and Emancipation during the Reconstruction of Indian Territory," *Journal of Southern History* 70 (February 2004): 63–95; see also the so-called whiteness scholarship, esp. David Roediger, *The Wages of Whiteness: Race and the Making of the American Working Class* (London, 1991); Eric Lott, *Love and Theft: Blackface Minstrelsy and the American Working Class* (New York, 1993); Noel Ignatiev, *How*

the *Irish Became White* (New York, 1995); Matthew Frye Jacobson, *Whiteness of a Different Color: European Immigrants and the Alchemy of Race* (Cambridge, 1998); George Lipsitz, *The Possessive Investment in Whiteness: How White People Benefit from Identity Politics* (Philadelphia, 1998). Much of this work uses W. E. B. Du Bois's concept of the "psychological wage," and some writers explicitly acknowledge that debt. On Europe and elsewhere, see T. Denean Sharpley-Whiting, *Black Venus: Sexualized Savages, Primal Fears, and Primitive Narratives in French* (Durham, 1999); Anne McClintock, *Imperial Leather: Race, Gender, and Sexuality in the Colonial Conquest* (New York, 1995); Ann L. Stoler, *Race and the Education of Desire: Foucault's History of Sexuality and the Colonial Order of Things* (Durham, 1995). Challenges to the idea of race from within the scientific study of genetics began to emerge when scholars realized that genetic diversity within people whom history has taught us to consider as members of the same "race" often exceeds that between people whom we are taught to regard as members of different "races"; see R. C. Lewontin, "The Apportionment of Human Diversity," *Evolutionary Biology* 6 (1972): 381–98; William B. Provine, "Geneticists and Race," *American Zoologist* 26 (1986): 857–87; Luigi Cavalli-Sforza and Francesco Cavalli-Sforza, *The Great Human Diasporas: The History of Diversity and Evolution*, trans. Sarah Thorne (Reading, 1995). Fields notes these developments in the second version of her article, "Slavery, Race and Ideology," *New Left Review* 181 (May–June 1990): 96.

23. Kathleen M. Brown, *Good Wives, Nasty Wenches, and Anxious Patriarchs: Gender, Race, and Power in Colonial Virginia* (Chapel Hill, 1996). See also Kirsten Fischer, *Suspect Relations: Sex, Race, and Resistance in Colonial North Carolina* (Ithaca, 2002); Morgan, *Laboring Women*.

24. On the transformations of African cultures and religions in the Afro-Atlantic world, see Gilroy, *Black Atlantic*; Joan Dayan, *Haiti, History, and the Gods* (Berkeley, 1995); John Thornton, *Africa and Africans in the Making of the Atlantic World* (Cambridge, 1994); Robert Farris Thompson, *Flash of the Spirit: African and Afro-American Art and Culture* (New York, 1983); Stuckey, *Slave Culture*; Sandra Barnes, ed., *Africa's Ogun: Old World and New*, (Bloomington, 1997); Michael Gomez, *Exchanging Our Country Marks: The Transformation of African Identities in the Colonial and Antebellum South* (Chapel Hill, 1998); Sharla M. Fett, *Working Cures: Healing, Health, and Power on Southern Slave Plantations* (Chapel Hill, 2002); Linda Heywood, ed., *Central Africans and Cultural Transformations in the American Diaspora*, (Cambridge, 2002); James H. Sweet, *Recreating Africa: Culture, Kinship, and Religion in the African-Portuguese World, 1441–1770* (Chapel Hill, 2003); Herman L. Bennett, *Africans in Colonial Mexico: Absolutism, Christianity, and Afro-Creole Consciousness, 1570–1640* (Bloomington, 2003); Whitney L. Battle, "A Yard to Sweep: Race, Gender, and the Enslaved Landscape," (Ph.D. Diss., Univ. Texas, 2004).

PART ONE

Gender and Slavery

"Some Could Suckle over Their Shoulder"

Male Travelers, Female Bodies, and

the Gendering of Racial Ideology

JENNIFER L. MORGAN

*P*rior to their entry onto the stage of New World conquests, women of African descent lived in bodies unmarked by what would emerge as Europe's preoccupation with physiognomy—skin color, hair texture, and facial features presumed to be evidence of cultural deficiency. Not until the gaze of European travelers fell upon them would African women see themselves—or one another—as defined by "racial" characteristics. In a sense, European racial ideology developed in isolation from those who became the objects of racial scrutiny, but ideologies about race would soon be as important to the victims of racial violence as it was to the perpetrators. For English slave owners in the Americas, neither the decision to embrace the system of slavery nor the racialized notion of perpetual hereditary slavery was natural. During the decades after European arrival to the Americas, as various nations gained and lost footholds, followed fairy-tale rivers of gold, traded with and decimated native inhabitants, and ignored and mobilized Christian notions of conversion and just wars, English settlers constructed an elaborate edifice of forced labor on the foundation of emerging categories of race and reproduction. The process of calling blackness into being and causing it to become inextricable from brute labor took place in legislative acts, laws, wills, bills of sale, and plantation inventories just as it did in journals and adventurers' tales of travels. Indeed, the gap between intimate experience (the Africans with whom one lived and worked) and ideology (monstrous, barely human savages) would ultimately be bridged in the hearts and minds of prosaic settlers rather than in the tales of worldly adventurers.[1] African women and men would have to scrutinize and navigate the settlers' ideas and praxis to survive. Nonetheless, I turn here to travel narratives to explore developing categories of race and racial slavery. The process by which "Africans" became "blacks" who became "slaves" was initiated—on the European side at least—through a series of encounters made manifest in literary descriptions and only later expanded by the quotidian dimensions of slave ownership and settlement. The publication of images fueled the imaginations of settlers and would-be colonists alike and constituted an essential component of the ideological arsenal that European settlers brought to bear on African laborers.

The connections between forced labor and race became increasingly important during the life of the transatlantic slave trade as the enormity of the changes wrought by the settlement of the Americas and the mass enslavement of Africans slowly came into focus for Europeans. Despite real contemporary issues of race and racism, however, the link between what race has come to mean and the wide range of emerging ideas about difference in the early modern period must not be overdetermined. A concept of race rooted firmly in biology is primarily a late-eighteenth- and early-nineteenth-century phenomenon.[2] Nonetheless, the fact that a biologically driven explanation for differences borne on the body owes considerable debt to the science of the Enlightenment should not erase the connection between the body and socially inscribed categories of difference in the early modern period. As travelers and men of letters thought through the thorny entanglements of skin color, complexion, features, and hair texture, they constructed weighty notions of civility, nationhood, citizenship, and manliness on the foundation of the amalgam of nature and culture. Given the ways in which appearance became a trope for civility and morality, it is no surprise to find gender located at the heart of Europeans' encounter with and musings over the connection between bodies and Atlantic economies.

In June 1647, Englishman Richard Ligon left London on the ship *Achilles* to establish himself as a planter in the newly settled colony of Barbados. En route, Ligon's ship stopped in the Cape Verde islands for provisions and trade. There Ligon saw a black woman for the first time. He recorded the encounter in his *True and Exact History of Barbados*: she was a "Negro of the greatest beauty and majesty together: that ever I saw in one woman. Her stature large, and excellently shap'd, well favour'd, full eye'd, and admirably grac'd. [I] awaited her comming out, which was with far greater Majesty and gracefulness, than I have seen Queen Anne, descend from the Chaire of State."[3] Ligon's rhetoric must have surprised his English readers, for seventeenth-century images of black women did not usually evoke the monarchy as a referent.

Early modern English writers, did, however, conventionally set the black female figure against one that was white and therefore beautiful. Scholars of early modern England have noted the discursive place of black women: Peter Erickson calls the image of the black woman a trope for disrupted harmony; Lynda Boose sees black women in early modern English writing as symbolically "unrepresentable," embodying a deep threat to patriarchy; Kim Hall finds early modern English literature and material culture fully involved with a gendered racial discourse committed to constructing stable categories of whiteness and blackness.[4] As these and other scholars have shown, male travelers to Africa and the Americas contributed to a European discourse about women that was already fully active by the mid-seventeenth century, when Barbados became England's first colony wholly committed to slave labor. While descriptions of naked native females evoked desire, travelers depicted black women as simultaneously unwomanly and marked by a reproductive value that was both dependent on their sex and evidence of their lack of femininity. Writers mobilized femaleness alongside an unwillingness to allow African women to embody "proper" female space, which in turn produced a focus for the notion of racial difference. And thus, over the course of his journey, Ligon came to another view of black women. He wrote that their breasts "hang down below their Navels, so that when they stoop at their common work of weeding, they hang almost to the ground, that at a distance you would think they had six legs." In this context, black women's monstrous bodies symbolized their sole utility—the ability to produce both crops and other laborers.[5] This dual value, sometimes explicit and sometimes lurking in the background of slave owners' decision-making processes, would come to define most critically women's experience of enslavement.

Seemingly because of Ligon's appraisal of beauty at Cape Verde, modern historians have characterized his attitude toward the enslaved as "more liberal and humane than [that] of the generality of planters."[6] Nevertheless, his text indicated the kind of symbolic work required of black women in early modern English discourse. As Ligon penned his manuscript while in debtor's prison in 1653, he constructed a layered narrative in which the discovery of African women's monstrosity helped to assure the work's success. Taking the female body as a symbol of the deceptive beauty and ultimate savagery of blackness, Ligon allowed his readers to dally with him among beautiful black women only to seductively disclose their monstrosity over the course of the narrative. Ligon's narrative is a microcosm of a much larger ideological maneuver that juxtaposed the familiar with the unfamiliar—the beautiful woman who is also the monstrous laboring beast. As the tenacious and historically deep roots of racialist ideology become more evident, it also becomes clear that through the rubric of monstrously "raced" African women, Europeans found a way to articulate shifting perceptions of themselves as religiously, culturally, and phenotypically superior to the black or brown persons they sought to define. In the discourse used to justify the slave trade, Ligon's beautiful Negro woman was just as important as her "six-legged" counterpart. Both imaginary women marked a gendered and, as Kim Hall argues, stabilized whiteness on which European colonial expansionism depended.[7]

Well before the mid-seventeenth-century publication of Ligon's work, Europe as a whole and England in particular had seen the publication of New World and African narratives that used gender to convey an emerging notion of racialized difference. By the time English colonists arrived in the Americas, they already possessed the ethnohistoriographical tradition of depicting imaginary "natives" in which Ligon's account is firmly situated.[8] Travel accounts, which had already proven their popularity by the time Ligon's *History of Barbados* appeared, relied on gendered notions of European social order to project African cultural disorder. Gender did not operate as a more profound category of difference than race; instead, racialist discourse was deeply imbued with ideas about gender and sexual difference that became manifest only in contact with each other. White men who laid the discursive groundwork on which the "theft of bodies" could be justified relied on mutually constitutive ideologies of race and gender to affirm Europe's legitimate access to African labor.[9]

Travel accounts produced in Europe and available in England provided a corpus from which subsequent writers borrowed freely, reproducing images of Native American and African women that resonated with readers. Over the course of the second half of the seventeenth century, some eighteen new collections with descriptions of Africa and the West Indies were published and reissued in England; by the eighteenth century, more than fifty new synthetic works, reissued again and again, had found audiences in England.[10] Both the writers and the readers of these texts learned to dismiss the idea that women in the Americas and Africa might be innocuous or unremarkable. Rather, indigenous women bore an enormous symbolic burden, as writers from Walter Raleigh to Edward Long used them to mark metaphorically the symbiotic boundaries of European national identities and white supremacy. The conflict between perceptions of beauty and assertions of monstrosity such as Ligon's exemplified a much larger process through which the familiar became unfamiliar as beauty became beastliness and mothers became monstrous, a process that ultimately buttressed racial distinctions. Writers who articulated religious and moral justifications for the slave trade simultaneously grappled with the character of a contradictory female African body—a body both desirable and repulsive, available and untouchable, productive and reproductive, beautiful and black. By the time an eighteenth-century Carolina slave owner could look at an African woman with the detached gaze of an investor, travelers and philosophers had already subjected her to a host of taxonomic calculations. The meanings attached to the female African body were inscribed well before the establishment of England's colonial American plantations, and the intellectual work necessary to naturalize African enslavement—that is, the development of racialist discourse—was deeply implicated by gendered notions of difference and human hierarchy.

Europe had long a tradition of identifying Others through the monstrous physiognomy or sexual behavior of women. Armchair adventurers might shelve Pliny the Elder's ancient collection of monstrous races, *Historia Naturalis*, which cataloged the long-breasted, wild woman, alongside Herodotus's *History*, in which Indian and Ethiopian tribal women bore only one child in a lifetime.[11] European readers may have perused Julian's arguments with Augustine, in which Julian wrote that "barbarian and nomadic women give birth with ease, scarcely interrupting their travels to bear children," or have pondered Aristotle's belief that Egyptian women had too many children and were therefore inclined to give birth to monsters.[12] Images of female devils included sagging breasts as part of the iconography of danger and monstrosity. The medieval wild woman, whose breasts dragged on the ground when she walked and could be thrown over her shoulder, was believed to disguise herself with youth and beauty to enact seductions that would satisfy her "obsessed . . . craving for the love of mortal men."[13] The shape of her body marked her deviant sexuality, and both shape and sexuality evidenced her savagery.

Writers commonly looked to sociosexual deviance to indicate savagery in Europe and easily applied similar modifiers to Others in Africa and the Americas to mark European boundaries. According to *The Travels of Sir John Mandeville*, "in Ethiopia and in many other countries [in Africa,] folk lie all naked, . . . and the women have no shame of the men." Furthermore, "they wed there no wives, for all the women there be common . . . and when [women] have children they may give them to what man they will that hath companied with them."[14] Deviant sexual behaviors reflected the breakdown of natural laws—the absence of shame, the inability to identify lines of heredity and descent. This concern with deviant sexuality, articulated almost always through descriptions of women, is a constant theme in the travel writings of early modern Europe. Explorers and travelers to the New World and Africa brought with them expectations of distended breasts and dangerous sexuality. Indeed, Columbus relied on the female body to articulate the colonial venture at the outset of his voyage when he wrote that the earth was shaped like a breast, with the Indies composing the nipple; his urge for discovery of new lands was inextricable from the language of sexual conquest.[15]

Richard Eden's 1553 English translation of Sebastian Münster's *A Treatyse of the Newe India* opened to English readers Amerigo Vespucci's 1502 voyage. Vespucci did not use color to mark the difference of the people he encountered; rather, he described them in terms of their lack of social institutions ("they fight not for the enlargeing of theyr dominion for as much as they have no Magis-trates") and social niceties ("at theyr meate they use rude and barbarous fash-ions, lying on the ground without any table clothes or coverlet"). Nonetheless, his descriptions are not without positive attributes, and when he turned his attention to women, his language bristled with illuminating contradiction:

> Theyr bodies are verye smothe and clene by reason of theyr often washings. They are in other thinges filthy and withoute shame. Thei use no lawful coniunccion of marriage, and but every one hath as many women as him liketh, and leaveth them again at his pleasure. The women are very fruiteful, and refuse no laboure al the whyle they are with childe. They travayle in maner withoute payne, so that the nexte day they are cherefull and able to walke. Neyther have they theyr bellies wimpeled or loose, and hanginge pappes, by reason of bearinge manye children.[16]

The passage conveys admiration for indigenous women's strength in pregnancy and their ability to maintain aesthetically pleasing bodies, but it also illustrates the conflict at the heart of European discourse on gender and difference. It hinges on both a veiled critique of European female weakness and a dismissal of Amerindian women's pain. After English men and women were firmly settled in New World colonies, they too would struggle with the notion of female weak-ness; they needed both white and black women for hard manual labor but also needed to preserve a notion of white gentlewomen's unsuitability for physical labor.

Vespucci's familiarity with icons of difference led him to expect American women whose hanging breasts, along with their efficient labors, would mark their difference; thus, he registered surprise that women's bodies and breasts were neither "wimpeled" nor "hanginge." And, indeed, the icon of sagging breasts is mobilized incompletely in relation to Native American women, who ultimately escaped an iconographical association designed to cement female bodies with manual labor. Vespucci's impulse to linger over the notion of savage women's pert breasts was inextricable from his description of their reproductive labors, which in turn became a central component of descriptions of Africa and Africans. Vespucci presented a preliminary, ambiguously laudatory account of Amerindian women. Sixteenth-century European writers had not arrived at any kind of consensus about the significance of Amerindian difference. Potentially either Christian or heathen, Native Americans would for some time present something of a conundrum to the European imagination. Vespucci, then, of-fered an analysis of native culture that depended on female physiognomy to chart the way toward clear cultural categories. He mobilized the place of women in society as a cultural referent that evoked the "fylth" and shamelessness of all indigenous people. Thus, the passage exposes early modern English readers' sometimes ambivalent encounters with narratives that used women's behavior and physiognomy to mark European national identities and inscribe racial hierarchy.[17]

That ambivalence is conveyed in Münster's narration of Columbus's voyage, where Münster situated women both as intermediaries between the intrusive and indigenous peoples and as animal-like reproductive units.[18] On arriving at Hispaniola, Columbus's men "pursewing" the women and men who had come down to the shore "toke a womanne whom they brought to theyr shyppe . . . fyllinge her with delicate meates and wyne, and clothing her in fayre apparel, & so let her depart . . . to her companie."[19] This woman figured as a pliable emissary who could be returned to her people as a sign of Spanish generosity (in the form of food and wine) and civility (in the form of clothes). She could be improved by the experience. Indeed, her ability to receive European goods—to be made familiar through European intervention—served as evidence of her people's savagery, disorder, and distance from civility.[20] Münster considered another role for indigenous women and children whose contradiction evokes the complicated assessment of native women and their bodies. Describing the behavior of so-called cannibals, Münster avowed that "such children as they take, they geld to make them fat as we doo cocke chikyns and yonge hogges. . . . Such younge women as they take, they keepe for increase, as we doo hennes to laye egges."[21] The metaphor of domesticated livestock introduced a notion that became a recurrent theme concerning indigenous and enslaved women's twofold value to the European project of expansion and extraction. This metaphor, however, did not fully encompass the complexity of dangers indigenous women presented for Europe. Despite his respect for female reproductive hardiness, at the end of the volume Vespucci fixed the indigenous woman as a dangerous cannibal: "There came sodeynly a woman downe from a mountayne, bringing with her secretly a great stake with which she [killed a Spaniard]. The other wommene foorthwith toke him by the legges, and drewe him to the mountayne. . . . The women also which had slayne the yong man, cut him in pices even win the sight of the Spaniardes, shewinge them the pieces, and rosting them at a greate fyre."[22] Vespucci later made manifest the latent sexualized danger inherent in the man-slaying woman in a letter in which he wrote of women biting off the penises of their sexual partners, thus linking cannibalism—an absolute indicator of savagery and distance from European norms—to female sexual insatiability.[23]

The label *savage* was not uniformly applied to Amerindian people. Indeed, in the context of European national rivalries, the indigenous woman became somewhat less savage. In the mid- to late sixteenth century, the bodies of women figured at the borders of national identities more often than at the edges of a larger European identity. Italian traveler Girolamo Benzoni, in his *History of the New World* (a 1572 narrative that appeared in multiple translations), used sexualized indigenous women both as markers of difference and as indicators of Spanish immorality. His first description of a person of the Americas (in Venezuela in 1541) occurred at the beginning of his story:

> Then came an Indian woman . . . such a woman as I have never seen before nor since seen the like of; so that my eyes could not be satisfied with looking at her for wonder. . . . She was quite naked, except where modesty forbids, such being the custom throughout all this country; she was old and painted black, with long hair down to her waist, and her ear-rings had so weighted her ears down, as to make them reach her shoulders, a thing wonderful to see. . . . [H]er teeth were black, her mouth large, and she had a ring in her nostrils . . . so that she appeared like a monster to us, rather than a human being.[24]

Benzoni's description draws upon a sizable catalog of cultural distance packed with meaning made visible by early modern conventions of gendered difference. His inability to satisfy his gaze speaks to an obfuscation Ligon enacted a hundred years later and one that Stephen Greenblatt argues is the defining metaphor of the colonial encounter. Benzoni's "wonder" created distance.[25] In the context of a society concerned with the deception of cosmetics, as Hall argues, the woman's black-faced body was both cause for alarm and evidence of a dangerous inversion of norms. Her nakedness, her ears, and her nose—all oddities accentuated by willful adornment—irrevocably placed her outside the realm of the familiar. Her blackened teeth and large mouth evoked a sexualized danger that, as Benzoni explicitly states, linked her and, by implication, her people to inhuman monstrosity.[26]

In evoking this singular woman—the like of whom he had never seen—Benzoni departed from his contemporaries. His used his description of her to open his narrative and, through her, placed his reader in the realm of the exotic. This "wonderful" woman alerted readers to the distance Benzoni had traveled, but he deployed another, more familiar set of female images to level a sustained critique of Spanish colonial expansion and thereby to insist on the indigenous woman's connection, or nearness, to a familiar European femininity.

> Capt. Pedro de Calize arrived with upward of 4000 slaves. . . . It was really a most distressing thing to see the way in which these wretched creatures naked, tired, and lame were treated [by the Spaniards]; exhausted with hunger, sick, and despairing. The *unfortunate mothers*, with two or three children on their shoulders or clinging round their necks, [were] overwhelmed with tears and grief, all tied with cords or with iron chains. . . . Nor was there a girl but had been violated by the depredators; wherefore, from too much indulgence, many Spaniards entirely lost their health.[27]

Benzoni used the pathetic figures of the fecund mother and the sexually violated young girl to condemn the Spaniards. Such a move was common in the aftermath of Las Casas's *In Defense of Indians* (ca. 1550) and amid European nations' intensified resentment of Spain's control to access to the Americas. In "Discoverie of the . . . Empire of Guiana" (1598), Raleigh stated that he "suffered not any man to . . . touch any of [the natives'] wives or daughters: Which course so contrary to the Spaniards (who tyrannize over them in all things) drewe them to admire her [English] majestie."[28] Although he permitted himself and his men to gaze at naked Indian women, Raleigh accentuated the restraint the Englishmen exercised. In so doing, he used the untouched bodies of Native American women to mark national boundaries and signal the civility and superiority of English colonizers in contrast to the sexually violent Spaniards. Moreover, in linking the eroticism of indigenous women to the sexual attention of Spanish men, Raleigh signaled the Spaniards' "lapse into savagery."[29] Benzoni, too, inscribed the negative consequences of too-close associations with indigenous women. For him, sexual proximity to local women depleted Spanish strength. As he prepared to abandon the topic of Indian slavery for a lengthy discussion of Columbus's travels, Benzoni again invoked motherhood to prove Spanish depravity: "All the slaves that the Spaniards catch in these provinces are sent [to the Caribbean] and even when *some of the Indian women are pregnant by these same Spaniards*, they sell them without any consciences."[30]

This rhetorical flourish, through female bodies, highlighted the contradictions of the familiar and unfamiliar in the Americas. Because of her nakedness and her monstrous adornments, the woman who opened Benzoni's narrative could not be familiar to conquistadors and colonizers, yet in her role as a mother, sexual victim, or even sexually arousing female she evoked the familiar. Benzoni sidestepped the tension inherent in the savage and violated mother by using her to publicize Spanish atrocity. In effect, the "black legend" created (among other things) this confusing figure of extractors and extracted, and the indigenous woman's familiarity had to be neutralized. Thus, the pathos of raped mothers ultimately could be laid at Europe's door, where it signified disdain for the Spanish and disregard for ultimately monstrous women.[31]

The monstrosity of the native mother had an important visual corollary. A mid-sixteenth-century Portuguese artist, for example, depicted the devil wearing a Brazilian headdress and rendered his demonic female companions with long, sagging breasts.[32] Toward the end of the century, a multivolume collection of travel accounts published in Latin and German augmented the evolving discourse of European civility and visual images of overseas encounters.[33] As Bernadette Bucher has shown, the early volumes of Theodor de Bry's *Grand Voyages* (1590) depicted the Algonkians of Virginia and the Timucuas of Florida as classical Europeans: Amerindian bodies mirrored ancient Greek and Roman statuary, modest virgins covered their breasts, and infants suckled at the high, small breasts of young attractive women (see figures 1, 2, and 3). As Joyce

Chaplin has illustrated, the English encounter with Native American bodies would ultimately "gesture towards racial identification of the body" as English settlers compared themselves favorably to Native Americans, whom they saw as weak.[34] Nonetheless, even years before the English arrived in the colonies, visual and literary images were laying the groundwork for an ideology of European superiority. Thus, the visual depictions of native women were always in flux. De Bry's third volume, *Voyages to Brazil*, published in 1592, portrayed the Indian as aggressive and savage and offered a changed representation of women's bodies. The new woman was a cannibal with breasts that fell below her waist. She licked the juices of grilled human flesh from her fingers and adorned the frontispiece of the map of Tierra del Fugo (see figures 4 and 5). Bucher argues that the absence of a suckling child in these depictions is essential to the image's symbolic weight.[35] Their childlessness signified the women's cannibalism—they consumed rather than produced. Although women alone did not exemplify cannibalism, women with long breasts came to mark such savagery in Native Americans for English readers. As depictions of Native Americans traversed the gamut from savage to noble, the long-breasted woman became a clear signpost of savagery, a stark contrast to her high-breasted counterpart. Other images of monstrous races, such as the headless Euaipanonoma, the one-footed Sciopods, and the Astomi, who lived on the aroma of apples, slowly vanished from Europe's imagined America and Africa. After Europeans reached Africa, however, the place of motherhood in the complex of savagery and race became central to the figure of the black woman. Unlike other monstrosities, the long-breasted woman—who, when depicted with her child, carried the full weight of productive savagery—maintained her place in the lexicon of conquest and exploration.

As he described one of the first European slaving voyages to West Africa, Portuguese trader Gomes Azurara pinpointed the precise location of African women for European slave traders and settlers in the economy of production and control:

> But rather they returned to their ship and on the next day landed a little way distant from there, where they espied some of the wives of those Guineas walking. And it seemeth that they were going nigh to a creek collecting shellfish, and they captured one of them, who would be as much as thirty years of age, with a son of hers who would be of about two, and also a young girl of fourteen years, who had well-formed limbs and also a favorable presence for a Guinea; but the strength of the woman was much to be marveled at, for not one of the three men who came upon her but would have had a great labour in attempting to get her on the boat. And so one of our men, seeing the delay they were making, during which it might be that some of the dwellers of the land would come upon them, conceived it well to take her son from her and to carry him to the boat; and love of the child compelled the mother to follow after it, without great pressure on the part of the two who were bringing her.[36]

Figure 1. Young virgin covering her breast. From Thomas Hariot, *A Brief and True Report of the New Found Land of Virginia*, in Thedor de Bry, *Grand Voyages*, vol. 1 (Frankfurt am Main, 1590), plate 6. Courtesy of the John Work Garrett Library of the Johns Hopkins University.

Figure 2. Woman suckling child. From *Eurom Quae in Florida . . .*, in Theodor de Bry, *Grand Voyages*, vol. 2 (Frankfurt am Main, 1591), plate 20. Courtesy of the John Work Garrett Library of the Johns Hopkins University.

Figure 3. Native American woman with her child, two views. From Thomas Hariot, *A Brief and True Report of the New Found Land of Virginia*, Theodor de Bry, *Grand Voyages*, vol. 1 (Frankfurt am Main, 1590), plate 10. Courtesy of the John Work Garrett Library of the Johns Hopkins University.

Figure 4. Woman (at left) holding leg. From *Memorabile Proviniciae Brasilae . . .* , in Theodor de Bry, *Grand Voyages*, vol. 3 (Frankfurt am Main, 1592), 179. Courtesy of the John Work Garrett Library of the Johns Hopkins University.

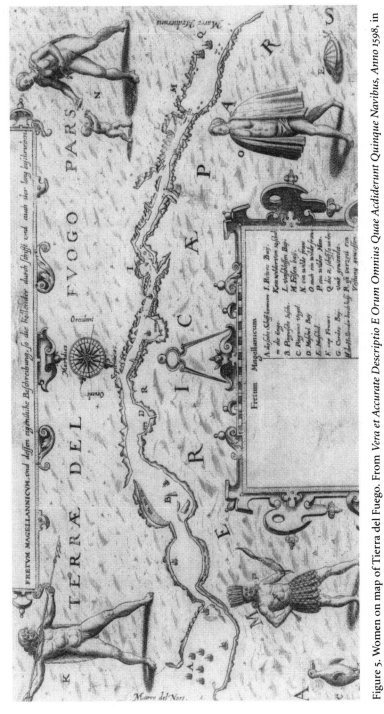

Figure 5. Women on map of Tierra del Fuego. From *Vera et Accurate Descriptio E Orum Omnius Quae Acciderunt Quinque Navibus, Anno 1598*, in Theodor de Bry, *Grand Voyages*, vol. 9 (Frankfurt am Main, 1602), 56. Courtesy of the John Work Garrett Library of the Johns Hopkins University.

Those who would capture African women to exploit their labors in the Americas would have to grapple with and harness those women's dual identity as workers and parents; having done so, the enslavers would inaugurate a language of race and racial hierarchy in which that dualism was reduced to denigration and mobilized as evidence of European distinction.

English travelers to West Africa drew on American narrative traditions in working to establish a clearly demarcated line that would ultimately define the English. Richard Hakluyt's collection of travel narratives, *Principal Navigations*, portrayed Africa and Africans in both positive and negative terms. The authors' shifting assessments of Africa and Africans "produc[ed] an Africa which is familiar and unfamiliar, civil and savage, full of promise and full of threat." Sixteenth-century ambivalence about England's role in overseas expansion required a forceful antidote. In response, Hakluyt presented texts that, through an often conflicted depiction of African peoples, ultimately differentiated between Africa and England and erected a boundary that made English expansion reasonable, profitable, and moral in the face of confused and uncivilized peoples.[37]

The bodies of women on the West African coast, like those of their New World counterparts, symbolized the parameters of the colonizing venture. But because England's contact with West Africa took place in a historical moment marked by the determination to "seed" valuable American colonies with equally valuable workers, the imagined African woman's body in English writings was more rigidly deployed and thus far less likely to appear as an object of lust or even potential beauty. English writers regularly directed readers' attention to the topic of African women's physiognomy and reproductive experience. In so doing, these writers drew attention to the complex interstices of desire and repulsion that shaped European men's appraisal of Amerindian and African women. Sixteenth- and seventeenth-century writers conveyed a sexual grotesquerie that ultimately made African women indispensable because it showed the gendered ways of putting African savagery to productive use. Although titillation was certainly a component of these accounts, to write of sex was also to define and expand the boundaries of profit through productive and reproductive labor.

The symbolic weight of indigenous women's sexual and childbearing practices moved from the Americas to Africa and continued to be brought to bear on England's literary imagination in ways that rallied familiar notions of gendered difference for English readers. John Lok's account of his 1554 voyage to Guinea, published forty years later in Hakluyt's collection, reinscribed Africans' place in the human hierarchy. Borrowing verbatim from Richard Eden's 1555 translation of Peter Martyr's description of the "New Worlde," Lok described all Africans as "people of beastly living." He located the proof of this in *women's* behavior: Among the Garamantes, women "are common: for they contract no matrimonie, neither have respect to chastitie."[38] This description of the Garamantes first appeared in Pliny, was reproduced again in Iulius Solinus's sixth-century *Polyhistor*, and reappeared in travel accounts through the Middle Ages and into the sixteenth and seventeenth centuries.[39] As he struggled to situate his new expertise on Brazil, sixteenth-century writer André Thevet noted that he was not surprised by the easy dissolution of family ties among native Brazilians because this was also the case among the "ancient Egyptians . . . before they had any laws."[40] Traders to the new worlds of Africa and the Americas did their homework before departure and grew adept at mobilizing symbols that resonated with their readers. Eden's Martyr has a long descriptive passage on African oddities; its reference to Garamante women's absence of "chastity" is followed by one to a tribe whose members "have no speeche, but rather a grynnynge and chatterynge. There are also people without heades cauled Blemines, havyinge their eyes and mouth in theyr breast."[41] Because he did not reproduce the entire paragraph, Lok suggested that by the end of the sixteenth century, the oddities of Africa could be consolidated into the particular symbol of women's sexual availability.

William Towrson's narrative of his 1555 voyage to Guinea, also published by Hakluyt in 1589, further exhibits this kind of distillation. Towrson depicted women and men as largely indistinguishable. They "goe so alike, that one cannot know a man from a woman but by their breastes, which in the most part be very foule and long, hanging downe low like the udder of a goate."[42] This perhaps represents the first time an Englishman in Africa explicitly used breasts as an identifying trait of beastliness and difference. He went on to maintain that "diverse of the women have such exceeding long breasts, that some of them will lay the same upon the ground and lie downe by them."[43] Lok and Towrson represented African women's bodies and sexual behavior as a means of distinguishing Africa from Europe. Towrson in particular gave readers only two analogies through which to view and understand African women—beasts and monsters.

Some thirty years after the original Hakluyt collections were published, other writers continued to mobilize African women to do complex symbolic work. In 1622, Richard Jobson's *The Golden Trade* appeared in London, chronicling his 1620–21 trading ventures up the Gambia River.[44] Jobson described strong and noble people on the one hand and barbarous and bestial people on the other, and African women personified his nation's struggle with the familiar and unfamiliar African, a struggle that can also be located along the axis of desire and repulsion. Jobson's associations with the "Fulbie" and "Maudingo" people furnishes evidence of this struggle. He described Fulbie men as beastlike, "seemingly more senseless, than our Country beasts," a state he attributed to their close association with the livestock they raised.[45] Unlike many of his contemporaries, Jobson regarded African women with admiration. In contrast to Fulbie men, the women were "excellently well bodied, having very good features, with long blacke haire."[46] He maintained that the discovery of a "mote or haire" in milk would cause these dairywomen to "blush, in defence of her cleanely meaning."[47] This experience of shame encapsulated a morality and civility to which only women had access. Among the "Maudingo" of Cassan, newly married women "observ[e] herein a shamefast modestie, not to be looked for, *among such a kind of black and barbarous people.*"[48]

Despite his well-meaning description of African women, Jobson recorded their civil behavior only when it deviated from what he and his readers expected. His appreciation of the Fulbie women and Maudingo people was predicated on their ability to exceed his expectations. This kind of appreciation of the exceptional is a rhetorical move that would recur again and again in the language of slave owners and legislators. Exceptional African women were rewarded only insofar as they reinforced white female behavioral norms. To Jobson, African women proved the precarious nature of African civility. His narrative, even at its most laudatory, always rested on the inferiority of African peoples. Although he described the history of kingship and the great importance of ancestral honor among the Maudingos, Jobson still contended that "from the King to the slave, they are all perpetuall beggers from us."[49] His "wonder" at women's modesty alerted his readers to the culture's abnormality and implicitly to its larger absence of civility. Even as he depicted them positively, women became part of the demonstration that despite kings and history, these Africans were barbarous and ripe for exploitation.

Unlike many of his contemporaries, Jobson leveled his open-eyed gaze primarily at male African sexuality. In a unique twist of consequences of the curse of Ham, Jobson maintained that African men carried the mark of the curse in the size of their sexual organs: they "are furnisht with such members as are after a sort burthensome unto them, whereby their women being once conceived with child . . . accompanies the man no longer, because he shall not destroy what is conceived." Jobson's interpretation of the penis corresponded to others' ideas about women's breasts. Both sexual organs were seen as pendulous and distended, somehow disembodied from their owner, and physically burdensome. He subsequently returned to the subject of women only in terms of their subjugation to men, certain that "there is no other woman [that] can be under more servitude."[50]

Other English publications continued to locate evidence of savagery and legitimate exploitation in women. After Hakluyt died, Samuel Purchas took up the mantle of editor and published twenty additional volumes in Hakluyt's series beginning in 1624.[51] In his translation of a fourteenth-century narrative by Leo Africanus, Purchas presented a West Africa sharply delineated from the civilized. Discussion of "the Land of Negros," for example, was preceded by and thus set apart from a long section on North Africa. "Negros," unlike their northern neighbors, lived "a bruitish and savage life, without any King, Governour, Common-wealth, or knowledge of Husbandry." To confirm this savagery, Leo Africanus asserted that the Africans were "clad in skinnes of beasts, neither had they any peculiar wives . . . and when night came they resorted . . . both men and women into one Cottage together . . . and each man choosing his [woman] which hee had most fanciee unto."[52] This indictment opened the descriptive passages on "Ghinea," thereby making women's sexual availability the defining metaphor of colonial accessibility and black African savagery. The nudity of African and Native American women was not incidental to their savagery. Nakedness was an essential part of most descriptions of native peoples in this period and became the precursor to discussions of women's physical and reproductive anomalies.[53]

In the next volume, Purchas published Andrew Battell's *Strange Adventures*.[54] Battell had spent seventeen years in Angola, from 1590 to 1607, some as captive, some as escapee, and some in service to King James. For sixteen months, Battell stayed near "Dongo" with the "Gaga" people, "the greatest Canibals and man-eaters that bee in the World."[55] Like sixteenth-century observers in Brazil, he highlighted women's unnatural reproductive behavior. This "tribe" of fighters and cannibals rejected motherhood. According to Battell, "the women are very fruitfull, but they enjoy none of their children: for as soon as the woman delivered of her Childe, it is presently buried quick [alive]; So that there is not one Childe brought up."[56] Battell positioned his discussion of this unnatural behavior in such a way as to close the debate on African savagery. Savagery began, in his account, with cannibalism and ended with mothers who consented to the killing of the children they bore.

Purchas also published a translation of Pieter de Marees's *A Description of Historicall Declaration of the Golden Kingdome of Guinea*. This narrative was first published in Dutch in 1602, was translated into German and Latin for the de Bry volumes (1603–34), and appeared in French in 1605. Plagiarism by seventeenth- and eighteenth-century writers gave it still wider circulation.[57] Here, too, black women embodied African savagery. De Marees began by describing the people at Sierra Leone as "very greedie eaters, and no lesse drinkers, and very lecherous, and theevish, and much addicted to uncleanenesse; one man hath as many wives as he is able to keepe and maintaine. The women also are much addicted to leacherie, specially, with strange Country people [and] are also great Lyers, and not to be credited."[58] As did most of his contemporaries, de Marees invoked women's sexuality to castigate the incivility of both men and women. Women's savagery does not stand apart. Rather, it indicts the whole: all Africans were savage. The passage displays African males' savagery alongside their access to multiple women. Similarly, de Marees located evidence of African women's savagery in their sexual desire. Given the association of unrestricted sexuality with native savagery, black female sexuality alone might have been enough to implicate the entire continent. But de Marees further castigated West African women: they delivered children surrounded by men, women, and youngsters "in most shameless manner . . . before them all."[59] This absence of shame (evoked explicitly, as here, or implicitly in the constant references to nakedness in other narratives) worked to establish distance. Readers, titillated by the topics discussed and thus tacitly shamed, found themselves further distanced from the shameless subject of the narrative. De Marees dwelled on the brute nature of shameless African women. He marveled that "when the child is borne [the mother] goes to the water to wash and make clean her selfe, not once dreaming of a moneths lying-in . . . as women here with us use to doe; they use no Nurses to helpe them when they lie in child-bed, neither seeke to lie dainty and soft. . . . The next day after, they goe abroad in the streets, to doe their businesse."[60] This testimony to African women's physical strength and emotional indifference is even more emphatic in the original Dutch. In the most recent translation from the Dutch, the passage continues, "This shows that the women here are of a cruder nature and stronger posture than the Females in our Land in Europe."[61]

De Marees went on to inscribe an image of women's reproductive identity whose influence persisted long after his original publication. "When [the child] is two or three monethes old, the mother ties the childe with a peece of cloth at her backe. . . . When the child crieth to sucke, the mother casteth one of her dugs backeward over her shoulder, and so the childe suckes it as it hangs."[62] Frontispieces for the de Marees narrative and the African narratives in de Bry approximate the over-the-shoulder breast-feeding de Marees described, thereby creating an image that could symbolize the continent (see figures 6 and 7). In 1634, Thomas Herbert drew the image of the female Hottentot "as a sort of she-devil nursing a child over her shoulder."[63] Herbert wrote a lengthy "description of the Savage Inhabitants" of the South African cape in which he treated men and women as identical. They were together uniformly marked—by nature or by culture—as surprisingly different from Europeans. Their hair "rather like wooll than haire, tis blacke and knotty," and "their eares are long and made longer by pondrous bables."[64] The only descriptions that distinguished women from men referred to alchemy of the bodies and behaviors of savagery that simultaneously marked the boundaries of English civility. "They are very ceremonious in thanksgiving, for wanting requitals, if you give a woman a piece of bread, she will immediately pull by her [loincloth] flap and discover her *pudenda*. A courtesie commended them, I suppose, by some Dutch-ill-bred Saylor, for taught it they are, they say, by Christians. And English men, I know, have greater modestie." While this detail was produced in service of English gentility and the titillation of readers, the easy and willing display of genitalia in exchange for bread spoke both to Hottentot immodesty and a relative state of undress. A brief note about their cannibalism was shortly followed by the illustration and a short descriptive paragraph that noted that "the women give their Infants sucke as they hang at their backes, the uberous dugge stretched over her shoulder."[65] Herbert's image is remarkable for the monstrous posture of the suckling child who apparently hangs from its mother's back with an almost insectlike tenacity while holding the "uberous dugge" between its teeth. Among the visual depictions of over-the-shoulder breast-feeding, this is undoubtedly the most violent.

The image, in more or less extreme form, remained a compelling one, offering a single narrative-visual moment evidence that black women's difference was both cultural (in this strange habit) and physical (in this strange ability). The word *dug*, which by the early seventeenth century meant both a woman's breasts and an animal's teats, connoted a brute animality that de Marees reinforced through his descriptions of small children "lying downe in their house, like Dogges, [and] rooting in the ground like Hogges" and of "boyes and girles [that] goe starke naked as they were borne, with their private members all open, without any shame or civilitie."[66] Herbert too elicited the animal connection by drawing the Hottentot woman clutching entrails in her hand while her child latched on with the intensity of a parasitic arthropod.

As Englishmen traversed the uncertain ground of nature and culture, African women became a touchstone for physical and behavioral curiosity both within Africa and in the Americas and Europe. Fynes Moryson wrote of Irish women in 1617 that they "have very great Dugges, some so big as they give their children suck over their Shoulders." But it is important that he connected this ability to being "not laced at all," or to the lack of corsetry.[67] While nudity—a state in which the absence of corsetry is certainly implicit—is constantly at play in descriptions of African women, the overwhelming physicality of the image is disaggregated from culture and instead becomes part of African female nature, something no amount of corsetry would set right. It is perhaps indicative of his national insularity in matters of the slave trade that Swiss physician Felix Spoeri commented on the length of enslaved women's breasts in seventeenth-century Barbados and explained it with an amalgam of nature and culture: "By nature slave women have very long breasts because they go about naked all the time."[68] In his 1670 publication on Africa, Nicolas Villaut suggested that the shape of African noses similarly resulted from the bad behavior of African mothers, "whose children sleeping many times whilst the mother is walking or at work, knock their noses against their shoulders and so in time they become flat; if they cry out for the teat, they throw their breasts over their shoulder and let them suck."[69] Drawing on Villaut, Robert Burton reproduced this speculation, noting that "they give them the breast over their shoulders, and this may be the reason of the flatness of their Noses by their knocking them continually against the Back and Shoulders of the Mother . . . for it is observed that the

INDIÆ ORIENTALIS
PARS VI.
VERAM ET HISTO-
RICAM DESCRIPTIONEM
AVRIFERI REGNI GVINEÆ, AD AFRICAM
PERTINENTIS, QVOD ALIAS LITTVS DE MINA VO-
cant, continens, Qua situs loci, ratio vrbium & domorum, portus
item & flumina varia, cum variis incolarum superstitionibus, e-
ducatione, forma, commerciis, linguis & moribus,
succincta breuitate explicantur & per-
censentur.

LATINITATE EX GERMANICO DONATA

Studio & opera

M. GOTARDI ARTHVS DANTISCANI.

Illustrata vero viuis, & artificiosissime in as incisis iconibus,
inque lucem edita

à

Iohanne Theodoro & Iohanne Israel de Bry fratribus.

Francofurti ad Mœnum ex Officina Wolfgangi Richteri, sumpti-
bus Iohan, Theodori & Iohan. Israel de Bry fratribus.

Anno M. DCIV.

Figure 6. Woman breast-feeding over her shoulder. Title page from *Verum et*
Historicam Descriptionem Avriferi Regni Guineaa, in Theodor de Bry, *Small Voyages*,
vol. 6 (Frankfurt am Main, 1604). Note the contrast between this later depiction and
the early representation of a Native American woman in figure 7. Courtesy of the John
Work Garrett Library of the Johns Hopkins University.

Figure 7. Women in Africa. From *Verum et Historicam Descriptionem Avriferi Regni Guineaa*, in Theodor de Bry, *Small Voyages*, vol. 6 (Frankfurt am Main, 1604), 3. Courtesy of the John Work Garrett Library of the Johns Hopkins University.

children of their Gentry whose Mothers do not labour nor carry their Infants about them; have very comely Noses."[70] Burton's addendum about class is quite important because it reflects the very real way in which the discursive landscape of appearance was disrupted by competing notions of class and sovereignty— the biological markers of racial difference that legitimate enslavement can here be interrupted by the behavior of the gentry, whose autonomy and freedom from enslavement might thus be assured. The confluence of mothers' abnormal bodies and their ability to inscribe racial characteristics on their children had long currency. Writing in the late eighteenth century, Johan Blumenbach also speculated that the pounding of a child's face on its mother's back shaped facial features. He claimed that the fact that such features could be seen on aborted fetuses was the result of a "natural degeneration" over time; thus, the African women again embodied the behavioral and physical characteristics that degraded an entire race of people.[71]

When John Ogilby compiled *America* in 1671, his more-than-six-hundred-page volume became the first comprehensive English introduction to the continent. His detailed and well-illustrated account of the Americas included the Columbus and Vespucci narratives (among many others) discussed previously. Readers learned of women in Hispaniola who "destroy'd the Infants in their Wombs, that they might not bear slaves for the Spaniards" and were again reminded of the ease with which Caribbean women give birth, an ease reinforced by the inversion of men taking to their beds for an extended celebratory "lying-in" on the birth of their first sons. Although replete with nudity, cannibalism, and warfare, the illustrations are almost uniformly of well-proportioned women: the sagging breasts of the fifteenth century have all but disappeared (see figure 8). However, in the last quarter of the text, the visual sense of Indian women is altered. Suddenly, the women on the maps of Granada and Guiana tell a familiar tale with their breasts. The tale is explicated in the appendix on Chile, where Ogilby explains that "some of them have such great breasts, that throwing them over their shoulders they suckle their Children."[72] These scattered images of sagging breasts in the late seventeenth century can only be read as distinct from the sixteenth-century evocations of Amerindian women's bodies. For Ogilby, the breasts seem to signify a set of concerns about Granada, Guiana, and Chile, perhaps as a means of situating them as distinct from other parts of the Americas. Just as African women's physiognomy became shorthand for savagery, the shifting image of America also became home to such physically inscribed differences (see figures 9, 10, and 11). But the enduring connection between African women's sexuality and difference at this point spoke specifically to the English market's increasingly apparent need for slaves and the inevitability that African women and men would satisfy that need.

Figure 8. High-breasted women illustrating America. From John Ogilby, *America* (London, 1671), frontispiece. Courtesy of New York Public Library.

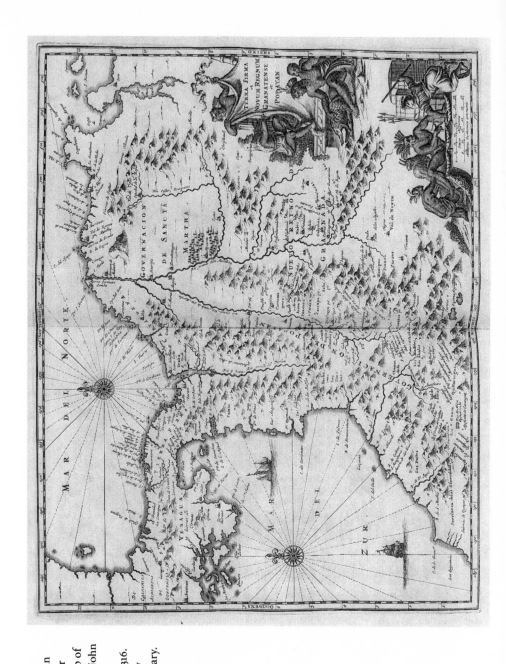

Figure 9. Native American woman suckling over her shoulder on map of Granada. From John Ogilby, *America* (London, 1671), 316. Courtesy of New York Public Library.

Figure 10. Native American woman with sagging breasts on map of Guiana. From John Ogilby, *America* (London, 1671), 341. Courtesy of New York Public Library.

Figure 11. Native American woman suckling over her shoulder in Chile. From John Ogilby, *America* (London, 1671), 360. Courtesy of New York Public Library.

African women's Africanness became contingent on the linkages between sexuality and a savagery that fitted them for both productive and reproductive labor. Women enslaved in the seventeenth and early eighteenth centuries did not give birth to men-children, but descriptions of African women in the Americas almost always highlighted their fecundity along with their capacity for manual labor.[73] Erroneous observations about African women's propensity for easy birth and breast-feeding reassured colonizers that these women could easily perform hard labor in the Americas; at the same time, such observations erected a barrier of difference between Africa and England. Seventeenth-century English medical writers, both men and women, equated breast-feeding and tending to children with difficult work, and the practice of wealthy women forgoing breast-feeding in favor of wet nurses was widespread.[74] English women and men anticipated pregnancy and childbirth with extreme uneasiness and fear of death, but they knew that the experience of pain in childbirth marked women as members of the Christian community.[75] As Saidiya Harman argues, the absence of pain—either in childbirth or at the receiving end of the lash or branding iron—becomes "absolutely essential to the spectacle of contented subjugation" and to the notion that Africans are in fact improved by slavery.[76] Pain-free and disinterested delivery of children could strike contemporary English readers only as a matter of astonishment and wonder. Upon further reflection, the connection between African women's reproductive lives and their suitability for hard manual labor would link their status with their bodies in a way distinct from but related to the biology of race. Roxann Wheeler has recently argued that "the performance of labor is a more reliable index of status than other activities or physical attributes."[77] But the double meaning of the terms *labor* and *travail* as well as the need to articulate a social space for Africans in the context of emerging socioeconomic ideologies of difference, biology, and lifelong forced labor collapsed the performance of work into the bodies of African women.

African women entered the developing discourse of national resources through an emphasis on what Europeans perceived as Africans' mechanical and meaningless childbearing. Metaphors of domestic livestock and sexually located cannibalism initially touched on notions of reproduction for consumption. Neither Native American women and men nor the children they produced—"fattened like capons"—added anything to English coffers. By about the turn of the seventeenth century, however, as England joined in the transatlantic slave trade, assertions of African savagery began to be predicated less on consumption and cannibalism and more on production and reproduction. African women came into the conversation in the context of England's need for productivity. Descriptions of these women that highlighted the apparent ease and indifference of their reproductive lives created a mechanistic image that ultimately became located within the national economy. Whereas English women's reproductive work took place solely in the domestic economy, African women's reproductive work embodied the developing discourses of extraction and forced labor at the heart of England's design for the Americas. By the eighteenth century, the contrasting connection between the "inscrutable and sexually polymorphous" African women and the "chaste maternal" English woman together offered the continent up for English consumption.[78]

By the eighteenth century, English writers rarely used black women's breasts or behavior for anything but concrete evidence of barbarism in Africa. In *A Description of the Coasts of North and South-Guinea*, begun in the 1680s and completed and published almost forty years later, John Barbot "admired the quietness of the poor babes, so carr'd about at their mothers' backs . . . and how freely they suck the breasts, which are always full of milk, over their mothers' shoulders, and sleep soundly in that odd posture."[79] William Snelgrave introduced his *New Account of Some Parts of Guinea and the Slave-Trade* with an anecdote designed to illustrate the benevolence of the trade. He described himself rescuing an infant from human sacrifice and reuniting the child with its mother, who "had much Milk in her Breasts." He accented the barbarism in those who had attempted to sacrifice the child and claimed that the reunion cemented his goodwill in the eyes of the enslaved, who, thus convinced of the "good notion of White Men," caused no problems during the voyage to Antigua.[80] Having used the figure of the breast-feeding woman to legitimize his slaving endeavor, Snelgrave went on to describe the roots of Whydah involvement in the slave trade and its defeat in war at the hands of the kingdom of Dahomey (both coastal cities in present-day Ghana). "Custom of the Country allows Polygamy to an excessive degree . . . whereby the land was become so stocked with people" that the slave trade flourished. Moreover, the wealth generated by the trade made the beneficiaries so "proud, effeminate and luxurious" that they were easily conquered by the more disciplined (that is, masculine) nation of Dahomey.[81] Polygamy and the abundance of women "unclaimed for monogamy," always an important trope of difference in travel accounts to Africa, signaled an unambiguous distance between Europe and Africa. Thus, women's fecundity undermined African society from without and within as it provided a constant stream of potential slaves and depleted the manhood of potentially dangerous adversaries.[82]

Eighteenth-century abolitionist John Atkins similarly adopted the icon of black female bodies in his writings on Guinea. "Childing, and their Breasts always pendulous, stretches them to so unseemly a length and Bigness that some . . . could suckle over their shoulder."[83] Atkins then considered the idea of African women copulating with apes. He noted that "at some places the Negroes have been suspected of Bestiality" and, while maintaining the ruse of scholarly distance, suggested that evidence "would tempt one to suspect the Fact." The evidence lay mostly in apes' resemblance to humans but was bolstered by the "Ignorance and Stupidity" of black women, who were unable "to guide or controll lust."[84] Abolitionists and antiabolitionists alike accepted the connections between race and black women's monstrous and fecund bodies. African women bridged other important differences between Atkins and Snelgrave. Although he was an avid slave trader, Snelgrave believed that Africans and Europeans shared a single origin, while Atkins, an abolitionist, was convinced that the two were separate species.[85] It is particularly noteworthy, then, that both men mobilized women's corporeal traits to further their quite different intellectual and political agendas.

The visual shorthand of the sagging-breasted African savage held sway for decades. In Peter Kolb's 1731 narrative of the Cape of Good Hope, a "Hottentot" woman sits smoking marijuana while her nursing child peers over her shoulder. The image, quite distinct from Herbert's monstrous Hottentot a century earlier, at first glance embodies a lethargy that might disrupt the notion of African women as constant workers. But she sits as if only for a moment, staff in hand, strong legs ready to be once again on the move, a woman not part of any discernable family or social group whose pipe, physique, and childbearing clearly lie outside the realm of European femininity (see figure 12).[86] In the 1785 edition of Ansham and John Churchill's *Collection of Voyages* (originally published in 1732 and reprinted three times by 1752), an illustration, "A Description of the Habits of Most Countries of the World," prefaces a discussion of clothing (see figure 13). The bottom half of the taxonomic illustration groups various seminude savages alongside Spaniards and Scots Highlanders, thus ensuring that readers understand the connection between savagery and civility. Outside of the complexion, the single most significant index of racial difference is to be found in the pendulous breasts of Hottentot and Negro women. Mexican, Virginian, and Floridian women appear nude, but they have high unused breasts that identify them as outside the category of perpetual laborer. Even the female Moor suffers from the dangers of proximity to Negro women (both in geography and on the page): peering out from beneath her veil, she appears to be burdened with breasts determined to slope downward.

The distortion of African women's bodies, then, became a given for eighteenth-century writers. Whether the connection forged by earlier travelers and philosophers was used to critique European woman, as a weak gesture of cultural relativism, or to cement the role of Africans as necessary slaves, it is a ubiquitous part of Europe's critique of and encounter with Africa. When William Smith embarked on a voyage to map the Gold Coast for the Royal Africa Company in 1727, he was initially disinterested in ethnography. His first description of people came more than halfway through the narrative, when he wrote, "But before I describe the Vegetables, I shall take Notice of the Animals of this

Figure 12. Hottentot woman suckling over her shoulder while smoking marijuana. From Peter Kolb, *The Present State of the Cape of Good Hope*, vol. 1 (London, 1731), plate 4. Courtesy of New York Public Library.

Figure 13. "A Description of the Habits of Most Countries in the World." From Ansham and John Churchill, *Collection of Voyages* (London, 1732). Courtesy of the Library Company of Philadelphia.

Country; beginning with the Natives, who are generally speaking a lusty strong-bodied People, but are mostly of lazy idle Disposition."[87] His short description, followed by a section on "Quadrepedes," is organized primarily around accusations of polygamy and promiscuity in which "hot constitution'd Ladies" are put to work by husbands who treat them like slaves. As the narrative continues, his ethnographic passages, while always brief, are also always organized around sexually available African women. In Whydah, for example, the reader encounters female priests inclined to whoredom, and Smith told of an anomalous queen in Agonna who satisfied her sexual needs with male slaves, handed down her crown to the resulting female progeny, and sold any male children into slavery.[88] Like de Marees a century earlier, Smith was not averse to using African women to critique European women's fashions:

> In Europe when our Children can go alone, how many Cares and Anxieties continually perplex us, nor do we think that we can ever take enough Care of them: but here they have none of this Trouble. Childrearing in this part of the World, is attended with no Expence of long Lying-in, Gossiping, etc. A Negro Woman, I have been told, has been deliver'd of a Child less than a Quarter of an Hour, and in their Labour they use no Shrieks or Cries; nay the very same Day it is customary for the Lying-in women to go to the Sea-Side and bathe herself, without ever thinking of returning to her Bed. Here are no Provision of any Necessaries for the newborn infant, and yet all its Limbes grow vigorous and proportionate, and I must deliver it as my Opinion the contrary Practice in Europe makes so many Crooked people.[89]

Despite the fact that throughout Smith's text, women and their sexual identities stand in both as evidence of African difference and as a backhanded criticism of European women, not until the final pages of the text does he perform an astonishing sleight of hand during which an African woman "speaks" of Africa and Europe. As Smith prepares to leave the coast, bound for Barbados and then England, he is heartened by the company of Charles Wheeler, who, Smith tells the reader, had been a factor for the Royal Africa Company for the past ten years and whose professed tales of Guinea "render'd his Company diverting." Smith then reproduces a first-person account that runs some twenty-one pages, much of which is taken up with conversations between Wheeler and "her Ladyship," an African concubine given to Wheeler during a visit to a king.[90] While initially loath to accept this woman as offered, Wheeler succumbs and finds himself entranced.

> Her lovely Breasts, whose Softness to the Touch nothing can exceed, were quite bare, and so was her Body to her Waste . . . and though she was black, that was amply recompenc'd by the Softness of her Skin, the beautiful Proportion and exact Symmetry of each Part of her Body, and the natural, pleasant and inartificial Method of

her Behavior. She was not forward, not yet coy, when I pressed her lovely Breasts, she gently stroak'd my Hand and smiling met my Salute with equal Ardour and Fervancy.[91]

Having located the legitimacy of his desire (he later says that "had she been White, I should have begg'd her of the King") and offered a veiled pornography of their encounter, he goes on to level a relentless critique of Europe's sexual behaviors through the voice of the savage "Lady." In response to her queries about the ways of the English, Wheeler (Smith) vents about the irrationality of English marital customs, of conventions ostensibly about chastity that lead to the ruin of England's best men and women, and ultimately about the civility of the savage. He closes his narrative by stating, "I doubt not by an impartial Examination of the Premises, it would be found, that we Christians have as many idle ridiculous Notions and Customs as the Natives of Guinea have, if not more."[92]

What is important about this use of the savage is not that it would have been particularly unusual at this time but rather that it occurs exclusively through the voice of a female informant and through the behavior of African women. Perhaps Smith—aware of the danger of his words and thus channeling them through not one but two secondary narrators—relied on her ladyship's queries not simply because of the titillating factor of having a savage woman say that "she believ'd, according to the Account I had given, few Women in Europe presented their Husbands with their Maidenheads" but because, as the sine qua non of savagery herself, her civility was that much more evocative. The rhetorical maneuver performed by Jobson's dairymaids and Ligon's Cape Verdean Queen Anne is echoed here, and its effect is to cement the position of African lady in opposition to her European counterpart. Whether English writers used the African woman to criticize British culture or to demonstrate British racial superiority, the images such writers used were the linchpins of England's emerging notion of itself.

One of a very few English woman in late-eighteenth-century West Africa, abolitionist Anna Falconbridge yearned for cultural relativism when she noted that women's breasts in Sierra Leone were "disgusting to Europeans, though considered *beautiful* and ornamental here."[93] But such weak claims of sisterly sympathy could hardly interrupt three hundred years of porno-tropical writing. By the 1770s, Edward Long's *History of Jamaica* presented readers with African women whose savagery was total, for whom enslavement was the only means of civilization. Long maintained that "an oran-outang husband would [not] be any dishonour to a Hottentot female; for what are these Hottentots?"[94] He asserted as fact that sexual liaisons occurred between African women and apes and made no reference to any sort of African female shame or beauty. Rather, Long used women's bodies and behavior to justify and promote the mass enslavement of Africans. By the time he wrote, the Jamaican economy was fully invested in slave labor and was contributing more than half of England's profits from the West Indies as a whole.[95] The association of black people with beasts—via African women—had been cemented: "Their woman are delivered with little or no labour; they have therefore no more occasion for midwifes than the female oran-outang, or any other wild animal. . . . Thus they seem exempted from the course inflicted upon Eave *and her daughters.*"[96] If African women gave birth without pain, they somehow sidestepped God's curse on Eve. If they were not Eve's descendents, they were not related to Europeans and could therefore be forced to labor on England's overseas plantations. Elaine Scarry has persuasively argued that the experience of pain—and thus the materiality of the body—lends a sense of reality and certainty to a society in times of crisis.[97] Early modern European women were so defined by their experience of pain in childbirth that an inability to feel pain was considered evidence of witchcraft.[98] In the case of England's contact with Africa and the Americas, the crisis in European identity was mediated by the construction of an image of pain-free reproduction that diminished Africa's access to certainty and civilization, thus allowing for the mass appropriation that was the transatlantic slave trade.

After Richard Ligon saw the black woman at Cape Verde, he pursued her around a dance hall, anxious to hear her voice, though she ultimately put him off with only "the loveliest smile that I have ever seen." The following morning he came upon two "pretties young Negro Virgins." Their clothing was arranged so that Ligon could see "their breasts round, firm, and beautifully shaped." He demurred that he was unable "to expresse all of he perfections of Nature, and Parts, the Virgins were owners of." Aware of the image of African womanhood already circulating in England, he assured his readers that these women should not be confused with the women of "high Africa . . . that dwell nere the River of Gambia, who are thick lipt short nos'd and commonly [have] low forheads."[99] As though their breasts did not adequately set these women apart, Ligon used these qualifiers to highlight the exception of their beauty. Along with many of his contemporaries, Ligon was quite willing to find beauty and allure in women who were exceptional—not "of high Africa"—but whose physiognomy and "education" marked them as improved by contact with Europe. Ligon encountered them in a domestic space, one familiar to him, and he sidestepped the discourse of savagery and painted a picture of seductive beauties that was understandable in part because of the familiarity of the setting.[100] In response to Ligon's pursuit, these women, like the beautiful woman he had met the evening before, remained silent. Ligon tried unsuccessfully to test the truth of their beauty through the sound of their speech. Language had marked monstrosity for centuries; Pliny identified five of his monstrous races as such simply because they lacked human speech.[101] It appears that for Ligon, decent language, like shame, denoted civility in the face of this inexplicable specter of female African beauty. Finally, Ligon begged pardon for his dalliances and remarked that he "had little else to say" about the otherwise desolate island.[102] To speak of African beauty in this context, then, was justified.

When Ligon arrived in Barbados and settled on a five-hundred-acre sugar plantation with one hundred slaves, his notion of African beauty—if it had ever really existed—dissolved in the face of racial slavery. He saw African men and women carrying bunches of plantains: "Tis a lovely sight to see a hundred hand-som Negroes, men and women, with every once a grasse-green bunch of these fruits on their heads . . . the black and green so well becoming one another." Here, in the context of the sugar plantation, where he saw African women work-ing as he had never seen English women do, Ligon struggled to situate African women as workers. Their innate unfamiliarity as laborers caused him to cast about for useful metaphors. He compared African people to vegetation; now they were only passively and abstractly beautiful, as blocks of color. Ligon at-tested to their passivity with their servitude: they made "very good servants, if they be not spoyled by the English."[103] But if Ligon found interest in beauty, as Jobson did in shame, Ligon ultimately equated black people with animals, declaring that planters bought slaves so that the "sexes may be equall [because] they cannot live without Wives," although the enslaved chose their partners much "as Cows do . . . for, the most of them are as near beasts as may be."[104] Like his predecessors, Ligon offered further proof of Africans' capacity for physical labor—their aptitude for slavery—through ease of childbearing. "In a fortnight [after giving birth], this woman is at worke with her Pickaninny at her back, as merry a soule as any is there."[105] In the Americas, African women's purportedly pain-free childbearing thus remained central. When Ligon reinforces African women's animality with descriptions of breasts "hang[ing] down below their Navels," he tethers his narrative to familiar images of black women that—for readers nourished by Hakluyt and de Bry—effectively naturalized the enslave-ment of Africans. Ligon's contemporary Felix Spoeri wrestled with the image of over-the-shoulder breast-feeding in 1661 when he noted that "when slave mothers go to work, they tie the young children to their backs. While they work they frequently give their children the breast, across the armpits, and let them suckle." In less outlandish terms, then, Spoeri worked to reconcile the tension between mothering and hard labor.[106]

By the time the English made their way to the West Indies, decades of ideas and information about brown and black women had predated the actual en-counter. In many ways, the encounter had already taken place in parlors and reading rooms on English soil, assuring that colonists would arrive with a bat-tery of assumptions and predispositions about race, femininity, sexuality, and civilization.[107] Confronted with an Africa they needed to exploit, European writers turned to black women as evidence of a cultural inferiority that ultimately became encoded as racial difference. Monstrous bodies became evidence of tangible barbarism. African women's "unwomanly" behavior evoked an immutable distance between Europe and Africa on which the development of racial slavery depended. By the mid-seventeenth century, what had initially marked African women as unfamiliar—their sexually and reproductively bound savagery—had become familiar. To invoke it was to conjure a gendered and racialized figure that marked the boundaries of English civility even as she naturalized the subjugation of Africans and their descendants in the Americas.

NOTES

This essay was previously published, under the same title, as chapter 1 of *Laboring Women: Reproduction and Gender in New World Slavery*, by Jennifer L. Morgan (Philadelphia, 2004), 12–49. Copyright © 2004 University of Pennsylvania Press. Published by permission of the University of Pennsylvania Press.

1. Sidney Mintz and Richard Price characterize the conflict between the imaginary savage and the human being with whom the slave owner has daily encounters as the contradictory characteristic of slave ownership in the Americas (*An Anthropological Approach to the Afro-American Past: A Caribbean Perspective* [Philadelphia, 1976]).

2. For an overview of the concept, see Henry Louis Gates Jr., "Introduction: Writing 'Race' and the Difference It Makes," in *Race, Writing, and Difference*, ed. Henry Louis Gates Jr. (Chicago, 1986), 1–20.

3. Richard Ligon, *A True and Exact History of the Island of Barbados* (London, 1657), 12–13.

4. Peter Erickson, "Representations of Blacks and Blackness in the Renaissance," *Criticism* 35 (Fall 1993): 514–15; Lynda Boose, " 'The Getting of a Lawful Race:' Racial Discourse in Early Modern England and the Unrepresentable Black Woman," in *Women, "Race," and Writing in the Early Modern Period*, ed. Margo Hendricks and Patricia Parker (New York, 1994), 35–55; Kim F. Hall, *Things of Darkness: Economies of Race and Gender in Early Modern England* (Ithaca, 1995), 4, 6–7.

5. Ligon, *True and Exact History*, 51.

6. P. F. Campbell, "Richard Ligon," *Journal of the Barbados Museum and Historical Society* 37 (1985): 259. For more on Ligon, see P. F. Campbell, "Two Generations of Walronds," *Journal of the Barbados Museum and Historical Society* 38 (1989): 253–85.

7. Hall, *Things of Darkness*, 29–61. In her masterful exploration of the interdependencies of "whiteness" and "blackness," Toni Morrison asserts that "the fabrication of an Africanist persona is reflexive; an extraordinary meditation on the [white] self; a powerful exploration of the fears and desires that reside in the writerly conscious. It is an astonishing revelation of longing, of terror, of perplexity, of shame, of magnanimity.

It requires hard work *not* to see this" (*Playing in the Dark: Whiteness and the Literary Imagination* [Cambridge, 1992], 17).

8. Peter Hulme, *Colonial Encounters: Europe and the Native Caribbean, 1492–1797* (London, 1986), 11, 18.

9. Arguments about the primacy of race or gender in the original construction of difference constitute an enormous theoretical literature. See, for example, Gates, "Introduction," 5, which asserts that "race had become a trope of ultimate, irreducible difference." Hortense J. Spillers similarly argues that racial slavery—the theft of the body—severed the captive from all that had been "gender-related [or] gender-specific" and thus was an "ungendering" process ("Mama's Baby, Papa's Maybe: An American Grammar Book," *Diacritics* 17 [Summer 1987]: 65–81). I believe that rather than creating a hierarchy of difference, simultaneous categories of analysis illuminate the complexity of racialist discourse in the early modern period. On the connections between categories of difference, see Anne McClintock, *Imperial Leather: Race, Gender and Sexuality in the Colonial Contest* (New York, 1995), 61. On simultaneous categories of analysis, see Elsa Barkley Brown, "Polyrhythms and Improvisations: Lessons for Women in History," *History Workshop Journal* 31 (Spring 1991): 85–90; for cautions on the dangers of erecting hierarchies of difference, see Ania Loomba, "The Color of Patriarchy: Critical Difference, Cultural Difference, and Renaissance Drama," in Hendricks and Parker, *Women, "Race," and Writing*, 17–34.

10. Anthony J. Barker, *The African Link: British Attitudes to the Negro in the Era of the Atlantic Slave Trade, 1550–1807* (London, 1978), 22.

11. Pliny the Elder, *Natural History*, trans. H. Rackham (Cambridge, 1938–63), 2:509–27; Herodotus, *The History*, trans. David Grene (Chicago, 1987), 4, 180, 191.

12. Elizabeth A. Clark, "Generation, Degeneration, Regeneration: Original Sin and the Conception of Jesus in the Polemic between Augustine and Julian of Eclanum," in *Generation and Degeneration: Tropes of Reproduction in Literature and History from Antiquity to Early Modern Europe*, ed. Valeria Finucci and Kevin Brownlee (Durham, 2001), 30; Valeria Finucci, "Maternal Imagination and Monstrous Birth: Tasso's *Gerusalemme Liberate*," in *Generation and Degeneration*, ed. Finucci and Brownlee, 65.

13. Richard Bernheimer, *Wild Men in the Middle Ages: A Study in Art, Sentiment, and Demonology* (Cambridge, 1952), 33–41, 34. See also Peter Mason, *Deconstructing America: Representation of the Other* (New York, 1990), 47–56.

14. John Mandeville, *The Travels of Sir John Mandeville: The Version of the Cotton Manuscript in Modern Spelling*, ed. A. W. Pollard (London, 1915), 109, 119.

15. Sharon W. Tiffany and Kathleen J. Adams, *The Wild Woman: An Inquiry into the Anthropology of an Idea* (Cambridge, 1985), 63. See McClintock, *Imperial Leather*, 22–23, for more on what she labels the "porno-tropic" tradition of European eroticized writing on Africa and the Americas.

16. Sebastian Münster, *A Treatyse of the Newe India by Sebastian Münster* (1553), trans. Richard Eden (microprint) (Ann Arbor, 1966), 57. See also Mason, *Deconstructing America*, 55, which links Vespucci's surprise at Indian women's firm breasts with expectations grounded in medieval imagery of wild women with sagging breasts. Language such as

"fylth" also evoked sodomy and treachery for English readers; see Alan Bray, "Homosexuality and the Signs of Male Friendship in Elizabethan England," in *Queering the Renaissance*, ed. Jonathan Goldberg (Durham, 1994), 48. The wording of Münster's passage materializes many ideas of difference.

17. It is significant that this association with sagging breasts, unusual childbearing, and monstrosity emerged so early. Not until the sixteenth century did elite European women begin to use corsets to impose an elevated shape to their bodies, and only then did the elevated breasts of corseted women become a marker of refinement, courtliness, and status. For more on corsetry, see Georges Vigarello, "The Upwards Training of the Body from the Age of Chivalry to Courtly Civility," in *Fragments for a History of the Human Body*, pt. 2, ed. Michael Feher, Ramona Naddaff, and Nadia Tazi (Cambridge, 1989), 154–55. Very soon thereafter, the "unused" breast, preserved among the elite by employing wet nurses for their children, embodied the "classic aesthetic ideal," according to Londa Schiebinger ("Why Mammals Are Called Mammals: Gender Politics in Eighteenth-Century Natural History," *American Historical Review* 98 [April 1993]: 401). For a broader discussion of breasts' symbolic valence, see Marilyn Yalom, *A History of the Breast* (New York, 1997).

18. Two years after the publication of Münster's *Treatyse*, Eden translated and published Peter Martyr, *The Decades of the New Worlde of West India* (1553; London, 1555), another description of the Columbus encounters.

19. Münster, *Treatyse*, 4; Martyr, *Decades of the New Worlde*, 2.

20. As Stephen Greenblatt has illustrated, the female "go-between" was crucial in encounter narratives. Greenblatt discusses the go-between through his analysis of Bernal Díaz's conquest narrative, arguing that Doña Marina, a native woman who becomes connected to the Spaniards, is the "object of exchange, agent of communication, model of conversion, the only figure who appears to understand the two cultures, the only person in whom they meet. . . . The site of the strategic symbolic oscillation between self and Other is the body of this woman" (*Marvelous Possessions: The Wonder of the New World* [Chicago, 1991], 143).

21. Münster, *Treatyse*, 5; Martyr, *Decades of the New Worlde*, 3.

22. Münster, *Treatyse*, quoted in Louis Montrose, "The Work of Gender in the Discourse of Discovery," *Representations* 33 (Winter 1991): 4.

23. Montrose, "Work of Gender," 5. For more on gender and cannibalism, see Carla Freccero, "Cannibalism, Homophobia, Women: Montaigne's 'Des Canibalies' and 'De l'amitie,'" in *Women, "Race," and Writing*, ed. Hendricks and Parker, 73–82; for the etymological relationship between Caribs and cannibalism, see Hulme, *Colonial Encounters*, 13–42.

24. Girolamo Benzoni, *History of the New World*, trans. by W. H. Smyth (1572; London, 1857), 3–4.

25. Greenblatt argues that "wonder is . . . the central figure in the initial European response to the New World, the decisive emotional and intellectual experience in the presence of radical difference" (*Marvelous Possessions*, 14).

26. Hall argues that "the painted woman often represents concerns over female unruliness, [and] the power of whiteness. . . . Male writers continually accuse women of

hiding their 'blackness' under the fair disguise of cosmetics" (*Things of Darkness*, 89–90). See also Paul-Gabriel Boucé for an early-eighteenth-century reference to popular English beliefs correlating the size of a woman's mouth to that of her vagina ("Some Sexual Beliefs and Myths in Eighteenth-Century Britain," in *Sexuality in Eighteenth-Century Britain*, ed. Paul-Gabriel Boucé (Totowa, 1982), 29–46, esp. 31–32.

27. Benzoni, *History of the New World*, 8. For an example of the consequences of the "black legend" for English settlers in the Americas, see Karen Ordahl Kupperman, *Providence Island, 1630–1641: The Other Puritan Colony* (Cambridge, 1993), 92–96.

28. Sir Walter Raleigh, "The Discoverie of the Large Rich and Beautiful Empire of Guiana," in Richard Hakluyt, *The Principal Navigations, Voyages, Traffiques and Discoveries of the English Nation* (1598–1600; Glasgow, 1903–5), 10:39, cited in Montrose, "Work of Gender," 20.

29. Karen Robertson, "Pocahontas at the Masque," *Signs* 21 (Spring 1996): 561, argues that "representation of an Indian woman does involve a dilemma for a male colonist, as expression of the erotic may signal his own lapse into savagery." See also Montrose, "Work of Gender," 21.

30. Benzoni, *History of the New World*, 11.

31. In eighteenth-century England, writers intent on displaying the "natural" role of motherhood for English women idealized the "savage mother" and in doing so created tension as the dichotomy of civilized English and savage Other slipped; see Felicity A. Nussbaum, *Torrid Zones: Maternity, Sexuality, and Empire in Eighteenth-Century English Narratives* (Baltimore, 1995), 48–53.

32. Hugh Honour, *The New Golden Land: European Images of America from the Discoveries of the Present Time* (New York, 1975), 54–55.

33. Theodore de Bry, ed., *Grand Voyages*, 13 vols. (Frankfurt am Main, 1590–1627). De Bry also published the series *Small Voyages* (12 vols., Frankfurt am Main, 1598–1628), chronicling voyages to Africa and the East India. Language training among the elite, particularly in Latin, meant that those with access to de Bry's volumes would possess the capacity to understand them; see Lawrence Stone, *The Crisis of the Aristocracy, 1558–1641* (Oxford, 1965), 672–702. For a discussion of the availability of books on reproduction and physiognomy, see Patricia Crawford, "Sexual Knowledge in England, 1500–1750," in *Sexual Knowledge, Sexual Science: The History of Attitudes to Sexuality*, ed. Roy Porter and Mikulas Teich (Cambridge, 1994), 86.

34. Bernadette Bucher, *Icon and Conquest: A Structural Analysis of the Illustrations of de Bry's Great Voyages*, trans. Basia Miller Gulati (Chicago, 1981); Joyce E. Chaplin, "Natural Philosophy and an Early Racial Idiom in North America: Comparing English and Indian Bodies," *William and Mary Quarterly*, 3rd ser., 54 (January 1997): 231.

35. Bucher, *Icon and Conquest*, 135, 145. Bucher's analysis introduces a complex discussion of the morphology of consumption and an explanation that locates the reversal of production with consumption at the heart of anthropophagi in the icon of the sagging breast (*Icon and Conquest*, 73–120). For the formulation of the long-breasted woman in the Americas, see also Mason, *Deconstructing America*, 47–60; for the late-seventeenth- and eighteenth-century use of the icon of sagging breasts, see Londa Schiebinger, *Nature's Body: Gender in the Making of Modern Science* (Boston, 1993), 160–63.

36. Gomes Eannes de Azurara, *The Chronicle of the Discovery and Conquest of Guinea*, in *Documents Illustrative of the History of Slave Trade*, ed. Elizabeth Donnan (Washington, D.C., 1930–35; repr., Buffalo, 2002), 1:40. I am grateful to Professor Stephanie Smallwood for drawing my attention to this passage and to its resonance for this project.

37. Emily C. Bartels, "Imperialist Beginnings: Richard Hakluyt and the Construction of Africa," *Criticism* 34 (Fall 1992): 519. For further discussion of the fluidity of images of Africa in the early modern European imaginary, see Winthrop D. Jordan, *White over Black: American Attitudes toward the Negro, 1550–1812* (Chapel Hill, 1968), 3–43. See also David Armitage, "The New World and British Historical Thought: From Richard Hakluyt to William Roberston," in *America in European Consciousness, 1493–1750*, ed. Karen Ordahl Kupperman (Chapel Hill, 1995), 52–75. The Hakluyt collection ultimately served as "a mythico-historical amalgam intended to introduce . . . conquest and colonization of Europeans" (Bucher, *Icon and Conquest*, 22).

38. "The Second Voyage [of Master John Lok] to Guinea . . . 1554," in Hakluyt, *Principal Navigations*, 6:167, 168. Pliny describes the "Garamantes" as an Ethiopian race that does not practice marriage. See John Block Friedman, *The Monstrous Races in Medieval Art and Thought* (Cambridge, 1981), 15.

39. Barker, *African Link*, 121.

40. André Thevet, *The New Founde Worlde, or Antarctike*, trans. by Thomas Hacket (London, 1568), 65–66, cited in Laura Fishman, "French Views of Native American Women in the Early Modern Era: The Tupinamba of Brazil," in *Women and the Colonial Gaze*, ed. Tamara Hunt and Micheline R. Lessard (New York, 2002), 72.

41. Martyr, *Decades of the New Worlde*, 356. In this paragraph, Martyr clearly borrows from Herodotus and Pliny. Monsters served a variety of functions in early modern literature, "from prodigies to pathology," and were an important part of descriptions of Africa "since Antiquity," according to Katharine Park and Lorraine J. Daston, "Unnatural Conceptions: The Study of Monsters in Sixteenth- and Seventeenth-Century France and England," *Past and Present* 92 (August 1981): 23, 37.

42. William Towrson, "The First Voyage Made by Master William Towrson Marchant of London, to the Coast of Guinea . . . in the Yeere 1555," in Hakluyt, *Principal Navigations*, 6:184. Jordan notes that "many chroniclers [of Africa] made a point of discussing the Negro women's long breasts and ease of childbearing," though he apparently takes such observations as fact rather than symbol (*White over Black*, 39–40). Schiebinger places the equation of African women's breasts with the udders of goats in a continuum of European imagery of and relationship to the breast. She notes that nineteenth-century ethnologists compared and classified breast size and shape much as they did skulls. Not surprisingly, they used African breasts, like African heads, to prove the linkage between Africans and animals; see Schiebinger, "Why Mammals Are Called Mammals," 402–3, 394. Philip Morgan asserts that beginning with Richard Ligon, "Barbadians were the first coherent group within the Anglo-American world to portray blacks as beasts or beast-like" ("British Encounters with Africans and African-Americans, circa 1600–1780," in *Strangers within the Realm: Cultural Margins of the First British Empire*, ed. Bernard Bailyn and Philip D. Morgan [Chapel Hill, 1991], 174).

43. Towrson, "First Voyage," 187. After he categorized women, Towrson relegated them to a passive role in the background of his interactions with Africans despite the fact that, as he noted, the women "worke as well as the men" (185).

44. Richard Jobson, *The Golden Trade; or, a Discovery of the River Gambra . . . by Richard Jobson* (1628; New York, 1968).

45. Ibid., 35.

46. Ibid., 33.

47. Ibid., 36.

48. Ibid., 56; emphasis added.

49. Ibid., 58.

50. Ibid., 58, 52, 54; Greenblatt, *Marvelous Possessions*, 14.

51. Samuel Purchas, *Hakluytus Posthumus, or, Purchas his Pilgrimes: Contayning a History of the World in Sea Voyages and Lande Travells by Englishmen and Others*, 20 vols. (1624; Glasgow, 1905–7).

52. Leo Africanus, "Observations of Africa, Taken Out of John Leo His Nine Bookes, translated by Master Pory . . . ," in *Purchas His Pilgrimes*, 5:517.

53. Drawing from Todorov's discussion of nudity in encounter narratives, Roxann Wheeler notes that remarks about African nudity are always qualified, as European observers concede that in fact they are witnessing only partial nudity and that high social rank is often signified by clothing (*The Complexion of Race: Categories of Difference in Eighteenth-Century British Culture* [Philadelphia, 2000], 117).

54. Andrew Battell, "The Strange Adventures of Andrew Battell," in *Purchas His Pilgrimes*, 6:367–517.

55. Ibid., 377–78.

56. Ibid., 32.

57. Pieter de Marees, *Description and Historical Account of the Gold Kingdom of Guinea*, edited and trans. Albert van Dantzig and Adam Jones (1602; Oxford, 1987), xvii.

58. Pieter De Marees, "Description and Historicall Declaration of the Golden Kingdome of Guinea," in *Purchas His Pilgrimes*, 6:251. I cite the Purchas edition rather than the modern edition to draw on the narrative that early modern English readers encountered.

59. Ibid., 258–59.

60. Ibid., 259.

61. De Marees, *Description and Historical Account*, 23.

62. De Marees, "Description and Historicall Declaration," 6:259.

63. Linda E. Merians, " 'Hottentot': The Emergence of an Early Modern Racist Epithet," *Shakespeare Studies* 26 (1998): 123–45, paragraph 26; available online at http://search.epnet.com/direct.asp?an=15311488&db=aph.

64. Thomas Herbert, *A Relation of Some Yeares Travaile Begunne Anno 1626* (London, 1634), 14; available online at http://wwwlib.umi.com/eebo.

65. Ibid., 17.

66. De Marees, "Description and Historicall Declaration," 6:261; *Oxford English Dictionary*, 2nd ed., 1989.

67. Fynes Moryson, *Shakespeare's Europe: A Survey of the Condition of Europe at the End of the Sixteenth Century, Being Unpublished Chapters of Fynes Moryson's Itinerary*, 2nd ed. (1617; New York, 1967), 485.

68. Alexander Gunkel and Jerome S. Handler, eds. and trans., "A Swiss Medical Doctor's Description of Barbados in 1661: The Account of Felix Christian Spoeri," *Journal of the Barbados Museum and Historical Society* 33 (May 1969): 7.

69. Nicholas Villaut, *A Relation of the Coasts of Africk . . .* (London, 1670), 157; available online at http://wwwlib.umi.com/eebo.

70. [Nathaniel Crouch], *A View of the English Acquisitions in Guinea, and the East Indies* (London, 1686), 8; available online at http://wwwlib.umi.com/eebo.

71. Londa Schiebinger uses Blumenbach's theories to highlight the connection between race and sex in the Enlightenment in "The Anatomy of Difference: Race and Sex in Eighteenth-Century Science," *Eighteenth Century Studies* 23 (Summer 1990): 392–93.

72. John Ogilby, *America* (London, 1671), 316, 360, 641.

73. Jordan, *White over Black*, 39.

74. Marylynn Salmon, "The Cultural Significance of Breastfeeding and Infant Care in Early Modern England and America," *Journal of Social History* 28 (Winter 1994): 247–70. For more on seventeenth-century wet nursing in England, see Valerie Fildes, *Wet Nursing: A History from Antiquity to the Present* (Oxford, 1988), 79–100.

75. Linda Pollock, "Embarking on a Rough Passage: The Experience of Pregnancy in Early Modern Society," in *Women as Mothers in Pre-industrial England*, ed. Valerie Fildes (New York, 1990), 45.

76. Saidiya Hartman, *Scenes of Subjection: Terror, Slavery, and Self-Making in Nineteenth-Century America* (New York, 1997), 51.

77. Wheeler, *Complexion of Race*, 65.

78. Nussbaum, *Torrid Zones*, 73–74. Ruth Perry argues that the valuation of motherhood developed in England alongside empire so that not until the nineteenth century did "the production of children for the nation and for the empire constitute childbearing women as a national resource" ("Colonizing the Breast: Sexuality and Maternity in Eighteenth-Century England," *Eighteenth-Century Life* 16, no. 1 [February 1992]: 204, 205). And, indeed, a growing literature explores the relationship between nineteenth- and twentieth-century imperialism and the intersections between childbearing and the national resources of colonial powers; see, for example, Anna Davin, "Imperialism and Motherhood," in *Tensions of Empire: Colonial Cultures in a Bourgeois World*, ed. Frederick Cooper and Ann Laura Stoler (Berkeley, 1997), 87–151. My work and that of Sharon Block, Kathleen Brown, Kirsten Fischer, and others suggest that the connections between reproduction and colonial identity were in fact in place some two hundred years earlier. See also Greenblatt, *Marvelous Possessions*, 7.

79. John Barbot, *A Description of the Coasts of North and South-Guinea*, in *A Collection of Voyages*, ed. A. Churchill (London, 1732), 36; see also J. D. Fage, " 'Good Red Herring': The Definitive Barbot," *Journal of African History* 34 (1993): 315–20.

80. William Snelgrave, introduction to *A New Account of Some Parts of Guinea and the Slave Trade* (1734; London, 1971).

81. Ibid., 3–4.

82. Nussbaum, *Torrid Zones*, 79.

83. John Atkins, *A Voyage to Guinea, Brazil, and the West-Indies* (1735; London, 1970), 50.

84. Ibid., 108.

85. Wheeler, *Complexion of Race*, 102.

86. Peter Kolb, *Present State of the Cape of Good Hope* (London, 1731), reproduced in Schiebinger, *Nature's Body*, 162.

87. William Smith, *A New Voyage to Guinea* (London, 1744), 142–43.

88. Ibid., 195, 208.

89. Ibid., 210.

90. Because of its length, its first-person narration, and its lack of appropriate punctuation, this section of Smith's narrative has been misunderstood as coming from him rather than his informant (Nussbaum, *Torrid Zones*, 78–79; Wheeler, *Complexion of Race*, 130).

91. Smith, *New Voyage to Guinea*, 253–54.

92. Ibid., 257, 266.

93. Falconbridge's observation immediately follows a description of childbearing: "A few years after a woman is delivered, she takes her child on her back to wherever her vocation leads her." And while Falconbridge ascribes endemic bowleggedness among adults to this maternal practice, she notably does not go on to suggest that women's long breasts allowed them to nurse the children on their backs (Anna Maria Falconbridge, "Two Voyages to Sierra Leone, during the Years 1791–2–3," in *Maiden Voyages and Infant Colonies: Two Women's Travel Narratives of the 1790s*, ed. Deirdre Coleman [London, 1999], 74).

94. Edward Long, "History of Jamaica, 2, with Notes and Corrections by the Author" (1774), Add. Ms., 12405, p364/f295, British Library, London. Long was not alone in his delight at suggesting interspecies copulation. Londa Schiebinger details seventeenth- and eighteenth-century naturalists' investigations of apes and notes that these writers "ascribed to [simian] females the modesty they were hoping to find in their own wives and daughters, and to males the wildest fantasies of violent interspecies rape" (*Nature's Body*, 78).

95. Robin Blackburn, *The Making of New World Slavery: From the Baroque to the Modern, 1492–1800* (London, 1997), 527–45.

96. Long, "History of Jamaica," p380/f304; emphasis added.

97. Elaine Scarry, *The Body in Pain: The Making and Unmaking of the World* (New York, 1985), 15, 185–91. Hortense Spillers argues that pain inflicted under slavery ungendered "female flesh," but I argue something different. While assertions about pain-free childbirth are, in a sense, an effort on the part of the slave owner to ungender female flesh to make it labor, the disgendered notions of differences between black women and black men include confidence in women's ability to do and proclivity for hard labor ("Mama's Baby, Papa's Maybe," 67–68).

98. Lyndal Roper, *Oedipus and the Devil: Witchcraft, Sexuality, and Religion in Early Modern Europe* (London, 1994), 203–4; see also Mary Poovey, *Uneven Developments: The Ideological Work of Gender in Mid-Victorian England* (Chicago, 1988), 24–50. Poovey shows that during mid-nineteenth-century debates over anesthesia for women in child-

birth, members of the medical and religious professions argued that to relieve women of pain would interfere with God and deprive women of the pain that ultimately civilized them. See also Diane Purkiss, "Women's Stories of Witchcraft in Early Modern England: The House, the Body, the Child," *Gender and History* 7 (November 1995): 408–32, for the connection between pain-free childbirth and accusations of witchcraft. On the connection between midwifery and accusations of witchcraft, Carol F. Karlson notes that "the procreative nurturing and nursing roles of women were *perverted* by the witches," in *The Devil in the Shape of a Woman: Witchcraft in Colonial New England* (New York, 1989), 144.

99. Ligon, *True and Exact History*, 13, 15–16.

100. Another example can be found in John Gabriel Stedman's relationship to the mulatto woman Johanna in his *Narrative of Five Years Expedition against the Revolted Negroes of Surinam: Transcribed . . . from the Original 1790 Manuscript*, ed. Richard Price and Sally Price (Baltimore, 1988). His attempts to persuade this almost-English woman to return to Britain with him failed in part because she understood what he did not— that her status as "exceptional" was contingent on her location in Surinam. Had she gone to England, she would have become in effect a "high African" woman. For a discussion of the symbolic importance of those who occupy the borders of colonial spaces, see Homi K. Bhabha, "Of Mimicry and Man: The Ambivalence of Colonial Discourse," *October* 28 (Spring 1984): 108.

101. Friedman, *Monstrous Races*, 29.

102. Ligon, *True and Exact History*, 17. Henry Louis Gates Jr. argues that the primary theme of Afro-American literature is the quest for literacy, a response to white assertions that blacks lacked "reason." Just as Phillis Wheatley's literacy had to be authenticated by thirteen white male signatories, so all Afro-American writing was an oppositional demonstration of authentic intellect that "was a political act." Ligon's need to hear the voices of the black women who excited his lust and curiosity suggests a precursor to the black literary link between reading and reason. "The spoken language of black people had become an object of parody at least since 1769," Gates writes (*Figures in Black: Words, Signs, and the "Radical" Self* [New York, 1987], 5–6). Ligon wrote during a period that predated that tradition of parody and instead located reason and civility in spoken language.

103. Ligon, *True and Exact History*, 44.

104. Ibid., 47.

105. Ibid., 51.

106. Gunkel and Handler, "Swiss Medical Doctor's Description," 7.

107. Greenblatt, *Marvelous Possessions*, 55.

Consciousness
and Calling

African American Midwives

at Work in the Antebellum South

SHARLA M. FETT

*L*ooking back on her life under slavery, Virginia midwife Mildred Graves remembered with satisfaction her ability to handle both difficult births and hostile white doctors. In a 1930s interview, Graves recounted arriving at the home of a well-to-do white woman to find two white doctors from Richmond already in attendance. The doctors, having reached the limits of their knowledge, wanted to call a third colleague to assist them. "I tol' dem I could bring her 'roun'," Graves recalled, "but dey laugh at me an' say, 'Get back darkie, we mean business an' don' won't any witch doctors or hoodoo stuff.'" Events soon turned in the midwife's favor, however, when the laboring mother dismissed her doctors and left Graves to bring both mother and son safely through their perilous passage. After that, Graves concluded, "Even de doctors dat had call me bad names said many praise fer me."[1] In the most immediate sense, Graves's story vindicated her skill and dignity in the face of the men who used racial epithets to disparage her training. Yet these memories can also draw us back into the antebellum period to consider how African American midwives forged identities in the midst of their work as enslaved and skilled women. Evidence concerning the last generation of enslaved midwives, who practiced roughly between 1840 and 1860, suggests that African American midwives sustained their calling by joining their skills as birth attendants to an astute consciousness of both intimate and public forms of power in antebellum slave society.

Despite a widespread consensus that the historical roots of African American southern midwifery lie in the era of slavery, the lives of these antebellum foremothers have been more assumed than studied.[2] Within the past two decades, a wealth of exciting scholarship on the twentieth century has charted the tensions between "traditional" African American midwifery and emerging public health regulation. Historians, sociologists, and anthropologists have examined the cultural biases and health effects of state-sponsored midwife training and licensing and have published important ethnographies and oral histories of twentieth-century black midwives.[3] Yet in-depth scholarship on the antebellum predecessors from whom "traditional" midwives are assumed to have emerged has lagged behind. The resulting gap risks rendering enslaved midwives as static culture bearers who served as vessels for conveying timeless African-based birthing practices to twentieth-century generations. A close look at the work of antebellum midwifery, including its social context as well as its practice, promises to historicize the antebellum generation while illuminating both continuities and changes within the broader span of African American midwifery.

For several decades, historians of U.S. slavery have acknowledged the social and cultural importance of African American midwives. In the 1970s explosion of scholarship on slave community and culture, John Blassingame upended previous assumptions about status ranking among slaves by suggesting that midwives and other healers occupied positions of high status within the social structure of enslaved communities.[4] A decade later, Deborah Gray White's cornerstone book on slave women highlighted the importance of older midwives to the gendered experience of enslavement and to enslaved women's collective labor and social networks.[5] Most recently, midwives and the politics of enslaved women's reproduction have received attention in studies of colonial slave women, antebellum plantation healing, and slave childhood.[6] Yet the insights of slavery studies have not been fully joined to the broader scholarship that considers African American midwifery as a historical practice reaching across enslavement, Reconstruction, and segregation. Today, the convergence of social history and cultural studies within the historiography of enslaved communities allows us to reread old sources in new lights. This chapter connects the work of midwifery to broader questions about how labor contexts and labor processes shaped enslaved women's culture and identity under slavery. This exploration will further the understanding of the interplay between expressive culture and slave labor as dual roots of enslaved women's consciousness.[7]

While government records and oral histories have painted a rich tapestry of twentieth-century midwives' lives and labors, antebellum sources on midwifery are far more scattered and fragmentary. Given the oral basis of African American midwifery practice and the exclusion of such voices from early archives, historians may search in vain for the African American–authored counterpart to Martha Ballard's diary. Instead, the evidence is embedded in oral histories of African American families, plantation records, planter and medical journals, and especially in the Federal Writers' Project "ex-slave" interviews (also known as the Works Progress Administration [wpa] interviews). Slaveholder and white physician records yield shards of evidence on the particulars of midwives' work, while twentieth-century interviews with elderly black men and women, read carefully, distill memories of what that work meant and how it was practiced in southern rural households.[8]

Working within antebellum households and communities, enslaved midwives displayed remarkable cultural and social versatility. Indeed, midwifery work frequently required enslaved women to move among many of the categories that historians have used to organize knowledge about antebellum slave communities. Midwives worked, for example, in slave quarters as well as white households. They hurried to their labor in day and night, thus blurring the boundaries between "own time" and "master's time." Some midwives toiled both at agricultural labor and at domestic tasks in the new mother's household. Furthermore, observes anthropologist Gertrude Fraser, midwives acted as "liminal figures" who mediated the spiritually charged events of birth and death, even staying to shroud the dead for burial if a mother or child failed to survive childbirth.[9] Within the context of antebellum slave society, black midwives routinely crossed lines of class, community, and race in ways that were unusual, especially for enslaved women. Such versatility presented enslaved midwives with both opportunity and danger. This chapter explores three arenas in which midwives traversed either ideological or spatial boundaries: (1) between the political economy of chattel slavery and enslaved African Americans' cultural definitions of birth; (2) between the spaces and economies of white and black southern households; and (3) between two domains of antebellum birthing knowledge—motherwit and obstetrics.[10] As antebellum midwives negotiated conflicting claims on their labor and knowledge, they developed keen insight into the social relations of southern society. The social context of midwifery work thus powerfully shaped the consciousness of antebellum African American midwives and contributed in critical ways to the legacy inherited by their twentieth-century granddaughters.

Between Conflicting Definitions of Birth and Caregiving

What the abolitionist minister James Pennington called the "chattel principle"—a principle that defined human beings as movable property in perpetuity through the mother's line of descent—profoundly shaped the political economy of African American birth under slavery.[11] From early colonial times onward, historian Jennifer Morgan argues, African women's "reproductive lives were at the heart of the entire venture of racial slavery."[12] In the antebellum period and particularly from the 1830s on, several major developments focused slaveholder attention on enslaved women's childbearing. The expansion of the U.S. plantation economy, the closing of the legal transatlantic slave trade, and the growth of an American-born slave population increased the vested interests of planters in enslaved women's reproduction and the involvement of white doctors in medical care for the enslaved.[13] This is not to argue that slaveholders' economic interests protected enslaved women from excessive labor and unhealthy pregnancies or ensured their children's survival—mortality studies show otherwise.[14] Rather, the political economy of African American birth gave slaveholders a stake in enslaved women's childbearing that added to the conflicting interests between masters and slaves.

Despite the delicacy with which slaveholders tiptoed around the subject of elite women's pregnancies, childbearing enslaved women received no such private shelter in planter rhetoric. The public writings of both planters and white doctors fused economic self-interest with the language of proslavery amelioration to argue that enslaved women's reproductive health comprised an important facet of a well-regulated plantation. Agricultural journals argued that planters too often sacrificed slave women's health (and thus planter wealth in persons) to the immediate demands of harvesting and planting. One county agricultural society warned that overwork "checks the increase of females" and cautioned fellow planters not to "kill the goose, to obtain the golden egg."[15] Medical doctors in the late antebellum period voiced similar concerns. "The principal value of the negro with us is his increase," wrote W. Fletcher Holmes, outlining a general plan for better health in upcountry South Carolina slave quarters.[16] Other physicians pondered the threat of contraceptive and abortifacient knowledge among enslaved women while arguing that the heavy field labor forced on pregnant and postpartum women contributed equally to miscarriage and infertility.[17]

A political economy that defined slave births in terms of slaveholder wealth implicitly linked the work of enslaved midwives to the property interests of slaveholders. African American midwives assisted birthing women in households across the antebellum South. Although obstetrics constituted an emerging field of nineteenth-century medical teaching and practice, most southern rural doctors attended relatively few births. Some elite southern families, like their urban northern counterparts, chose medical doctors as birth attendants, but many planter families relied on free and enslaved midwives unless serious complications arose.[18] White doctors, even when present for other kinds of slave medical care that included considerable gynecological work, usually attended slave births only when called by slaveholders to difficult deliveries.[19] Thus, the vast majority of enslaved newborns (as well as many white babies) came into the world in the hands of African American midwives.

By necessity, enslaved midwives worked self-consciously between two definitions of their labor: as plantation health work and as gifted vocation. In this respect they shared much with a larger group of enslaved healers designated by slaveholders as "doctor women" or "nurses." Midwifery skills routinely overlapped with other kinds of doctoring. For some women, like Mississippi midwife Rena Clark, this meant specializing in "most everything that ails the women folks."[20] Others served an even broader range of health needs. John Sneed, for example, described his Tennessee-born enslaved mother, Sarah, as a "pneumonia doctor" and a midwife.[21] South Carolina planter Alexander Telfair directed his overseer to midwife Elsey as "Doctress of the Plantation." A slave trader advertised "Clarissa, midwife and nurse" as one who could be "trusted to mix and administer medicine."[22]

Like other enslaved healers, most midwives on southern plantations belonged to the ranks of older women reassigned to other tasks because of their declining endurance for fieldwork. Although some still labored periodically in the fields, these older women also worked at child care and subsistence production in plantation outbuildings and yards. For example, a sale broadside designated Doll, of Christ Church Parish, as a field hand, a dairy maid, and a midwife.[23] Not all midwives came out of the communities of fieldworkers, but most combined midwifery with other tasks commonly assigned to older enslaved women, including weaving, sewing, cooking, domestic work, and sick care.[24] As profiled in plantation inventories and deeds of sale, midwifery work represented an efficient distribution of enslaved women's labor: midwives' primary purpose was to ensure plantation production and the reproduction of slaveholder wealth.[25]

Authors of plantation management advice typically depicted the enslaved midwife and more commonly the plantation "nurse" as "elderly" but "trustworthy and intelligent." In this idealized image, the black midwife derived her authority from the planter and sought guidance from the neighborhood's best white doctor. Such an "office," according to one author, was "one of no little responsibility and importance on a Southern plantation."[26] Interestingly, the same advice literature had little to offer in the realm of childbirth techniques and care of newborn and mother. The slave-management articles in the late antebellum decades included ample advice about the work, clothing, housing, and pregnancies of enslaved laborers but rarely explicitly mentioned midwives or childbirth.[27] These writers appeared far more concerned with the midwife's subservience than with her birthing techniques.

Yet the planter view of midwives as deferential older nurses was a partial one that failed to include midwives' critical social and spiritual contributions to enslaved communities. Women healers became visible in historical records not only because slaveholders appointed them but also because enslaved communities affirmed the effectiveness of their work. Many elder midwives arrived at plantation-wide healing responsibilities through earlier healing work for their own families as well as apprenticeships with older women.[28] While they shared with planters the goal of thriving infants and healthy mothers, African American midwives helped to create an alternative meaning of slave birth that confronted the objectification of the chattel principle and attempted to place the newborn infant within the context of kinship and spiritual protection.

The combination of practical advice and spiritual leadership offered by enslaved midwives extended far beyond the physical events of labor and delivery. Fragmentary evidence suggests the possibility that enslaved midwives helped pregnant women understand cycles of fertility and the onset of labor in terms of a lunar calendar.[29] Furthermore, midwives advised pregnant women, whose swelling bodies were understood to be more vulnerable to both natural and spiritual forces, concerning protection from illness and conjuration. During and after the birth, midwives provided advice, prayers, and herbal medicines to protect mothers and infants. They covered the umbilical cord of each newborn with a piece of scorched linen, wrapped the mother's abdomen in a white "belly band," and properly disposed of the placenta so that it could not be mishandled for ill purposes. If unusual circumstances accompanied the birth, such as the birth of twins or the presence of the "veil" (amniotic sac) over the face, signaling a gift of spiritual insight, midwives became ritual specialists who worked to contain dangerous forces. To the extent that overseers and slave masters allowed, midwives oversaw the parturient mother's nine-day "lying in" period of seclusion within the birthing room, facilitated the transition of the mother back into the broader community life of the slave quarters, and sometimes participated in the child's naming.[30] Planters, overseers, and white doctors could and did violate African American birth rituals and proscriptions with their own agenda for labor and dominance, but such intrusions reinforced rather than diminished the importance of the midwife's intermediary presence.

Working between the desires of planters and the hopes of enslaved families, some African American midwives became skilled translators of the different meanings of slave birth. Frances Kemble Butler, an English actress who lived briefly on her husband's Georgia plantations, noted the efforts of Sackey, one of the "chief nurses" (and most likely a birth attendant), to intervene on behalf of new mothers. Sackey drew Kemble's attention to the health hazards of a recently shortened postpartum recovery period for enslaved mothers. The recorded encounter suggests Sackey's ability to act as intermediary by translating the suffering of her charges into the language of plantation productivity. According to Kemble, Sackey mentioned only the physical dangers of shortened seclusion, not the spiritual risk of exposing the new mother and baby too early to an unpredictable world. She translated the enslaved mothers' fears into the language of the chattel principle by warning that the practice threatened to "utterly [destroy] all the breeding women" of the Butler estate. The irritated responses of both the overseer and Kemble's husband to this warning suggest that even in this veiled petition, Sackey transgressed her appointed role.[31]

The dual roles of plantation caregiver and community leader exposed midwives to charges of interfering in both slave reproduction and the broader social order of planter rule. A Georgia midwife faced the first charge when she was taken into court for allegedly assisting an enslaved mother in killing her newborn. Charles Colcock Jones reported that in this case, the midwife had used her position as caregiver to deny that a birth had taken place, even after a "full-formed" infant's body had been discovered. Much remains unexplained in this incident, and we are left to reflect on a mother's motives and a midwife's decisions.[32] Nevertheless, the incident illustrates both the vulnerabilities and opportunities of midwives, who by virtue of their planter-delegated work could mediate or even oppose slaveholders' vested interests.

The second (and less common) charge that midwives used their social authority to encourage resistance to slavery is illustrated in a series of dramatic events involving a free black midwife in Maryland, probably in the late 1850s. Thomas Foote told a Federal Writers' Project interviewer that his freeborn mother, Eliza Myers, acquired knowledge of herbal medicines, midwifery, and literacy in her work for a homeopathic white doctor north of Baltimore. Her reputation as a "doctor woman" and midwife spread quickly. Although she was at times hired by wealthy whites, she was, according to her son, "suspected by the white people but confided in by the colored people both for their ills and their troubles." When a man who had recently consulted her escaped his bondage, local whites accused Myers of "voodooism." They jailed and interrogated Myers and eventually forced her to choose between a sentence of enslavement or expulsion from the state. In this incident, Eliza Myers's free status almost certainly heightened her vulnerability to planter hostility.[33] Nevertheless, her story indicates the social threat that whites ascribed to African American midwives who developed independent relations with their clientele and acted from a complex sense of their authority and identity outside of white elite oversight or sponsorship.

Brief glimpses of midwives at work remind us that antebellum African American midwives were a large and varied group of southern practitioners. In making the argument that midwives worked between two potentially conflicting definitions of birth, I am not contending that all midwives uniformly chose African American concepts of social and spiritual relations over the slaveholder's underlying property interests. In truth, there was no single moment in which any enslaved midwife could declare such an allegiance and permanently resolve the contradictions of her labor. Rather, as midwives accumulated lifetimes of experience with birthing babies, they also by virtue of their position within the antebellum political economy acquired varying degrees of sophistication in negotiating the conflicting and unequal claims of slaveholders and enslaved families.

Between Black and White Households

If antebellum black midwives shared the burden of planter suspicion with other doctoring women, they were distinguished from this larger group by their frequent mobility across what historian Stephanie Camp has called the plantation's "geography of containment."[34] The most consistent phrase that African Americans in the 1930s used to describe the work of antebellum midwives was some variation on the expression "midwife to black and white."[35] Though legally bound to particular slaveholders, enslaved midwives frequently attended African American births in other households. The lower cost of midwives and doubts about white medical doctors' competence created demand for black midwives in white households outside the ones in which they were enslaved. This demand for midwives gave them unusual access to geographic mobility and sometimes even cash.

In an era of numerous restrictions on slave mobility, readiness to travel was a built-in requirement of midwifery work. Elsey, midwife and doctor woman for the Telfairs' Thorn Island Plantation, for example, traveled regularly to white households as well as the slave quarters of other plantations. Her frequent travels contrasted starkly with a regimen of passes, tickets, and outright prohibitions on "visiting" between two Telfair family plantations.[36] Although enslaved male artisans, hostlers, and boatmen traveled openly, midwives had one of the few skilled female occupations that required movement across plantation boundaries. The mobility of midwives is mentioned as frequently in Federal Writers' Project interviews as are the varied means of transportation. Cornelia Winfield's mother, a Georgia seamstress and house slave, rode a "horse and buggy" to attend births at other plantations. Sarah Pittman's grandmother in Louisiana rode sidesaddle on a "big old bay horse," and Jennie Ferrell's North Carolina–born grandmother rode horseback "far and near" as a midwife in Mississippi. Buggies, surreys, and horses signified the urgent dependence of white households on midwives' work. Ferrell identified access to elite modes of transportation as a distinctive feature of the antebellum political economy when she concluded her description of her grandmother's horseback travels by saying, "After freedom she walked."[37]

Along with unusual mobility, enslaved midwives derived a certain measure of autonomy through the nature of their responsibilities. Birthing babies was an unpredictable business, requiring practitioners to make independent decisions in response to the mother's changing condition. Moreover, nineteenth-century midwifery work extended beyond the birth to postpartum care and other domestic work in the mother's household. Some planters expected midwives to stay with the enslaved families they attended for up to a fortnight after the child's birth.[38] Wealthy white mothers often hired midwives for the duration of the confinement rather than simply the day of the birth. Thus, in one sense, the attributes of mobility, unpredictability, and distance from the slaveholder lent the midwife's work a certain leeway comparable to that of some male skilled labor. At the same time, however, the performance of the work within the heart of white households or plantation slave quarters in the presence of a birthing woman's relatives distinguished midwifery from the solitary work of enslaved fishermen, hunters, or male artisans.[39]

Victoria McMullen, speaking to Federal Writers' Project interviewers, captured the distinctive nature of midwifery in her description of her Grandmother Katy, a "nurse," "midwife," and "real good doctor." "In slavery times," according to McMullen, "my grandma was almost as free as she was in freedom because of her work."[40] Her statement was not simply the kind of nostalgic evasion that typically appears in some WPA interviews, for McMullen minced no words in describing the violence of her grandmother's enslavement. Rather, McMullen emphasized the rare and limited measure of control that Katy achieved over her labor through her travels as a midwife.

Carrie Pollard's memories of her aunt echoed this sense of autonomy but added to it the vulnerability that travel entailed for antebellum African American women. Pollard's aunt, Cynthia, a freeborn midwife, bore nine children with an enslaved man, Tom, who lived on a neighboring farm near Gainesville, Alabama. Although Tom's owner coveted Cynthia's children, he was unable to enslave them because of their legal status as children of a free mother. On one occasion, when Cynthia traveled roughly eight miles to Sumterville to attend a white woman in childbirth, Tom's owner kidnapped the children and carried them along with Tom to De Kalb, Mississippi. Cynthia drew on the whites in the household she was then attending, along with her legal white guardian, to organize a rescue party of white men on horseback. The successful retrieval of the children and Tom's subsequent reunion with Cynthia became a cornerstone of Carrie Pollard's family history, a memory intimately tied to Cynthia's identity as a midwife. Cynthia's mobility produced several contradictory results. Her absence from home heightened her children's vulnerability to abduction, while her midwifery work in white households allowed her to mobilize other whites to rescue her children. Her work as a midwife lent her insight into the interests of various whites in her neighborhood and how she might best attempt to gain a limited amount of security for her family.[41]

Slaveholders' ability to appropriate fees earned by enslaved midwives further underscored the tenuous nature of their autonomy. In their narratives, formerly enslaved midwives and their families closely linked the attributes of mobility and autonomy with the money earned. Antebellum midwife fees generally ranged between one and three dollars a visit, a sum less than that charged by white doctors but nevertheless significant within local economies.[42] The *Southern Cultivator* magazine noted the earning power of midwifery work and attempted to make political hay of this fact when it described enslaved "nurses" who were hired by the "most respectable families, especially in obstetrical cases." Enslaved midwives, argued this proslavery article, thus amassed "considerable income," far surpassing that of women in Europe's laboring class.[43] In actuality, birthing babies proved far less lucrative for enslaved women than this author suggested. Indeed, the theme of rightful ownership of birthing fees surfaced frequently in accounts of slave women's midwifery.

Whereas freedwomen such as Cynthia did indeed attempt to make a living through midwifery, slaveholders considerably hindered enslaved midwives' access to their hard-earned fees.[44] In 1837, well into Elsey's years as the Thorn Island midwife, the plantation instruction book read, "Many persons are in debt to Elsey for attending upon their negroes. I wish you to see them or send to them for the money."[45] But who would profit by the payment of Elsey's debt? Telfair's phrase, "in debt to Elsey," could imply that midwifery gave enslaved women access to cash and the internal slave economy.[46] The Federal Writers' Project interviews, however, support a more cautious interpretation. Mildred Graves's Virginia owner hired her out as a midwife and nurse for white families. "Sho he let me go," she told her interviewer, "twas money fer him, you know." Graves received "a few cents," while the owner collected the rest. Echoing this experience, Arkansas midwife Clara Walker asserted, "I made a lot o' money for old miss."[47] Crossing into white households thus also brought enslaved midwives a deeper awareness of how slaveholders exploited their slaves' valued labor.

Moving back and forth between black and white households gave African American midwives a distinctive perspective on southern social relations. Among enslaved women, midwives possessed a cherished mobility that allowed them to move across the geographic boundaries normally set by slaveholders. Indeed, formerly enslaved elders and their children distilled this mobility in memory as a way of describing the midwife's skill and importance to her local neighborhood. Midwives entered the intimate spaces of white households and observed white elite women and men in vulnerable moments of pain, fear, and joy. Finally, the cash that midwives generated through their labor for other whites underscored slaveholders' property interests in enslaved midwives' birthing skills. Whereas the culture of antebellum slave quarters contained an implicit critique of slave owning as the theft of African American bodies, enslaved midwives found in owners' claims on their fees an added theft of wages earned.[48]

Between Motherwit and Obstetrics

As enslaved midwives traveled among southern households, they also found it necessary to negotiate two contrasting worlds of birthing knowledge: an older African American concept of motherwit and the newly emerging medical field of obstetrics. Writing about the early twentieth century, Gertrude Fraser observes that the story of African American midwifery's encounter with medical science "does not lend itself to interpretations derived from a 'before' and 'after' model of change." In other words, rural black Virginians on the brink of public health regulation did not necessarily see a mutually exclusive relationship between a midwife and a physician. "Coexistence with scientific medicine," Fraser writes, "was neither alien nor untenable."[49] Fraser's insights can be extended back to the antebellum period, when slaveholders' vested interests in both midwives and enslaved infants shaped an uneasy coexistence between motherwit and obstetrics. Attributions of mentorship and training suggest that early African American midwives necessarily moved between these contrasting apprenticeship systems. It is clear that not every nineteenth-century African American midwife equally embraced each approach, yet evidence does suggest that enslaved midwives' work required greater familiarity with antebellum medical approaches to childbirth than one might gather from studies of twentieth-century midwifery.

In the absence of extended first-person reflections by antebellum African American midwives, I have found it useful instead to look at attributions of apprenticeship found within the WPA interviews and other oral histories, by which I mean the accounts given by midwives and their descendants regarding the midwives' training. Who introduced each woman to the world of childbirth and whom did she credit for her knowledge? For example, Margaret Charles Smith, a rural African American midwife for much of the twentieth century, obtained her license from the state of Alabama but drew her identity from a line of midwives reaching back into slavery. "I took training courses," she said, "but the midwife had already trained me, Ella Anderson. . . . [E]verything, everything I learned, I learned from Miss Anderson."[50] Although antebellum midwives did not have to concern themselves with the state apparatus of licensing, as Smith did, the earlier generation nevertheless shared her strong sense of occupation emerging from apprenticeship with older practitioners.

In the first category of apprenticeship narratives, midwives credited their skills to "motherwit," a blend of God-given wisdom, common sense, and the instruction of older women. According to this tradition, the transmission of knowledge took place in the context of a woman's emerging identity as a fully practicing midwife. Motherwit proceeded from oral instruction passed through a succession of African- and American-born foremothers and grounded itself in religious and ancestral authority.[51] A woman in the South Carolina Sea Islands expressed her commitment to her mother's knowledge with the following assertion: "My moder taught me day way, started me dat way, [I] keep up de way she started me."[52] Midwife Lula Russeau connected this matrilineal line of instruction to spiritual empowerment, maintaining that her enslaved mother, a midwife, "learnt me all I know." Russeau's calling as a midwife, however, preceded her training: "I wuz born" a midwife, she asserted, "God made me dat way."[53]

Choosing a successor (often a younger relative) through the guidance of dreams, visions, and signs was a momentous decision in an elder midwife's life (and one of the first prerogatives of African American midwives targeted by twentieth-century reform). We do not yet know enough about how slaveholders disrupted these lines of succession in the antebellum years, whether through sale and forced migration or by designating their own choice of birth attendant. Nevertheless, evidence from twentieth-century midwives suggests that their enslaved grandmothers found ways to pass on the calling to acceptable successors.[54] Onnie Lee Logan, a twentieth-century Alabama midwife, described her vocation as a legacy: "My grandmother inspired me," she told her interviewer, "and it still is in me today."[55]

Another, not necessarily contradictory, set of apprenticeship narratives identified a second line of instruction between young enslaved or free African American midwives and older white male professional doctors. Clara Walker, for example, was thirteen when her mistress hired her out to a white doctor. Walker worked with this man for five years, attending births in the slave quarters of many southern Arkansas plantations. As her skills increased, she reported, "he sit down an I'd do all de work."[56] Elizabeth Brannon's grandmother had been sold as a girl to a Virginia doctor, who "learned her to be a midwife."[57]

These references to white medical mentors present an interpretive puzzle. On the surface, they simply confirm that the antebellum political economy made it convenient for physicians to train young enslaved women as midwives who could assist their work, be profitably hired out, or sold as skilled laborers.[58] Training by a medical doctor may have represented an alternative path to nineteenth-century African American midwifery. The physician-trained women certainly learned about birthing at a much younger age than most enslaved midwives, who usually bore their own children before beginning to attend other families. Furthermore, the location of a small cluster of these women in Arkansas and Texas suggests that slaveholders may have trained younger enslaved women to do midwifery work on frontier settlements where established ties to older midwives had been broken by forced migration or the domestic slave trade.

On a more complicated level, however, apprenticeship narratives generated by WPA interviews require close attention to the way that formerly enslaved informants remembered, spoke, and kept silent about midwifery in the 1930s.[59] It would not be at all surprising, in a period when public health programs were bringing rural black midwifery under a racialized hierarchy topped by white physicians, that midwives and their family members would emphasize a white doctor as mentor. Furthermore, the interviews contain glimpses of other teachers and alternative sources of authoritative practice. Clara Walker's African-born mother may very well have played a role in her education, and Walker's birth with the "veil" over her face distinguished her as a person with spiritual gifts.[60] Sarah, who began attending births as a young enslaved assistant to a wealthy North Carolina planter and physician, also learned herbal medicines from her African-born mother.[61] Such evidence at the least suggests that African American midwives and their families navigated coexisting domains of knowledge about childbirth, choosing in various contexts which teachers to emphasize and credit.

Finally, accounts of young slave women trained by white physicians must be read alongside white doctors' considerable antipathy toward older enslaved midwives, which is evident in antebellum medical journals. White physicians took for granted the subordinate social position of their enslaved assistants and, unlike African American elder midwives, did not assume that their instruction implied a transfer of spiritual and social authority. Although mid-nineteenth-century southern physicians did not mount organized campaigns for antimidwife legislation, their public writings certainly reflected antimidwife rhetoric.[62] Antebellum southern doctors' efforts to label elder African American midwives ignorant, dirty, and incompetent thus proved less effective than twentieth-century campaigns did in eventually displacing midwives but were nonetheless significant in heightening many antebellum midwives' awareness of their practice within a racialized slave society.

White physicians blamed a host of reproductive disorders, birth complications, and high infant mortality on African American midwives. Some doctors accepted midwives as an ordinary feature of rural health care, but a more vocal component saw them as a southern health problem.[63] One aspiring medical student from Charleston attributed the prevalence of prolapsed uteruses in slave women to the "improper management" of "ignorant" enslaved midwives, who, he charged, used aggressive techniques to hurry the delivery of the placenta.[64] Other physicians attributed the high mortality of enslaved infants to midwives' "nasty nostrums" and aggressive manual intervention in labor.[65] From the 1840s on, the debate over the causes of the fatal disease neonatal tetanus focused particular criticism on, as one writer put it, the "unskillful management of negro midwives who do not know how to take care of the navel."[66]

Neonatal tetanus served as the grounds for one Savannah doctor's extended

confrontation with an enslaved midwife, who clearly found herself caught between motherwit and obstetrics. In an 1847 article in the *Southern Medical and
Surgical Journal*, P. M. Kollock presented his version of the story. Like other
medical practitioners in the period before the discovery of the tetanus bacil-
lus, Kollock believed that contamination or irritation of the navel was the most
likely cause of neonatal tetanus. According to his account, Kollock "severely rep-
rimanded" an enslaved midwife on a "neighboring plantation" for persisting
with the common practice of placing a scorched piece of cloth on the navel.
Substituting his own method, Kollock directed the woman to dress the navel
with cerate ointment and wash it twice daily with warm water.[67] For a time, the
midwife complied, but when she later returned to her original method, Kollock
enlisted the authority of the slaveholder to threaten her "with punishment." In
this case, the scientific interests of the doctor joined with the slaveholder's property interests. Physical coercion, not state bureaucracy, became the instrument
of attempted control.

Read against the grain, Kollock's comments reveal enslaved women's resistance, however veiled, to obstetric reforms. The doctors went on to report that
he waged his personal campaign to reform local midwifery practices "notwithstanding the occasional broad, and not to be misunderstood hints, on the part
of the *sage femmes*, that I was meddling with what was no business of mine."[68] If
white male doctors had any accepted role in birth, these Georgia midwives perceived it as ending with delivery. Postpartum care of mother and child, which
in African American culture held spiritual as well as physiological significance,
belonged to the midwife.[69] In this particular instance, obstetrics served not as a
parallel source of birthing knowledge but rather as a hostile intruder on motherwit. As with earlier sections of this chapter, the point here is not whether
enslaved midwives identified with the authority of obstetrics or the wisdom
of motherwit but the fact that African American midwives under slavery on a
mundane basis negotiated both realms. Such daily negotiations between socially
unequal practitioners deepened midwives' consciousness of the relationship between health and power and honed their skills of translation between forms of
birthing knowledge.

"Culture is not a fixed condition but a process," historian Lawrence Levine
has observed.[70] In this light, African American midwifery under slavery was
a changing art shaped by the constant negotiations of enslaved women at work.
Slaveholders enlisted African American midwives as health workers in service of
slaveholder wealth. At the same time, African American midwifery was, among
enslaved communities, a cultural institution that met physical and spiritual
needs. African American midwives based much of their authority and training
as healers in the cultural and religious values of enslaved communities. Their

work took them, literally and figuratively, across the boundaries of southern black and white households, where they witnessed both the value of their skills and the theft of their fees. Their practice required a keen consciousness of both their designated role as subservient plantation health workers and their identities as respected doctor women. As the primary birth attendants of the rural South, antebellum midwives confronted the emerging conflict between the domain of black-woman-authored midwifery knowledge and a white male domain of obstetrical science. In short, African American midwives faced white efforts to control their work, define their roles, and appropriate their skills well in advance of Progressive Era legislation.

It is important to realize both the small amount of time and the large historical shifts that lie between the last generation of enslaved midwives and the first generation of African American midwives subjected to systematic, state-sponsored public health regulation. In the aftermath of emancipation, transformations of labor and economy dramatically reduced both white doctors' involvement in and white planters' vested interests in African American birth. African American midwives, however, continued to function as valued healers for black families in the context of grossly unequal access to biomedical care.[71] When early-twentieth-century public health boards and medical professionals began their intensive "reeducation" of African American midwives, they engaged women whose mothers and grandmothers had long ago developed strategies for negotiating contentious racial politics alongside difficult births. These strategies, as well as the spiritual and cultural meanings of birth, formed an important legacy of antebellum African American midwives to their twentieth-century daughters.

NOTES

For comments on previous versions of this paper, I thank Peter Lindert and Tracy McKenzie. I am also grateful for Stephanie Camp's advice as friend and editor and for the insightful remarks of this volume's anonymous reviewer. This chapter is an extension and further development of material from my book, *Working Cures: Healing, Health, and Power on Southern Slave Plantations* (Chapel Hill, 2002).

1. Charles L. Perdue Jr., Thomas E. Barden, and Robert K. Phillips, eds., *Weevils in the Wheat: Interviews with Virginia Ex-slaves* (Charlottesville, 1976), 120–21.

2. Book-length studies of antebellum midwifery focus on the North and largely exclude African American women; see Laurel Thatcher Ulrich, *A Midwife's Tale: The Life of Martha Ballard, Based on Her Diary, 1785–1812* (New York, 1990); Richard W. Wertz and Dorothy C. Wertz, *Lying-In: A History of Childbirth in America* (New York, 1977); Jane Donegan, *Women and Men Midwives: Medicine, Morality, and Misogyny in Early America* (Westport, 1978); Judith Walzer Leavitt, *Brought to Bed: Childbearing in Amer-*

ica, 1750–1950 (New York, 1986); Janet Bogdan, "Care or Cure? Childbirth Practices in Nineteenth-Century America," *Feminist Studies* 4 (June 1978): 92–99.

3. Molly Ladd-Taylor, " 'Grannies' and 'Spinsters': Midwife Education under the Sheppard-Towner Act," *Journal of Social History* 22 (Winter 1988): 255–75; Gertrude Jacinta Fraser, *African American Midwifery in the South: Dialogues of Birth, Race, and Memory* (Cambridge, 1998); Susan Smith, *Sick and Tired of Being Sick and Tired: Black Women's Health Activism in America, 1890–1950* (Philadelphia, 1995), 118–48; Beatrice Mongeau, Harvey L. Smith, and Ann C. Maney, "The 'Granny' Midwife: Changing Roles and Functions of a Folk Practitioner," *American Journal of Sociology* 66 (March 1961): 497–505; Holly F. Mathews, "Killing the Medical Self-Help Tradition among African Americans: The Case of Lay Midwifery in North Carolina, 1912–1983," in *African Americans in the South: Issues of Race, Class, and Gender*, ed. Hans A. Baer and Yvonne Jones (Athens, 1992), 60–78. Margaret Charles Smith and Linda Janet Holmes, *Listen to Me Good: The Life Story of an Alabama Midwife* (Columbus, 1996); Onnie Lee Logan, *Motherwit: An Alabama Midwife's Story* (New York, 1989); Louvenia Taylor Benjamin and Linda Janet Holmes, "Louvenia Taylor Benjamin, South Lay Midwife: An Interview," *SAGE* 2 (Fall 1985): 51–54; Beverly J. Robinson, *Aunt (Ānt) Phyllis* (Berkeley, 1989); Deborah Anne Susie, *In the Way of Our Grandmothers: A Cultural View of Twentieth-Century Midwifery in Florida* (Athens, 1988).

4. John W. Blassingame, "Status and Social Structure in the Slave Community: Evidence from New Sources," in *Perspectives and Irony in American Slavery*, ed. Harry P. Owens (Jackson, 1976), 137–51.

5. Deborah Gray White, *Ar'n't I a Woman? Female Slaves in the Plantation South* (New York, 1985), 128–30; see also Jacqueline Jones, *Labor of Love, Labor of Sorrow: Black Women, Work, and the Family from Slavery to the Present* (New York, 1985), 40–41.

6. Jennifer L. Morgan, *Laboring Women: Reproduction and Gender in New World Slavery* (Chapel Hill, 2004); Sharla M. Fett, *Working Cures: Healing, Health, and Power on Southern Slave Plantations* (Chapel Hill, 2002), 45–55, 129–30; Marie Jenkins Schwartz, *Born in Bondage: Growing Up Enslaved in the Antebellum South* (Cambridge, 2000), 37–42.

7. Lawrence W. Levine, *Black Culture and Black Consciousness: Afro-American Folk Thought from Slavery to Freedom* (New York, 1977); Ira Berlin and Philip D. Morgan, "The Slaves' Economy: Independent Production by Slaves in the Americas," *Slavery and Abolition* 12 (May 1991): 1–30. On enslaved women and political consciousness, see Gayle T. Tate, *Unknown Tongues: Black Women's Political Activism in the Antebellum Era, 1830–1860* (East Lansing, 2003), 4–11.

8. While historians have debated extensively the merits and drawbacks of Federal Writers' Project interviews, each of the types of sources mentioned here must be read carefully and in context. For an excellent discussion of sources on antebellum slave life and thought and additional references to the debates on the WPA interviews, see Mia Bay, *The White Image in the Black Mind: African-American Ideas about White People, 1830–1925* (New York, 1999), 114–16.

9. Fraser, *African American Midwifery*, 43, 142–43; on midwives and burial preparation, see Logan, *Motherwit*, 69; Margaret Charles Smith and Holmes, *Listen to Me Good*, 79–81.

10. One type of boundary crossing that I will not address here is the intermediary role of midwives between state bureaucracy and southern households. Antebellum midwives were much less subject to this role than twentieth-century midwives, who were legally coerced into participation in state record keeping through mandated birth certificates; see Fraser, *African American Midwifery*, 44–49, 53–54, 55, 62–64, 65–67, 74–76. State-level collection of vital statistics had only just begun to emerge in the late antebellum period. An 1858 South Carolina statute required "all physicians and midwives" to keep birth and death registries and instructed them in the different data required for slave versus free entries. Virginia also began to collect birth and death statistics in 1853 but directed county commissioners of revenue to carry out the task. Although some of these efforts named midwives, it is likely that enslaved midwives did not regularly participate in collecting these early population statistics, and it appears that no legislation enforced the record keeping requirements. See *State Slavery Statutes, 1789–1860: South Carolina* (Frederick, 1989), no. 4410, 1858; Todd L. Savitt, *Medicine and Slavery: The Diseases and Health Care of Blacks in Antebellum Virginia* (Urbana, 1978), 136.

11. James W. C. Pennington, "The Fugitive Blacksmith," in *Great Slave Narratives*, ed. Arna Bontemps (Boston, 1969), 196, 198.

12. Jennifer L. Morgan, *Laboring Women*, 4.

13. Gavin Wright, *The Political Economy of the Cotton South: Households, Markets, and Wealth in the Nineteenth Century* (New York, 1978), 24; White, *Ar'n't I a Woman?* 67–70, 99–105; Savitt, *Medicine and Slavery*, 166, 195–201.

14. Richard H. Steckel, "A Dreadful Childhood: The Excess Mortality of American Slaves," *Social Science History* 10 (Winter 1986): 427–65; John Campbell, "Work, Pregnancy, and Infant Mortality among Southern Slaves," *Journal of Interdisciplinary History* 14 (Spring 1984): 793–812; Cheryll Ann Cody, "Cycles of Work and of Childbearing: Seasonality in Women's Lives on Low Country Plantations," in *More than Chattel: Black Women and Slavery in the Americas*, ed. David Barry Gaspar and Darlene Clark Hine (Bloomington, 1996), 61–78.

15. John A. Calhoun, E. E. DuBose, Virgil Bobo, "Management of Slaves," *Southern Cultivator* 4 (August 1846): 1–2; see also John M. Turner, "Plantation Hygiene," *Southern Cultivator* 15 (1857): 140.

16. W. Fletcher Holmes, "Typhoid Fever, as Observed in Newberry District, S.C.," *Charleston Medical Journal and Review* 7 (1852): 60.

17. John H. Morgan, "An Essay on the Causes of the Production of Abortion among Our Negro Population," *Nashville Journal of Medicine and Surgery* 19 (1860): 117–23; E. M. Pendleton, "On the Comparative Fecundity of the Caucasian and African Races," *Charleston Medical Journal and Review* 6 (1851): 351–56. For a doctor's implication that "many negro women" welcomed miscarriage and sought to avoid childbearing, see M. Troy, "Case of Retention of the Foetus for Three Weeks after Rupture of the Membranes and the Escape of the Liquor Amnii," *New Orleans Medical and Surgical Journal* 15 (July 1858): 581; William L. McCaa, "Observations on the Manner of Living and Diseases of the Slaves on the Wateree River" (medical school thesis, University of Pennsylvania, 1823, Waring Historical Library, Charleston, S.C.), 12.

18. Steven M. Stowe, "Obstetrics and the World of Doctoring in the Mid-Nineteenth-Century American South," *Bulletin of the History of Medicine* 64 (Winter 1990): 540–

66; Sally G. McMillen, *Motherhood in the Old South: Pregnancy, Childbirth, and Infant Rearing* (Baton Rouge, 1990), 70; Logan, *Motherwit*, 47.

19. L. S. Joynes, "Remarks on the Report of the Auditor of Public Accounts to the General Assembly of Virginia relative to the Registration of Births, Marriages, and Deaths," *Virginia Medical Journal* 7 (1856): 7; Savitt, *Medicine and Slavery*, 182; Stowe, "Obstetrics and the World of Doctoring," 548–49, 556; Eugene D. Genovese, *Roll, Jordan, Roll: The World the Slaves Made* (New York, 1976), 497; Bennett H. Wall, "Medical Care of Ebenezer Pettigrew's Slaves," *Mississippi Valley Historical Review* 37 (December 1950): 451–70. On the question of whether slaves or slaveholders chose the birth attendants for enslaved mothers, see Schwartz, *Born in Bondage*, 33–37.

Only rarely do medical account books note doctors attending complications such as "delivering adherent placenta" or "instrumental delivery of wench on plantation" (John Ogilvie, Medical Account Books, 1845–70, March 23, 1848, March 24, 1860, South Caroliniana Library, University of South Carolina, Columbia; W. B. Boyd, Account Book, September 16, 1858, South Caroliniana Library; C. V. Barnes Account Book, vol. 1, 1858–59, pp. 10, 12, South Caroliniana Library; Andrew Hasell Medical Account Book, South Carolina Historical Society, Charleston (hereafter SCHS); Henry Ravenel Medical Daybook, January 28, [1816?], January 21, 1816, SCHS.

20. George P. Rawick, *The American Slave: A Composite Autobiography* (Westport, 1972–78), supp. ser. 1, vol. 7, pt. 2, p. 409.

21. John Sneed, "Texas Narratives" 16:49; Thomas Foote, "Maryland Narratives," 8:14; Rebecca Hooks, "Florida Narratives," 3:171; Dellie Lewis, "Alabama Narratives" 1:256; unless otherwise noted, all state ex-slave narratives are cited from "Born in Slavery: Slave Narratives from the Federal Writers' Project, 1936–1937," available at http://memory.loc .gov/ammem/snhtml/snhome.html. See also Logan, *Motherwit*, 48.

22. Thorn Island Rule and Direction Book, June 11, 1832, 1837; "List of Negroes at Thorn Island," 1836, Telfair Family Papers, Georgia Historical Society, Savannah; sale broadside, January 23, 1860, Louis D. De Saussure Papers, SCHS. For other evidence that midwives were also charged with sick care and/or child care on southern plantations, see "Susannah, midwife and hospital nurse," in Gordon Gang slave list, n.d., Ford/Ravenel Papers, SCHS; "Phoebe, midwife and nurses children," 1849 sale list, William Ravenel Papers, SCHS; Frances Anne Kemble, *Journal of a Residence on a Georgian Plantation in 1838–1839*, ed. John A. Scott (Athens, 1984), 66, 98–99.

23. Sale broadside, January 21, 1859, De Saussure Papers; see also sale broadside, n.d., De Saussure Papers; Jennie Ferrell, "Arkansas Narratives," 2:282; Sarah Whitmore, "Arkansas Narratives," 2:141.

24. Cornelia Winfield, "Georgia Narratives," 4:177; Isaiah Green, "Georgia Narratives," 4:51; Clara Walker, "Arkansas Narratives," 2:22; Elizabeth Brannon, "Arkansas Narratives," 2:237; Victoria McMullen, "Arkansas Narratives," 2:33; Jennie Wormly Gibson, "Arkansas Narratives," 2:17; Sneed, "Texas Narratives," 16:49; Everett Ingram, "Alabama Narratives," 1:215.

25. For an extended analysis of enslaved women's health work on plantations, see Fett, *Working Cures*, 111–41.

26. "Note—'Nurse' on a Southern Plantation," *Southern Cultivator* 5 (May 1847): 67; see also P[hilip] Tidyman, "A Sketch of the Most Remarkable Diseases of the Negroes

of the Southern States," *Philadelphia Journal of the Medical and Physical Sciences*, n.s., 3 (1826): 332. On slaveholder expectations that midwives would assist the planter in monitoring pregnancies of enslaved women, see Schwartz, *Born in Bondage*, 30.

27. Of forty-seven slave-management articles appearing in three popular agricultural journals—*De Bow's Review* (New Orleans), *Southern Planter* (Richmond, Va.), and *Southern Cultivator* (Augusta, Ga.)—between 1847 and 1860, only two articles referred to the activities of slave "midwives," one to enslaved "doctor women," and one to the obstetrical activities of plantation "nurses"; see W. C. Daniell, "Health of Young Negroes," *De Bow's Review* 20 (June 1856): 746; P. C. Weston, "Management of a Southern Plantation," *De Bow's Review* 22 (January 1857): 41; R. W. Gibbes, "Southern Slave Life," *De Bow's Review* 24 (April 1858): 321–22, 324; Ed. Farm. Lib., "Note—'Nurse' on a Southern Plantation," *Southern Cultivator* 5 (May 1847): 67.

28. White, *Ar'n't I A Woman?* 111, 124–30; Fett, *Working Cures*, 75–76, 130–131; Blassingame, "Status and Social Structure," 142–43.

29. Fraser, *African American Midwifery*, 215–16; Schwartz, *Born in Bondage*, 37.

30. Fraser, *African American Midwifery*, 218–24, 226–28, 230–37, 239–47; Schwartz, *Born in Bondage*, 37–39; Mongeau, Smith, and Maney, " 'Granny' Midwife," 501–3; Lula Russeau, 58, Federal Writers' Project Microfiche Collection, Southern Historical Collection, University of North Carolina, Chapel Hill; Ophelia Settle Egypt, J. Masuoka, and Charles S. Johnson, eds. *Unwritten History of Slavery: Autobiographical Account of Negro Ex-slaves* (1945; Westport, 1972), 39; Rawick, *American Slave*, supp. ser. 1, vol. 7, pt. 2, p. 409. Evidence for African American midwifery practices comes largely from postemancipation sources, including folklore collections and former slave interviews. Historians working with these postemancipation sources must keep in mind how the conditions of slavery both impeded and allowed certain popular birth practices.

31. Kemble, *Journal of a Residence*, 293. For an emphasis on the "ideal midwife" as one who could maneuver between slave and slaveholder expectations, see Schwartz, *Born in Bondage*, 40.

32. This incident is discussed in White, *Ar'n't I A Woman?* 126, citing Robert Myers, *The Children of Pride: A True Story of Georgia and the Civil War* (New Haven, 1972), 528, 532, 542, 544, 546. On the broader subject of enslaved women's resistance to bearing children under slavery, see Darlene Clark Hine and Kate Wittenstein, "Female Slave Resistance: The Economics of Sex," in *The Black Woman Cross-Culturally*, ed. Filomina Chioma Steady (Cambridge, 1981), 289–99. The scarcity of sources illuminating the involvement of midwives in enslaved women's resistance against rape and childbearing under slavery leads to one of the painful silences in the history of African American midwifery (Michele Mitchell, "Silences Broken, Silences Kept: Gender and Sexuality in African-American History," *Gender and History* 11 [November 1999]: 433–44).

33. Foote, "Maryland Narratives," 8:15. Foote goes on to say that under interrogation, Eliza Myers either inadvertently or deliberately supplied information that led to the fugitive's recapture.

34. Stephanie Camp applies this phrase, coined by Houston Baker, to southern antebellum plantations in *Closer to Freedom: Enslaved Women and Everyday Resistance in the Plantation South* (Chapel Hill, 2004), 6, 28–33.

35. See Ferrell, "Arkansas Narratives," 2:282; Whitmore, "Arkansas Narratives," 2:140;

Walker, "Arkansas Narratives," 2:21; Sara Pittman, "Arkansas Narratives," 2:354; Mc-Mullen, "Arkansas Narratives," 2:33; Foote, "Maryland Narratives," 8:14; Nancy Boudry, "Georgia Narratives," 4:113; Brannon, "Arkansas Narratives," 2:237.

36. Thorn Island Rule and Direction Book, June 11, 1832, Telfair Family Papers. Some of the largest plantations, such as the Butler Island plantation described by Frances Kemble, contained several slave settlements, thereby requiring enslaved women doctors to travel considerable distances even within plantation boundaries.

37. Winfield, "Georgia Narratives," 4:177; Pittman, "Arkansas Narratives," 2:354; Ferrell, "Arkansas Narratives," 2:282. For a description of another doctor woman (not named as a midwife) traveling on horseback, see Rawick, *American Slave*, supp. ser. 1, 4:449; see also Logan, *Motherwit*, 48.

38. Richard J. Arnold to I. Swanston, May 22, 1837, Richard J. Arnold to Mr. Sanford, [May 19, 1840], Arnold and Screven Family Papers, Correspondence, ser. 1.1, Southern Historical Collection.

39. See, for example, the potential for quasi independence among enslaved fishermen, discussed in David S. Cecelski, *The Waterman's Song: Slavery and Freedom in Maritime North Carolina* (Chapel Hill, 2001), 25–56, 67.

40. McMullen, "Arkansas Narratives," 2:33.

41. Carrie Pollard, "Alabama Narratives," 1:318–19.

42. Savitt, *Medicine and Slavery*, 182.

43. "Note—'Nurse' on a Southern Plantation," *Southern Cultivator* 5 (May 1847): 67.

44. On midwives earning a living after emancipation, see Jacqueline Jones, *Labor of Love, Labor of Sorrow*, 56, 89–90.

45. Thorn Island Rule and Direction Book, 1837, Telfair Family Papers. For a North Carolina merchant and planter whose account books include midwife fees, see Thomas Carroll Account Book, 1844–67, Duke University Library, Durham, N.C. Carroll paid fees directly to black and white midwives (April 19, 1853, March 1, December 29, 1859) as well as to men who may have hired out enslaved midwives (August 25, 1849).

46. On property and gender within enslaved communities, see Berlin and Morgan, "The Slaves' Economy"; Dylan C. Penningroth, *The Claims of Kinfolk: African American Property and Community in the Nineteenth-Century South* (Chapel Hill, 2003); Larry E. Hudson Jr., *To Have and to Hold: Slave Work and Family Life in Antebellum South Carolina* (Athens, 1997), 32–78.

47. Perdue, Barden, and Phillips, *Weevils in the Wheat*, 120–21; Walker, "Arkansas Narratives," 2:21–22; see also Fanny Smith Hodges, "Mississippi Narratives," 9:69, who confirmed that midwifery brought "good money" but did not comment on who profited.

48. On African American vernacular analysis of slaveholders' claims to human property, see Levine, *Black Culture and Black Consciousness*, 130–31; Michael A. Gomez, *Exchanging Our Country Marks: The Transformation of African Identities in the Colonial and Antebellum South* (Chapel Hill, 1998), 199–207; Fett, *Working Cures*, 30–34.

49. Fraser, *African American Midwifery*, 259.

50. Margaret Charles Smith and Holmes, *Listen to Me Good*, 75.

51. Fraser, *African American Midwifery*, 197–200.

52. Elsie Clews Parsons, *Folk-Lore of the Sea Islands, South Carolina* (New York, 1923),

197. At times midwife and planter choices for successor may have converged. James Henry Hammond noted in his plantation rulebook that when midwives attended the women in childbirth, "some other woman learning the art usually assists her." Hammond does not indicate how the woman in training was selected (James H. Hammond, "Plantation Manual of James H. Hammond of Beach Island, South Carolina," [c. 1834], typescript of original in Joseph I. Waring Research Files, Waring Historical Library).

53. Lula Russeau, 54, Federal Writers' Project Microfiche Collection, Southern Historical Collection.

54. Fraser, *African American Midwifery*, 190–197; Mongeau, Smith, and Maney, " 'Granny' Midwife," 501–2; Susie, *In the Way of Our Grandmothers*, 13–16.

55. Logan, *Motherwit*, 48. Networks of instructions in African American doctoring were not exclusively female. For example, one African-born midwife in coastal Georgia taught her grandson, Jack Waldburg, how "tuh make medicine from root" (Georgia Writers' Project, Savannah Unit, ed., *Drums and Shadows: Survival Studies among the Georgia Coastal Negroes* [Athens, 1940], 68).

56. Walker, "Arkansas Narratives," 2:21.

57. Brannon, "Arkansas Narratives," 2:237; see also Sneed, "Texas Narratives," 16:49. The WPA interviews also contain descriptions of doctors training African American women who then became midwives just after emancipation; see Bell Williams, "Arkansas Narratives," 2:149; Cyntha Jones, "Arkansas Narratives," 2:139.

58. Mongeau, Smith, and Maney suggest partnerships, though hierarchical and "with a division of labor along class and color lines," between white rural doctors and African American midwives in the early twentieth century (" 'Granny' Midwife," 502–3).

59. Gertrude Fraser provides a sophisticated reading of the silences and ambivalent opinions encountered in her late-twentieth-century informants' comments on African American midwifery and birthing. Silences, she argues, result from cultural perspectives of a particular generation of rural African Americans on the private nature of birth-related experiences as well as the outcome of a constellation of shame, punishment, and intrusion represented by public health regulation and Jim Crow health systems (*African American Midwifery*, 139–61, 261–63).

60. Walker, "Arkansas Narratives," 2:19.

61. Margaret C. Albert, "John and Sarah: Triumph over Slavery," *Pittsburgh History* 81 (Spring 1998): 20; see also Schwartz, *Born in Bondage*, 40.

62. McMillen, *Motherhood in the Old South*, 17–18.

63. Ibid., 19. Neutral to positive physician references to African American midwives include Troy, "Case of Retention," 583; William A. Patteson, "On the Operation of Hysterotomy," *Virginia Medical Journal* 6 (January 1856): 1–6.

64. F[ranklin] Perry Pope, "A Dissertation on the Professional Management of Negro Slaves" (thesis, Medical College of the State of South Carolina, 1837, Waring Historical Library), 13, 14.

65. James P. Jervey, "Rupture of Uterus from Manual Violence," *Southern Journal of Medicine and Pharmacy* 2 (1847): 34; Thomas Affleck, "On the Hygiene of Cotton Plantations and the Management of Negro Slaves," *Southern Medical Reports* 2 (1850): 435.

66. Affleck, "On the Hygiene," 435; P. C. Gaillard, "Remarks on Trismus Nascentium,"

Southern Journal of Medicine and Pharmacy 1 (1846): 503; Sally G. McMillen, " 'No Uncommon Disease': Neonatal Tetanus, Slave Infants, and the Southern Medical Profession," *Journal of the History of Medicine and Allied Sciences* 46 (July 1991): 301, 308, 309; Deborah Kuhn McGregor, *From Midwives to Medicine: The Birth of American Gynecology* (New Brunswick, 1998), 29.

67. P. M. Kollock, "Case of Traumatic Tetanus Cured by Strychnine," *Southern Medical and Surgical Journal* 3 (October 1847): 601. Cerate is a fatty ointment mixed with wax or resin. Conflict over African American midwives' practice of dressing the navel continued into the twentieth century; see Fraser, *African American Midwifery*, 230–37.

68. Kollock, "Case of Traumatic Tetanus," 601.

69. Schwartz, *Born in Bondage*, 38–39.

70. Levine, *Black Culture and Black Consciousness*, 5. The full quotation reads, "Culture is not a fixed condition but a process: the product of interaction between the past and present. Its toughness and resiliency are determined not by a culture's ability to withstand change, which indeed may be a sign of stagnation not life, but by its ability to react creatively and responsibly to the realities of a new situation."

71. The years between emancipation and twentieth-century regulation represent a little-researched period of African American midwifery. This may have been the period in which whites intruded least on African American midwifery practices, if only because of systemic exclusion and discrimination on the part of white health care providers and institutions (Fraser, *African American Midwifery*, 32).

The Pleasures of Resistance

Enslaved Women and Body Politics
in the Plantation South, 1830–1861

STEPHANIE M. H. CAMP

*A*s a young woman, Nancy Williams joined other enslaved people and "cou'tin' couples" who would "slip 'way" to an "ole cabin" a few miles from the Virginia plantation where she lived. Deep in the woods, away from slaveholding eyes, they held secret parties at which the slaves amused themselves by dancing, performing music, drinking alcohol, and courting. A religious woman in her old age, Williams admitted only reluctantly to her interviewer that she had enjoyed the secular pleasures of dressing up and going to these outlaw dances. "Dem de day's when me'n de devil was runnin roun in de depths o' hell. No, don' even wanna talk 'bout it," she said. However, Williams ultimately agreed to discuss the outlaw parties she had attended, reasoning, "Guess I didn' know no better den," and remembering with fondness that, after all, "Dem dances was somepin."[1]

Musicians played fiddles, tambourines, banjos, and "two sets o' [cow] bones" for the dancers. Williams was a gifted and enthusiastic dancer; she would get "out dere in de middle o' de flo' jes' a-dancin'; me an Jennie, an' de devil. Dancin' wid a glass o' water on my head an' three boys a bettin' on me." Williams won this contest by dancing the longest while balancing the glass of water on her head without spilling a drop. She "jes' danced ole Jennie down." Like the other women in attendance, Williams took pride in her outfits at these illicit parties, and she went to great trouble to make them. She adorned one dress with ruffles and dyed others yellow or red. Her yellow dress even had matching yellow shoes; they were ill fitting, as many bondpeople's wooden brogans were, and "sho' did hurt me," but "dat ain' stop me f'om dancin'." By illuminating a part of everyday life that bondpeople kept hidden, Nancy Williams's account of attending outlaw slave parties helps uncover one part of the story of enslaved women's lives: the role that the body played in slaveholders' endeavors to control their labor force and in black resistance to bondage in the nineteenth-century plantation South. Despite planters' tremendous efforts to prevent such escape, enslaved women and men sporadically "slip[ped] 'way" to take pleasure in their bodies.[2]

At the heart of the process of enslavement was a geographical impulse to locate bondpeople in plantation space. Winthrop D. Jordan found that confinement, "more than any other single quality," differentiated slavery from servitude in the early years of American slavery's formation. Not only a power or labor relation, "enslavement was captivity." Accordingly, black mobility appears to have been the target of more official and planter regulations than other aspects of slave behavior.[3] Slaveholders strove to create controlled and controlling landscapes that would determine the uses to which enslaved people put their bodies. But slaveholders could not dictate body politics in the Old South. To the contrary, slave owners' attempts to control both black movement and other aspects of black bodily experience created a terrain on which bondpeople would contest slaveholding power. Bondpeople, who had their own plans for their bodies, violated the boundaries of space and time intended to demarcate and consolidate planters' patriarchal power over plantation households. This alternative negotiation and mapping of plantation space might best be called, in Edward Said's phrase, a "rival geography." Enslaved people's rival geography was not a fixed spatial formation, for it included quarters, outbuildings, woods, swamps, and neighboring farms as opportunity permitted. Where slaveholders' mapping of the plantation was defined by rigid places for its residents, the rival geography was characterized by motion: the secret movement of bodies, objects, and information within and around plantation space. Together but differently, women and men took flight to the same woods and swamps that planters had intended as the borders of the plantation's "geography of containment."[4] There the slaves held clandestine and illegal parties. These parties were sporadic affairs, contingent as they were on opportunity (itself informed by the season), on the availability of resources, and no doubt on the emotional climate within local black communities and between enslaved people and their owners. This chapter studies the personal and political meanings of bodily pleasure made and experienced at these parties, focusing on the activities of women.

No mere safety valve, bondpeople's rival geography demands to be understood in multiple ways. To a degree, black mappings and uses of southern space were the result and expression of the dialogic of power relations between owner and owned—part of day-to-day plantation relations characterized by a paternalistic combination of hegemonic cultural control and violent discipline. To a large extent, however, the paternalist framework fails to explain everyday slave resistance. The paternalist model offers an apt theory of plantation management but a fundamentally incomplete perspective on plantation—and particularly black—life. Viewing resistance other than organized rebellion or running away as only partial or even as co-optative distracts us from interesting and important possibilities for understanding black politics during slavery, such as the hidden, everyday acts that help to form overt resistance. The tendency to draw a sharp line between material and political issues on the one hand and aesthetic, spiritual, and (emotionally and physically) intimate issues on the other also limits our understanding of human lives, especially those of women, in the past.[5]

Evidence is spare but comes to us consistently from both the Upper and Lower South in slaveholders' diaries and journals, in state legislative records, in nineteenth-century autobiographies, and in twentieth-century interviews of the formerly enslaved.[6] Many recent studies on American slavery focus on a subregion, a crop, or a county. This trend has deepened our understanding of the variations of work and culture in American slavery, has furthered our sense of important differences among enslaved people, and has added texture and detail to our picture of day-to-day life in bondage. At the same time, studying slavery as a wider regional system of domination, profit, and racial formation remains a valuable practice, as recent innovative and informative works on the slave past have also demonstrated.[7] Throughout the antebellum period and across the plantation South, enslaved people took flight to nearby woods and swamps for the secret parties they occasionally held at night.[8]

This chapter pieces together the story and politics of these illicit parties, arguing that these celebrations and the bodily pleasures that accompanied them occupied the wide terrain of political struggle between consent and open, organized rebellion.[9] The bondpeople who participated in activities in the rival geography expressed, enjoyed, and used their somatic, or bodily, selves in terms other than those of their relationship to their owners. They took pleasure in their bodies, competed with other enslaved people with them, and contested their owners' power over them. Bondpeople's everyday somatic politics had more than symbolic value: they resulted in temporal and material gains for enslaved people and in some loss of labor for slaveholders. If bondpeople's uses of their bodies and their time were contingent on the season, the ignorance of their owners, and the ability to find a safe location (and they were), these uses nonetheless also undermined slaveholders' claims to slaves' bodies and time. Everyday resistance to pass laws and plantation rules was an endemic problem in the rural South, with real and subversive effects on slaveholding mastery and on plantation productivity, both of which rested on elite white spatial and temporal control of enslaved bodies.

The body, as French historian Dorinda Outram has written, is at once the most personal, intimate thing that people possess and the most public. The body, then, provides a "basic political resource" in struggles between dominant and subordinate classes. As second-wave feminists put it, the personal is political. C. L. R. James, Grace C. Lee, and Pierre Chaulieu have previously argued that "ordinary . . . people . . . are rebelling every day in ways of their own invention [to] regain control over their own conditions of life and their relations with one another"; often, "their struggles are on a small personal scale." Enslaved people's everyday battles to regain control—albeit temporally limited—took place on this very personal terrain.[10]

Enslaved people possessed multiple social bodies.[11] Inhabitants of a premodern society, they were made to suffer domination largely through the body in the form of exploitation, physical punishment, and captivity. Theorists of colonialism have analyzed the effects of somatic suffering in other, analogous contexts. Describing the consequences of European colonialism for twentieth-century Africans, Frantz Fanon wrote, "In the white world the man of color encounters difficulties in the development of his bodily schema. Consciousness of the body is solely a negating activity. It is a third-person consciousness. The body is surrounded by an atmosphere of certain uncertainty." Caught in the white gaze, Fanon argued, blacks were "sealed in that crushing objecthood." Under colonialism, experiences of the body were negating activities in which identification with the colonizer resulted in degrees of self-hatred and humiliation. Students of American slavery will find much with which to agree in Fanon's analysis of black bodily experience. Violent attacks by white people, brutal and exhausting labor, sickness brought on by diseased environments such as South Carolina's rice swamps, and exposure on the auction block were basic characteristics of life in slavery. Indeed, these characteristics were, in combination with confinement of the black body on the property of whites, the essence of bondage.[12]

However, brutality did not constitute the whole of black bodily experience. For people who, like bondpeople and women generally, have experienced oppression through the body, the body becomes an important site not only of suffering but also (and therefore) of resistance, enjoyment, and potentially transcendence. Studying the body as both the target of containment and the means of transgression grants us access to new perspectives on resistance and the workings of gender difference within enslaved plantation communities. Thinking about the black body in space allows us to think about it materially and to watch as the prime implement of labor in the Old South moved in ways inconsistent with the rigors of agricultural production. And attention to the body also facilitates thinking about issues beyond the material, such as the roles of movement and pleasure in the culture of opposition developed by enslaved people. A somatic approach, such as the one employed here, risks objectifying people, but the point is the opposite: to demonstrate how enslaved people claimed, animated, politicized, personalized, and enjoyed their bodies—flesh that much of American society regarded as no more than biddable property.

Most of all, attention to uses and experiences of the body is mandatory for those interested in the lives of women in slavery. Actual and imagined reproductive labor and the unique forms of bodily suffering (notably sexual exploitation) distinguished the lives of women from those of men. Feminist scholars have shown us that to study women's lives requires posing different questions of our sources, using new methods to interpret them, and fundamentally changing how we think about politics.[13] Historians of enslaved women have revealed the falseness of the dichotomy between the material/political and the personal, in large measure by showing how the body, so deeply personal, is also a political arena. Their work has demonstrated the extent to which women's bodies were unique sites of domination under slavery, yet this scholarship has also shown that enslaved and formerly enslaved women used their bodies as sites of resistance.[14] Women employed their bodies in a wide variety of ways, from seizing control over the visual representation of their physical selves in narrative and photographic forms (both of which were in enormous demand among nineteenth-century northerners) to abortion.[15] In addition to the body's reproductive and sexual capacities and its representations, however, enslaved women's bodily pleasure was a resource for resistance to slavery.

Recent scholarship has shown that perceptions of the proper uses of the black body and especially the female body were central, materially and symbolically, to the formation of slaveholding mastery. As the English became entrenched in the slave trade in the second half of the seventeenth century, their preexisting ideas of Africans developed into constructions of blackness and representations of bodily difference that justified the economically expedient turn to enslaved black labor. Jennifer L. Morgan has demonstrated that these constructions relied in large part on sixteenth- and seventeenth-century male travelers' representations of African women's bodies as inherently laboring ones—as female drudges who stood in stark distinction to the idealized idle and dependent English woman. Male travelers to Africa in the earliest years of contact remarked on what they saw as African women's sexual deviance: the women lived in "common" (polygamously) with men and bared much of their bodies, most remarkably their breasts, with "no shame." Europeans depicted African women's breasts ("dugs") as large and droopy, "like the udder of a goate," as one traveler put it. Animal-like, African women's exposed dugs struck male observers as evidence of Africa's savagery and inferiority. To European eyes, African women's reproductive bodies also demonstrated physical strength: they gave birth "withoute payne," suggesting that "the women here [Guinea] are of a cruder nature and stronger posture than the Females in our Lands in Europe." Confirming this conclusion was the fact that African women commonly worked in agriculture. Unencumbered by the delicacy that prevented the ideal English woman from such arduous work, African women were seen as naturally fit for demanding agricultural and reproductive labor.[16]

Englishmen began to encode ideas of protoracial difference based on perceptions of African women's laboring bodies into law in Virginia in 1643. In that year, the colonial legislature declared free African women tithables (meaning that their labor could be taxed), along with all free white men and male heads of households. Because white women were viewed as dependents—as "good wives" who performed household rather than agricultural labor—they remained untaxed. The very different treatment of African and English women, based on conceptions of their capacity to work in the fields, articulated very different projections of the roles each would play in the life of the colony. Two years later, African men also became tithables and thus fell within the legal construction of African bodies as inherently laboring ones. Buttressed by ideas of Africans as savages that relied heavily on representations of African women's sexual and reproductive bodies, English lawmakers could, by 1670, force non-European servants who had arrived in Virginia "by shipping" (Africans) to serve lifelong terms of servitude, while those who had "come by land" (Indians) served limited terms. This law, combined with an earlier 1667 measure banning the manumission of Africans converted to Christianity, helped to crystallize the racial form of the emergent slave economy.[17] In the context of slavery, issues of representation of the black body—especially the female black body—and material expropriation could not be separated.

Enslaved people, then, possessed at least three bodies. The first served as a site of domination; it was the body on which slaveholders acted. Early constructions of African and black women's bodies and sexuality played a central role in rationalizing the African slave trade. They also gave license to sexual violence against enslaved women. Colonial and antebellum slaveholders believed that strict control of the black body—in particular, its movement in space and time—was key to their enslavement of black people. By the late antebellum years, planters were working energetically to create strategies for mastering such black bodily minutiae as nourishment, ingestion of alcohol, and even dress, all as part of paternalist management strategies. In the Old South, the slave body, most intensely the female body, served as the "bio-text" on which slaveholders inscribed their authority.[18]

The second body was the subjective experience of this process. It was the body lived in moments and spaces of control and force, of terror and suffering. This was the colonized body that, in Fanon's terms, the person "of color" experienced "in the white world," where "consciousness of the body is solely a negating activity." Within the "white world"—within planters' controlled and controlling landscapes, vulnerable to sale, sexual and nonsexual violence, disease, and exploitative labor—enslaved bodies were surely "surrounded by an atmosphere of certain uncertainty."[19]

Yet within and around the plantation, enslaved people's bodies were a hotly contested terrain of struggle. Again and again, enslaved people violated planta-tion boundaries of space and time; in the spaces they created, runaway party-goers celebrated their bodies and did what they could to reclaim them from planter control and view. This reclaimed body, this outlawed body, was the bondperson's third body: the body as site of pleasure and resistance. For en-slaved women, whose bodies were so central to the history of black bondage, the third body was significant in two ways. First, their third body was a source of pleasure, pride, and self-expression. The enormous amount of energy, time, and care that some bondwomen put into such indulgences as making and wearing fancy dresses and attending illicit parties indicates how much they valued such activities. Pleasure was its own reward for those experiencing it, and it must be a part of our understanding of the lives of people in the past, even people who enjoyed little of it. Second, just as exploitation, containment, and punishment of the body were political acts, so too was enjoyment of the body. Bondwomen's third body was therefore a political site, an important symbolic and material re-source in the plantation South, and its control was fiercely contested between owner and owned. Far from accommodating bondage or acting as a safety valve within it, everyday somatic politics acted in opposition to slavery's symbolic systems and its economic imperatives.

By the nineteenth century, the centerpiece of the theory of mastery that elites laid out in law books and in plantation journals was a geography of containment that aimed to control slave mobility in space and in time. In his memoir of life in bondage, Charles Ball summarized what he called the "principles of restraint" that governed black movement. "No slave dare leave" the plantation to which she or he belonged, he said, not even for "a single mile" or a "single hour, by night or by day," except by "exposing himself to the danger of being taken up and flogged."[20] At stake was nothing less than the good functioning of the plantation itself. One slave-management manual instructed its readers that "no business of any kind can be successfully conducted without the aid of system and rule." In pursuit of "system and rule," the manual prescribed two core "maxims": first, "that there must be a time for everything and everything done in its time"; and second, that there must be "a rule for everything and everything done according to rule."[21]

Together, lawmakers and planters created the rules governing spatial and temporal order. Laws forbade bondpeople everywhere to leave their owners' property without written passes. Responsibility for enforcing the laws was shared unequally by nonelite whites, who most often manned slave patrols to police rural and urban areas, and slaveholders, who also did their best to enforce compliance with the law by insisting that the people they owned leave only with written permission. Even when planters did grant permission to travel off the plantation, they specified the spatial and temporal boundaries of a pass's tenure by writing the bondperson's destination and the pass's expiration date.[22] Enslaved women experienced the limits of the plantation's geography of containment in especially intense ways. Because most of the work that took bondpeople off the plantation was reserved for men and because slaveholders almost always granted visiting privileges only to husbands with abroad marriages and not to wives: women left farms and estates much less frequently than men did. Women were thus fixed even more firmly than men within plantation boundaries.[23]

Recognizing the potential for trouble nevertheless, slaveholders focused much of their managerial energy on regulating black movement in the nighttime. Almost all enslaved people were forbidden to leave the plantation at all in the evenings, and some were prohibited from even stirring from their quarters. In December 1846 Mississippi planter William Ethelbert Ervin codified his ideal of slave behavior by setting to paper the rules that were to govern his human property. Total control over his bondpeople's bodies was central to Ervin's conception of the master-slave relationship: two of the four fundamental rules on Ervin's estate sought to control slave mobility. First, he indicated that plantation borders not only marked the edges of his estate but also hemmed in his bondpeople: No one was to "leave the place without leaf of absence." Second, within those spatial borders, he added temporal limits that bound enslaved people's movement even more: "At nine o'clock every night the Horn must be blown Which is the signal for each to retire to his or her house and there to remain until morning." Doing his best to guarantee a rested and orderly workforce, Ervin directed his overseers to check on people in the quarters: anyone found "out of their places" would be "delt with" "according to discretion." Most often, transgressors of boundaries of space and time were dealt with violently. Only as long as, in the words of one former bondwoman, "slaves stayed in deir places" were they not "whipped or put in chains."[24]

The nineteenth-century plantation system symbolized larger social relations, however. The importance of rules of containment went beyond plantation efficiency and issues of production, striking at the core of what it meant to be a master in the antebellum years. Seeking to restrain black bodies even further, some planters used plantation frolics as a paternalist mechanism of social control. Plantation parties, which carefully doled out joy on Saturday nights and on holidays, were intended to seem benevolent and to inspire respect, gratitude, deference, and, importantly, obedience. As North Carolinian Midge Burnett noted sardonically, his owner held plantation frolics on holidays and gave bondpeople Christmas trees in December and an Easter egg hunt in the spring—all "ca[u]se Marse William intended ter make us a civilized bunch of blacks."[25]

Most of all, these sponsored frolics were supposed to control black pleasure by giving it periodic, approved release. Paternalist slaveholders accomplished this goal by attending and surveilling the parties. Indeed, the most important component of paternalistic plantation parties was the legitimating presence of the master. It was common for whites to "set around and watch" while bond-people danced and sang.[26] Though sanctioning black pleasure, the slaveholders' gaze oversaw and contained that pleasure, ensuring that it would not become dangerous. For example, to make certain that the alcohol, music, dancing, "sun-drie articles," and "treat[s]" he provided his bondpeople at holiday time served the dual purpose of giving limited expression to and restraining bodily plea-sure in time as well as space, John Nevitt made sure to "s[i]t up untill 2 oclock in the morning to keep order with them."[27] Both former slave Henry Bibb and former slaveholder Robert Criswell remembered the surveillance role that the slaveholders' presence played at plantation frolics, and both men illustrated the constrictive effects of that gaze in their memoirs of antebellum plantation life (see figures 1 and 2).

Alcohol proved an important lubricant for production at plantation affairs. Neal Upson watched adults set a rhythm for their work of shucking a season's corn harvest by singing. As they sang and shucked, "de little brown jug was passed 'round." The "little brown jug" of alcohol gave the workers just enough liquor to warm their muscles and their spirits to the enterprise at hand: "When [the jug] had gone de rounds a time or two, it was a sight to see how fast dem Niggers could keep time to dat singin'. Dey could do all sorts of double time den when dey had swigged enough liquor." Similarly, Bill Heard's owner provided "plenty of corn liquor" to his bondpeople at corn shuckings to speed up the work. "You know dat stuff is sho to make a Nigger hustle," Heard remembered. "Evvy time a red ear of corn was found dat meant a extra drink of liquor for de Nigger dat found it."[28] Even as planters attempted to master black bodily movement and pleasure in these ways, however, some enslaved people were not satisfied with official parties. They sought out secret and secular gatherings of their own making.

Bondwomen and -men who worked in the gang system, the predominant form of work organization in the Old South, worked hard all day, almost every day of the year, with breaks only on Sundays and some holidays. "Dey wucks us from daylight till dark, an' sometimes we jist gits one meal a day," Charlie Crump said of his slavery experience.[29] Slaves in South Carolina and parts of Georgia who worked under the task system did not necessarily have to wait for the evening to end their toil, but they, like bondpeople employed in gang labor, were prohibited from leaving their home farms without passes. Even bad weather meant only a change in routine—respite only from field labor but not from plantation maintenance chores. As they worked, bondpeople, in the words of one folk song sung by women textile workers in Virginia, kept their "eye on

Figure 1. *The Sabbath among Slaves.* This illustration shows plantation festivities as Henry Bibb, a man who had been enslaved, remembered them. Enslaved people dance, play music, lounge, tussle, and drink while four elite whites on the left watch, amused. The plantation patriarch, to the right of center, distributes alcohol to a respectful bondman who has removed his hat and gratefully bows slightly. Note the very strong presence of a "fence": it is on the right, here represented as a wall. The wall on the right is joined by the wall of four white onlookers to contain and control this scene of black pleasure. From Henry Bibb, *Life and Adventures* (New York, 1849). Courtesy of the Library Company of Philadelphia.

Figure 2. *The Festival.* This illustrated memory, from a former slaveholder's autobiography, represents the centrality of white surveillance at plantation parties. From R. Criswell, *Planter's Home* (New York, 1852). Courtesy of the Library Company of Philadelphia.

de sun," watching it cross the sky as the day wore long. Because "trouble don' las' always," they anticipated the end of the workday and on occasion planned illicit parties in the woods.[30]

Speaking for enslaved people everywhere, Charlie Crump recounted that "we ain't 'lowed ter go nowhar at night. . . . [D]at is," he added, "if dey knowed it." In violation of the planters' boundaries of space and time, Crump and many of the young people he knew who had worked "from daylight till dark" left at night. At the risk of terrible punishment, blacks "from all ober de neighborhood [would] gang up an' have fun anyhow." Similarly, Midge Burnett and his friends knew that "de patterollers 'ud watch all de paths leadin' frum de plantation" to prevent bondpeople from running away. What the patrollers did not know, however, was that "dar wus a number of little paths what run through de woods dat nobody ain't watched ca[u]se dey ain't knowed dat de paths wus dar." Many partygoers traveled to their covert events along just such paths (see figure 3).[31]

"Yes, mam, they had dances all right," Georgian Jefferson Franklin Henry remembered. "That's how they got mixed up with paterollers. Negroes would go off to dances and stay out all night."[32] Because secrecy demanded a high level of planning, the outlaw gatherings were often prepared well in advance. Austin Steward and his neighbors and friends in rural Virginia were well aware of the laws and rules that forbade enslaved people from leaving "the plantation to which they belong, without a written pass." Nonetheless, they occasionally left their plantations to visit family, to worship, and sometimes to hold parties. One spring the enslaved people on a nearby estate held an Easter frolic with the permission of their owner. But word of this legitimate "grand dance" quickly spread to "a large number of slaves on other plantations," who intended to attend the party whether or not they could obtain official passes.[33]

Meanwhile, the hosts began preparations. Reappropriation was the main way of obtaining the goods they needed. "They took, without saying, 'by your leave, Sir,' " the food and drink they wanted, Steward wrote, "reasoning among themselves, as slaves often do, that it can not be stealing, because 'it belongs to massa, and so do we, and we only use one part of his property to benefit another.' " The women took the ingredients and moved their owners' culinary property "from one location to another," a relocation that made an enormous difference in the purposes of both the frolic and the food. With the ingredients in hand, women hid themselves in "valleys," swamps, and other "by-places" to cook in secret at night. "Night after night" this went on: women prepared dishes late into the night and then headed back to the cabin in the morning, "carefully destroy[ing] everything likely to detect them" on their way. At the same time, the "knowing ones" continued to plan the celebration, encouraging each other's high spirits "with many a wink and nod."[34]

Finally, the appointed night arrived. A little after ten o'clock, the music began

Figure 3. *A Live Oak Avenue.* Avenues around the plantation, the concourses of slaveholding leisure and business, branched off into smaller paths known only to enslaved people. Bondpeople used these paths to reach the secret spaces in the woods where they held outlaw slave parties. From *Harper's New Monthly Magazine*, November 1859, 733. Courtesy of the Library Company of Philadelphia.

when an "old fiddler struck up some favorite tune," and people danced until midnight, when it was time to feast. The food was "well cooked," and the wine was "excellent," Steward reported. But he recalled more than the events: he went to the trouble of recording the effect of the moment. Steward had noted that planters believed that enslaved people hobbled through life "with no hope of release this side of the grave, and as far as the cruel oppressor is concerned, shut out from hope beyond it." Yet despite—or perhaps in part because of—their abject poverty and the humiliations and cruelties of bondage, here at the party, "Every dusky face was lighted up, and every eye sparkled with joy. However ill fed they might have been, here, for once, there was plenty. Suffering and toil was forgotten, and they all seemed with one accord to give themselves up to the intoxication of pleasurable amusement." In the context of enslavement, such exhilarating pleasure gotten by illicit use of the body was important and meaningful enjoyment, personal expression, and an oppositional use of the body.[35]

But there were limits to alternative uses of the body for the enslaved. Late at night, the fiddler suddenly stopped playing and adopted "a listening attitude." Everyone became quiet, "listening for the cause of the alarm." The dreaded call came to them when their lookout shouted, "Patrol!" and perhaps ran away from the party, a common technique to throw off patrols. If the lookout at this party did so, he was unsuccessful, for the slave patrol, whose job it was to ensure that enslaved people (in Steward's words) "know their place" and stay in it, found the party and broke it up. Many people had run away immediately after the call came, but others, including Steward, had only managed to hide themselves and overheard the patrolmen talking.[36]

Two of the patrolmen debated the wisdom of a few white men attempting to disband a meeting of so many bondpeople. One hesitated to push the matter, arguing that the slaves might "resist." After all, "they have been indulging their appetites, and we cannot tell what they may attempt to do." His colleague mocked his apprehension and wondered if he was really "so chicken-hearted as to suppose those d——d cowardly niggers are going to get up an insurrection?" The first patrolman defensively clarified that he worried only that the partygoers "may forget themselves at this late hour." This man's concerns were based on the realities at hand. In these woods, on the figurative if not the literal margins of the host plantation, there was a black majority. This particular black majority was made up of those who already had proven their lack of deference to white authority and their willingness to defy rules. While unprepared and perhaps unwilling to "get up an insurrection," they just might have been capable of "forgetting themselves" by challenging white authority to an incalculable extent. Indeed, in a sense they already had forgotten themselves, having abandoned "their place" in the plantation spatial and temporal order—and the "self" they had to be there—in favor of their own space and their own place.[37]

The most important part of preparing a night meeting, as Austin Steward's remembered party shows, was evading slave patrols. In addition to doing their best to keep their own movements stealthy, bondpeople carefully monitored patrol activity. Inverting the dominant ideal of plantation surveillance, household, skilled, and personal slaves watched their surveillants and sometimes learned of a patrol's plan to be in the area. These bondpeople would pass the word along using a code, "dey bugs in de wheat," meaning that the scheduled party had been found out. Sometimes they canceled the party; when they did not, some bond-people would avoid the party while others would attend anyway, alert and ready to leap out of windows and sprint out of sight when the patrol arrived. Revelers also protected their space by constructing borders of their own. They stretched vines across paths to trip patrolmen and their horses and posted lookouts at key locations along the periphery.[38]

Young people also gathered in spaces outside of their owners' view. Very often they met, like Nancy Williams and the people she knew, in unoccupied cabins in the woods. At other times they simply came together in the open air (see figures 4 and 5). Occasionally, on very large plantations where outbuildings could be quite a distance from the slaveholder's house, enslaved people gathered in barns or in the quarters. Male musicians performed for their friends and neighbors, playing fiddles, banjos, and tambourines. They also made instruments; for example, the popular "quill" was created in places where sugar was grown. Ten or so cane stems were cut to different lengths, and a hole was drilled in the top of each. They were then bound together to make a flute. Musicians also improvised instruments out of reeds and handsaws to perform the melody and created the percussion with spoons, bones, pans, and buckets, playing such popular songs as "Turkey in the Straw."[39]

Outlaw partygoers also made music with their voices, singing lyrics sure to amuse. According to Dosia Harris, one went "somepin' lak dis":

Oh! Miss Liza, Miss Liza Jane!
Axed Miss Liza to marry me
Guess what she said?
She wouldn't marry me,
If de last Nigger was dead.[40]

Dancers also sang, perhaps gloatingly, of their subterfuge:

Buffalo gals, can't you come out tonight,
Come out tonight, an' dance by the light of de moon?[41]

As morning approached, those who had caroused the night away warned each other of the approach of day and the danger of violating that temporal boundary (which located them properly at work): "Run nigger run, pattyrollers ketch you, run nigger run, it's breakin' days."[42] A variant elaborated,

Figure 4. *A Negro Funeral*. Enslaved people gathered for funerals, religious services, and secret, secular parties in the remote spaces in the woods bordering plantations. *Harper's New Monthly Magazine*, November 1859, 731. Courtesy of the Library Company of Philadelphia.

Figure 5. *The Country Church.* Deep in some woods were abandoned or simply unoccupied church buildings, old barns, and other outbuildings such as this one. Enslaved people occasionally used these structures to hold outlaw parties. *Harper's New Monthly Magazine*, November 1859, 729. Courtesy of the Library Company of Philadelphia.

Run nigger run, de patterrollers ketch you—
Run nigger run, fer hits almos' day,
De nigger run; de nigger flew; de nigger los'
His big old shoe.[43]

Dance tunes contained political meanings as well as entertainment value. The self-deprecating song about the rejected lover is one example: Liza Jane, the object of affection, is called by a title, "Miss," a sign of respect that whites denied bondpeople. Other songs were bolder. Mississippian Mollie Williams danced to and sang a song inflected by the spirit of resistance nurtured at outlaw parties:

Run tell Coleman,
Run tell everbody
Dat de niggers is arisin'![44]

Together, women and men performed a variety of period dances. Many formerly enslaved people described the dances of their youth as proper and respectable (without the "man an woman squeezed up close to one another," as Fannie Berry put it). When she was young, Liza Mention danced "de cardrille [quadrille] de virginia reel, and de 16-hand cortillion." Mention insisted, "Dances in dem days warn't dese here huggin' kind of dances lak dey has now."[45] Instead, bondpeople chose physically expressive but still respectable dances like "pigeon wings" (flapping the arms like a bird and wiggling the legs, while "holdin' yo' neck stiff like a bird do"), "gwine to de east, an' gwine to de west" (leaning in to kiss one's dance partner on each cheek but "widout wrappin' no arms roun' like de young folks do today"), "callin' de figgers" (following the fiddler's challenging calls), and "hack-back" (in which couples stood facing one another and "trotted back and forth"). Other dances included "set de flo'" (partners began by bowing to each other at the waist, with hands on the waist, and then tap-danced, patting the floor firmly, "jus' like dey was puttin' it in place"), "dancin' on de spot" (the same as "set de flo'" except that dancers had to remain within the circumference of a circle drawn in the ground), "wringin' and twistin'" (the early basis of the twist), the "buzzard lope," "snake hips," and the "breakdown."[46]

Competition was a common form of amusement at outlaw dances and sometimes forged camaraderie among equals. To win a dance competition required expertly executing complex dance moves while maintaining a cool and controlled outward demeanor. For example, as mentioned earlier, Nancy Williams competed with another woman, Jennie, to see who could dance most deftly and with the most mastery of her body. To make the challenge even greater, the two women danced with glasses of water on their heads; the winner was she who maintained her cool, making the performance look easy. Dance competition allowed some women to demonstrate the strength and agility of their bodies, as compared with men's, whose physical power was usually recognized as greater. Jane Smith Hill Harmon "allus could dance" and enjoyed, even as an old woman, "cut[ting] fancy steps now sometimes when I feels good." Her talent inspired awe, and she regularly competed with men. "One night when I wuz young," she related, "I danced down seben big strong mens, dey thought dey wuz sumpin'! Huh, I danced eb'ry one down!" Dance competition could provide women moments of relief from black gender hierarchies as well as from slaveholding control.[47]

Such an issue as violence between women and men at secret parties is difficult to access in the sources. We know that enslaved families, like free ones, were home to resentment, betrayal, anger, and other disappointments of family life. Physical and verbal abuse between spouses was a part of life in the quarters from Virginia to Mississippi.[48] James Cornelius, who had been enslaved in Mississippi, openly told his interviewer about the time he hit his wife in the postbellum years. During their marriage ceremony, Cornelius had interrupted the preacher to make his wife promise never to accuse him of lying. She promised, and Cornelius reciprocated; he pronounced the exchange " 'a bargain' an' den de preacher went on wid de weddin'." A few years later, his wife became suspicious about his whereabouts one evening, and when his excuse failed to convince her, she told him, "That's a lie." Cornelius responded in the manner he viewed as appropriate: "Right den I raised my han' an' let her have it right by de side of de head, an' she niver called me a liar ag'in. No ma'm, dat is somethin' I won't stand for." While rates of domestic violence may have changed in the transition from slavery to freedom, incidents such as this one were certainly not new. Cornelius and many other men, both slave and free, believed that they had the right to use violence against their wives, and a major influence on his conception of domestic life must have been his own (enslaved) family.[49] Violence was also a common aspect of drinking culture among both whites and blacks. It is therefore difficult to imagine that violence, a part of life both in the quarters and in drinking culture, did not occur between men, between women, and between men and women at outlawed parties. In particular, men's drinking must have created some difficulties for bondwomen. But men were not the only ones to use violence. Sometimes slave parties gave space for the continuation of rivalries between women who were not always or even often motivated by feelings of honorable competition between equals. Women's competition could turn viciously bitter and have tragic results. For example, when two women, Rita and Retta, misunderstood "Aunt" Vira's laughter at a party as directed at them, they poisoned both Vira and her infant.[50]

While women and men danced together, outlaw parties were also characterized by gender differences in ideas of pleasure. Women, more than men, reclaimed their bodies through dressing up, and men, more than women, enjoyed drinking alcohol. Dress was a contested terrain: planters attempted to use it for disciplinary purposes, and women utilized it for purposes inconsistent with the social demands and economic imperatives of slave society. Under cover of night, women headed for secret frolics wearing their best fancy dress, marking on their bodies the difference between the time that belonged to the master and the time that was their own.[51] While at work, when their bodies were in the service of their owners, bondpeople looked, according to one observer, "very ragged and slovenly." Planters imprinted slave status on black bodies by vesting bondpeople in clothing of the poorest quality, made of fabric reserved for those of their station. In the summer, enslaved people wore uncolored cotton or tow, a material made from rough, unprocessed flax. Many women's dresses were straight, shapeless, and stintingly cut, sometimes directly on the body to avoid wasting fabric. Charity McAllister's clothes were "poor. One-piece dress made o' carpet stuff, part of de time." Others were cut fuller, tapered at the waist, and most dresses were long. Almost all bondpeople's clothes were homemade, not store-bought, and those who wore them appreciated the difference. Fannie Dunn disagreed with her mother's assessment of conditions under slavery in North Carolina on the basis of the clothes she was forced to wear: "My mother said dat we all fared good, but of course we wore handmade clothes an' wooden bottomed shoes."[52]

Some planters, as part of their system of rule, annually or biannually distributed clothes with dramatic flair to represent themselves as the benevolent source of care and sustenance and thereby instill loyalty in their bondpeople. On other plantations, neglect and avarice rather than paternalistic management systems characterized slaveholder behavior. Year after year, for example, Roswell King, Pierce Butler's Georgia overseer, pleaded with Butler, who lived in Philadelphia, to provide his bondpeople with clothing. King subscribed to the paternalist school's combination of cruel violence, stern order, and benevolent encouragement of disciplined behavior, but he could not find an ally in Butler. "Do you recollect," King wrote to Butler on one occasion, "that you have not given your Negroes Summer clothing but twice in fifteen years past?" Old, torn, shredded, and dirty clothing certainly saved costs for slave owners, but it also had social effects. Poor-quality clothing reflected and reified slaves' status and played a role in their subjugation. Harriet Jacobs wrote bitterly in her 1861 narrative of life as a bondwoman that the "linsey-woolsey dress given me every winter" by her mistress was "one of the badges of slavery."[53]

Another badge of slavery was the blurring of gender distinctions that some experienced, effected by the grueling work routines that many women followed during much of their lives. With a mixture of pride and bitterness, Anne Clark recalled that during her life in bondage she had worked like a man. She "ploughed, hoed, split rails. I done the hardest work ever a man ever did." "Women worked in de field same as de men. Some of dem plowed jes' like de men and boys," George Fleming remembered. Fleming claimed that the women he knew even resembled men in the fields: he "couldn't tell 'em apart in de field, as dey wore pantelets or breeches."[54]

Conversely, when bondpeople, especially women, dressed for their own occasions, they went to a great deal of trouble to create and wear clothes of quality and, importantly, style. When possible, women met with white itinerant traders to exchange homespun goods, garden produce, and pelts for good-quality or decorative cloth, beads, and buttons. In South Carolina, the slaves' independent economy enabled women to purchase cloth, clothing, and dye. But even in Virginia, Frederick Law Olmsted noticed that some women "purchase[d] clothing for themselves" and on their own time "look[ed] very smart." Enslaved women located near ports or major waterways probably had more opportunities to barter with black boat workers, who carried on a lively trade with the plantation bondpeople encountered while traveling.[55] Most women, however, procured fancy dress—when they could at all—simply by eking out time at night to make it, from beginning to end: they grew and processed the cotton, cultivated and gathered the roots and berries for the dye, wove the cloth, and sewed textiles into garments.

When they dressed up and when they refused to perform the regular nightly toil demanded of them so that they had time to make fancy dress, enslaved women asserted that some Saturday nights, Sundays, holidays, and occasionally weeknights were their own. Women, whose bodies were subject to sexual exploitation, dangerous and potentially heartbreaking reproductive labor, and physically demanding agricultural labor, tried not to miss the opportunity to reclaim themselves from the brink of degradation at the hands of their masters. Even though women's bodies were sources of suffering and sites of planter domination, women also worked hard to make their bodies spaces of personal expression, pleasure, and resistance.

Fancy dress offered a challenge to status-enforcing clothing because dressing up was heterodox behavior. Pierre Bourdieu defines *doxa* as the "naturalization" of the social order accomplished through a number of social and symbolic mechanisms, including assumptions by dominant classes about the "uses" and presentation of the body. Within the reigning doxa, the black body was vested in slave dress, which enforced and naturalized its status. Enslaved women sporadically engaged in heterodox behavior—behavior that was conscious of the doxa, exposed its arbitrariness, and challenged it. When they adorned their bodies in fancy dress rather than in the degrading rough and plain clothing, rags, or livery provided by slaveholders, they challenged the axiomatic (doxic) quality of their enslaved status. In particular, women fashioned new identities that highlighted their femininity and creativity.[56]

Finally, women's heterodox style—expressed as they transgressed the plantation's boundaries of space and time—allowed them to take pleasure in their bodies while simultaneously denying that their bodies had exclusively fiduciary value and that the sole use of the body was to labor for their owners.[57] Indeed, the act of slipping out of plantation boundaries to attend parties withheld labor: enslaved people who failed to rest properly for the next day's chores worked less efficiently, much to the outrage of their owners. In the Old South, issues of representation of the black body and material expropriation could not be separated from one another.

When women adorned themselves in fancy dress of their own creation, they distanced themselves from what it felt like to wear slaves' low-status clothing. "Aunt" Adeline was, as her mother had been, an accomplished dyer. On one occasion she wore a dress that she would never forget "as long as I live. It was a hickory stripe dress they made for me, with brass buttons at the wrist bands." She was "so proud of that dress"; with her identity refashioned by it, she "felt so dressed up in it, I just strutted!" Some of the reactions to the young women who dressed up also reveal the heterodox aspects of fancy dress. One time, the young Amelia walked out of her house on her way to church in a hoopskirt she adored. To her mortification, the other children laughed at her and accused her of "playin' lady"—of affecting a status beyond her own to which she had no right. She was so hurt by their mockery of her status transgression, now seen as presumption, that she took off the offending skirt "and hide it in de wood." Enslaved people, young or adult, did not uniformly appreciate disrespect for the Old South's racial etiquette.[58]

In addition to the symbolic value dress held for plantation blacks and whites, clothing held more tangible meanings as well. The production, distribution, and use of King Cotton—and cotton products such as clothing—were very material issues in the slave South. Textile production complicated the plantation's temporal order along gender lines: the nighttime was less neatly "off" time for bondwomen than it was for men. While women and men could both quit working for their owners at sunset, many women began a second shift of labor at night, and sometimes on Saturdays or Sundays, working for their families. At these times women worked in their homes, performing reproductive labor that allowed families to survive and grow—cooking, cleaning, gardening, washing, and candle and soap making. Henry James Trentham saw women plowing during the day, working hard to "carry dat row an' keep up wid de men," then quit at sunset "an den do dere cookin' at night." Moreover, in their "off" time and during the winters, women were responsible for some to all of the production of textiles for plantation residents, black and white. Only on the very largest plantations was some of this work concentrated in the hands of women specialists.[59]

Most enslaved women, then, worked grueling first and second shifts. Their second shift of labor, however, also presented an opportunity, which they exploited, to devote a bit of their time to heterodox activity. Women spent some of their evenings turning the plain, uncolored tow, denim, hemp, burlap, and cotton they had spun into decorative cloth. Morris Sheppard remembered his mother's handiwork: "Everything was stripedy 'cause old Mammy liked to make it fancy." Catharine Slim's mother, a talented weaver, wove stripes of red, white, and blue as well as flowers into the cloth she sewed into dresses for her daughter. Women dyed the coarse material allotted them with colors that they liked. Nancy Williams's dedication to style was unusual, but it remains instructive. "Clo'es chile? I had plenty clo'es dem days," she claimed. "Had dress all colors. How I get 'em? Jes' change dey colors. Took my white dress out to de polk berry bush an' jes' a-dyed it red, den dyed my shoes red. Took ole barn paint an' paint some mo' shoes yaller to match my yaller dress." Women set the colors fast in their cloth with saline solutions, vinegar and water, or "chamber lye" (urine). They hung the cloth on lines to dry and from there sewed the fabric into garments. Women also traded the products of their nighttime labor—their crafts such as quilts and baskets, the produce of their gardens, the eggs they collected, the berries they picked in the woods, and the skins of animals they hunted—for calico and fine or decorative cloth as well as for ornamental objects.[60]

After they had the cloth, enslaved women went to great effort to make themselves something more than the cheap, straight-cut dresses they were rationed. When possible, women cut their "dress-up" dresses generously to cover the length of the body and to sweep dramatically and elegantly. Some women accentuated the fullness of their skirts by crisply starching them. Annie Wallace remembered that when her mother went "out at night to a party some of the colored folks was havin'," she would starch her skirts with "hominy water." "They were starched so stiff that every time you stopped they would pop real loud." Wallace's mother instructed her children to listen carefully for her return in case the party was broken up by the arrival of Virginia's rural patrols. "And when we heared them petticoats apoppin' as she run down the path, we'd open the door wide and she would get away from the patteroll."[61]

Other women liked to draw attention to their skirts with hoops made from grapevines or tree limbs. Though Salena Taswell's owner "would not let the servants wear hoops," she and the other household bondwomen sometimes swiped "the old ones that they threw away." Secretly, they "would go around with them on when they were gone and couldn't see us." Hoopskirts came into fashion during the early 1850s, coinciding with the emergence of the cult of domesticity, and stayed in style until the pressures of the Civil War made them both impractical and expensive. Among the elite women who wore them, however, hoopskirts symbolized "Victorian ideals of domesticity and . . . of a separate woman's sphere," as Drew Gilpin Faust has suggested. The style flaunted high levels of consumption and idleness because the skirts made physical labor tricky. Consistent with Victorian ideals of respectable womanhood, the hoopskirt also hid the body. No doubt bondwomen's skirts were smaller than those of their owners, which could measure up to five feet in diameter. Nonetheless, Camilla Jackson recalled that hoopskirts "were the fad in those days" among black as well as white women, a fad that enabled bondwomen to appropriate a symbol of leisure and femininity (and freedom) and denaturalize their slave status. "In dem days de wimen wore hoops. . . . De white folks dun it an' so did the slave wimen," Ebenezer Brown said.[62]

Yet black women's style did not simply mimic slaveholding women's fashions. Enslaved women's use of accessories most accentuated their originality. Topping off many women's outfits were head wraps or elaborate hairstyles. Nineteenth-century bondwomen made the head wrap into a unique expressive form. Some women wore their favorite head wraps to outlaw parties, and many others removed their wraps to display their hair—in cornrows, plaits, or straightened. Women could straighten or relax their curls by wrapping sections of their hair in string, twine, or bits of cloth and then covering it during the week to hide the wrappings and to keep their hair clean and protected from the sun. On special occasions, such women removed their head wraps and the strings, and their hair fell down straightened or in looser curls. Although accessories were more difficult to obtain, they were not overlooked. Some women made straw hats from "wheat straw which was dried out." They also made buttons and ornaments for their clothing out of "li'l round pieces of gourds" covered with cloth and from "cows and rams horns."[63]

Shoes posed a special problem for women engaged in the work of refashioning their bodily identities. Many bondpeople wore no shoes at all during the warm months and received wooden clogs against the cold only once a year. On some farms women received footwear even more infrequently. Perhaps because even their agricultural labor was denigrated as "women's work" and therefore considered easier work, some women received no shoes at all. W. L. Bost was appalled at the hardships women faced, especially their inadequate dress in cold weather: "They never had enough clothes on to keep a cat warm. The women never wore anything but a thin dress and a petticoat and one underwear. I've seen the ice balls hangin' on to the bottom of their dresses as they ran along, jes like sheep in a pasture 'fore they are sheared. They never wore shoes."[64]

Women's creation and appropriation of cloth and clothing helped them to express their personalities and senses of style, but their uses of clothing also raised material issues. Women's alternative uses of dress laid claim to the product of their labor: they seized the cotton that they had raised and harvested and used it for their own purposes. "How I get 'em?" Nancy Williams seemed pleased with her interviewer's question and eager to tell of her ingenuity. Perhaps exaggerating, Williams said she had "plenty" of clothes during her life in bondage, though not as a result of any generosity from her owner. In addition to dyeing the plain cloth she was allotted, Williams reappropriated what she needed. For example, she "had done stole de paint" to make yellow shoes to go with a yellow dress she wore to an illicit dance.[65]

Similarly, Mary Wyatt's Virginia owner had a dress that Wyatt adored. "Lawdy, I used to take dat dress when she warn't nowhere roun' an' hole it up against me an' 'magine myself wearin' it." One Christmas season, Wyatt decided to wear the dress to a plantation frolic. "De debbil got in me good," she admitted. "Got dat gown out de house 'neath my petticoat tied rounst me an' wore it to de dance." Donning the fancy dress of her mistress, Wyatt shed the most outward markers of her slave status and adopted instead a symbol of freedom. Like other women who reappropriated their owners' clothing, when Mary Wyatt stole her owner's dress she committed not only a symbolic transgression of place by imagining herself in a dress that was made of a design and material reserved for the free white women who could afford it but also an act of material consequence. She reclaimed the product of her own labor. Women like her had picked the cotton, processed it, and made it into a dress; the institution of slavery made the dress her owner's, but Mary Wyatt made it hers. In Wyatt's case, the act of reappropriation was brief. She returned the dress, putting it "back in place de nex' day." But even as the terror that gripped her while she stole and wore the dress indicates the power of her owners, Wyatt's act also reveals the strength of her commitment to wearing the dress.[66]

Bondwomen took tremendous risks in procuring and wearing fancy dress to plantation frolics and outlawed slave parties, and the potential extent of this personal endangerment is also a measure of the significance of the otherwise seemingly trivial concerns of dress and style. By dressing up to go to outlaw parties, bondwomen flagrantly violated the doxa of plantation social hierarchy as well as plantation boundaries of space and time. The degree of danger involved in donning conspicuous fancy dress and running away for an evening and women's willingness to take the chance suggest just how urgent some of them believed it was to extricate themselves from their "proper" places. Frances Miller, a slaveholding woman, encountered such determination as she endeavored to impose a "system of management" within her Virginia household. She rose at 4:30 every morning, in advance of her bondpeople, to wake them and prod them to work, not at all shying away from physical violence when their "insubordination" proved too much for her. Miller dedicated herself, in what she described as a "herculean" manner, to "always righting things up." Thanks to the "open rebellion, impudence and unfaithfulness of domestics," things seemed "never righted" in her household.[67]

Among the most egregious acts of "unfaithfulness" and "insubordination" that Miller witnessed in her household was the determination of one unruly woman, Rose, to sneak away at night to a party. On her way to bed one night, Miller encountered Rose on her way out of the house, "dressed up as I supposed for a night's jaunt." Caught, Rose thought on her feet and, thrusting the candle that she held to light her passage toward Miller, asked Miller to carry it back for her. Miller had been hardened by Rose's long history of disobedience, however, and was not distracted from the issue at hand. When Miller sarcastically "asked her why she did not do it herself," Rose claimed that "she was going to wash." Rose's explanation for still being awake and heading out, when, according to the late hour, she ought to have been in bed in her room was not convincing. Miller could tell by the way Rose was "dressed so spry" that she was not at all going to wash and so "did not believe her." Instead, she reminded Rose of her curfew and of where she ought to be, telling her that "it was bedtime and she must go directly upstairs." Rose "refused" and remained determined to go out to "wash." Rose's plans were thwarted only after Miller "shut the door and locked it." With no key, Rose had no way out. Angered that she would now miss the party, Rose insulted Miller, telling her "that I was the most contrary old thing that she ever saw."[68]

As punishment for attempting to disobey the household's boundaries of space and time as well as for her effrontery, Miller promised to flog Rose, prompting Rose to assert that she "would not submit to any such thing and that she would go to the woods first." Rose, however, did not carry out her threat. Perhaps because she was so disappointed about having been prevented from going out, Rose "yielded with less difficulty than usual" to the bondman William's "switches." Miller succeeded in stopping Rose from leaving the household, but the whole incident left Miller "sorely grieved—sorely." She was frustrated "that the necessity had existed" to whip Rose. Rose's transgression of place mandated, to Miller's mind, the deployment of violence, which contradicted Miller's ideal of a mastery so effective as not to warrant its explicit use.[69]

Black women's and men's absentee nightly pleasures, such as sneaking off to parties to stay up late dancing and drinking, compromised slaveholding authority and plantation productivity. Julia Larken noted that her owner "never laked for nobody to be late in de mornin'," presumably because of the disorder and the inefficiency that tardiness caused. Nonetheless, lateness and fatigue were not unusual. When enslaved people stayed up late into the night worshiping, for example, they would be "sho tired" the next day. Charlie Tye Smith recalled that no matter how late bondpeople had been up the night before, they "had better turn out at four o'clock when ole Marse blowed the horn!" They dragged themselves through the motions of their chores all morning and at lunchtime collapsed in the field. Those who had not attended the religious meeting looked upon a field "strowed with Niggers asleep in the cotton rows" until the midday break ended, and they all resumed work.[70]

And so it was after illicit parties. Jefferson Franklin Henry remembered how other bondpeople—but not he—"would go off to dances and stay out all night; it would be wuk time when they got back." These revelers valiantly "tried to keep right on gwine," but they were worn out; "the Good Lord soon cut 'em down." These mornings did not inhibit future parties, however, nor did the Christian objections of other blacks make an impact: "You couldn't talk to folks that tried to git by with things lak that," Henry regretted. "They warn't gwine to do no diffunt, nohow."[71]

An extraordinary document survives that articulates not the success of slave resistance using the body but, given the extent to which the body was a point of conflict between slaves and their owners, what meanings the latter group ascribed to that conflict. In the mid-1840s, slaveholders in the Edgefield and Barnwell districts of South Carolina formed the Savannah River Anti–Slave Traffick Association to put a stop to the practice of selling alcohol to bond-people. Slave drinking and the theft and black-marketeering that bondpeople engaged in to obtain liquor and other goods from obliging nonelite whites resulted in what the Savannah River group deemed "very considerable losses." Bondwomen and -men—like association member James Henry Hammond's Urana—appropriated property from slave owners by breaking into "dwelling houses, barns, stables, smoke houses," and so forth with "false keys which abound among our negroes," or by picking locks "with instruments at which they have become very skilful" at crafting and using. Moreover, the neighbors complained that their crops were also vulnerable to appropriation: "Not content with plundering from Barns, our standing crops are beginning to suffer depredation." Thanks to these various activities, the Savannah River neighbors thought they had noticed their profits decline. "Often when a Farmer has expected to sell largely, he finds himself compelled to use the most stringent economy to make his provisions meet his own wants, and sometimes has actually to buy."[72]

Slaves' trading, stealing, and drinking were not the only "evils" worrying these South Carolina planters. Equally vexatious was the practice of "prowling" off to "night meetings." Because of the "too great negligence of slave owners in maintaining wholesome discipline," every night, or so it seemed, bondpeople could be found sneaking "abroad to night meetings." The association claimed that "hundreds of negroes it may be said without exaggeration are every night, and at all hours of the night, prowling about the country," stealing, trading, drinking, and meeting, almost certainly for secular affairs.[73]

The association weighed heavily the financial loss its members believed that they incurred when enslaved people were too hung over and tired to work well. "The negroes themselves are seriously impaired in physical qualities," the group noted. The association's regulations further detailed that these "nightly expeditions are followed by days of languor." Seeing their "owners, and especially their overseers, as unjust and unfeeling oppressors," bondpeople, it seemed to these South Carolinians, responded with insubordination and work characterized by "sullenness [and] discontent."[74]

The Savannah River neighbors were mobilized to action by what they saw as a second pernicious effect of black nightly "prowling." In addition to the damage nightly pleasures inflicted on productivity and the theft associated with such parties, association members complained of the resulting corrosion of slave-holding mastery. Black "minds are fatally corrupted" by these nighttime activities, these South Carolinians believed. In the revisionist history that the association wrote, bondpeople were beginning to dissent from the paternalist contract that supposedly governed planters' estates. "Formerly Slaves were essentially members of the family to which they belonged, and a reciprocal interest and attachment existing between them, their relations were simple, agreeable, easily maintained, and mutually beneficial," the association contended. It seemed that the freedom bondpeople tasted at night compromised their willingness to be deferential and obedient during the day. The association complained of the "difficulty in managing" the bondpeople because night activity appeared to encourage many to see their masters as their "natural enemies." This perspective facilitated more disorderly behavior, and the members of the Savannah River organization were forced to admit to one another that they were having trouble "preserving proper subordination of our slaves."[75]

The apocalypse was clear to the Savannah River residents: in alarmist tones, they predicted the end of slavery as they knew it if such unruliness continued. Reappropriating the "fruits of their own labors," working only with "sullenness [and] discontent," and skeptical of the authority of their masters, bondpeople in their neighborhood were creating "such a state of things [that it] must speedily put an end to agriculture or to negro slavery." Engaging in these small, outlawed activities, the association argued, the "negro ceases to be a moral being, holding a position in the framework of society, and becomes a serpent gnawing at its vitals or a demon ready with knife and torch to demolish its foundations."[76]

Drinking and dancing at night rather than resting for the next day's work could not and did not bring down the house of slavery. Nonetheless, the histrionics of the Savannah River Anti–Slave Traffick Association are more than amusing; they are revealing. When engaged in these activities, enslaved people ceased, their owners thought, to hold a proper "position in the framework of society" because they disregarded slaveholders' control over their bodies.

Stealing time and space for themselves and for members of their communities, those who attended secular parties acted on the assumption that their bodies were more than inherently and solely implements of agricultural production. While many planters desired and struggled for a smooth-running, paternalistic machine, some bondpeople created, among other things, a gendered culture of pleasure that "gnawed" at the fundamentals—the "vitals"—of slaveholding schemes for domination of the black body, a body that slaveholders had (ideally) located in a particular "position in the framework of society."

In a context where control and degradation of the black body were essential to the creation of slave-owning mastery—symbolically, socially, and materially—bondwomen's and -men's nighttime pleasures insulted slaveholders' feelings of authority. Mastery demanded respect for spatial and temporal boundaries, but bondpeople sometimes transgressed these borders and forged spaces for themselves. While slave owners' drive for production required rested slave bodies, bondpeople periodically reserved their energies for the night and exhausted themselves at play. Perhaps most important of all, enslaved women and men struggled against planters' inclination to confine them and thus created the space and time to celebrate and enjoy their bodies as important personal and political entities in the plantation South.

NOTES

Reprinted with permission from the *Journal of Southern History* 68, no. 3 (August 2002): 533–73 (copyright The Southern Historical Association). For generous insights and careful criticisms I am indebted to Houston Baker, Edward E. Baptist, Douglas R. Egerton, Drew Gilpin Faust, Farah Jasmine Griffin, Lani Guinier, Diannah Jackson Leigh, Nell Painter, Uta G. Poiger, Carroll Smith-Rosenberg, Lynn M. Thomas, and the Brown Bag Seminar of the McNeil Center for Early American Studies. I am also grateful to the *Journal of Southern History*'s anonymous reviewers for tough and inspiring comments. Many thanks to the Organization of American Historians, the Virginia Historical Society, the Library Company of Philadelphia, the departments of history at the University of Pennsylvania and Vassar College, and the MacBride Faculty Fund and the Walter Chapin Simpson Center for the Humanities at the University of Washington for support of research and writing.

1. Charles L. Perdue Jr., Thomas E. Barden, and Robert K. Phillips, eds., *Weevils in the Wheat: Interviews with Virginia Ex-slaves* (Charlottesville, 1976), 316. Williams was fourteen years old when the Civil War began. Before slavery ended, however, she had reached young adulthood; she told her interviewer that she had "growd up" when she left the slaveholding house for field work. At about the same time, she "start[ed] dis cou'tin.'" Like many but not all formerly enslaved interviewees in the 1930s, Williams had more than a child's memories of bondage. She offers, as do other interviewees, the remembrances of young adulthood.

2. Ibid.

3. Winthrop D. Jordan, *White over Black: American Attitudes toward the Negro, 1550–1812* (Chapel Hill, 1968), 55–56, 107; Philip J. Schwarz, *Twice Condemned: Slaves and the Criminal Laws of Virginia, 1705–1865* (Baton Rouge, 1988), 22; Ira Berlin, *Many Thousands Gone: The First Two Centuries of Slavery in North America* (Cambridge, 1998), 113. For more on the social geography of the colonial and antebellum South, see Rhys Isaac, *The Transformation of Virginia, 1740–1790* (Chapel Hill, 1982), 11–57; Stephanie McCurry, *Masters of Small Worlds: Yeomen Households, Gender Relations, and the Political Culture of the Antebellum South Carolina Low Country* (New York, 1995), 10–15; David Goldfield, *Region, Race, and Cities: Interpreting the Urban South* (Baton Rouge, 1997), 69–86, 103–44.

4. Anne Godlewska and Neil Smith cited in Matthew Sparke, "Mapped Bodies and Disembodied Maps: (Dis)placing Cartographic Struggle in Colonial Canada," in *Places through the Body*, ed. Heidi J. Nast and Steve Pile (London, 1998), 305. John Michael Vlach discusses the "black system of place definition," its emphasis on movement, and its rejection of fixity in *Back of the Big House: The Architecture of Plantation Slavery* (Chapel Hill, 1993), 13–17. The phrase "geography of containment" is Houston Baker's from his response to Michael Hanchard, "Temporality, Transnationalism, and Afro-Modernity" (paper presented to the Reshaping Afro-American Studies seminar at the Center for the Study of Black Literature and Culture, University of Pennsylvania, March 27, 1997).

5. Ulrich B. Phillips, *American Negro Slavery: A Survey of the Supply, Employment, and Control of Negro Labor as Determined by the Plantation Regime* (1918; Baton Rouge, 1966), 327; Eugene D. Genovese, *Roll, Jordan, Roll: The World the Slaves Made* (New York, 1972), 3–7. Genovese's paternalism thesis has been the subject of intensive debate since the publication of his monumental *Roll, Jordan, Roll*. Among the many questions at issue is the extent to which enslaved people could resist bondage and the importance of such resistance. Some historians have agreed that paternalist, slaveholding hegemony determined the shape of every feature of black life and, further, that the lives of bondpeople must be understood primarily in terms of their exploitation and oppression by slaveholders. Slaveholding power, in this view, flattened the possibility of meaningful oppositional activity except for running away and organized rebellion: everyday forms of resistance "qualify at best as prepolitical and at worst as apolitical" (Genovese, *Roll, Jordan, Roll*, 3, 6, 7, 22, 90–91, 125, 143–44, 284, 598). See also Elizabeth Fox-Genovese, *Within the Plantation Household: Black and White Women of the Old South* (Chapel Hill, 1988), 30, 49–50, 319; Bertram Wyatt-Brown, "The Mask of Obedience: Male Slave Psychology in the Old South," *American Historical Review* 93 (December 1988): 1228–52; William Dusinberre, *Them Dark Days: Slavery in the American Rice Swamps* (New York, 1996), 235, 248, 265, 270–71, 273. The focus on hegemony overestimates the extent of consent at the expense of the determining role of force. Other historians in the traditional debate have placed black communities, their struggles, and their sufferings—not slaveholders and their hegemonic aspirations—at the center of bondpeople's lives. This chapter builds on this tradition, which includes Herbert Aptheker, *American Negro Slave Revolts* (New York, 1943); George P. Rawick, *From Sundown to Sunup: The Making of the Black Community* (Westport, 1972); John W. Blassingame, *The Slave Community: Plantation Life in*

the Antebellum South, rev. ed. (New York, 1979); Lawrence W. Levine, *Black Culture and Black Consciousness: Afro-American Folk Thought from Slavery to Freedom* (New York, 1977); Charles Joyner, *Down by the Riverside: A South Carolina Slave Community* (Urbana, 1984); Roger D. Abrahams, *Singing the Master: The Emergence of African American Culture in the Plantation South* (New York, 1992); Douglas R. Egerton, *Gabriel's Rebellion: The Virginia Slave Conspiracies of 1800 and 1802* (Chapel Hill, 1993); Shane White and Graham White, *Stylin': African American Expressive Culture from Its Beginnings to the Zoot Suit* (Ithaca, 1998); Douglas R. Egerton, *He Shall Go Out Free: The Lives of Denmark Vesey* (Madison, 1999). This chapter departs from this literature and this debate, however, in its focus on women, gender difference and conflict, and cultural politics as well as in its attention not to lore or religion (that is, to the intellectual and moral history of enslaved communities) or to organized rebellion but to values embodied in the everyday physical use of space, to political belief put into movement.

6. All of these sources present difficulties, and alone none tells all we might want to know. For all of the difficulties of plantation records and legal sources, however, historians of slavery tend to focus their methodological critiques on the interviews of ex-bondpeople. The criticisms contend that the interviews collected by the Works Progress Administration (WPA) were conducted decades after emancipation, after too much had transpired in the lives of the informants to make their recollections creditable. Many of the interviews were also done by whites, further warping the information respondents gave. I do not dispute the problems inherent in the WPA interviews, but I do not conclude from these difficulties that the source is unworkable. This article gathers material from a range of sources—including black and white, contemporaneous and subsequent, and written and oral sources—building a story out of their agreements and common accounts as well as from the insights offered by their differences. These sources also explain the periodization of this article. Because the WPA interviews refer primarily to the last decades of slavery and because black autobiographies proliferated in the same period, this chapter focuses on the years between 1830 and the beginning of the Civil War.

7. Thomas D. Morris, *Southern Slavery and the Law, 1619–1860* (Chapel Hill, 1996); Christopher Morris, "The Articulation of Two Worlds: The Master-Slave Relationship Reconsidered," *Journal of American History* 85 (December 1998): 982–1007; Walter Johnson, *Soul by Soul: Life Inside the Antebellum Slave Market* (Cambridge, 1999). For all of the important differences caused by farm size, crop, type of work, and subregion, American slavery was, above all, a system of economic exploitation and racial subjugation that, when studied in a broad geographic range, reveals strong continuities as well as differences. We have much to learn about the interplay of local and individual experiences of enslavement, about slavery as a system, and about resistance to it as a practice with patterns and trends. In particular, the fragmentary nature of the evidence on a topic such as women's everyday forms of resistance demands a broad geographic sweep.

8. Bondpeople living on farms, in neighborhoods, and in states with small numbers of other enslaved people (like Florida or Delaware) would certainly have enjoyed far less frequent, if any, illegal parties. There would have been differences between the Upper South and the Lower South, but the scarcity of sources precludes knowing for certain. It is possible to note, however, that while it might appear that illicit movement would have

been more common in the Upper South because of its proximity to the free North, the evidence does not support this hypothesis. Bondpeople in the Lower South also formed an active rival geography and organized and attended secret parties. Indeed, these forms of movement may have taken on special importance in the Lower South precisely because bondpeople had little chance of escaping as fugitives. In particular, South Carolina's black majority no doubt enjoyed a great deal of discretion and autonomy when having parties. But enslaved South Carolinians were not the only ones to know life as a black majority: in 1850 about half (50.6 percent) of all bondpeople in the South lived on farms that had at least twenty enslaved people (with a significant minority of 13.1 percent living on holdings with fifty to a hundred enslaved people) (Lewis Cecil Gray, *History of Agriculture in the Southern United States to 1860*, 2 vols. [Washington, D.C., 1933], 1:530). Locally, then, many enslaved people inhabited communities among and near enough others to make independent socializing viable.

9. For the theory of everyday forms of resistance that undergirds the approach taken here, which sees day-to-day resistance as neither a safety valve nor as revolutionary but as a form of political struggle before and behind open political organization, see James C. Scott, *Weapons of the Weak: Everyday Forms of Peasant Resistance* (New Haven, 1985), esp. xv–xvi, 35–36, 285–303, 317; James C. Scott, *Domination and the Arts of Resistance: Hidden Transcripts* (New Haven, 1990), esp. 66, 178, 184–88. Historians who have skillfully employed Scott's theories to study U.S. slave resistance include Alex Lichtenstein, " 'That Disposition to Theft, with Which They Have Been Branded': Moral Economy, Slave Management, and the Law," *Journal of Social History* 21 (Spring 1988): 413–40; Marvin L. Michael Kay and Lorin Lee Cary, *Slavery in North Carolina, 1748–1775* (Chapel Hill, 1995). Critics of Scott's work include Rosalind O'Hanlon, "Recovering the Subject: Subaltern Studies and Histories of Resistance in Colonial South Asia," *Modern Asian Studies* 22 (February 1988): 189–224; Sherry B. Ortner, "Resistance and the Problem of Ethnographic Refusal," *Comparative Studies in Society and History* 37 (January 1995): 173–93.

10. Dorinda Outram, *The Body and the French Revolution: Sex, Class and Political Culture* (New Haven, 1989), 1; C. L. R. James, Grace C. Lee, and Pierre Chaulieu, *Facing Reality* (Detroit, 1974), 5; James C. Scott, *Weapons of the Weak*, 289–99. Dagmar Herzog and Uta Poiger have demonstrated that German feminist analyses connecting the personal and the political grew out of broader German New Left efforts to do the same. American and German feminist movements in the 1970s may have popularized the concept and applied it in especially liberatory ways to women's lives, but they did not invent it (Herzog, " 'Pleasure, Sex, and Politics Belong Together': Post-Holocaust Memory and the Sexual Revolution in West Germany," *Critical Inquiry* 24 [Winter 1998]: 393–444; Poiger, *Jazz, Rock, and Rebels: Cold War Politics and American Culture in a Divided Germany* [Berkeley, 2000], 219, 269 n.32).

11. This discussion is informed by the work of anthropologists and philosophers who have posited the body as an important terrain of conquest and as a site for the reproduction of the social order. They have also detailed what, following Mary Douglas's account of "two bodies," may be called a second body: the social imprint on the body that shapes and limits the experience of the body. See Frantz Fanon, *Black Skin, White Masks*, trans. Charles Lam Markmann (New York, 1967), 109–40; Mary Douglas, *Natural Symbols:*

Explorations in Cosmology (New York, 1970), chap. 5; Michel Foucault, *Discipline and Punish: The Birth of the Prison,* trans. Alan Sheridan (New York, 1977). Recent scholarship has demonstrated that the black body has been more than a site of racial subjugation and suffering. Historians of black bodily joy include Robin D. G. Kelley, *Race Rebels: Culture, Politics, and the Black Working Class* (New York, 1994); Tera W. Hunter, *To 'Joy My Freedom: Southern Black Women's Lives and Labor after the Civil War* (Cambridge, 1997); Helen Bradley Foster, *"New Raiments of Self": African American Clothing in the Antebellum South* (New York, 1997); Shane White and White, *Stylin'*.

12. Fanon, *Black Skin, White Masks,* 110–11. There are at least two criticisms to be made of Fanon's point here. First, Fanon equates the experience of "being black" with domination, allowing for no experience of blackness that is something other than oppressive or Othering. Fanon also goes too far in arguing for a space outside of ideology. Resistance is not created outside of hegemonic ideologies and other forms of domination but is constituted within them. Domination not only calls forth resistance but also establishes the terrain over which struggle ensues. Slaveholders, who understood the importance of regulating the body to social control, identified the black body as a site of domination. Enslaved people responded by rendering their bodies a site of political struggle and enjoyment. This is no neat teleology, for everyday forms of resistance were not the mere shaping or measure of repression (though they were that as well), as critics of everyday politics would have it. Everyday resistance also reveals the formation of genuine black subjectivities and the expression of human agency. These objections notwithstanding, Fanon's suggestion that in spaces away from the white gaze, colonial subjects may experience some freedom from domination is instructive. See also Ann Farnsworth-Alvear, "Orthodox Virginity/Heterodox Memories: Understanding Women's Stories of Mill Discipline in Medellin, Columbia," *Signs* 23 (Autumn 1997): 71–101; James C. Scott, *Weapons of the Weak,* 299.

13. Mary Douglas, *Purity and Danger: An Analysis of Concepts of Pollution and Taboo* (London, 1966); Douglas, *Natural Symbols*; Carolyn Kay Steedman, *Landscape for a Good Woman: A Story of Two Lives* (New Brunswick, 1987); Joan Wallach Scott, *Gender and the Politics of History* (New York, 1988); Elizabeth Faue, *Community of Suffering and Struggle: Women, Men, and the Labor Movement in Minneapolis, 1915–1945* (Chapel Hill, 1991); Evelyn Brooks Higginbotham, "African-American Women's History and the Metalanguage of Race," *Signs* 17 (Winter 1992): 251–74.

14. For work on the somatics of bondwomen's enslavement, see Darlene Clark Hine and Kate Wittenstein, "Female Slave Resistance: The Economics of Sex," in *The Black Woman Cross-Culturally,* ed. Filomena Chioma Steady (Cambridge, 1981), 289–300; Deborah Gray White, *Ar'n't I a Woman? Female Slaves in the Plantation South* (New York, 1985); Stephanie J. Shaw, "Mothering under Slavery in the Antebellum South," in *Mothering: Ideology, Experience, and Agency,* ed. Evelyn Nakano Glenn, Grace Chang, and Linda Rennie Forcey (New York, 1994), 237–58; Nell Irvin Painter, *Sojourner Truth: A Life, a Symbol* (New York, 1996); Leslie A. Schwalm, *A Hard Fight for We: Women's Transition from Slavery to Freedom in South Carolina* (Urbana, 1997). Many southern women's historians are also blurring the dichotomy between the personal and creative and the political and material; see, for example, Elsa Barkley Brown, "Negotiating and Transform-

ing the Public Sphere: African American Political Life in the Transition from Slavery to Freedom," *Public Culture* 7 (Fall 1994): 107–46; Kathleen M. Brown, *Good Wives, Nasty Wenches, and Anxious Patriarchs: Gender, Race, and Power in Colonial Virginia* (Chapel Hill, 1996); Hunter, *To 'Joy My Freedom*; Jacquelyn Dowd Hall, " 'You Must Remember This': Autobiography as Social Critique," *Journal of American History* 85 (September 1998): 439–65. Paul Gilroy's work also informs the discussion here; see "One Nation under a Groove: The Cultural Politics of 'Race' and Racism in Britain," in *Anatomy of Racism*, ed. David Theo Goldberg (Minneapolis, 1990), 274.

15. White abolitionists used graphic representations of the exploited, abused, or degraded enslaved body to garner support for the antislavery cause; see Phillip Lapsansky, "Graphic Discord: Abolitionist and Antiabolitionist Images," in *The Abolitionist Sisterhood: Women's Political Culture in Antebellum America*, ed. Jean Fagan Yellin and John C. Van Horne (Ithaca, 1994), 201–30; Elizabeth B. Clark, " 'The Sacred Rights of the Weak': Pain, Sympathy, and the Culture of Individual Rights in Antebellum America," *Journal of American History* 82 (September 1995): 463–93. Scholars of nineteenth-century slave narratives have demonstrated that black writers—especially women—used rhetorical strategies to draw attention away from their bodies to emphasize their political voices rather than titillate white audiences; see Anthony G. Barthelemy, introduction to *Collected Black Women's Narratives*, ed. Henry Louis Gates Jr. (New York, 1988), xxix–xlviii; Carla L. Peterson, *"Doers of the Word": African-American Women Speakers and Writers in the North (1830–1880)* (New York, 1995), esp. 22; Jeannine DeLombard, " 'Eye-Witness to the Cruelty': Southern Violence and Northern Testimony in Frederick Douglass's 1845 Narrative," *American Literature* 73 (June 2001): 245–75.

16. Jennifer L. Morgan, " 'Some Could Suckle over Their Shoulder': Male Travelers, Female Bodies, and the Gendering of Racial Ideology, 1500–1770," *William and Mary Quarterly*, 3d ser., 54 (January 1997): 179, 170, 184, 181, 171.

17. Kathleen M. Brown, *Good Wives, Nasty Wenches, and Anxious Patriarchs*, 116–19, 125, 135–36. For more on notions of racial difference and their relation to the expansion of the African slave trade and American slavery, see Edmund S. Morgan, *American Slavery, American Freedom: The Ordeal of Colonial Virginia* (New York, 1975), 295–337; Jordan, *White over Black*; Alden T. Vaughn, "The Origins Debate: Slavery and Racism in Seventeenth-Century Virginia," *Virginia Magazine of History and Biography* 97 (July 1989): 311–54; Peter Kolchin, *American Slavery, 1619–1877* (New York, 1993), 11–12, 17.

18. "Bio-text" is John O'Neill's phrase, from *The Communicative Body: Studies in Communicative Philosophy, Politics, and Sociology* (Evanston, 1989), 3.

19. Fanon, *Black Skin, White Masks*, 110–11.

20. Charles Ball, *Slavery in the United States: A Narrative of the Life and Adventures of Charles Ball* (1836; Detroit, 1970), 125.

21. The manual's instructions are printed on the inside cover of the Richard Eppes Diary, 1858, Eppes Family Papers, Virginia Historical Society, Richmond (hereafter cited as VHS). Mark M. Smith demonstrates the increasing importance of time discipline to plantation production during the antebellum period in the following works: "Time, Slavery, and Plantation Capitalism in the Ante-bellum American South," *Past and Present* 150 (February 1996): 142–68; "Old South Time in Comparative Perspective," *American*

Historical Review 101 (December 1996): 1432–69; *Mastered by the Clock: Time, Slavery, and Freedom in the American South* (Chapel Hill, 1997).

22. For a single example, Virginia slaveholder John Bassett wrote a pass for an enslaved person named Edward: "Edward is sent to Rich[mon]d. To remain till Monday next[.] Feby 25th 1826. John Bassett." The note at the bottom of the pass confirmed Edward's movements: "I have recd five Dollars by your Boy Edward[.] R[.] Brooks" (section 17, Bassett Family Papers, VHS). More passes can be found in section 4, Hundley Family Papers, VHS; sections 5, 42, and 86, Spragins Family Papers, VHS. On slave patrols, see Gladys-Marie Fry, *Night Riders in Black Folk History* (Knoxville, 1975); Sally E. Hadden, *Slave Patrols: Law and Violence in Virginia and the Carolinas* (Cambridge, 2001).

23. Deborah Gray White, *Ar'n't I a Woman?* 75; see also the passes cited in n.22. Women occasionally were able to procure (legal) passes and leave the plantation, usually to perform labor. For example, enslaved women on the Hunter family's Virginia estate obtained written permission to take their cloth to a dressmaker (Mary Evelina [Dandridge] Hunter Papers, box 10, Hunter Family Papers, VHS).

24. William Ethelbert Ervin Diaries, December 31, 1846, #247-z, Southern Historical Collection, University of North Carolina at Chapel Hill; George P. Rawick, ed., *The American Slave: A Composite Autobiography* (Westport, 1972–79), vol. 13, pt. 3, 128. Andrew Boone recalled, "If you wus out widout a pass dey would shore git you. De paterollers shore looked after you. Dey would come to de house at night to see who wus there. If you wus out of place, dey would wear you out" (Rawick, *American Slave*, 14:134).

25. Rawick, *American Slave*, 14:157; see also Genovese, *Roll, Jordan, Roll*, 3–7, 570, 577–80, 584. Roger D. Abrahams has shown how bondpeople sometimes turned paternalistic events like corn shuckings into rituals of their own meaning (*Singing the Master*, 83–106).

26. Rawick, *American Slave*, 16:23. Some WPA informants reported that attending plantation frolics was an activity reserved for white men. For example, George Fleming said, "White ladies didn't go to de frolics, but some of de white men did" (Rawick, *American Slave*, supp. ser. 1, 9:128).

27. John Nevitt Diary, December 27, 1828, #543, Southern Historical Collection. "Treat[s]" are mentioned in the December 25, 1827, December 25, 1829, and December 27, 1830, entries.

28. Rawick, *American Slave*, vol. 13, pt. 4, p. 68; vol. 12, pt. 2, p. 142.

29. Ibid., 14:213.

30. The lyrics, as Bob Ellis remembered them, were, "Keep yo' eye on de sun, / See how she run, / Don't let her catch you with your work undone, / I'm a trouble, I'm a trouble, / Trouble don' las' always" (Perdue, Barden, and Phillips, *Weevils in the Wheat*, 88; for another version see 309).

31. Rawick, *American Slave*, 14:213, 156.

32. Ibid., vol. 12, pt. 2, p. 188.

33. Austin Steward, *Twenty-two Years a Slave, and Forty Years a Freeman*, introduction by Jane H. Pease and William H. Pease (1857; Reading, 1969), 19–22.

34. Ibid., 20.

35. Ibid., 15, 21.

36. Ibid., 20–24.

37. Ibid., 23–24.

38. Hadden, *Slave Patrols*, 109; Fry, *Night Riders*, 93; Perdue, Barden, and Phillips, *Weevils in the Wheat*, 93, 297; Rawick, *American Slave*, vol. 13, pt. 4, p. 80; vol. 14, pt. 1, p. 213; 16:49–50.

39. Perdue, Barden, and Phillips, *Weevils in the Wheat*, 316; Rawick, *American Slave*, vol. 13, pt. 4, pp. 306, 40, 64, 124; vol. 15, pt. 2, p. 132; supp. ser. 1, 11:128.

40. Rawick, *American Slave*, vol. 12, pt. 2, p. 110.

41. Ibid., 7:161.

42. Ibid., 126.

43. Ibid., 162.

44. Ibid., 161.

45. Perdue, Barden, and Phillips, *Weevils in the Wheat*, 49–50; Rawick, *American Slave*, vol. 13, pt. 3, p. 124.

46. The "pigeon wings," "gwine to de east, an' gwine to de west," "callin' de figgers," "set de flo'," and "dancin' on de spot" are described in Perdue, Barden, and Phillips, *Weevils in the Wheat*, 49–50; the "hack-back" is described in Rawick, *American Slave*, supp. ser. 1, 11:127–28; the remaining dances are described in Katrina Hazzard-Gordon, *Jookin': The Rise of Social Dance Formations in African-American Culture* (Philadelphia, 1990), 19.

47. Hazzard-Gordon, *Jookin'*, 20; Perdue, Barden, and Phillips, *Weevils in the Wheat*, 316; Rawick, *American Slave*, vol. 12, pt. 2, p. 99.

48. Brenda E. Stevenson, *Life in Black and White: Family and Community in the Slave South* (New York, 1996), 23, 255; Christopher Morris, *Becoming Southern: The Evolution of a Way of Life, Warren County and Vicksburg, Mississippi, 1770–1860* (New York, 1995), 63.

49. Rawick, *American Slave*, 7:30. Domestic violence was a source of both comedy and moral judgment in the folk song "Old Dan Tucker," in which Tucker, "a mighty mean man" who "beat his wife wid a fryin' pan," ends up passed out drunk in a "red hot" fire. Dora Franks remembered singing this song with other enslaved youth in Mississippi (Rawick, *American Slave*, 7:53).

50. Ibid., vol. 13, pt. 4, p. 104.

51. For more on black style under slavery, see Patricia K. Hunt, "The Struggle to Achieve Individual Expression through Clothing and Adornment: African American Women under and after Slavery," in *Discovering the Women in Slavery: Emancipating Perspectives on the American Past*, ed. Patricia Morton (Athens, 1996), 227–40; Foster, *"New Raiments of Self"*; Shane White and White, *Stylin'*.

52. Frederick Law Olmsted, *The Cotton Kingdom: A Traveller's Observations on Cotton and Slavery in the American Slave States*, ed. Arthur M. Schlesinger Sr. (1953; New York, 1984), 82; Rawick, *American Slave*, vol. 12, pt. 1, p. 4; 15:62, 14:272.

53. Drew Gilpin Faust, *James Henry Hammond and the Old South: A Design for Mastery* (Baton Rouge, 1982), 100–103; Genovese, *Roll, Jordan, Roll*, 5–7; Roswell King to Pierce Butler, December 7, 1812, April 20, 1816, July 6, 1817, Butler Family Papers, box 3, folder 9, Historical Society of Pennsylvania, Philadelphia; Harriet A. Jacobs, *Incidents in the Life of a Slave Girl, Written by Herself*, ed. Jean Fagan Yellin (Cambridge, 1987), 11.

54. Rawick, *American Slave*, vol. 4, pt. 1, p. 223; supp. ser. 1, 11:130; see also supp. ser. 2, 8:2990. As historians of enslaved women have pointed out, this "masculinization" of bondwomen at work was never complete, and rarely did it define enslaved women's gender identities. At work in their specialized labor, their gender-segregated or gender-specific agricultural labor, and the reproductive labor they performed for their families, enslaved women constructed their own meanings and expressions of womanhood. See Deborah Gray White, *Ar'n't I a Woman?* Jacqueline Jones, *Labor of Love, Labor of Sorrow: Black Women, Work, and the Family from Slavery to the Present* (New York, 1985); Schwalm, *Hard Fight for We*.

55. Joyner, *Down by the Riverside*, 74; Foster, *"New Raiments of Self,"* 111–12; Schwalm, *Hard Fight for We*, 60; Rawick, *American Slave*, vol. 13, pt. 3, pp. 2, 186; Olmsted, *Cotton Kingdom*, 82; Thomas C. Buchanan, "The Slave Mississippi: African-American Steamboat Workers, Networks of Resistance, and the Commercial World of the Western Rivers, 1811–1880" (Ph.D. diss., Carnegie Mellon University, 1998), 175–84.

56. Pierre Bourdieu, *Outline of a Theory of Practice*, trans. Richard Nice (Cambridge, 1977), 164–71.

57. Ibid., 165.

58. Rawick, *American Slave*, vol. 13, pt. 4, pp. 212, 220.

59. Ibid., vol. 13, pt. 3, p. 72; 15:364; *Aunt Sally; or, The Cross the Way of Freedom: A Narrative of the Slave-Life and Purchase of the Mother of Rev. Isaac Williams, of Detroit, Michigan* (Cincinnati, 1858), 47; Octavia V. Rogers Albert, *The House of Bondage; or, Charlotte Brooks and Other Slaves* (1890; New York, 1988), 64; see also Rawick, *American Slave*, vol. 13, pt. 4, pp. 80, 183; 15:129, 179; Foster, *"New Raiments of Self,"* 104.

60. Foster, *"New Raiments of Self,"* 112, 114, appendix 3; Perdue, Barden, and Phillips, *Weevils in the Wheat*, 316–17; Rawick, *American Slave*, 11:52–53, 14:184; Olmsted, *Cotton Kingdom*, 82.

61. Perdue, Barden, and Phillips, *Weevils in the Wheat*, 294.

62. Rawick, *American Slave*, 17:306, vol. 12, pt. 2, p. 297, supp. ser. 1, 6:249; Drew Gilpin Faust, *Mothers of Invention: Women of the Slaveholding South in the American Civil War* (Chapel Hill, 1996), 223. Robert Shepherd similarly said, "De white ladies had nice silk dresses to wear to church. Slave 'omans had new calico dresses what dey wore wid hoopskirts dey made out of grapevines" (Rawick, *American Slave*, vol. 13, pt. 3, p. 253).

63. Shane White and Graham White, "Slave Hair and African American Culture in the Eighteenth and Nineteenth Centuries," *Journal of Southern History* 61 (February 1995): 70–71; Rawick, *American Slave*, supp. ser. 1, 11:57; Foster, *"New Raiments of Self,"* 115, 252.

64. See clothing distribution lists, 1802, in Jane Frances Walker Page Commonplace Book, vhs; "List of negroes who received clothes," April 1846, November 1846, George J. Kollock Plantation Journals, vol. 6, #407, Southern Historical Collection; Foster, *"New Raiments of Self"*, 243–44; Rawick, *American Slave*, 14:139.

65. Perdue, Barden, and Phillips, *Weevils in the Wheat*, 316. For more on women's use of clothing to exhibit their individuality, see Hunt, "Struggle," 227–40.

66. Perdue, Barden, and Phillips, *Weevils in the Wheat*, 333.

67. Frances (Scott) Miller diary, July 3, 5, 1858, Armistead, Blanton, and Wallace Family Papers, section 10, VHS.

68. Ibid., February 7, 1857.

69. Ibid.

70. Rawick, *American Slave*, vol. 13, pt. 3, pp. 39, 276.

71. Ibid., vol. 12, pt. 2, pp. 188–89. Fatigue and its effects on plantation production constituted a problem after paternalist frolics as well. Some slaveholders accounted for exhaustion and allowed some time the day following frolics for naps. For example, Addie Vinson remembered how after a dance given by her owner, "Niggers dat had done danced half de night would be so sleepy when de bugle sounded dey wouldn't have time to cook breakfast. Den 'bout de middle of de mawnin' dey would complain 'bout bein' so weak and hongry dat de overseer would fetch 'em in and have 'em fed. He let 'em rest 'bout a hour and a half; den he marched 'em back to de field and wuked 'em 'til slap black dark" (Rawick, *American Slave*, vol. 13, pt. 4, p. 109).

72. *Preamble and Regulations of the Savannah River Anti–Slave Traffick Association* (n.p., 1846), 3, 4. For Hammond's complaints about drinking and theft among the enslaved population at Silver Bluff, see James Henry Hammond, plantation records for Silver Bluff, October 16, 1835, South Caroliniana Library, University of South Carolina, Columbia, available on microfilm in Kenneth M. Stampp, ed., *Records of Ante-bellum Southern Plantations from the Revolution through the Civil War*, set. A, pt. 1, reel 1.

73. *Preamble and Regulations of the Savannah River Anti–Slave Traffick Association*, 3, 4, 5, 8.

74. Ibid., 3, 5. Slaveholders' fears about the effects of slave drinking were not strictly racial in nature; elites attempted to curb poor whites' drinking as well. Many antebellum Americans believed that regular or excessive drinking impinged on a person's productivity and stimulated flashes of anger. One newspaper editorialist, for example, opined that "in proportion as men become drunkards, they cease to be useful to themselves, to their families, or to society. . . . When a common laborer becomes a drunkard, his family is soon reduced to the utmost need. The more he drinks the less he works, and the greater are his expenditures." Furthermore, the journalist warned, "An early effect of habitual drinking . . . is IRASCIBILITY OF TEMPER" (*Natchez [Miss.] Southern Galaxy*, July 17, 1828, 1). There were, nonetheless, racial aspects to slaveholders' extreme concerns regarding slave drinking. Decreased productivity in a working white man cost others only indirectly; the worker "ceas[ed] to be useful" to "society" generally. But an enslaved person's decreased productivity directly cost her or his owner. Moreover, alcohol, when imbibed by a black body, was widely believed to unleash black impulses—that is, innate African savagery and violence—otherwise repressed under slavery's ostensible civilizing influence (Denise Herd, "The Paradox of Temperance: Blacks and the Alcohol Question in Nineteenth-Century America," in *Drinking: Behavior and Belief in Modern History*, ed. Susanna Barrows and Robin Room [Berkeley, 1991], 354–75).

75. *Preamble and Regulations of the Savannah River Anti–Slave Traffick Association*, 3–5. Everywhere in the slave South that blacks traded for and drank alcohol, slaveholders worried, as the Savannah River neighbors did, about the integrity of their property

rights and the stability of slave subordination. Kentucky's Supreme Court tellingly worried in 1845 that trading liquor to bondpeople would "tempt them to petty larcenies, by way of procuring the means necessary to buy." Equally important, access to alcohol threatened to "lead them to dissipation, insubordination and vice, and obstruct the good government, well being and harmony of society." Many white southerners, even those in the cities, would have concurred with the Savannah River Anti–Slave Traffick Association that black marketing and drinking gave bondpeople ideas inappropriate to their station and inspired behavior threatening to those who sought to maintain black "subordination." For example, in 1846 one Charleston jury pronounced that "the unrestrained intercourse and indulgence of familiarities between the black and white . . . are destructive of the respect and subserviency which our laws recognize as due from the one to the other and which form an essential feature in our institutions." Just a few years later, in 1851, another Charleston jury argued that slave liquor trafficking brought "the negro slave in such familiar contact with the white man, as to . . . invite the assertion of equality, or draw from him exhibitions of presumption and insubordination" (*Smith v. Commonwealth*, 6 B. Mon. [Ky.] 22 [September 1845]; Charleston juries quoted in Richard C. Wade, *Slavery in the Cities: The South, 1820–1860* [New York, 1964], 157).

76. *Preamble and Regulations of the Savannah River Anti–Slave Traffick Association*, 3–5.

PART TWO

Race, Identity, and Community

Genealogies to a Past

Africa, Ethnicity, and Marriage in Seventeenth-Century Mexico

HERMAN L. BENNETT

*D*espite colonial Mexico's exceedingly rich historiography of ethnicity, a curious omission prevails—the dearth of social and cultural inquiries on persons of African descent. In light of the African population's numerical ascendancy over Spaniards throughout the colonial period, this omission seems glaring. But when we acknowledge that during the same period, the principal urban centers—the sites of Spanish power—registered slave and free black majorities, this absence becomes rather ominous. Indeed, this void highlights how much speculation figures in our understanding of the African past in Mexico and perhaps elsewhere in Latin America.

Basic social and cultural questions still need to be framed. We know so little about the domestic arrangements of persons of African descent that even our knowledge about which questions we need to ask about gender, sexual, and family conventions among Africans and their descendants remains provisional. Did a family structure exist among enslaved Africans? If so, what was its nature, and on what social logic did it rest? How did the family structure of the enslaved change over time? What social consequences, if any, flowed from the changing family structure? What were the cultural implications, if any, of these structural changes? Did the existence of the family and its structural changes enable access to freedom? While underscoring the neglect of family life, these elemental questions also reveal how little we know about the enslaved and the cultures they forged. In light of this tradition of neglect, the story of the African past still remains mired in a narrative of revelation whereby successive generations of scholars express surprise at the presence and significance of New Spain's African past.

Slavery and the Postconquest Narrative

In the wake of the Spanish conquest of Tenochtitlán (1519–21), a steady trickle of Africans augmented central Mexico's initial black population. Fifty years later, the African population outnumbered the viceroyalty's Spanish population. Most of the sixteenth-century arrivals originated in West Africa, but West-Central Africans steadily proliferated among the seventeenth-century slave trade (1595–1640). By 1640, the Spaniards had imported nearly two hundred thousand West and West-Central Africans into New Spain. The survivors of the dreaded Middle Passage constituted a subject of much concern. As the Spanish community composed of royal officials, ecclesiastics, and Spaniards of various means engaged in a protracted struggle to put into practice their competing social visions—largely formulated around labor and land—the institution of African slavery occupied a prominent role in their thinking. Moving from their initial location in New Spain's urban domestic economy, where they worked as servants attending to Spanish needs, many Africans found themselves in the countryside employed in the expanding commercial economy. In rural areas, the majority of Africans, and in particular their descendants, staffed Spanish agricultural and livestock estates of a different scale. The Spaniards also employed a sizable number of Africans in other commercial activities, most notably mining, that sprung up throughout the countryside. Finally, the Spaniards relied on those of African descent as vital cogs in the transport sector of the commercial economy. In this capacity, peoples of African descent guided the innumerable pack mules that moved goods to local and regional markets. Even as the Spaniards formulated new land and labor practices, they tied the enslaved African presence to an increasingly extensive commercial economy that revolved around commodification.

Africans represented their masters' property, employed as the masters saw fit. But the diverse nature of urban and rural slavery resulted in many forms of bondage. Identifying a person as a slave said little about the nature of his or her slave experience. Slavery always reflected the nature of the enterprise in which the enslaved were engaged and, more importantly, mirrored the master's whims and circumstances. The wide range of occupations in which Africans and their descendants worked makes it difficult, if not impossible, to generalize about the slave experience in Spanish America. Slavery, in short, assumed numerous configurations. Although obvious, scholars of slavery often overlook the implications of this statement.

We must question decontextualized formulations of the slave experience. Even in discussions of the African past, the subject of this chapter, our analysis needs to privilege the contingent nature of experience over the myth of structural and cultural continuity. Karl Marx, an ardent structuralist, eloquently questioned the notion of historical transcendence by asking "What is a Negro slave?" His answer: "a man of the black race. . . . [H]e only becomes a slave in certain relations."[1] Slave owners, slaves, and others who profited from certain relations thus continually had to be made. Africans in the seventeenth century were made into slaves through specific relations of domination that marked them as distinct both from sixteenth-century arrivals and from others who experienced slavery in seventeenth-century New Spain. This chapter describes that historical process.

Ethnicity in the Catholic Crucible

On July 11, 1633, two Angolans, Angelina and Jusepe, entered Mexico City's cathedral intent on winning sanction for their desired marriage. Upon receiving their request, the vicar, Fray Luís de Cifuentes, asked the couple to provide evidence of their unmarried status. At that moment, two other Angolans, Juan and María de la Cruz, who had accompanied Angelina and Jusepe on their mission, stepped forward to testify that neither was married and that the two were not closely related. A day later, after weighing the evidence, Luís de Cifuentes granted the couple their wish. Unless someone came forward with incriminating evidence in the next twenty-one days (which corresponded to three consecutive readings of the banns), Angelina and Jusepe would marry. Since no one challenged the match, the couple wed in August 1633.[2]

Angelina and Jusepe were not unusual. Throughout the colonial period, numerous couples solemnized their unions in the Catholic church. Angolans, like Angelina and Jusepe, represented no exception. As believers in a polytheistic pantheon in which their beliefs existed in a Christian cultural context, many embraced the sacrament of a Christian marriage. Though some hesitated to do so under normal circumstances, on the threshold of death even the culturally recalcitrant often renounced their common-law arrangements (*amancebamiento*).[3] Moral imperatives led many Africans residing in common-law arrangements to petition for absolution of their mortal sins. Even individuals who refused to abide by Christian values in other aspects of their lives ascribed symbolic importance to a church-sanctioned union. Fear of eternal hell, perhaps an index of an individual's degree of creolization, often prompted those residing in a state of *amancebamiento* to marry, revealing the degree to which Christianity had permeated their consciousness. This Christian worldview is of interest, but so are the ethnic and racial identities informing spouse selection, kinship networks, and friendships. As we shall see, identities and social networks were mutually constitutive. The union of Angelina and Jusepe epitomized their Christian consciousness. Similarly, the marital alliances of thousands of Africans and those of their descendants illustrate how their New World identities assumed tangible expressions around well-defined but not immutable boundaries. One guiding question maintained and reproduced such boundaries: "Do *we* intermarry with *them*?"[4]

Before examining the cultural practices that highlight the construction of ethnic ties, we must note that slavery, like Angelina and Jusepe's marriage, existed in the crucible of Christianity. To ignore the centrality of this crucible oversimplifies Christianity's pervasive power in Spanish American urban centers and the myriad of ways that it defined the colonial experience. Seventy years after the conquest, New Spain's clergy routinely received marriage petitions. But the frequency of these petitions increased after the viceroyalty's first inquisitor general, Pedro de Moya y Contreras, became archbishop and in accordance with the Council of Trent (1545–63) introduced ecclesiastical reforms. In 1569, Pedro de Moya y Contreras arrived in Mexico City intent on inaugurating the era of Catholic renewal in New Spain. As the newly named inquisitor general of the tribunal of the Holy Office of the Inquisition, Moya y Contreras acted decisively to secure the realm for Catholicism and the Spanish sovereign, Philip II. Moya y Contreras and the Inquisition asserted both royal authority and clerical reforms designed to bolster the ecclesiastical structure through which the Crown insinuated its dominion over the behavior and therefore the souls of the faithful. Thus, the tribunal directed its proceedings against Protestant heretics, *conversos* suspected of still being Jews, and the amorphous *republica de los españoles*, whose composition included Spaniards, mestizos, and the variously defined descendants of Africans. After Moya y Contreras installed the tribunal and then presided over a series of spectacular autos-da-fé (public proceedings of faith to which the Catholic clergy subjected sinners, he was appointed archbishop of Mexico, a position that enabled him to impose his reformist zeal directly on the clergy, the social group explicitly concerned with the spiritual life of the faithful. These reforms led to greater discipline and regulation.

After New Spain held the Third Provincial Council (1585), which affirmed the Tridentine reforms and set ecclesiastical policy for the colony's diverse inhabitants, the marriage petition (*informacion matrimonial*) appeared with regularity, thus underscoring, at least in the viceregal capital, the ascendance of Catholic renewal. From the ecclesiastical perspective, the marriage petition symbolized order (*policía*) in the Christian commonwealth (*república Cristiana*), an order that organically tied individuals through conjugality to the temporal and sacred sovereigns. Marriage, the petitioners' intent, linked the realm of Spain's sovereign with those of wedding party, thereby insuring both social order and legitimacy. The marriage petition and the rituals surrounding it became standard features of social life in seventeenth-century urban New Spain.

As a customary practice, Christian matrimony underscores how Catholicism insinuated itself into the lives of Africans and their creolized descendants. As a measure of Christian faith, Christian matrimony and its ritualized proceedings also signify how patrimonial authority gained currency among persons of African descent. By embracing Christian matrimony, Africans legitimized their desire to forge ethnic and other affinity ties. But in affirming this desire, Christian matrimony instilled Christian identities—identities that were in conformance with Catholic sovereignty. In short, the power of Catholic rituals resided not solely in the ethnic legitimacy they accorded but also in the authority to which they bound the Christian faithful. On this journey into Catholic patrimonialism, persons of African descent ventured of their own volition. In most instances, neither masters nor the clergy played a visible role in this cultural appropriation of Catholicism. For strategic reasons, Africans and their descendants forged solitary paths.

Catholic absolutism steadily registered the regulatory and specific ritual instances involving persons of African descent that in turn highlighted their desires. In and through these recorded instances of desire, a culture emerged.[5] In this sense, I view spouse and sponsor selection among persons of African descent as an expression of cultural desire. While the legally sanctioned marriages were by definition Christian, this does not imply that cultural imperatives prompting Africans and their descendants to marry always reflected the workings of a Christian conscience. Persons of African descent married for various reasons, both in and out of the Catholic church. In the process of spouse and sponsor selection, however, a perceived link between social interaction, community, and cultural formation flourished. Our task then is to discern the cultural logic of this process.

Rules, prescriptions, and taboos serving as the web of cultural signification shaped patterns of marriage, kinship, and descent. Communities and their members abide by prescriptive norms to avoid violating existing taboos or engaging in defiling acts of pollution. For anthropologists, such behavior has long underscored the cultural as opposed to the natural dimension of kinship practices. Social practices constitute cultural cues that individuals internalize in the course of being socialized as part of a particular community. But from where do these practices and the norms that sustain them derive? How are we to understand the emergence of a new set of practices and norms among recent cultural outsiders, people whose various ancestors and kin adhered to different practices and norms? Why and when did these practices take hold? What purpose did they initially serve? In posing these questions, the cultural logic that prompted Christian notions of reckoning is brought into relief, explaining how individuals such as Jusepe and Angelina utilized Christian marriage to effect ethnic ties but did so with profound consequences—the internalization of Christian norms.

As agencies of social control, slavery, and Christianity defined acceptable cultural expressions and provided a sociocultural arena in which transplanted

African social institutions acquired different functions. Although West-Central African and Western European families exhibited common features, the form manifested distinctive imperatives in different cultures. The atomized conjugal unit, Christian kinship and descent patterns, and incipient Western European individualism represented alien notions to seventeenth-century West-Central Africans. Modifications in their social structure and kinship ideology, produced by Christianity in the form of suppression or conversion, thus precipitated changes in their cultural practices and identities.[6]

When Angelina and Jusepe petitioned to have their union legitimized, they were departing from the practices of their "Angolan" ancestors. For West-Central Africans, the Christian conjugal unit, the role of free will in the process of spouse selection, monogamy, and normative assumptions about gender and domestic relations required cultural modifications that threatened the always already fragile social organization and values. Christianity and its family structure challenged West-Central Africans because their cultural identities, like those of others, were the products of contextualized family and kinship systems.

Despite the implications of cultural loss that conversion to Christianity entailed, thousands of West-Central Africans, like Angelina and Jusepe, sought marriage in the Catholic church. What were the cosmological and personal imperatives leading Angolans to embrace the Christian conjugal unit? What was their understanding of Christianity, its family and kinship structure, and marriage? More importantly, how did they adjust to the potential cultural conflict between their African and Christian identities, a persistent feature of the seventeenth century as Angolans in particular forged, maintained, and sanctioned their ethnic cohesiveness through Christianity? Clear answers will always remain elusive, but the prevalence and recurrence of behavioral patterns show that the Christian family was instrumental in Angelina's and Jusepe's lives since they used it to construct their particular New World communities.

Before the ecclesiastical authorities in 1633, Juan testified that he and Angelina had "come together to this kingdom." Juan then noted that "for six years I have communicated with Angelina in Mexico City." If by 1633 they had resided in New Spain for six years, they probably arrived in 1627 on the *Nuestra Señora de la Piedad*, the only registered slave ship for that year, which arrived with 152 West-Central Africans.[7] After disembarking in Veracruz, the survivors were inspected by royal officials and rested briefly in the port's mosquito-ridden and oppressive humidity. After several days, these Africans faced hordes of interested buyers, who violated and humiliated them with touches and penetrating stares. Angelina and Juan may have been purchased by their respective owners, Doña Mariana Namino de Aguilar and Francisco de Lorenzana, either in Veracruz or in Mexico City. In any event, they and their remaining shipmates next had to endure the arduous journey from Veracruz to the viceregal capital. Upon completing the steep and difficult climb from the tropics of Veracruz to Mexico City's temperate climate, Angelina's and Juan's new lives as Mexican slaves began.

Variations on the African Past

Separation, death, deprivation, and humiliation marked the contours of Angelina's and Juan's forced migration from Angola to New Spain. Merchants' ledgers underscore mortality rates and profits but remain silent on the cultural, psychological, and spiritual toll the Middle Passage extracted. As they recovered from the physical horrors of their transatlantic voyage, African survivors also had to make tremendous cultural adjustments, the most profound of which transpired in the cosmological realm. The experiences of Angelina, Jusepe, María, and Juan suggest that they had undergone this scrutinizing process and had embraced certain changes. They were Africans for whom ethnicity found expression in spouse selection and friendship ties. Ethnically aware, Angelina, Jusepe, María, and Juan also became Christians, thus indicating the coexistence of dual—if not pluralistic—and potentially conflicting identities. The nature and implications of this adjustment encouraged both continuity and change in the lives of Africans during the seventeenth century.

Among scholars of Mexican history, however, the lack of interest in the African past from which people such as Angelina, Jusepe, María, and Juan had been uprooted raises conceptual difficulties for the study of cultural formation. These scholars tend in their colonial narratives to depict Africans as culturally bereft people. This intellectual practice stands in marked contrast to the ways scholars engage the indigenous past. Even for a population whose members, in lieu of corporate structures, engaged colonialism as individuals, the past played some role in the colonial encounter. Yet the claim that Africans were individualistic serves to excuse historians' lack of engagement with the African past.[8] But what they call individualism was in fact a process. Armed with an understanding of the African past, we can see that so-called individuality conceals the ways by which seventeenth-century arrivals from West-Central Africa emerged as Angolans and then formulated ethnic communities through Christian matrimony.

Instead of looking closely, Mexicanists ascribe a deep and inexplicable void to the African past. Nonetheless, for Western-trained historians, the transition from African to Western cosmologies, which was part of the "Angolans'" reformulation of identity, poses several methodological and interpretive problems. How do we demonstrate that Central African cosmologies matter when Western rules of evidence configure the relevant archive in decidedly narrow ways? Also, in discussing the African cultural past, how do we adhere to historicizing to avoid charges of mythical or structuralist interpretations? Despite these conceptual dilemmas, New Spain's African past demands more than Mexicanist scholars' current lack of engagement with African cultural history. In fact, the existing void in historians' writings is akin to social death—the severing and denial of a past before slavery.[9] But slaves such as Angelina and Jusepe had an African past into which they had been socialized as children.

From childhood, seventeenth-century West-Central Africans had been acquainted with Mpemba, "the land of the death," located in the west across a large body of water in which deceased spirits with white skins ruled. According to a prophecy retold by local elders, "A man's soul does not dwell in the grave after his death but leaves it to become a ghost [*n'kuyu*] in the land of the dead, which is called *ku mpemba a fula*. In the land of the dead there are villages, waters, and hills as there are here [*vava nsi*]. He must first cross the water, climb the hill, and descend to arrive in the country [*mu si*] of *Mpemba a Fula*. . . . When he arrives, they paint him with *tukula*-red so that his body becomes parti-colored [*mfumfukutu*]. They are healthier than we. They go to the Europeans to travel and to buy things. They work and have plenty to eat."[10]

For the approximately seventy-five thousand West-Central Africans who arrived in Mexico between 1595 and 1640, the prophecy surrounding Mpemba appeared to have been fulfilled. Although they were physically alive and the prophecy stated that only the souls of the dead made the voyage, perhaps the enslaved saw themselves as having experienced a spiritual death. In fact, the widely shared BaKongo cosmology identified two juxtaposed worlds, "this world" and the "land of the dead." Death defined the space beyond what was known—life outside of the village and separation from one's lineage.

As the ship that carried Angelina and Juan tossed on the waves of the Atlantic, the Mpemba mythology must have assumed the frightening air of reality. Those unaware of the BaKongo prophecy had different legacies through which they saw Europeans, interpreted the significance of the Middle Passage, and understood their arrival in the Americas. Even after sustained European and African contact along the Bight of Biafra, Olaudah Equiano, an Ibo, interpreted his fate among Europeans in supernatural terms: "I was now persuaded that I had gotten into a world of bad spirits and that they were going to kill me. Their complexions too differing so much from ours, their long hair and the language they spoke (which was very different from any I had ever heard) united to confirm me in this belief."[11] Even if we question the veracity of Equiano's account and his claims to be African—as have a number of prominent historians—it is still critical to acknowledge that Africans brought their own beliefs into the encounter with Europeans. West and West-Central Africans filtered their experiences through myths, beliefs, or prophecies that predated the arrival of the Europeans. For West-Central Africans, the Portuguese phenotypes, the voyage across the Atlantic, and the Spanish presence in New Spain probably heightened the levels of anxiety about the Mpemba prophecy.

For the enslaved West-Central Africans, the relevance of the Mpemba prophecy did not cease with the Middle Passage. The elders had predicted that a man "must first cross the water, climb the hill, and descend to arrive in the country of *Mpemba a Fula.*"[12] Such a route characterized the voyage from Angola to Mexico City. After disembarking at Veracruz, the enslaved Africans had to climb the mountainous road to Mexico City; after reaching the valley of Mexico, they descended into the city. The topographical coincidence between the Mpemba prophecy and the journey from Angola to Mexico City surely reinforced many West-Central Africans' conviction that they had arrived in the "land of the dead." Even the most dubious must have had their cosmology reaffirmed after witnessing another prophecy fulfilled when they saw swarthy Spaniards dominating and exploiting the reddish-brown indigenous peoples.

For the thousands of West-Central Africans, the perception that they had arrived in Mpemba had profound cultural implications. West-Central Africans not only had to reaffirm ancestral beliefs but also had to be simultaneously predisposed to embracing the beliefs of the *bamindele* (white people). Although the Mpemba prophecy helped rationalize the Middle Passage and later experiences, believers must have grown increasingly suspicious over time. Contact between new and earlier African arrivals and social intercourse with black creoles would have undermined the explanatory power of the Mpemba prophecy. Some Africans probably began to blame individual or collective failure to propitiate the ancestors or deities, witchcraft and sorcery, or the omnipotence of the Christian god. In their quest to attribute blame, Africans became increasingly predisposed to a process of ritual remediation through which they sought to improve their lives in Mpemba and their status with African deities. When this failed, some Africans began to view the Christian god with awe and became willing to embrace aspects of Christianity. Yet Africans did not abandon their ancient cosmos or become exclusively Christian. Selected African beliefs coexisted alongside aspects of Christianity. Africans, like others in New Spain, could both be good Christians and adhere to ancestral beliefs. Only as the memory of the African deities faded did Christianity come to dominate the black cosmos. Even then, ancestral beliefs and practices continued to influence the lives of Africans and their descendants.

Although intangible manifestations of culture persisted, African marriage and kinship patterns, social relations, and social organization often were transformed to the point where they resembled those of other sociocultural groups in New Spain. Practical considerations reinforced by the peculiarities of the slave trade and slavery, a new sociocultural environment, and the ideological and structural dimensions of Christian social control affected Africans' cultural practices in innumerable ways. Initiated in the sixteenth and seventeenth centuries, the creolization of the African population and its cultural practices was never complete. In a colonial context, cosmological and practical considerations provided a strong impetus for change.

Although the Mpemba myth prophesied that the inhabitants of the "land of the dead" were distinguished by their white and red phenotypes, the preponderance of blacks in central Mexico must have startled the West-Central Africans who arrived during the first half of the seventeenth century. Was it not prophesied that blacks would be transformed into whites? How did new arrivals interpret the black presence, which included kin, friends, and various peoples who defined themselves as Bran, Wolof, and Biafra, among others? The black presence surely fostered doubts about the prophecy and about whether New Spain was indeed the "land of the dead." These doubts probably gained strength as the new arrivals interacted with "the dead," who after a time less and less resembled spirits, ghosts, or ancestors. This realization awoke many people to the reality of New World slavery. One must ponder Angelina and Juan's feelings when they learned that Mpemba was in actuality Mputo, the "land of the whites."

For readers dubious of cosmological renderings of the Central African past, one might offer a more familiar (that is, Western) narrative. Here the emphasis resides on discerning where seventeenth-century Africans originated. Here the rules of evidence privilege numbers derived from merchant ledgers and imposed early modern European notions of polity, ethnos, and cultural proclivities. Even this empirically driven context requires cultural speculation, as the student of colonial Mexico must link Western configurations of African history with specific peoples as they emerged as slaves.

Thousands of West-Central Africans were uprooted by the consolidation of the Kongo kingdom in the late fifteenth century, the rise of the Mbundu kingdom, the Jaga invasions of the Kongo kingdom in the sixteenth century, the gradual disintegration of the Kongo kingdom, and the various Angolan wars erupting in the seventeenth century.[13] Military conflicts and dependent exchanges created the initial slaving frontiers and meant that people sold to the Portuguese slave traders who operated in West-Central Africa tended to come from certain ethnic groups. This was especially evident in New Spain between 1595 and 1640, when most enslaved Africans came from the region west of the Kwango River, south of the Zaire River, and north of the port of Benguela. Consequently, those who defined themselves as being from the land of Angola used this label to refer to linguistic and cultural similarities they shared with specific ethnic groups. This coincided with the Iberian tendency to homogenize Africans on the basis of their port of embarkation. In other words, Africans may have identified themselves to Spaniards by geographical origins and simultaneously distinguished among themselves on the basis of linguistic and cultural differences. During the slave trade, "Angola" included the ports of embarkation along the Luandan coast, including Luanda, Lobito, and Benguela. While Europeans simply defined the enslaved from the region as being from the "land of Angola" or the "land of the Congo," Africans themselves did not forget primary identities that the Mbundu, Ovimbundu, Imbangala, Pende, Sonyo, Kongo, Soso, Zombo, and Tyo (Teko) peoples, among others, carried with them to the Americas.

In the initial years of the slave trade, many West-Central Africans sold to Europeans came from a reservoir of dependents, including male slaves, impoverished cultivators, and individuals uprooted by war, drought, famine, and/or debt.[14] Exchange of dependents took place within an elite reciprocal trading network extending from the interior to the coast; the enslaved ultimately found themselves in Portuguese hands as payment for European goods. Although it is impossible to establish the number or percentage of dependents thus transferred into European hands, their presence was substantial.

Slaves and dependents probably did not seek to re-create the ideological basis on which their status in Africa had rested. As socially degraded beings in Angola, those who were most likely to be enslaved in the seventeenth-century New World had no reason to embrace the more lowly aspects of their Old World status. Cross-cultural examples have demonstrated a propensity among the marginalized to discard stifling, oppressive practices when new opportunities arose. This was true even when the cost of discarding oppressive practices involved changing cultural identity. Perhaps the victims of the transatlantic slave trade chose this course by re-creating an African past devoid of the ideology and practice that had legitimized their subordination. If this process did transpire, a new cultural synthesis had to emerge.[15]

Of course, the principal victims of the transatlantic slave trade—the youth and the marginalized—carried a particular but often imperfect understanding of the worlds they had left behind. They filtered their cultural understanding through the prism of gender, age, status, and lineage. Despite the social and cultural interdependence between males and females, subordinates and elites, youth and their elders, no one was likely to reproduce in its entirety the corpus of African beliefs, symbols, and cultural and situational meanings. Consequently, victims of the transatlantic slave trade carried a cultural perspective that largely mirrored their gender, age, and status. Such individuals were differently suited than were free Africans—also victims of the "Atlantic complex" (the economic, political, and cultural process that characterized the slave trade and its consequences for Africa, the Americas, and Europe)—to reconstruct cultural forms and practices. Anthropologist Richard Price has remarked that "the tenacious fidelity to 'African' forms is, in many cases, an indication of a culture finally having lost meaningful touch with the vital African past. Certainly, one of the most striking features of West African cultural systems is their internal dynamism, their ability to grow and change."[16] In the final analysis, what mattered to enslaved Africans in the Americas was not the authenticity of certain cultural forms or practices but their efficacy in making daily life bearable. The forms and practices that Africans introduced and created had, above all else, to be functional. Indeed, as victims of the slave trade encountered alien peoples, grappled with unpredictable realities, and met an array of new cultural forms, they had to scrutinize existing ontologies and cosmologies—what one observer has termed "the functional revaluation of the categories."[17] In this process, Africans discarded, retained, and modified some old forms and borrowed selectively from others, thus effecting a cultural transformation.

When Angelina and Juan arrived in 1627, they found themselves in the midst of a critical mass of West-Central Africans. From the evidence presented before the ecclesiastical authorities, Juan and Angelina clearly maintained contact after being separated in Mexico City, which is not surprising since they were siblings.[18] Having endured the process of enslavement and the horrors of the Middle Passage together, Juan and Angelina probably came to depend substantially on one another as they together confronted an alien environment, encountered foreign peoples, and witnessed strange customs. As they sought to impose meaning on their experience, the siblings also relied on the presence of other Angolans, including Jusepe and María de la Cruz, with whom the siblings shared linguistic and cultural similarities. Although the circumstances surrounding their courtship remain unknown, Jusepe and Angelina apparently had sufficient opportunities to see one another regularly. In fact, Angelina and Juan probably both met Jusepe in 1628. The marriage witnesses, Juan and María de la Cruz, stated that Jusepe and Angelina "ordinarily interacted in this city," suggesting that they had some freedom of movement. Such mobility was related to a person's occupation and the errands at hand. Angelina and Juan, for example, belonged respectively to a shopowner and merchant, both of whom plied their trade in the plaza. During their working hours, they had opportunities to interact with family and friends. The West-Central African presence, in tandem with Christianity, enabled Angolans to establish networks of relationships along socially reconstituted lines of endogamy; in the process, they affirmed and maintained their ethnic cohesiveness.

Strategic Conjugality

Given the structure of slavery in seventeenth-century Mexico City, where the enslaved were employed largely as domestics and artisans, most Angolans actually resided with a small multiracial nucleus of household staff. Among the

330 identified Angolan married couples in Mexico City's wealthiest parishes in the first half of the seventeenth century, only 100 had the same master, including Manuel and María, owned by Juan Bautista de Avilar.[19] Couples such as Manuel and Gracía or Domingo and Inés were rather fortunate since they resided on the same street, albeit in different households.[20] Cristóbal and Luisa also had different masters yet resided in the same neighborhood.[21] But spatial proximity acquired its real meaning in relationship to the whims of the masters and the resourcefulness of the slaves. In this context, exogamy—availing oneself of a differently identified partner in the same household—represented a viable option. Nonetheless, Angolans forged ties with other Angolans living on different streets, distant barrios, and even remote towns. Despite the hardships that continuation of such contracts entailed and in spite of their daily interaction with members of different ethnic and racial groups, the majority of Angolans established their most intimate associations with persons similarly defined.

Spouse selection clearly affirmed perceived distinctiveness. Despite the restrictions that slavery imposed, persons of African descent used the social system's flexibility to claim social and cultural space for themselves. By establishing the foundations of their lives in the act of marriage, Angolans insured that their identities and boundaries were mutually reinforcing and in turn they reproduced those identities through ties of consanguinity and affinity. Indeed, from their earliest presence in New Spain, peoples of African descent manifested the dialectical relationship between identities and boundaries in their social interaction. In the dynamic process of redefining themselves in the New World, Africans established a sphere of relative autonomy.

Angolan marriage practices were not, however, classical expressions of endogamy. The peculiarities of the transatlantic slave trade prevented Angolans from reproducing preexisting marriage and kinship patterns. Moreover, Angolans and their descendants were denied the institutional power crucial to enforcing and transmitting cultural norms. As such, Angolans relied on family and community pressures, social conformity, and socially constructed personal preference to find solace with individuals of similar heritage. This behavior was not peculiar to Angolans. In the absence of institutionally enforced laws, collective sentiment played a greater role in establishing community norms and shaping personal choices. The decision of an Angolan to select another Angolan as a mate reflected individual choice conditioned by the prevailing sentiment of ethnicity.

Ethnic sentiment did not, however, insulate Africans from the burdens of slavery and the weight of Christian colonialism intent on regulating their souls. Cohesiveness and ethnic boundaries protected the enslaved but were simultaneously porous and malleable. After cultural osmosis occurred, new mutations emerged. The multiple identities manifest among persons of African descent reflected the dynamic relation between slavery and Christianity. But racial slavery and racial oppression simply did not fuse the identities and experiences among peoples of African descent. Since the various Africans viewed the world through related but different prisms, they ascribed different values to and had varied understandings of endogamy, the rigidity of boundaries, and social relations. This pattern was similarly manifest among the diverse population of creoles.

Arguably, no collective African identity existed in New Spain. Only through their contact with the non-African Other did Africans manifest a tenuous collective consciousness. In some instances, they internalized an imposed Africanity, but one cannot document this phenomenon as generally true for Africans in New Spain or throughout the hemisphere. Uprooted and atomized as they confronted circumstances over which they had no control, the various coffle- and shipmates, drawn from diverse ethnic groups because of their common plight, forged a tenuous collective consciousness.

Shared experiences alone could not forge an enduring collective identity. Some enslaved Africans subsumed their internal differences in the crucible of racial slavery, while in other cases they transported preexisting ethnic rivalries to the Americas.[22] Yet the enslaved grew increasingly predisposed to renegotiating their identities. Shared circumstances were largely incapable of destroying ethnic rivalries. But the seventeenth-century slaving frontier made new collective identities more likely, bestowing a shifting geographical concentration among the victims of the slavers that in turn enabled a linguistic and cultural convergence under which temporal ethnicity flourished.[23]

The cultural dynamism of the slaving frontier, the slave trade, and planter preference undermines the once prevalent yet facile assumption that racial oppression alone enabled a single, collective African consciousness. In their mundane daily lives and most intimate choices, Africans made distinctions on the basis of ethnicity, thereby affirming Sidney Mintz and Richard Price's critique of the homogenization explicit in the idea that two and only two discrete cultures—African and European—encountered each other in the New World.[24] In fact, we must question scholarly assertions that New World Africans established communities in which intra-African ethnicity did not prevail.[25] Such assertions wrongly attribute to Africans cultural homogeneity, cultural stasis, and mythical racial and slave consciousness, generalizations that reveal much about historians' perceptions of culture and consciousness but very little about African realities. During some moments of crisis—usually slave rebellions and collective flight—ethnic identities were subordinated to an overarching African, black, or slave consciousness. Such episodes were unusual, brief, and rarely if ever manifested among the total slave population. Indeed, such expressions resembled ethnic alliances rather than the subordination of ethnicity. After the need for cooperation had waned, in fact, ethnic distinctions, including rivalries, resurfaced.[26]

Ethnicity's importance resides primarily in the function it performed among Africans in sixteenth- and seventeenth-century New Spain. The functional boundary depended less on authentic differences than on perceived and imposed linguistic and cultural similarities. Sensitive to boundary formation, one observer has stated, "The ethnic boundary channelizes social life—it entails a frequently quite complex organization of behavior and social relations. The identification of another person as a fellow member of an ethnic group implies a sharing of criteria for evaluation and judgment. . . . On the other hand, a dichotomization of others as strangers, as members of another group implies a recognition of limitations on shared understandings, differences in criteria for judgment of value and performance, and a restriction of interaction to sectors of assumed common understanding and mutual interest."[27] Even an impressionistic examination of seventeenth-century African marriages such as that of Angelina and Jusepe magnifies the existence of such boundaries.

In general, African patterns of spouse selection in the New World were neither random nor indiscriminate. Africans differentiated themselves through perceived ethnic criteria. The evolution from an ethnic African to black creole population apparently did not involve a pan-African transitional period. In part, this resulted from the primacy of ethnicity—real and imposed—and the supposed cultural orientation of the creole child. The Spaniards invariably classified the child of two Angolans as a *negro criollo*, a term that also implied a Hispanicized sociocultural heritage. Framed differently, the African population manifested ethnic cohesion that as a cultural dynamic simply could not be transferred intact to later generations. The decline of African imports in the third decade of the seventeenth century complicated the creolization process. When the slave trade to New Spain declined after 1640, ties of African ethnicity also waned. As creoles, Afro-Mexicans could not reproduce the ethnicity of their parents. Only the African-born could accomplish that task. The mass of incoming West Africans had been the harbingers of African ethnicity in sixteenth-century New Spain. When West-Central Africans and Angolans in particular came to outnumber West Africans in the seventeenth century, they by means of spouse selection and the construction of an elaborate network of relationships emerged as the principal architects of African ethnicity. Ironically, they legitimized their ethnicity through Christian matrimony.

Still, black creoles were not divorced from the African past, despite the assumption of the historiography of colonial Mexico that there was a rupture from the African past. Regardless of their efforts, neither Africans nor creoles re-created an African cultural environment, yet African parents and ancestors molded their ethnic heritage through and to fit American circumstances.

Superficial and even profound changes notwithstanding, Africans and their descendants on the whole maintained their relatively autonomous identities and boundaries. In the course of the seventeenth century, Africans and creoles initiated or culminated the structuring of boundaries through spouse selection. Coexisting and overlapping boundaries reflected the multiple identities and consciousness manifested by the black population. Although consciousness—ethnic, racial, and color—defined boundary formation throughout the colonial period, the process was never static. Even the most enduring boundaries changed over time. Although social and cultural changes affected consciousness and boundaries in dynamic ways, this symbiosis was ascendant in the seventeenth century and never lost its primacy in the colonial period, highlighting the need to reexamine the centrality accorded to social death.[28]

Over the past twenty years, social death has emerged as the organizing metaphor through which scholars of slavery and therefore black life represent the slaves' experience and that of their new world progeny. As a metaphor, social death centers power as the defining category informing slave life and culture. The representative slave emerges as the ultimate nonperson constrained from asserting an independent existence. As chattel, the slave allegedly did not constitute a being beyond the master's confining grasp. Arguably, only the master possessed the authority and will to imagine an autonomous slave existence. Even as a person, the slave did not have sufficient authority to insist on an acknowledgment of her/his humanity. In a slave society and society with slaves, social death aptly characterized an important, if not the defining, component of the slave and thus black experience. But in relationship to colonial Mexico—where the slave acquired a juridical identity as a vassal and person with a soul—this formulation needs to be questioned. Asked differently, when was social death? The complex configurations of gender and ethnicity that shaped the desire to contract marriage and the resulting kinship ties that subsequently emerged beg the question. As the narrative of the slave experience, social death assumes a uniform African, slave, and ultimately black subject rooted in a static New World history whose logic originated in being property and remains confined to slavery. It absorbs and renders exceptional evidence that underscores the contingent nature of experience and consciousness. Thus, the normative assumptions about the experiences of peoples of African descent assert a timeless, ahistorical, epiphenomenal "black" cultural experience—a perspective I call black structuralism. But in the first half of the seventeenth century, ethnic networks reigned ascendant among New Spain's African population. Within the dual contours of Christianity and slavery, a shallow ethnic interiority emerged. Through Christian marriages, Africans inaugurated and sustained the process of ethnogenesis, the creation of social networks inside the structures of domination.

Christianity enabled African ethnicity even as it insinuated itself among the African population. By means of Christianity, some slaves became ethnics. In light of the process of cultural formation manifest among seventeenth-century persons of African descent, we must again ponder why colonial Mexican historiography positions the African and slave experiences between a tradition of scholarly neglect and black structuralism.

NOTES

I thank Jennifer L. Morgan, Edward Baptist, and Stephanie Camp for their engaged reading of this chapter.

1. Karl Marx, *Wage Labour and Capital* (Beijing, 1978), 29.

2. Archivo General de la Nación (Mexico City, Mexico), Matrimonios, ser. 1, tomo 47, expediente 8, folios 17–18. Hereafter cited as AGN, Matrimonios.

3. The Catholic church defined *amancebamiento* as the state of concubinage. Examples include AGN, Matrimonios, tomo 81, expediente 35, folios 102–3; tomo 29, expediente 95, folios 233–34; tomo 113, expediente 69, folio 176; tomo 7, expediente 85, folio 274; tomo 126, expediente 18, folio 54.

4. E. R. Leach, "Characterization of Caste and Class Systems," in *Caste and Race: Comparative Approaches*, ed. Anthony de Reuck and Julie Knight (Boston, 1967), 19.

5. The point here is that these instances—composed of ritual declarations and testimonies—are by act of being recorded granted valence in a Christian society. In the process, recorded experiences compete with other manifestations of history and memory. Consequently, a degree of tension if not conflict informs the coexistence of competing modalities that shape the self and the collective. While other modalities may flourish beyond regulatory proceedings, recorded instances steadily gain authority through legitimacy in the legalistic culture characterizing Spanish and Christian colonialism. Over time, as a result of its unintended structural support from church and state, the recorded acquires a degree of persistence, enabling its claims to persevere.

6. Richard Price has captured this phenomenon among the Saramakas in Suriname. Aware that literacy would allow them greater understanding of and access to the "white world," the Saramakas sought to have some of their children educated by the Moravian missionaries. According to Price, the "toll exacted over the centuries for this privilege remained constant: intense pressure to renounce 'heathen' ways and break off relations with non-Christian family and kinfolk. Saramakas then as now were caught in this terrible bind, knowing that literacy was a password to an understanding of the outside world and the key to being able to manipulate it, but also knowing that its acquisition entailed what was, for them, a truly Faustian bargain, the willingness to sell their souls" (*Alabi's World* [Baltimore, 1991], 67–68).

7. In 1633, Juan is quoted as saying that "for six years I have communicated" with Angelina in Mexico City (AGN, Matrimonios, tomo 47, expediente 8, folios 17–18). Enriqueta Vila Vilar has compiled a list of registered slave ships for the sixteenth and seventeenth

centuries. Based on her research, the *Nuestra Señora de la Piedad* was the only registered slave ship that entered the Veracruz port in 1627; see Enriqueta Vila Vilar, *Hispanóamerica y el Comercio de Esclavos* (Seville, 1977), appendix.

8. Claudio Lomnitz-Adler, *Exits from the Labyrinth: Culture and Ideology in the Mexican National Space* (Berkeley, 1992), 268–74.

9. Orlando Patterson has written extensively and brilliantly on "social death" in slave societies. In his most recent discussion of the phenomenon, *Slavery and Social Death: A Comparative Study* (Cambridge, 1982), he distinguishes between intrusive and extrusive manifestations of social death, an outgrowth of his earlier work, *The Sociology of Slavery: An Analysis of the Origins, Development, and Structure of Negro Slave Society in Jamaica* (1967; Kingston, 1973), 145–81. According to Patterson, "In the intrusive mode the slave was conceived of as someone who did not belong because he was an outsider, while in the extrusive mode the slave became an outsider because he did not (or no longer) belonged" (*Slavery and Social Death*, 44).

10. Wyatt MacGaffey, *Religion and Society in Central Africa: The BaKongo of Lower Zaire* (Chicago, 1986), 45–46; see also Wyatt MacGaffey, "Cultural Roots of Kongo Prophetism," *History of Religions* 17 (November 1977): 177–93; Wyatt MacGaffey, "Kongo and the King of the Americans," *Journal of Modern African Studies* 6 (August 1968): 171–81.

11. Olaudah Equiano, *Equiano's Travels: His Autobiography; the Interesting Narrative of the Life of Olaudah Equiano or Gustavus Vassa the African*, ed. Paul Edwards (London, 1967), 25.

12. MacGaffey, *Religion and Society in Central Africa*, 46.

13. Useful studies that document the political evolution of West-Central Africa include David Birmingham, *Trade and Conflict in Angola: The Mbundu and Their Neighbours under the Influence of the Portuguese, 1483–1790* (Oxford, 1966); Anne Hilton, *The Kingdom of Kongo* (Oxford, 1985); Joseph C. Miller, *Kings and Kinsmen: Early Mbundu States in Angola* (Oxford, 1976); Joseph C. Miller, *Way of Death: Merchant Capitalism and the Angolan Slave Trade, 1730–1830* (Madison, 1988); Thomas Q. Reefe, *The Rainbow and the Kings: A History of the Luba Empire to 1891* (Berkeley, 1981); John K. Thornton, *The Kingdom of Kongo: Civil War and Transition, 1641–1718* (Madison, 1983); Jan Vansina, *Kingdoms of the Savanna* (Madison, 1966); Jan Vansina, *The Children of Woot: A History of the Kuba Peoples* (Madison, 1978).

14. *Dependents* refers to individuals who were beholden to elites or their patrons. For example, junior kin, women, children, and slaves were dependent on the lineage head, who in turn existed as a cultivator, soldier, or vassal in a state of dependency with regard to an elite patron (Miller, *Way of Death*, 40–104).

15. This insight flows from selective readings, including Victor Turner, *The Ritual Process: Structure and Anti-structure* (Ithaca, 1969); Claire C. Robertson, *Sharing the Same Bowl: A Socioeconomic History of Women and Class in Accra, Ghana* (Bloomington, 1984).

16. Richard Price, introduction to *Maroon Societies: Rebel Slave Communities in the Americas*, 2nd ed., ed. Price (Baltimore, 1979), 29–30.

17. Marshall Sahlins, *Islands of History* (Chicago, 1985), ix.

18. In his testimony, Juan stated, "Since I can remember I have known Angelina . . .

for she is my sister and we have come to this kingdom together" (AGN, Matrimonios, tomo 49, expediente 8, folios 17–18). It is possible that Juan employed the term *hermana* as he would have in West-Central Africa. According to Anne Hilton, "Throughout their known history the Kongo normally reckoned descent for the purposes of land-holding in terms of their relationships with *kanda*, not with individuals. Thus the term 'brother' was applied to all members of ego's *kanda* who could also be called collectively 'mother,' 'father' referred to all members of ego's father clan and 'child' referred to all member of ego's child's clan. A free man could normally depend upon four 'chiefs' to interest themselves in his affairs. These were the lineage heads of his mother's [i.e., his], his father's and his paternal and maternal grandfather's *kanda* or *kanda* segment" ("Family and Kinship among the Kongo South of the Zaire River from the Sixteenth to the Nineteenth Centuries," *Journal of African History* 24, no. 2 [1983]: 190). Igor Kopytoff and Suzanne Miers have cautioned scholars that "the metaphorical use of kin terms may be deceptive and should not, above all, be taken at their Western face value" (*Slavery in Africa: Historical and Anthropological Perspectives* [Madison, 1977], 25).

19. AGN, Matrimonios, tomo 10, expediente 69, folio 166; tomo 5, expediente 43, folio 151; tomo 5, expediente 101, folio 278.

20. Ibid., tomo 63, expediente 68, folios 17–18; tomo 10, expediente 153, folio 355.

21. Ibid., tomo 29, expediente 96.

22. The exchange between Monica Schuler and Richard Price in "Afro-American Slave Culture" suggests that the identities of enslaved Africans manifested themselves, on the one hand, in ethnic consciousness and, on the other, in panethnicity. The phenomenon was invariably linked to the slave trade and a society's ethnic composition. The preponderance of a given ethnolinguistic group, as in the case of Jamaica, often resulted in stratification along ethnic lines. Slave societies such as Suriname and British North America that received a wider range of enslaved Africans than did Jamaica tended to experience panethnic consciousness very early on. As the Suriname case makes clear, panethnic alliances were often intersected by a collective consciousness based on legal status (maroon versus enslaved), the estate to which individuals belonged, and New World lineage ties; see Price, "Commentary Two," *Historical Reflections* 5 (Summer 1979): 141–49; Price, *Alabi's World*. In seventeenth-century New Spain, both phenomena—narrowly defined ethnicity and panethnicity—coexisted among persons of African origin.

23. Miller has defined the "slaving frontier" as the "moving frontier zone of slaving violence." Its geographical contours "took shape with the first border raids of the newly centralized Kongo kingdom shortly after 1500 and continued in the shudders that ran through that state in the late sixteenth century. . . . The Kongo violence fed the initial Portuguese purchases of slaves in west central Africa. The sixteenth-century growth of the Mbundu kingdom of the Ngola a Kiluanje and a similar collapse of its conquered domains into partisan struggles in the 1620s, though complicated by the interference of Portuguese armies in the internal politics of the African state in the 'Angolan Wars' of the seventeenth century, advanced the slaving frontier south from the Kongo beyond the Kwanza. It also set Luanda-based slaving on the war footing it featured for the first half of the seventeenth century" (*Way of Death*, 141). Birmingham, *Trade and Conflict in Angola*, also provides a geographical sketch of the "slaving frontier."

24. In a seminal book, Sidney W. Mintz and Richard Price suggest that Afro-Americanists have viewed the early interaction between Europeans and Africans too narrowly as a one-dimensional encounter between two distinct cultures. Mintz and Price criticize this "encounter model" on the basis that it grossly oversimplifies the African and European experiences and conclude that it "needs considerable rethinking" (*An Anthropological Approach to the Afro-American Past* [Philadelphia, 1976], 4). Despite Mintz and Price's caution, scholars continue to homogenize the experiences of Africans and their diverse cultural heritage. Some scholars, in fact, have even made conclusions about West and West-Central Africans based on the cultural practices and experiences of East Africans. In her discussion of time among black Virginians, Mechal Sobel, for example, relied on ethnographic accounts of the Nuer, an East African ethnic group. Most, if not all, black Virginians were descendants of West and West-Central Africans (*The World They Made Together: Black and White Values in Eighteenth-Century Virginia* [Princeton, 1987], 26–29).

25. This is especially true for some recent works on Africans in what today constitutes the United States. Sterling Stuckey, for example, has stated that "what we know of slave culture in the South, and of that of blacks in the North during and following slavery, indicates that black culture was national in scope, the principal forms of cultural expression being essentially the same. This is attributable mainly to the similarity of the African regions from which blacks were taken and enslaved in North America and to the patterns of culture shared more generally in Central and West Africa" (*Slave Culture: Nationalist Theory and the Foundations of Black America* [New York, 1987], 82). For a similar argument, see Margaret Washington Creel, *"A Peculiar People": Slave Religion and Community-Culture among the Gullahs* (New York, 1988).

26. Very little is known about ethnicity among enslaved Africans. Recent works, however, have shown great sensitivity in their discussion of the African-creole dichotomy. See, for example, Monica Schuler, "Akan Slave Rebellions in the British Caribbean," *Savacou* 1 (June 1970): 8–31; David Barry Gaspar, *Bondmen and Rebels: A Study of Master-Slave Relations in Antigua, with Implications for Colonial British America* (Baltimore, 1985). A number of other works, including Mary C. Karasch, *Slave Life in Rio de Janeiro, 1808–1850* (Princeton, 1987), 3–28, 254–301; Mieko Nishida, "Ethnicity and Manumission in Urban Slavery: Salvador, Brazil, 1808–1888," paper presented at the Carolinas Colonial Latin America Seminar, Durham, N.C., April 1991; and João José Reis, *Slave Rebellion in Brazil: The Muslim Uprising of 1835 in Bahia*, trans. Arthur Brakel (Baltimore, 1993), transcend the traditional African-creole dichotomy and are quite suggestive with regard to ethnicity. Current inquiries reveal the usefulness of ethnicity as a category of analysis—alongside race, gender, status, and age—in New World slave societies. Nevertheless, ethnicity, like Africanity, still needs to be contextualized along lines of gender, age, and status since it may have constituted the primary nexus in which enslaved Africans most frequently operated. See also Richard Price, *First-Time: The Historical Vision of an Afro-American People* (Baltimore, 1983); Brackette F. Williams, *Stains on My Name, War in My Veins: Guyana and the Politics of Cultural Struggle* (Durham, 1991); Leroy Vail, ed., *The Creation of Tribalism in Southern Africa* (Berkeley, 1989); John Comaroff and Jean Comaroff, *Ethnography and the Historical Imagination* (Boulder, 1992);

Peter Wade, *Race and Ethnicity in Latin America* (London, 1997); Michael A. Gomez, *Exchanging Our Country Marks: The Transformation of African Identities in the Colonial and Antebellum South* (Chapel Hill, 1998); Paul E. Lovejoy, ed., *Identity in the Shadow of Slavery* (London, 2000); Linda M. Heywood, *Central Africans and Cultural Transformation in the American Diaspora* (New York, 2002); Maureen Warner-Lewis, *Central Africa in the Caribbean: Transcending Time, Transforming Cultures* (Kingston, 2003); Herman L. Bennett, *Africans in Colonial Mexico: Absolutism, Christianity, and Afro-Creole Consciousness, 1570–1640* (Bloomington, 2003).

27. Fredrik Barth, introduction to *Ethnic Groups and Boundaries* (Boston, 1969), 15.

28. The phrase *primary associations* is a slight semantic modification of Milton M. Gordon's *primary relationships* and refers to the most intimate ties of friendship and kinship. Gordon defined *primary relationships* as "personal, intimate, emotionally affective, and . . . bring[ing] into play the whole personality, as contrasted with *secondary relationships*, which are impersonal, formal, and segmentalized, and tend not to come very close to the core of personality" (*Assimilation in American Life: The Role of Race, Religion, and National Origins* [New York, 1964], 32).

Kinship and Freedom

Fugitive Slave Women's Incorporation into Creek Society

BARBARA KRAUTHAMER

*I*n the second half of the eighteenth century, enslaved black women in colonial Georgia regularly ran away from their masters to escape the psychic and corporeal ravages of bondage. The majority of these women runaways sought to ameliorate their enslavement with short-term respites and ran off to visit with relatives enslaved on neighboring plantations. Many enslaved women, however, fled with little or no intention of returning, taking advantage of the demand for female domestic labor in urban areas and hiding out in the anonymity of bustling port cities such as Savannah or Charleston. A limited number of fugitive women ventured farther still, severing all ties to their families and masters on coastal plantations and heading inland to the Creek Indian towns that stretched out along the Chattahoochee, Coosa, and Tallapoosa rivers in present-day western Georgia and northern Florida. In the late eighteenth and early nineteenth centuries, Creeks' attitudes toward black people varied widely as growing numbers of Creeks increasingly embraced Anglo-Americans' racial distinctions and the association of blackness with enslavement. While not all Creeks were inclined to offer sanctuary to fugitive slaves, many Creeks, especially those in the Lower Creek towns near the Chattahoochee River, eschewed colonial categories of race and status and harbored runaway slaves, eventually incorporating fugitive women as adopted relatives into the matrilineal kin groups or clans that composed Creek settlements. When enslaved African and African American women ran away from low-country masters to Lower Creek towns, the refugees secured freedom from chattel slavery by remaking their lives in kinship-based communities that valued their presence as women whose labor generated vital resources and whose reproduction enhanced the kin group's size and strength. While motherhood and marriage under slavery left women vulnerable to their masters' coercion and the loss of loved ones to death or sale, the kinship ties forged between fugitive women and their Creek hosts had emancipatory potential that likely resonated with enslaved women's knowledge of their African pasts.

The runaway women who remained among the Creeks were distinctive because they escaped as well as because of their destination. Charting enslaved women's flight to Creek territory and incorporation into Creek communities illuminates an unexamined juncture of two usually discrete historiographies— that is, studies of fugitive slaves and of black-Indian contact. Too often, studies of contact between fugitive slaves and Native Americans in the colonial Southeast focus mainly on men. Scholars have devoted much attention to the insurgent martial solidarity forged between fugitive slave men and Indian men who identified each other as allies and coconspirators in the webs of partnership and enmity that bounded geopolitics in the Southeast.[1] Historians have examined, for example, the ways in which Spain deployed Indian and African surrogates to fight on its behalf in the ongoing Spanish-English imperial contest for dominance along the eastern seaboard during the eighteenth century. After the American Revolution, military alliances between black and Indian men continued well into the antebellum era as runaway slave men and Indian warriors joined forces in efforts to stave off the extension of white settlement and U.S. authority into the southeastern territory claimed and inhabited by maroons and Indians. In the 1830s and 1840s, runaway slave men in Florida took up arms alongside the Seminoles who had harbored them. Together, Seminole and black warriors faced the U.S. military in a series of wars for territorial control of Florida. While black women are not wholly absent from such studies, their intermittent contact and sustained relations with southeastern Indian peoples have not been the focal point in studies of black-Indian relations, and the conditions of enslaved women's lives have not been integral to the discussions of fugitive slaves' strategies for remaking their lives by connecting with nearby Indian peoples. Military alliances fostered bonds of reciprocity and affinity between black and Indian men but were not the only means by which fugitive slaves could safeguard their distance from chattel slavery. Enslaved women could permanently escape bondage by forming lasting kinship ties with hospitable Creeks. The distinctive experience of these women points to the need to investigate the gendered meanings and outcomes of enslaved women's impulse to run away and seek refuge among the Creeks.

Much of our understanding of women's escape from enslavement has been shaped by evidence pointing to the infrequency of women's flight. In the late-eighteenth-century Georgia and South Carolina low country, runaway slave men vastly outnumbered runaway women, especially among those fugitives who sought a permanent escape from bondage. The higher incidence of men's flight stems in part from the lower numbers of women in the enslaved population.[2] Beyond sheer numbers, the gendered aspects of enslaved labor served to keep women tethered to plantations and enslaved communities. Slave men rather than women engaged in skilled occupations. Whether hired out or simply dispatched to work for their masters, men labored as boatmen, blacksmiths, woodworkers, and wagoners and traveled beyond the limits of their owners' plantations, gaining familiarity with the surrounding region and expanding their knowledge of the local roads and waterways that could serve as avenues for escape to distant sites. Enslaved women, by contrast, were generally not diverted from plantation field labor and thus had fewer opportunities to gain firsthand knowledge about their surroundings.[3] Enslaved women did, of course, run away, but they often did not attempt to escape slavery forever and instead hid out in nearby woods and swamps or with relatives on neighboring plantations or farms. In his study of runaway advertisements in colonial South Carolina newspapers, for example, Philip Morgan determined that of some 665 fugitive women, more than four-fifths were presumed to have gone to see family members.[4] Women temporarily absented themselves from work, seizing a respite from the bone-crushing demands of rice plantation labor and sustaining family connections with personal contact. If the proximity of loved ones prompted slave women to engage in truancy rather than escape, the obligations of caring for children further heightened women's reluctance to flee. Unwilling either to abandon their children or to increase the risks of running away by bringing along a child, many enslaved women opted not to flee at all or sought only temporary relief by stealing away to visit loved ones.[5]

Emotional ties and the demands of parenting undoubtedly shaped women's decisions about whether and how to attempt an escape from slavery, but framing motherhood primarily as a constraint against escape diverts attention from the instances of women's successful flight with or without their children. One cannot reduce enslaved women to what historian Jennifer L. Morgan has described as the mythic image of "selfless women working endless hours to support their children—mamas with expansive hearts and bosoms and a ferocious protectiveness."[6] The prevailing conclusion that women did not attempt permanent escape because of the obligations of motherhood erroneously implies that all enslaved women had children. From 1751, when Georgia's trustees repealed the colony's 1735 ban on the importation of black slaves, to 1773, nearly fifteen thousand slaves were transported from West Africa, the West Indies, and South Carolina to Georgia, where they engaged in the arduous and often debilitating labor of rice cultivation. Whether from the devastating physical toll of rice labor, skewed sex ratios, or intentional use of contraceptives and abortifacients, in colonial Georgia as in South Carolina, a low rate of natural increase among the enslaved persisted well into the late eighteenth century.[7] Low birthrates in conjunction with high infant mortality rates meant that between 1755 and 1777 the average number of children per enslaved woman in Georgia was less than one. According to historian Betty Wood's survey of the inventories of colonial Georgia plantations, 43 percent of enslaved couples who lived together either had no children or had been separated from their offspring.[8]

One cannot ignore the paramount importance of family ties in the lives of the enslaved, but a maternal desire to remain with and care for offspring did not always stifle women's impulse to flee. Between 1763 and 1790, almost one-third of the advertisements for runaways placed in Georgia newspapers announced the escape of female slaves, and the majority of these 273 runaway women fled without children. Only 33 women ran away with children, 5 pregnant women fled, and another 15 escaped with both their husbands and their children; still, less than 20 percent of the women runaways in late-eighteenth-century Georgia fled with children.[9] An April 1786 advertisement in Savannah's *Gazette of the State of Georgia* detailed the escape of a woman named Hannah. When she ran off from her mistress, Hannah took her five-year-old daughter but left behind her nursing infant.[10] For enslaved women in the colonial low country who did bear and retain their children, the experiences and expectations of parenting were informed as much by the shattering violence and dislocations of their enslavement and the appropriation of their children as property as by familial bonds of affection, and both factored into decisions about escape.[11]

Women did indeed escape slavery. Once they did, the meanings of reproduction and family ties shifted, especially for the women who fled to Indian settlements. Enslaved women who fled their masters for Creek settlements instead of Savannah or Charleston, for example, found immediate relief from the backbreaking labor of plantation agriculture. Yet securing a socially sanctioned position as a free person in a Creek community was another matter entirely. Freedom in the Creeks' world did not necessarily mean that individuals lived as autonomous persons unfettered by relations of obligation or subordination. Rather, Creek conceptions of freedom entailed an array of expectations and commitments that bound people within families and linked kinship groups together, uniting them not in an idealized, harmonious world but in mutual yet hierarchical relations of, for example, gender and age.[12] African and African American women who ran away to Lower Creek settlements in the late eighteenth and early nineteenth centuries entered communities that identified these fugitives as strangers who had to be transformed into relatives through kinship relations if they were to remain among the Creeks. Marriage and motherhood as well as adoption and the bonds of fictive kinship could cement runaway women's places as free women in Creek communities. Family formations had exposed the brutal contradictions of black women's lives under chattel slavery. In the Creek towns that harbored fugitive women, family formations served instead as the means for establishing freedom, making Lower Creek settlements an attractive destination for runaway African and African American women in the second half of the eighteenth century.[13]

Immediately after slavery was officially permitted in Georgia, planters purchased and imported slaves from South Carolina and the West Indies. Within a decade, the colony began importing slaves directly from the West African coast; more than half the slaves brought to Georgia between 1751 and 1773 were African born. As low-country rice plantations boomed, Georgia's enslaved black population expanded rapidly, increasing from about five hundred in 1751 to nearly fifteen thousand by 1773. South Carolina, however, remained the largest importer of African slaves in the North American colonies in the eighteenth century. On the eve of the American Revolution, the colony's black majority population totaled more than eighty thousand, more than one-third of them born in Africa.[14]

The definitions and patterns that organized the social and economic relations of slavery and freedom in African kin-based societies, as in Native American societies, were never static, nor did they simply determine behavior and experience.[15] This chapter does not argue for a static African past or an unmediated, timeless continuity between Africa and America, but it does draw on scholarship in African history and the African diaspora in the Americas to inform a discussion of fugitive slave women's flight to Creek settlements. In many eighteenth-century West African societies, kinship informed people's identities and status, including enslavement. Relations of reciprocity as well as hierarchy linked biological and fictive kin alike. Kinlessness and subordinate status might be mitigated over time as fictive kinship allowed for slaves' absorption into their master's lineage.[16] Yet the processes of incorporating the kinless necessarily entailed ongoing conflict, with masters and slaves struggling over the extent of slaves' inclusion in the local community and its institutions. Africans enslaved in North America went to great lengths to safeguard their knowledge and memories of life in Africa prior to capture and bondage. While they were unable to replicate their past, the enslaved improvised, creating new associations and relationships that served as a bridge between the past and present.[17] In Spanish Florida, similarities between Spanish and African notions of extended kinship allowed women of African descent to use to their advantage the gendered conceptions of freedom and the protections of women's property rights embedded in Spanish law and custom.[18] Fugitive slave women found similar opportunities in the Creeks' kinship-based society.[19] Specifically, when runaway slaves and Creeks encountered each other against the backdrop of rapidly expanding plantation monoculture and chattel slavery, the Creek idiom of kinship offered fugitive women an appropriate language for negotiating their freedom and remaking their lives in Creek communities.

From their vantage point on the edge of the Deep South, Creek Indians witnessed the development on their horizon of chattel slavery and plantation agriculture. No strangers to social hierarchy or even coerced labor, Creeks had brokered trade relations with early Carolinian colonists in the late seventeenth century, selling deerskins, foodstuffs, and Indian captives to British traders.[20] Creeks, like other southern Indians, however, did not simply endorse trade and military alliances with the British but continually strove to counter the devastating effects of epidemic disease, Indians' enslavement, and colonial violence. In 1715, some Creek towns joined the indigenous insurgency against the British, fighting in the Yamasee War. After their defeat, some towns sought to align themselves with the French or Spanish.[21] A wide range of factors informed Creeks' choice of European trade partners and allies and the growth of the British colonies' plantation complex.[22] South Carolina's enslaved population outnumbered its free population for the first time in 1708, and by 1720 British enslavement of Indians had dwindled but the number of African slaves (12,000) had risen to nearly double the number of free white colonists (6,525).[23] The growth of South Carolina's large-scale commodity crop production contributed to the marginalization of the deerskin trade and heightened colonists' interests in Indian lands. But the starkly oppressive labor regime commanded Creeks' attention and generated serious concern in many Creek towns throughout the eighteenth century and into the early nineteenth century.

Loathing coercion, the Creek peoples had long organized their society in ways that sought to balance power through rituals of oration and persuasion and with a division of authority. Creeks identified themselves as members of their families and towns, which were bound together through an extensive web of connections. Within any Creek town were multiple extended matrilineal families that belonged to a specific kin group or clan, and each clan had members in several towns. Because Creeks chose marriage partners from clans other than their own, kin ties also bridged clans.[24] Clans and towns were divided into two moieties, red and white, that took the lead in matters of war and peace, respectively. Only after extensive deliberation and negotiation between representatives of the red and white paths did a Creek town decide on a particular course of action. The balance or tension between red and white extended to gender relations. Women orators used ridicule as a means of checking men's authority and of voicing opposing views.[25] Within kin groups and towns, Creeks strove to ensure that power and authority did not accrue to any one person or clan but were distributed and balanced. Struck by its distinctiveness, James Oglethorpe of Georgia described the Creek decision-making process, in which leaders summoned "their old men and captains together" and reasoned "together with great temper and modesty till they have brought each other into some unanimous resolution."[26] Social structure and institutions, of course, did not dictate individual behavior but set forth the rules and expectations that people accepted and adapted according to particular circumstances.

Understandings of kinship bound people in reciprocal relationships within their clans and towns and informed how Creeks defined and related to outsiders. Only people who had acknowledged kinship ties to a Creek clan were considered fully human; others were merely "dunghill fowl," creatures of little consequence that could be easily subdued.[27] Well before their contact with Europeans, Creeks dealt with outsiders, usually Indian war captives, in one of two ways: male captives were killed, while after a period of subordination, women were adopted into a clan as daughters or wives.[28] In the 1770s, Philadelphia naturalist William Bartram wrote of his travels through the Southeast and his encounters with the region's indigenous peoples. The Yamasee captives held as slaves by a Creek chief, Bartram noted, were permitted to marry Creeks, and their children were considered free and equal members of the society.[29] By the end of the eighteenth century, economic, social, political, and demographic changes in the Americas reverberated through the Creeks' world, altering the meanings of Creek slavery. Yet the pace of change proceeded unevenly across time and space. Some Creek ideas and practices of property ownership shifted significantly to allow for ownership of black people as chattel, while other Creeks retooled older definitions of slavery to fit with newer circumstances.[30] Through the first decades of the nineteenth century, many Creeks, whose conceptions of property varied widely, continued to construe servitude or enslavement (now of Africans rather than Indian captives) in relation to kinship.

Bartram's descriptions of the Creek towns he visited include a number of accounts of slavery, and his writings suggest the ways in which black women were incorporated into Creek kin groups. In one instance, Bartram described an encounter with a man named Boatswain, the son of a British trader and Creek woman, who received the northern traveler into his home, where the men enjoyed "excellent Coffee served up in China Dishes by young Negro Slaves." After feasting on corn cakes, barbecued venison, and assorted sweets, Bartram took stock of Boatswain's agricultural endeavors. He had close to one hundred acres of fertile land fenced in and under cultivation, and those responsible for planting and tending the crops were "his own private family, which consists of about Thirty People, among which were about 15 Negroes."[31]

Neither Bartram nor Boatswain understood the ties between the Indians and blacks in this "family" in terms of the paternalism espoused by nineteenth-century slaveholders to veil the racial ideology and sexual violence of chattel slavery.[32] Like Europeans, however, Creeks took note of the physical differences between themselves and the African men and women they encountered in the

Southeast. Yet outsider status—meaning the absence of biological or fictive kin ties—was far more significant for categorizing people than was physical appearance. At times, however, especially in diplomatic relations with Europeans, the Creeks employed a system of color symbolism as a useful measure for distinguishing themselves from new arrivals in the Southeast. By the early eighteenth century, some southern Indians, drawing on their red path/white path dualism and responding to English settlers' use of color—white—to identify themselves, had begun referring to themselves as red people. According to historian Nancy Shoemaker, Indians "were engaged in the same mental processes" as Europeans. The natives revisited old ideas about divine origins and considered new ideas about human appearance to explain and manage the changing American social and political landscape.[33]

Still, through the early years of the nineteenth century, Creeks classified outsiders by factors other than their appearance or other European notions of race. Instead, the Creeks focused on individual behavior and personal relationships. Boatswain's "family" consisted of female biological relatives and other women in his clan, including slaves, who were linked to each other and to Boatswain through hierarchical relations of kinship rather than property. Furthermore, several of the black women in Boatswain's family, according to Bartram, "were married to Indians and enjoy equal privileges with the Indians, but they are slaves until they marry, when they become Indians, or Free Citizens."[34]

Black women held as subordinates in Creek clans would have had little choice about the work they performed, owing their labor to their host family. Like captive Indian women before them, black women would have labored alongside Creek women as agricultural workers, acquiring the skills and knowledge expected of women in Creek clans and towns. Creek women were the primary agricultural laborers in their towns, although the status imputed to Creek women's labor as farmers changed during the eighteenth century with the rise of Creek men's roles as hunters and traders of deerskins. By learning the labor patterns of Creek women and men, outsider women gained more than technical knowledge: they became familiar with the gendered meanings of labor and power in Creek clans and towns.[35]

The friction, such as daily negotiations over the allocation of work or the selection of a marriage partner, as well as the affinity that developed between black women subordinates and their Creek hosts are not readily apparent in Bartram's account but must have been central to black women's experiences of incorporation into Creek society. Definitions of freedom in Creek society, which entailed clear constraints on autonomy and required outsiders' temporary subordinate status and compulsory labor, bore little resemblance to liberal conceptions of freedom taking shape in the late eighteenth century. For many fugitive women, however, Creek meanings of freedom through the bonds of kinship resonated with the African past even as they provided a sense of security against the threat of reenslavement in the colonies.

The Creeks were primarily Muskogee speakers, but by the eighteenth century some leaders had had extensive contact, including intermarriage, with British traders. Consequently, a growing number of Creeks both spoke and wrote the English language.[36] As they did throughout the Americas, black people in Creek towns acquired the language of their hosts. Benjamin Hawkins, the U.S. Indian agent to the Creeks after the revolution, arrived among the Creeks in 1796 to initiate the government's plans for civilizing southern Indians through the promotion of cotton agriculture and women's textile production. In one town, Hawkins's Creek host provided him with "a negro woman for [an] interpreter."[37] The ability to speak English proved invaluable for fugitives hoping to find work and pass for free in southern cities, but for those who reached the Creek nation it offered access to a key role in the Creeks' expanding network of trade and diplomatic relations with their Euro-American neighbors. Serving as a linguistic intermediary likely advanced black women's efforts to translate their subordinate status into one of kinship and inclusion.[38]

Enslaved women who ran away from their Anglo-American masters and headed toward the Creek settlements likely chose this path because they had some knowledge of the nearby Indian populations. Contact between African slaves and indigenous peoples in the Southeast dated back to the earliest years of British settlement in Carolina, when members of both groups were held in bondage. Africans and Indians lived and labored alongside each other, and intermarriage was not uncommon.[39] Personal relationships, however, were only one strand of a wider web linking Africans and Indians in the Southeast. Slaves gained critical information about the Creeks' locations as well as their social relations and antipathy for chattel slavery simply by listening attentively to their masters and other free whites. By midcentury, these exchanges would have included discussion of the potential for black-Indian alliances, especially those facilitated by the Spanish, and some Indians' refusal to return fugitive slaves.

Keenly aware of fugitives' attempts to flee to the backwoods and Indian settlements and eager to safeguard their property, colonists aimed to foster animosity between their slaves and nearby Indian peoples. Colonists encouraged Creeks to capture and redeem fugitives, which also assuaged nagging fears of a united black-Indian rebellion.[40] Treaties and agreements between colonial authorities in South Carolina and Georgia and the leaders of Creek Indians involved negotiations regarding the fate of the runaway slaves who arrived in Indian settlements. In the early summer of 1767, John Stuart, the southern superintendent of Indian affairs, met with the Creeks to negotiate trade relations, which necessarily encompassed a discussion of fugitive slaves. Determined to prevent the

Indians' territory from becoming an "asylum for Negroes," Stuart insisted that the Creeks return runaway slaves to the colonists.[41] Subsequent agreements between South Carolina authorities and the Creeks reiterated the expectation that the Creeks would surrender any "Negroes harbored in Creek Country."[42]

Creeks occasionally turned over fugitives. Often, however, whites' attempts to control not the enslaved but those who might assist them proved only marginally successful. Enslaved Africans knew that the Creeks did not always return fugitives and knew how to reach the Creek country. British colonial trade relations with Creeks had brought a number of enslaved African men into contact with Creeks and created conditions that allowed them to obtain ample knowledge of Creeks' locations and language that might be shared with other slaves. Traders living in Creek territory routinely ignored colonial prohibitions against keeping slaves at their stores. These traders owned men to tend horses, to perform manual labor in storehouses, to raise small crops, and to act as personal servants. Slave men owned by merchants and other colonists connected to the Anglo-Indian trade worked as horsemen and boatmen and thus became well acquainted with the location and language of Creek towns.[43] In one case from the winter of 1771, a man named Jack took off from his master, John Stuart, and fled to the Indians. Having previously been owned by a trader to the Creeks, Jack had worked in a Creek town and had learned "the Creek Language tolerably well." Jack also knew the roads that led in and out of Creek territory, enabling him to plot his escape route.[44] When slaveholders did regain possession of runaways who had reached the Creeks' territory, the victory was mitigated by the return of someone who had gained considerable information about life in Creek settlements.

From careful attention to their masters' conversations and from slaves' networks of communication, enslaved women learned of escape routes leading to the Creeks. Cassandra and her husband, Harry, for example, took off from Augusta in the autumn of 1769, and while their master considered the possibility that they might head to Mobile to be near Cassandra's parents, he believed that they had gone "to the Indian nation."[45] Information about escape routes and potential Indian allies swirled through the continual streams of communication that linked black people across the low country and kept them abreast of important events and sites in the Southeast.[46]

The American Revolution and the repeated transfer of control over Florida between the British and Spanish drastically altered the geopolitical climate in the Southeast but did not deter black people from discerning ways of protecting themselves from the multiple modes of violence at the heart of plantation agriculture. During the war, in fact, many slaves took advantage of the chaos to run away in numbers large enough that one historian has likened their flight to "a type of slave revolt."[47] One slaveholder placed an ad in 1783 for a family of five runaways who had fled four years earlier. The group retreated from Savannah with the Indians days before the British besieged the city.[48] Slaves' flight during and after the war suggests that despite some Creeks' growing interest in acquiring black slaves as chattel, many others continued to offer some form of refuge to runaways. In 1786, for example, a large group of runaways, consisting of Juba and her husband, Isaac; Phebe and her husband, Pate; Quahobe and her husband, Battes; and Sue, her husband, Ned, and their two young children, fled West Florida for the Creeks' territory.[49]

In the wake of the revolution, low-country planters pushed into Georgia's backcountry, where the rivers and streams that had formed the core of the Creek territory would soon serve as the major arteries linking inland cotton plantations to coastal markets. Facing pressure from the federal and state governments, Creek leaders ceded the land between the Oconee and Ocmulgee rivers in central Georgia in 1802; in 1821, they ceded land up to the Flint River; and in 1826 they relinquished claim to land as far west as the Chattahoochee River, which marks Georgia's western boundary.[50] Creek leaders, many of whom had distanced themselves from the older models of power sharing and negotiation, ceded hunting grounds that were vital to most Creeks' subsistence. The loss of much of their land, coupled with a poor 1804 harvest and subsequent food shortage, exacerbated divisions between whites and Creek towns and fueled Creeks' discontent with the land-hungry newcomers.[51] Even as white Georgians pushed to seize more land from southern Indians, they also pushed to import more slaves before the Constitution's 1808 ban on the transatlantic slave trade took effect. Some forty thousand Africans were imported into Charleston between 1804 and 1807. During the following years, an equally brutal domestic slave trade would channel millions of African American slaves from the Upper South to the bone-crushing labor of the Deep South's cotton plantations.

In the early nineteenth century, the interests of many Creeks and runaway slaves converged at least to the degree that members of both groups were searching for ways to undermine or at least escape the terrors wrought by the expansion of commercial plantation agriculture. In 1802, an East Florida planter complained that two of his slave men had run off to the Indians; in addition, "an Indian Negro" had stolen a slave woman and her child. The slave woman, moreover, had given birth to another child after leaving her master's plantation.[52] Although planters contended that Indians stole slaves, those who were captured often established new lives as free people by forging family bonds with their captors. Creek conceptions of kinship and incorporation allowed for the inclusion of fugitive women and their children into Creek clans and towns. Although increased rates of intermarriage with white men precipitated shifts in the ways Creeks mapped kin ties, most Creeks in the early nineteenth century continued to trace descent through the female line. At first glance, this might suggest that they would have been reluctant to incorporate outside women through marriage. Foreign women, of course, had no kin in the community, making it virtually impossible to establish their children's lineage at the outset. But black women incorporated into Creek kinship groups as subordinates to Creek women and men acquired fictive relatives, making them eligible for marriage to Creek men and ensuring their children's lineage. Theda Perdue's study of a Cherokee Deer clan family's adoption of a black woman named Molly in the 1770s makes clear that while southern Indians' ideas about race, property, and slavery were in flux, many people continued to acknowledge and abide by the primacy of kinship.[53]

Neither Creeks nor runaway slave women left behind accounts of their interactions, but documents generated by slaveholders attempting to regain ownership of fugitive women provide clear evidence of the ways in which black women and their children were incorporated into Creek society. In 1796, for example, a slaveholder from Liberty County, Georgia, claimed that a "party of Indians" had "inveigled" a slave couple, Adam and Fanny, away from his plantation and brought them to a Creek village. While Adam was soon killed, Fanny continued to reside in the town. By 1822 she reportedly had eighteen children and grandchildren.[54] Fanny clearly had been incorporated into a Creek kinship network, where she married, bore children, and lived peacefully. Her fate in the Creek nation—specifically, her marriage and reproduction—attracted the continued attention of her master, who sought compensation from the state not only for the loss of his two slaves but also for the value of Fanny's offspring. Slaveholders' capacious understanding of their patriarchal rights of ownership over black women's bodies allowed them to bequeath unborn children and insist on possessing children born beyond the plantation confines.[55]

Creeks took a dim view of slaveholders' arguments that the children born to fugitive slave women in Creek towns were white slaveholders' rightful property. Lower Creeks not only refused to surrender fugitive women and their children but also articulated distinct understandings of descent and identity. In May 1793, the overseer of William Smith's plantation, also in Liberty County, Georgia, noticed that slaves who should have been working in the rice fields were "running in every direction," and he saw Indians leading them away. Seven men and six women escaped from the plantation: some were eventually retrieved, but several remained with the Creeks. In 1821, when Smith filed suit with the state for compensation for his losses, he indicated that one of the fugitive women, Mary, had four children living among the Creeks. Smith had been unable to regain possession of the children, complaining that "the Indians kept them because they were born upon their hands." The Creeks' insistence on keeping Mary's children suggests to the extent to which she had been woven into their social fabric and was granted the protection afforded to members of the community despite her initial outsider status.[56] When some Creeks recognized Mary's children as members of a Creek family and wider community, furthermore, they made clear their rejection of American notions of slavery's descent through the mother and conveyed their disinterest in American categories of race.

At least through the early nineteenth century, Creeks continued to accept fugitive slaves into their settlements. Some historians have contended that the absence of commercial agriculture allowed Creeks to continue their older patterns of retaining captives as slaves but not as property.[57] Yet such a formulation suggests that economic institutions and practices rather than Creek ideas and values organized their society. Even as prominent Creeks adapted their ideas about property and became exceedingly comfortable with individual property ownership, including the ownership of black people as chattel, and the accumulation of personal wealth, the shift did not occur in a single moment or unilaterally. In the late eighteenth and early nineteenth centuries, black people's status varied widely throughout the Creeks' territory, reflecting Creeks' disparate views and practices of race, kinship, and slavery. Like other southern Indians, many Creeks embraced older patterns of kinship and incorporation, relying on clans to give shape and meaning to their social relations even as they adopted newer modes of governance, property ownership, and social hierarchy.

Well into the antebellum era, the intimacy between Creeks and black women continually alarmed and infuriated white southern slaveholders. When they looked at the fugitive slaves who gained freedom in Creek towns and even at the black slaves owned as property by some Creeks, American slaveholders did not see the complex and changing dynamics of kinship and slavery; instead, they saw Creeks as a dangerous and dismally flawed alternative to whites' racial and social order. American chattel slavery rested on the abject racial and sexual degradation of African and African American women. The denial of blacks' humanity through the denial of their legal rights as persons required the continual policing of boundaries of race and gender. Slaveholders owned black women's bodies, physical labor, and reproductive potential.[58] When Anglo-American slaveholders looked at the Creeks' towns, however, they witnessed black women possessing their own bodies and labor, moving freely and retaining control of much of what they produced. Slaveholders' saw that many Creeks recognized black women's offspring as legitimate children rather than added value—a scene that contradicted all of the principles of race, gender, and property informing the social, economic, and political foundations of chattel slavery.

Nothing revealed this confusion more clearly than the writings of the men directed by the federal government to take a census of the Creeks in 1832, on the eve of their forced removal from the South to the West. The census takers entered the Creeks' territory and began the process of going from town to town, recording the name of each household head and tallying the number of men and women, including slaves, in each family. At every turn, the census takers encountered households that defied their categorization scheme. They found households in which free black women headed families; black women identified as slaves named free Indian men as husbands; and free men and women who appeared to the census takers' eyes to be black labeled themselves Indian. In the end, the census enumerated nearly one thousand black slaves and fourteen free black families, nine of which were headed by women; one entry, a woman named Juba who claimed her black husband as one of her five "slaves," suggests the presence of the 1786 runaways from West Florida.[59] All of the free black women in the census claimed black slaves as members of their household, and some indicated that their "slaves" included their husbands and children.

African and African American women in the Creeks' territory, like the Creeks who adopted and incorporated them, organized their lives in accordance with their own understandings of what it meant to be enslaved or free. For the African women and their American-born daughters who sought refuge from chattel slavery in the Creek territory, the clan-based, matrilineal organization of the Creek world offered certain kinds of freedom not necessarily available in southern port cities or other sites of refuge. When they entered Creek towns, black women found local societies compatible with the communities left behind in West Africa. This is not to say that slaves replicated their African past but that Creek patterns of subordination and liberation, as well as Creek gender roles, family structure, and division of labor, might not have been entirely alien to fugitive women. Enslaved women knew too well that family ties and childbearing left them vulnerable to their masters' ability to undermine those relationships through labor demands or sale. Women who ran away to the Creek territory recognized that inclusion in Creeks' family and kin relations signaled freedom from bondage. Meanings of family or kin relations and freedom informed enslaved women's decisions about running away and shaped Creeks' responses to the fugitive women who arrived in the Creek villages. Examining enslaved women's flight from chattel slavery to incorporation in Creek communities reveals new aspects of the gendered meanings of family and freedom in the late-eighteenth- and early-nineteenth-century Southeast.

NOTES

1. See, for example, Kevin Mulroy, *Freedom on the Border: The Seminole Maroons in Florida, the Indian Territory, Coahuila, and Texas* (Lubbock, 1993); Kenneth Wiggins Porter, *The Negro on the American Frontier* (New York, 1971); Claudio Saunt, *A New Order of Things: Property, Power, and the Transformation of the Creek Indians, 1733–1816* (New York, 1999), chap. 12; J. Leitch Wright Jr., *Creeks and Seminoles: The Destruction*

and *Regeneration of the Muscoculge People* (Lincoln, 1986); Jane Landers, *Black Society in Spanish Florida* (Urbana, 1999), chap. 2.

2. Peter Wood, *Black Majority: Negroes in Colonial South Carolina from 1670 through the Stono Rebellion* (New York, 1975), chap. 5; Betty Wood, "Some Aspects of Female Resistance to Chattel Slavery in Low Country Georgia, 1763–1815," *Historical Journal* 30 (September 1987): 606; Daniel E. Meaders, "South Carolina Fugitives as Viewed through Local Colonial Newspapers with Emphasis on Runaway Notices, 1732–1801," *Journal of Negro History* 60 (April 1975): 292.

3. Philip D. Morgan, *Slave Counterpoint: Black Culture in the Eighteenth-Century Chesapeake and Lowcountry* (Chapel Hill, 1998), chap. 4; Betty Wood, *Women's Work, Men's Work: The Informal Slave Economies of Lowcountry Georgia* (Athens, 1995); Stephanie Camp, *Closer to Freedom: Enslaved Women and Everyday Resistance in the Plantation South* (Chapel Hill, 2004).

4. Philip D. Morgan, "Colonial South Carolina Runaways: Their Significance for Slave Culture," *Slavery and Abolition* 6 (December 1985): 67; Peter Wood, *Black Majority*, 240–68.

5. Stephanie Camp, " 'I Could Not Stay There': Enslaved Women, Truancy, and the Geography of Everyday Forms of Resistance in the Antebellum Plantation South," *Slavery and Abolition* 23 (December 2002): 1–20; Deborah Gray White, *Ar'n't I a Woman? Female Slaves in the Plantation South* (New York, 1985).

6. Jennifer L. Morgan, *Laboring Women: Reproduction and Gender in New World Slavery* (Philadelphia, 2004), 113.

7. Judith Carney, *Black Rice: The African Origins of Rice Cultivation in the Americas* (Cambridge, 2001); Betty Wood, *Slavery in Colonial Georgia* (Athens, 1984), chap. 6; Julia Floyd Smith, *Slavery and Rice Culture in Low Country Georgia, 1750–1860* (Knoxville, 1985).

8. Betty Wood, *Slavery in Colonial Georgia*, 106; Betty Wood, "Some Aspects of Female Slave Resistance," 609; Philip Morgan, *Slave Counterpoint*, chap. 1. Jennifer Morgan surveyed the inventories of South Carolina plantations in 1742 and found that the number of women without children was greater than that with children (*Laboring Women*, 141). For a comparison of the birthrates for black and white women, see Peter Wood, *Black Majority*, 162.

9. Lathan Windley, comp., *Runaway Slave Advertisements: A Documentary History from the 1730s to 1790*, vol. 4, *Georgia* (Westport, 1983).

10. *Gazette of the State of Georgia*, April 20, 1786, in ibid., 140.

11. For a comprehensive and insightful discussion of the intricate connections between enslaved women's reproductive lives and chattel slavery, see Jennifer Morgan, *Laboring Women*; Kirsten Fischer, *Suspect Relations: Sex, Race, and Resistance in Colonial North Carolina* (Ithaca, 2002); White, *Ar'n't I a Woman?*

12. Fischer's *Suspect Relations*, a study of illicit sexual relations in colonial North Carolina, has even further enhanced understandings of the colonial-era workings of race, gender, and status by placing nonelite women and men, including Native Americans, at the center and illuminating the complexity of their roles as guardians and transgressors of social and legal categories.

13. Tiya Miles, *Ties That Bind: The Story of an Afro-Cherokee Family in Slavery and Freedom* (Berkeley, 2005); Theda Perdue, "Clan and Court: Another Look at the Early Cherokee Republic," *American Indian Quarterly* 24 (Fall 2000): 562–69.

14. Betty Wood, *Slavery in Colonial Georgia*, 98–99; Philip Morgan, *Slave Counterpoint*, chap. 1; Smith, *Slavery and Rice Culture*, chap. 2; Elizabeth Donnan, ed., *Documents Illustrative of the History of the Slave Trade to America*, vol. 4 (Washington, 1930–35).

15. Jonathon Glassman, "The Bondsman's New Clothes: The Contradictory Consciousness of Slave Resistance on the Swahili Coast," *Journal of African History* 32 (1991): 277–312; Frederick Cooper, "The Problem of Slavery in African Studies," *Journal of African History* 20 (1979): 103–25. The debates about kinship, marginality, and African slavery begin with Igor Kopytoff and Suzanne Miers, "African 'Slavery' as an Institution of Marginality," in *Slavery in Africa: Historical and Anthropological Perspectives*, ed. Igor Kopytoff and Suzanne Miers (Madison, 1977), and Claude Meillassoux, *The Anthropology of Slavery: The Womb of Iron and Gold*, trans. Alide Dasnois (Chicago, 1991).

16. Iris Berger and E. Frances White, *Women in Sub-Saharan Africa: Restoring Women to History* (Bloomington, 1999).

17. For the debate over the loss or retention of African identities, see, for example, Melville Herskovits, *The Myth of the Negro Past* (New York, 1941); Sidney Mintz and Richard Price, *The Birth of African-American Culture: An Anthropological Perspective* (Boston, 1992); Lawrence Levine, *Black Culture and Black Consciousness: Afro-American Folk Thought from Slavery to Freedom* (New York, 1977); Michael Gomez, *Exchanging Our Country Marks: The Transformation of African Identities in the Colonial and Antebellum South* (Chapel Hill, 1998), chap. 1.

18. Landers, *Black Society*, chap. 6.

19. Peter Wood, *Black Majority*, 260.

20. Kathryn E. Holland Braund, *Deerskin and Duffels: The Creek Indian Trade with Anglo-America, 1685–1815* (Lincoln, 1993); Alan Gallay, *The Indian Slave Trade: The Rise of the English Empire in the American South, 1670–1717* (New Haven, 2002).

21. William L. Ramsey, " 'Something Cloudy in Their Looks': The Origins of the Yamasee War Reconsidered," *Journal of American History* 90 (June 2003): 44–75; Gallay, *Indian Slave Trade*, 327–40.

22. Claudio Saunt, " 'The English Has Now a Mind to Make Slaves of Them All': Creeks, Seminoles, and the Problem of Slavery," in *Confounding the Color Line: The Indian-Black Experience in North America*, ed. James F. Brooks (Lincoln, 2002), 52.

23. Peter Wood, *Black Majority*, 147–48.

24. John Reed Swanton, *Social Organization and Social Usages of the Indians of the Creek Confederacy* (Washington, 1928); Robert Ethridge, *Creek Country: The Creek Indians and Their World* (Chapel Hill, 2003), 109–11.

25. Theda Perdue, *Cherokee Women: Gender and Culture Change, 1700–1835* (Lincoln, 1998).

26. James Oglethorpe quoted in Charles C. Jones, *Historical Sketch of Tomo-Chi-Chi, Mico of the Yamacraws* (1868; Millwood, 1975), 45.

27. Saunt, *New Order of Things*, 112; James Merrell, "The Racial Education of the Catawba Indians," *Journal of Southern History* 50 (August 1983): 363–84.

28. Theda Perdue, *Slavery and the Evolution of Cherokee Society, 1540–1866* (Knoxville, 1979), chaps. 1, 2; Kathryn E. Holland Braund, "The Creek Indians, Blacks, and Slavery," *Journal of Southern History* 57 (November 1991): 601–4.

29. William Bartram, *Travels through North and South Carolina, Georgia, East and West Florida, the Cherokee Country, the Extensive Territories of the Muscogulges or Creek Confederacy and the Country of the Chactaws* (Philadelphia, 1791), reprinted in William Bartram, *Travels and Other Writings* (New York, 1996), 166.

30. For a full history of Creeks' changing meanings and practices of property, including slavery, see Saunt, *New Order of Things.*

31. William Bartram, *Observations on the Creek and Cherokee Indians,* (1789; New York, 1853), reprinted in *William Bartram on the Southeastern Indians,* ed. Kathryn E. Holland Braund and Gregory A. Waselkov (Lincoln, 1995), 186.

32. Eugene Genovese, *Roll, Jordan, Roll: The World the Slaves Made* (New York, 1972); Elizabeth Fox-Genovese, *Within the Plantation Household: Black and White Women of the Old South* (Chapel Hill, 1988).

33. Nancy Shoemaker, "How Indians Got to Be Red," *American Historical Review* 102 (June 1997): 643; Merrell, "Racial Education of the Catawba Indians."

34. Bartram, *Observations,* reprinted in *William Bartram,* ed. Braund and Waselkov, 187.

35. Braund, "Creek Indians, Blacks, and Slavery," 602–3; Theda Perdue, "Women, Men, and American Indian Policy: The Cherokee Response to 'Civilization,' " in *Negotiators of Change: Historical Perspectives of Native American Women,* ed. Nancy Shoemaker (New York, 1995), 90–114.

36. On Creeks acquiring written literacy in English, see Saunt, *New Order of Things,* chap. 8.

37. Benjamin Hawkins, November 30, 1796, in *The Collected Works of Benjamin Hawkins, 1796–1810,* ed. Thomas Foster (Tuscaloosa, 2003), 20.

38. On fugitives' linguistic abilities, see Betty Wood, "Some Aspects of Female Slave Resistance," 616; Philip D. Morgan, "Colonial South Carolina Runaways," 67.

39. Jack D. Forbes, "The Manipulation of Race, Caste, and Identity: Classifying Afroamericans, Native Americans and Red-Black People," *Journal of Ethnic Studies* 17 (Winter 1990): 1–51.

40. Merrell, "Racial Education of the Catawba Indians"; Martha Condray Searcy, "The Introduction of African Slavery into the Creek Indian Nation," *Georgia Historical Quarterly* 66 (Spring 1981): 21–32; William S. Willis, "Divide and Rule: Red, White, and Black in the Southeast," *Journal of Negro History* 48 (July 1963): 157–76.

41. Daniel F. Littlefield Jr., *Africans and Creeks from the Colonial Period to the Civil War* (Westport, 1979), 19.

42. Quoted in Meaders, "South Carolina Fugitives," 305.

43. William McDowell, ed., *Documents Relating to Indian Affairs, May 21, 1750 to August 7, 1754* (Columbia, 1958), 88.

44. *South-Carolina and American General Gazette,* January 14–21, 1771, *South-Carolina Gazette,* October 23, 1752, August 9, 1768, in *Runaway Slave Advertisements,* compiled by

Windley, vol. 3, *South Carolina*, 436, 115, 637. On traders using black boatmen, see Peter Wood, *Black Majority*, 114–15, 123–24.

45. *Georgia Gazette*, July 13, 1768, October 25, 1769, *South-Carolina Gazette*, December 6, 1751, in *Runaway Slave Advertisements*, compiled by Windley, 4:30, 40, 3:110.

46. Julius Scott, "The Common Wind: Currents of Afro-American Communication in the Era of the Haitian Revolution" (Ph.D. diss., Duke University, 1987); Peter Linebaugh and Marcus Rediker, *The Many-Headed Hydra: Sailors, Slaves, Commoners, and the Hidden History of the Revolutionary Atlantic* (Boston, 2000); Jeffrey Bolster, *Black Jacks: African American Seamen in the Age of Sail* (Cambridge, 1997); Landers, *Black Society*.

47. Sylvia Frey, *Water from the Rock: Black Resistance in a Revolutionary Age* (Princeton, 1991), 81.

48. *Gazette of the State of Georgia*, May 15, 1783, in *Runaway Slave Advertisements*, compiled by Windley, 4:105.

49. *Georgia State Gazette*, October 21, 1786, in ibid., 182.

50. Joseph P. Reidy, *From Slavery to Agrarian Capitalism in the Cotton Plantation South: Central Georgia, 1800–1880* (Chapel Hill, 1992).

51. Saunt, *New Order of Things*, chap. 9.

52. Quoted in ibid., 210. For a similar account of Indians stealing slaves from Georgia planters and then marrying the captive women, see William Dallam Armes, ed., *The Autobiography of Joseph Le Conte* (New York, 1903), 19–21.

53. Perdue, "Clan and Court," 567.

54. Affidavit of John A. Cuthbert, August 8, 1835, in *Indian Depredations, 1787–1825*, ed. Mrs. J. E. Hays (Atlanta, 1938–40), vol. 2, pt. 1, p. 17.

55. Jennifer Morgan's *Laboring Women* offers an elegant and pathbreaking analysis of enslaved black women's labor and reproduction in seventeenth-century Barbados and South Carolina.

56. Affidavit of William Smith, June 4, 1821, in *Indian Depredations*, ed. Hays, vol. 2, pt. 2, p. 628. Thanks to Claudio Saunt for bringing these cases to my attention.

57. Littlefield, *Africans and Creeks*, 44.

58. Margaret Burnham, "An Impossible Marriage," *Law and Inequality* 5 (July 1987): 187–225; Peter Bardaglio, " 'Shamefull Matches': The Regulation of Interracial Sex and Marriage in the South before 1900," in *Sex, Love, Race: Crossing Boundaries in North American History*, ed. Martha Hodes (New York, 1999): 112–40.

59. 1832 Census of Creek Indians Taken by Parsons and Abbott, National Archives, Washington, D.C., microfilm publication T-275; B. S. Parsons to Lewis Cass, September 7, 1832, in J. H. Jonston, "Documentary Evidence of the Relations of Negroes and Indians," *Journal of Negro History* 14 (January 1929): 37.

My People, My People

The Dynamics of
Community in Southern Slavery

DYLAN C. PENNINGROTH

> When somebody else eats fried fish, bananas, and a mess of peanuts and throws all the
> leavings on the floor, they gasp, "My skin-folks but not my kinfolks." And sadly over
> all, they keep sighing, "My People, My People!"
>
> ZORA NEALE HURSTON, *Dust Tracks on a Road*

*W*ho are "my people"? Josiah Henson faced this question when he was only six years old. His master sold him away from his mother to another plantation. And then, he recalled, the new master "put me into his negro quarters with about forty others, of all ages, colours, and conditions, all strangers to me. Of course nobody cared for me. . . . All day long I [was] left alone . . . lying on a lot of rags, thrown on a dirt floor . . . crying for water, crying for mother; the slaves, who left at daylight, when they returned cared nothing for me." Henson nearly died from neglect before he was sold back near his mother, "my best friend on earth."[1]

The way we think about slave communities has been shaped by decades of revisionist historical writing that has put slaves squarely at the center of their own history—indeed, at the center of southern history. Much of this revisionism has relied on two interpretive themes: the debate over cultural survival and acculturation and the dialectic of accommodation and resistance. These themes are sometimes fused into a framework that might be called acculturation and resistance. Viewed through this framework, slave communities and families were tough, resilient havens that helped black people survive the oppression of slavery and Reconstruction. Lately, a spirited counterrevisionist critique has emerged, warning that the emphasis on slave agency—in the family, in gardens, in the "infrapolitics" of master-slave negotiation—is making us forget the raw realities of slavery: the system was about making black people work for white people, and the whites had all the guns.[2]

But such critiques do not bring us closer to understanding stories such as Josiah Henson's. How do we, as historians, interpret evidence of neglect and loneliness in the "negro quarters"? Emphasizing the struggles between blacks and whites can make the black community by contrast seem more or less homogeneous, harmonious, even—as some historians have argued—"egalitarian."[3] This approach is not well suited for explaining conflict and difference *between* blacks. As Nell Irvin Painter and Evelyn Brooks Higginbotham have shown, assumptions about "strong black people" and "the overdeterminacy of race [have] tended to devalue and discourage attention" to "problems of gender, class, and sexual orientation internal to black communities."[4] Both the resistance framework and its counterrevisionist critics focus on conflict between the races, especially the master-slave relationship. That emphasis tends to obscure the experiences of black people, whose understanding of economic and social life involved far more than their relations with white people. To understand African American communities under slavery—how they decided who was and who was not "my people"—we might turn to a subject that has received increasing attention in recent years: the "slaves' economy." Studying how slaves acquired, held, traded, borrowed, and talked about property opens new possibilities for African American history, both because it illuminates the struggles between masters and slaves and because it reveals how slaves negotiated among themselves over power and resources.

Community and property were interrelated in the slave South: property helped create and define community at the same time that community ties "made" property. Before exploring that idea in more depth, I will briefly sketch the contours of property ownership among southern slaves. In U.S. history, despite a growing number of case studies, the "slaves' economy" is often viewed as a "special" case, unique to the low country with its absentee landowners and peculiar habit of working slaves by the task rather than in gangs. We will probably never know exactly how common it was for slaves to own property.[5] Yet evidence of slaves' ownership of property is everywhere—in antislavery narratives by fugitive slaves and accounts by travelers from England and the North, in the docket books of county courts in the 1820s and the case files of a federal compensation commission that existed during the 1870s. Perhaps most telling is the fact that when southerners mentioned their dealings with enslaved property owners, they did it almost without comment. Perhaps the closest we can come to a statistical snapshot is in the records of the Southern Claims Commission, a federal board that compensated loyal southerners for property lost during the

Civil War. Of the 5,004 "allowed" claims whose records survive, ex-slaves filed 498, about 10 percent of the total. Their claims were scattered over 121 counties in every southern state except Texas and West Virginia, both of which sent very few claims of any kind.[6] Ex-slaves' claims were not confined to task-system areas or privileged slaves. Two-thirds of the successful claims by ex-slaves (331 claims) came from counties outside the low country.[7] Hundreds of claims came from former field hands, suggesting that the "slaves' economy" reached far beyond the narrow band of house servants and artisans who masters believed made up the privileged class in the quarters.[8]

Testimony from former slaves and their witnesses (many of whom were white neighbors or even former masters) suggests that property ownership was far from a special case but rather was generic among slaves. Slaves seized hold of the everyday processes that made up the institution of slavery and used them to create property. They usually did not own very much—the typical claim was for three hundred dollars worth of such items as corn, hogs, and pots and pans, with an occasional horse or featherbed. Moreover, no court would have protected a slave's claim to those items because slaves did not have property rights. Still, although slaves' property ownership posed a legal conundrum, it was perfectly compatible with the institution of slavery.[9]

What does the slave community look like if we know that slaves commonly owned property? First, it begins to reveal a tangled web of social relationships, both between slaves and whites and among the slaves themselves. Time rather than land represented the scarce resource for slaves. Consequently, when slaves accumulated property, they usually did so with at least one other slave's contribution of time and labor. A few slaves hired others for jobs or used their status as drivers to command labor. Most slaves, however, lacked that status in the master's hierarchy and instead got access to other people's time through kin and communal relationships. In other words, in regions with a flourishing slaves' economy, being part of a family or community often meant having to work for other slaves. Such inequality and power dynamics within slave communities are an underexplored part of U.S. history. Although historians have long been aware that hierarchies existed in the quarters, scholars have struggled to distinguish those distinctions that masters imposed (where butlers and drivers stood at the top of a pyramid) from those that came from the slaves themselves (where, for example, elders and healers were venerated). One major conceptual problem has been the assumption that property, the most obvious marker of inequality, was impossible for slaves. Knowing that many slaves owned property allows us to rethink slaves' internal relations—of gender, family, community, and more—in ways that account for inequality and potential conflict without resorting to hierarchies imposed by masters.[10] And, in so doing, we need not think of conflict among slaves as a reflection of white oppression or as something inimical to the making and survival of black communities.[11]

Other strands in slaves' social networks reached out to touch fellow slaves, masters, white neighbors, and shopkeepers. All of these groups participated in the informal economy, and their participation turned something that legally was nonsense into something that most southerners simply took for granted. Some places had laws to regulate slaves' ownership of property, often by requiring slaves to carry "tickets" or written permissions to trade, and some masters complied with these measures, but spoke of them as "customs" rather than as "laws."[12] "It was customary among us," testified a former Mississippi slave owner, "when we sold a horse to a slave to say to his master when I first met him, that 'I have sold so and so a horse is it all right?' "[13] Many whites did not even bother to do that. As Louisiana's high court pointed out, white passengers on steamboats and stagecoaches, "cannot be expected to lose time in inquiring whether the boy be a slave or a free person [or] whether he has his owner's permission. The law forbids the purchase of anything from a slave, without a written permission from his master, yet, many times, the most correct of our citizens buy a melon, or other trifling article, without the production of this permit. In such a case, the act is considered as justified by the maxim, *de minimis non curat lex*, or the proverb, *lo poco por nada se reputa* [the law does not concern itself with trivial matters]."[14] Whites' disagreements about slaves' ownership of property tapped into deep splits among different segments of white society as well as ongoing problems in the system of law.

White people argued all the time over what to do about slave-owned property, and larger changes in politics and the plantation economy may have curtailed slaves' independent economic activity by the 1860s. Especially as worldwide demand for cotton surged during the 1850s, slave owners in the cotton regions may have tried harder than ever to gobble up more of the slaves' time. Still, the evidence suggests that slaves held remarkably secure claims to their things. Joseph Bacon understood that slaves had no legal right to property but insisted that "a master who would take property from his slaves would have a hard time." His master, Bacon said, "never interfered with me and my property at all."[15] Why not?

Slaves protected their claims to property by using public occasions and public spaces to display their possessions and to secure acknowledgment from their masters and fellow slaves. The physical arrangement of the plantation was essential to this practice. Most big southern plantations clustered the slaves' cabins together in rows somewhere near where the master or the overseer, if there was one, lived. Slave owners liked this layout because it kept slaves under supervision.[16] But slaves used the plantation layout for their own purposes.

In the absence of legal protection, slaves' claims to property seem to have depended on their long association with an item, an association that had to be visible to as many eyes as possible. "I seen it in her possession, and her master knew it, and everyone considered it her property," said a witness in an Alabama case.[17] What from a legal perspective might have seemed merely rights of use or possession translated over time into real claims of ownership. As another witness put it, "I know it was his because it was right there under his 'control-ment' & no one else claimed it."[18] In effect, by dragging their personal property into public view, the slaves cemented their claims to owning property in a society whose laws did not admit that possibility. In a very real sense, community "made" property in the nineteenth-century South. And slaves were not alone in this. After all, many white people also lacked written records of ownership in the 1800s and relied heavily on social relationships with kin and neighbors in matters of work and property.[19]

By the same token, however, property "made" community. The historiography of U.S. slave families has long been preoccupied with a hunt for structure, largely because so many observers then (and now) denied that slaves even had families. Today, Herbert Gutman's basic premise—that slaves created and maintained families despite incredible obstacles—is widely accepted, and scholars have turned to historicizing and complicating what had been a somewhat static and general portrait of "the black family." For example, Ann Patton Malone shows that "the real strength of the slave community was its multiplicity of forms, its tolerance for a variety of families and households, its adaptability, and its acceptance of all types of families and households as functional and contributing." Ira Berlin, Steven F. Miller, and Leslie S. Rowland see a creative expansion of family ties during and after the Civil War.[20] Building on such insights, I propose four strategies for reconceptualizing slave social ties. First, growing evidence that slaves had multiple and changing family structures suggests that structure might not be the most useful object of inquiry; instead, we might look for process—the shifts and slippages that helped make slave communities so contingent. In this sense, we can think of kinship not only as a set of facts (biological, social, two-parent, and so on) but also as an ideology, shaped but not determined by blood and marriage, that slaves deployed to pursue their interests. Third, we might think more about exclusion as well as expansion, the moments when slaves chose to reject kin or communal ties as well as the moments of embrace. Focusing on kinship's limits anchors it firmly back in its historical contexts and reminds us that although it could be adaptable and expansive, black kinship was never universal or automatic.[21] And fourth, combining analysis of an ideology of kinship with a focus on property can help address issues of power and inequality among nineteenth-century black people, struggles that, in Armstead Robinson's words, "emanated" not solely from their relations with whites but also from "the social structures of [slavery and] postslavery Afro-American communities."[22]

Like thousands of enslaved people between 1810 and 1850, Charles Ball got sold down the river, forced by his master to trudge from the Chesapeake to a new plantation in western Georgia. What happened to Ball and those like him, young adults sent to live among strangers? Ball's narrative suggests that they needed to make kin, relatives who would help in dealing with grief and anger and who would provide loans, gardens, and extra hands to help the newcomers to start earning property (which often was needed just to stay alive). Ball's master put him in a cabin with another slave family, but being black and enslaved did not automatically render them anything more than strangers to one another. For the next fifty pages, Ball's narrative never even mentions their names, dwelling instead on his sadness at losing his wife and children back in Maryland.[23] Only when they agreed to share property and labor did Ball really become involved with the people in this cabin: "I therefore proposed to her and her husband [Nero] . . . that whilst I should remain a member of the family, I would contribute as much towards its support as Nero himself; or, at least, that I would bring all my earnings into the family stock, *provided I might be treated as one of its members*, and be allowed a portion of the proceeds of their patch or garden. This offer was very readily accepted, *and from this time we constituted one community*, as long as I remained among the field hands on this plantation."[24] Agreeing to share economic interests went hand in hand with the formation of new social ties, so that a newcomer such as Ball became a "member of the family," part of their "community," at the moment when he began to participate in its economic life. This and other testimony suggests that there was nothing automatic about either kinship or community among enslaved people. In some cases, at least, such matters had less to do with being black or being enslaved than with people's interests in property.

Indeed, being part of the same community did not rule out the possibility of conflict among slaves. Asked to testify about what Jacob Quarterman, one of the field hands, had owned, Joseph Bacon testified that he "knew all about what he owned & what was his" except for his money. "He is a man what had money," Bacon insisted, but people "never see his money. [H]e too cunning to show any body his money."[25] When someone did steal, slaves dealt with it by skillfully manipulating the power of the spoken word and the physical landscape of the countryside. Journalist Charles Raymond was relaxing on a big-house veranda when one of his host's slaves began to chant,

"Oh-h-h-h, Jesus! Oh-h-h-h, Jesus!
An' dey make long prayers,
An' dey sing long psalms,

But dey steal my chick-ins, Lord;
Oh-h-h, Jesus! Oh-h-h, Jesus!"

Then, as an interlude, would follow a continuous humming sound, as if gathering up her feelings into metrical shape; and again would the plaint burst forth:

" . . . But dey'll all be damned
In dat drefful day;
For dey steal my chick-ins, Lord." [26]

Slaves used words to display their claims of ownership, name their suspicions about the theft, and mobilize their social ties with other slaves to retrieve property. Sometimes they set up special committees that publicly questioned suspects and used such divination objects as string-tied Bibles and graveyard dirt to detect thieves. [27] Away from the eyes of their masters, slaves' verbal jousting became less oblique, more pointed. An enslaved Virginia man named West sarcastically told a fellow slave named Hubbard "to be more of a Gentleman" and pay back the fifty cents he owed; West added "that he was the rong man for Hubbard to fool with." [28] Whites almost never noticed disputes between African Americans unless one of their slaves seemed likely to end up dead (which is what happened to West). [29] Indeed, because of the constraints of the slavery system, slaves could not use public display in their conflicts over property and social relationships as easily as they used it to secure their claims of ownership. Masters controlled the physical layout of plantations and had an interest in suppressing any disputes among slaves that might hurt the plantation's profits. More often, the plantations' physical layout and the threat of harsh punishment from masters prompted slaves to manipulate words and public spaces as an alternative way of dealing with a whole range of disagreements, of which stealing was just one. Black people's words darted and drifted on the air of the South, ignored by whites and thus safe from censure because much of what they said was aimed at other black people.

Furthermore, conflict in slave communities did not necessarily happen along lines of color or status. Since field hands could own property right alongside carpenters and house slaves, conflict among slaves spilled out in all sorts of messy, unpredictable ways: although field hands complained about drivers, husbands also grumbled about their wives, and neighbors argued with each other as well as with strangers. In short, black-black conflict over property sheds light on what slave communities looked like and what it meant to be part of them.

These tensions and negotiations among black people are a rich part of black history, one that overlapped with but was not determined by African Americans' struggles with whites. While some observers claim that slavery's tendency to break up black families, its corrosion of supposedly traditional African gender roles, and especially slaves' utter lack of property ingrained a legacy of "dysfunction" in black communities,[30] others think that the dysfunction argument is tantamount to blaming black people for their own victimization. Rather than a source of continuing dysfunction, proponents of this view argue, the black family, the black community, and black traditions of property ownership have been the only things keeping black people from total annihilation. Acknowledging both the power of white oppression and black people's resistance to it, we might instead be guided by the principle that black people's lives involved far more than their relations with whites. "When you find a set of folks who won't agree on a thing," Zora Neale Hurston wrote, "those are My People."[31] And this tongue-in-cheek critique of the 1940s contains a challenge for historians of the nineteenth century: to consider what was at stake between slaves as a way of understanding the solidarities, differences, and conflicts that defined who slaves were to each other.

NOTES

I thank Stephanie Camp, Ed Baptist, the participants at the 2002 New Studies in American Slavery symposium, and an anonymous reader for the University of Georgia Press for their helpful critiques and suggestions.

1. Josiah Henson, "Autobiography of the Reverend Josiah Henson," in *Four Fugitive Slave Narratives*, ed. Robin W. Winks (Reading, 1969), 18.

2. For an early statement of this counterrevisionism, see Peter Kolchin, "Reevaluating the Antebellum Slave Community: A Comparative Perspective," *Journal of American History* 70 (December 1983): 579–601. For other examples, see Ann Patton Malone, *Sweet Chariot: Slave Family and Household Structure in Nineteenth-Century Louisiana* (Chapel Hill, 1992), 254–58; William Dusinberre, *Them Dark Days: Slavery in the American Rice Swamps* (New York, 1996); Peter A. Coclanis, "The Captivity of a Generation," *William and Mary Quarterly*, 3rd ser., 61, no. 3 (2004), 550–55 (review of Ira Berlin, *Generations of Captivity* [Cambridge, 2003]). Wilma A. Dunaway is blunt: "Too many recent studies have the effect of whitewashing from slavery the worst structural constraints. . . . Notions like 'windows of autonomy within slavery' or an 'independent slave economy' seriously overstate the degree to which slaves had control over their own lives, and they trivialize the brutalities and inequities of enslavement" (*The African-American Family in Slavery and Emancipation* [New York, 2003], 4).

3. On "egalitarianism," see Deborah Gray White, *Ar'n't I a Woman? Female Slaves in the Plantation South* (New York, 1999), 153, 158; Philip D. Morgan, *Slave Counterpoint: Black Culture in the Eighteenth-Century Chesapeake and Lowcountry* (Chapel Hill, 1998), 533. The issue of conflict in slave communities is difficult to integrate into the resistance framework but is not new to historians. Several scholars, including White and Morgan, have discussed the subject and concluded that, whatever the conflicts among slaves, those conflicts were overshadowed by, subsumed within, or by-products of the conflict between slaves and masters.

4. Nell Irvin Painter, "Soul Murder and Slavery: Toward a Fully Loaded Cost Accounting," in *U.S. History as Women's History*, ed. Linda K. Kerber, Alice Kessler-Harris, and Kathryn Kish Sklar (Chapel Hill, 1995), 125–46; Evelyn Brooks Higginbotham, "African-American Women's History and the Metalanguage of Race," in *Feminism and History*, ed. Joan W. Scott (New York, 1992), 200–201.

5. Peter Kolchin, *American Slavery, 1619–1877* (New York, 1993), 153.

6. Because these states sent very few claims to Washington—seventeen from Texas, forty-three from West Virginia—the absence of claims by ex-slaves can be seen as statistically insignificant. Amounts calculated from Case Files, Southern Claims Commission, Records of the Third Auditor, Allowed Case Files, Records of the U.S. General Accounting Office, Record Group 217, National Archives, Washington, D.C. (hereafter cited as scc). An additional 2,088 allowed claims are not considered here because they were either lost or filed with the records of other agencies. Claims were judged item by item, and most claims were disallowed at least in part. Allowed claims were those that proved that the claimant stayed loyal to the Union, that the claimant owned the property in question, and that the property had been taken by Union soldiers for legitimate army use. Overall, more than 22,000 people filed claims, but fewer than one-third of them passed these rigorous tests.

7. I include the following counties in the low country (number of allowed claims by ex-slaves appears in parentheses). Georgia: Camden (1), Glynn (0), McIntosh (0), Liberty (91), Bryan (0), Chatham (43). South Carolina: Beaufort (23), Colleton (0), Charleston (1), Georgetown (4), Horry (0). North Carolina: Brunswick (0), New Hanover (1), Onslow (0), Carteret (2), Craven (0), Pamlico (0), Beaufort (1), Hyde (0), Tyrell (0), Dare (0). Florida: Nassau (0), Duval (0), Saint Johns (0). Amounts calculated from scc.

8. This statistic is inexact because many claimants did not state their occupation during slavery.

9. Seen in a global perspective, this was not unusual; many slave societies throughout history have permitted slaves to own property. For examples, see Richard Roberts, *Warriors, Merchants, and Slaves: The State and the Economy in the Middle Niger Valley, 1700–1914* (Stanford, 1987), 112–26; Richard Roberts, "Conflicts over Property in the Middle Niger Valley at the Beginning of the Twentieth Century," *African Economic History* 25 (1997): 91; Jan Hogendorn, "The Economics of Slave Use on Two 'Plantations' in the Zaria Emirate of the Sokoto Caliphate," *International Journal of African Historical Studies* 10, no. 3 (1977): 378; Orlando Patterson, *Slavery and Social Death: A Comparative Study* (Cambridge, 1982), 182–86; Gyan Prakash, *Bonded Histories: Genealogies of Labor Servitude in Colonial India* (Cambridge, 1990); Baas Terwiel, "Bondage and Slavery in Early Nineteenth-Century Siam," in *Slavery, Bondage, and Dependency in Southeast Asia*, ed. Anthony Reid (New York, 1983), 118–37; Ira Berlin and Philip D. Morgan, eds., *Cultivation and Culture: Labor and the Shaping of Slave Life in the Americas* (Charlottesville, 1993).

10. One potential line of inquiry is whether, as Larry E. Hudson Jr. argues for nineteenth-century South Carolina, the slaves' economy fostered "clear social and economic differences . . . among slave families" that were significant enough that "the best-organized families dominated the slave quarter community" (*To Have and to Hold: Slave Work and Family Life in Antebellum South Carolina* [Athens, 1997], xiv, xxi).

11. On black-black conflict as a reflection of white oppression, see Malone, *Sweet Chariot*, 228–29; Lawrence McDonnell, "Money Knows No Master: Market Relations and the American Slave Community," in *Developing Dixie: Modernization in a Traditional Society*, ed. Winfred B. Moore Jr., Joseph F. Tripp, and Lyon G. Tyler Jr. (Westport, 1988), 38; Ira Berlin and Philip D. Morgan, introduction to *Cultivation and Culture*, ed. Berlin and Morgan, 38–39; Ira Berlin, *Many Thousands Gone: The First Two Centuries of Slavery in North America* (Cambridge, 1998), 138. Dusinberre extends this argument even further and attributes nearly all evidence of conflict among slaves to the masters' divide-and-conquer strategy (*Them Dark Days*, 177).

On black-black conflict as a destructive force within black communities, see Kolchin, *American Slavery*, 109; Brenda Stevenson, "Distress and Discord in Virginia Slave Families, 1830–1860," in *In Joy and in Sorrow: Women, Family, and Marriage in the Victorian South, 1830–1900*, ed. Carol Bleser (New York, 1991), 103–24; Orlando Patterson, *Rituals of Blood: Consequences of Slavery in Two American Centuries* (Washington, 1998), 3. Studies dealing with domestic violence among white Americans generally do not make such arguments. See Elizabeth Pleck, "Wife Beating in Nineteenth-Century America," *Victimology* 4, no. 1 (1979): 60–74; Christine Stansell, *City of Women: Sex and Class in New York, 1789–1860* (New York, 1986); Pamela Haag, "'The Ill-Use of a Wife': Patterns of Working-Class Violence in Domestic and Public New York City, 1860–1880," *Journal of Social History* 25 (Spring 1992): 447–77; Hendrik Hartog, *Man and Wife in America: A History* (Cambridge, 2000).

12. Testimony of Benjamin P. McCrany in claim of John Langford, p. 9, Madison County, Alabama, scc; James Benson Sellers, *Slavery in Alabama* (Tuscaloosa, 1994), 233; testimony of James Fraser in claim of John Bacon Sr., p. 24, Liberty County, Georgia, scc.

13. Testimony of J. H. Ledbetter in claim of William Hardeman, pp. 6–7, Hinds County, Mississippi, scc.

14. *Rice v. Cade*, 10 La. 288, 1836 WL 746 (La.); see also Thomas Read Rootes Cobb, *Inquiry into the Law of Negro Slavery* (Athens, 1999), 235.

15. Claim of Joseph Bacon (1873) in Philip D. Morgan, "The Ownership of Property by Slaves in the Mid-Nineteenth-Century Low Country," *Journal of Southern History* 49 (August 1983): 411. Many Louisiana plantations had house-search policies yet rarely exercised them (Roderick A. McDonald, *Economy and Material Culture of Slaves: Goods and Chattels on the Sugar Plantations of Jamaica and Louisiana* [Baton Rouge, 1993], 148).

16. Emily P. Burke, *Reminiscences of Georgia* (Oberlin, 1850), 112. Burke goes on to describe the slaves' gardens, their after-task work, their trading, and their purchases. On plantation layouts in North Carolina, see *Robert McNamara v. John Kerns et al.* (1841) 24 N.C. 66; on Virginia, see Larry McKee, "The Ideals and Realities behind the Design and Use of Nineteenth Century Virginia Slave Cabins," in *The Art and Mystery of Historical Archaeology: Essays in Honor of James Deetz*, ed. Anne Elizabeth Yentsch and Mary C. Beaudry (Boca Raton, 1992), 200–210; on Louisiana and Tennessee, see John B. Rehder, *Delta Sugar: Louisiana's Vanishing Plantation Landscape* (Baltimore, 1999), 93–94, 99–100; Brian W. Thomas, "Power and Community: The Archaeology of Slavery at the Hermitage Plantation," *American Antiquity* 63 (October 1998): 537–39.

17. Testimony of George Richardson in claim of Emily Frazier, p. 20, Limestone County, Alabama, scc.

18. Testimony of Brister Fleming in claim of Prince Stevens, p. 18, Liberty County, Georgia, SCC.

19. Michael Merrill, "Cash Is Good to Eat: Self-Sufficiency and Exchange in the Rural Economy of the United States," *Radical History Review* 4 (Winter 1977): 42–71; Steven Hahn, *The Roots of Southern Populism: Yeoman Farmers and the Transformation of the Georgia Upcountry, 1850–1890* (New York, 1983); Christopher Clark, *The Roots of Rural Capitalism: Western Massachusetts, 1780–1860* (Ithaca, 1990); deposition of Peter Perkins in *Sarah T. Thornton v. Lunsford A. Paschall*, May 31, 1862, 044.928.14, Granville County, Civil Action Papers Concerning Slaves and Free Persons of Color, 1846–1875, North Carolina State Archives, Raleigh.

20. Malone, *Sweet Chariot*, 258; Ira Berlin, Steven F. Miller, and Leslie S. Rowland, "Afro-American Families in the Transition from Slavery to Freedom," *Radical History Review* 42 (1988): 89–121.

21. For analyses that seem to conflate kinship with community or the slave quarter, see Berlin, Miller, and Rowland, "Afro-American Families," 89; Jon F. Sensbach, *A Separate Canaan: The Making of an Afro-Moravian World in North Carolina, 1763–1840* (Chapel Hill, 1998), 270; Morgan, *Slave Counterpoint*, 511.

22. Armstead L. Robinson, "Beyond the Realm of Social Consensus: New Meanings of Reconstruction for American History," *Journal of American History* 68 (September 1981): 291–93; see also Darlene Clark Hine, "Rape and the Inner Lives of Black Women in the Middle West: Preliminary Thoughts on the Culture of Dissemblance," *Signs* 14 (Summer 1989): 912–20.

23. Charles Ball, *Slavery in the United States* (Lewistown, 1836), mentions the family several times in these pages but refers to them as "a middle-aged man" (142), "my new friend" (142), "the mistress [of] this humble abode" (143), "my companions" (145), and "the man with whom I lived" (189).

24. Ibid., 192–93; emphasis added.

25. Testimony of Joseph Bacon in claim of Jacob Quarterman, p. 9, Liberty County, Georgia, SCC.

26. Charles A. Raymond, "The Religious Life of the Negro Slave," *Harper's New Monthly Magazine* 27 (November 1863): 824–25.

27. Jacob Stroyer, *My Life in the South* (Salem, 1889), 57–59.

28. Testimony of Milly in *Trial of Hubbard*, January 20, 1817, Southampton County, Virginia, box 3, Condemned Slaves File, Virginia State Library, Richmond.

29. See, for example, *Trial of Peter*, October 16, 1828, Essex County Court Order Book, 45, microfilm reel 94, Virginia State Library.

30. Orlando Patterson, *Rituals of Blood*, 3–7, 25–42; Dinesh D'Souza thinks slavery did not destroy "the two-parent black family unit" but did foster "a culture of self-defeating and irresponsible attitudes and behavior among black Americans" (*The End of Racism: Principles for a Multiracial Society* [New York, 1995], 97).

31. Zora Neale Hurston, "My People, My People!" in *Dust Tracks on a Road* (New York, 1991), 215–18.

PART THREE

The Politics of Culture in Slavery

Spiritual Terror and Sacred Authority

The Power of the Supernatural

in Jamaican Slave Society

VINCENT BROWN

*I*n his 1801 history of the British West Indies, Jamaican planter and slave-holder Bryan Edwards admitted that "in countries where slavery is established, the leading principle on which the government is supported is fear: or a sense of that absolute coercive necessity which, leaving no choice of action, super-sedes all questions of right."[1] Yet slave masters did not achieve the fear requi-site to maintaining control over the enslaved by physical force alone. They in fact asserted their right to rule by trying to terrorize the spiritual imaginations of the enslaved.[2] To do so, slave masters projected their authority symbolically through spectacular punishments visited upon the bodies of the dead. As an-thropologist Katherine Verdery has noted, dead bodies carry great symbolic weight: "They evoke awe, uncertainty, and fear associated with 'cosmic' con-cerns, such as the meaning of life and death."[3] Moreover, when dead bodies are managed with political intent, "their corporeality makes them important means of *localizing* a claim."[4] In other words, the physical presence of a corpse connects its meaningful associations to its tangible location. Using dead bodies as symbols, masters marked territory with awesome icons of their power.

The use of spectacular terror to capture the imaginations of the enslaved was a staple feature of social control in slave society. Yet even more menacingly, slaveholders supplemented physical coercion with "government magic," as they harnessed the affective power of the dead and awe of the afterlife in an attempt to turn legal mastery into sacred authority.[5] Though their intent was to dom-inate the imagination, the routinization of terrifying spectacles inspired novel understandings of the relationships among dead bodies, haunting spirits, and political authority, understandings that could also enhance the sacred authority of slaves who were willing to resist or to rise up and strike their masters. For their part, the enslaved established competing discourses of authority by invoking the spirits of the dead and by selectively appropriating the symbolic power of the master class for their own purposes.[6] Both masters and slaves tried to elevate their authority by connecting it to the transcendent. In other words, they attached worldly power to otherworldly concerns.

Slaveholders faced a persistent threat of dispossession by suicide. The harshness of the labor regime, social isolation, and diminished status as well as the longing to return to ancestral lands prompted many among the enslaved to destroy themselves. Henry Coor, who worked for fifteen years as a millwright in the Jamaican parish of Westmoreland, observed that unbearable workloads, physical punishment, and incessant hunger prompted many Africans to cut their own throats or hang themselves. "I remember fourteen Slaves," he told a British House of Commons committee in 1791, "that it was generally said, and I believe it was, from bad treatment, that them [sic] rise in rebellion on a Sunday, who ran away into the woods, and all cut their own throats together."[7] For some, harsh treatment only aggravated the general indignity of lost social status. One plantation doctor who served in Jamaica from 1755 to 1765 told the same committee about an African "man of consequence" who reportedly refused to work for any white man. Even after being punished by his overseer, the African told the overseer to warn his owner that "he would be a slave to no man." Fearing that the man was an incorrigible rebel, the owner ordered him removed to another plantation. "His hands were tied behind him; in going over a bridge, he jumped headlong into the water, and appeared no more."[8] Less esteemed Africans still faced the kind of disorienting social isolation that could lead to unrecoverable depression. The same plantation doctor owned a boy who "detested the idea of slavery so much that he refused all support, which brought on a dropsy, and terminated in his death."[9] New African immigrants were known to kill themselves more often than seasoned slaves; creoles (those born on the island) only rarely committed suicide. Commenting on higher death rates for newly arrived men than for women, former overseer William Fitzmaurice testified in 1791 that entering into relationships and being taken as domestic servants afforded women social roles and protections unavailable to men. Consequently, he surmised, men were more depressed and committed suicide in Jamaica more often than women.[10] Recently arrived Africans "constantly told me," he said, "that they preferred dying to living."[11]

Perhaps many Africans were sanguine about suicide because they believed they would return to their ancestral lands after death and there be reunited with lost kin and friends as spirits and ancestors.[12] Mark Cook, a clerk, schoolmaster, and small planter in Jamaica, knew of several men and women, all Africans, who had hanged or shot themselves. Claiming to be acquainted with African funerals, he recognized that they made "great rejoicings on those occasions, because, as I have understood from them, they thought their countrymen were gone back to their own country again."[13] When Lieutenant Baker Davidson of the Seventy-ninth Regiment testified before a committee of the House of Commons in 1790, he was asked if he knew of any cases of Africans "expressing themselves with affection of their native country, and desiring to return to it."[14] "I did," Davidson replied, "as I brought a Guinea woman to England who wished much to be sent back to her own country; and it is very common for Negroes when they are sick to say, they are going back to their own country." "Do they say it with apparent satisfaction?" the committee asked. "They certainly do," Davidson said, "as they express always a great deal of pleasure when they think they are going to die, and say that they are going to leave this Buccra country."[15]

Slave masters throughout the Caribbean used spiritual terror to deter Africans from self-destruction. At least as early as the mid-seventeenth century, British West Indian planters hoped that mutilating the dead would impress Africans with the planters' power over the spiritual fate of the enslaved. Richard Ligon, a seventeenth-century chronicler of slave society in Barbados, lamented that Africans "believe in a Resurrection, and that they shall go into their own Country again, and have their youth renewed. And lodging this opinion in their hearts, they make it an ordinary practice, upon any great fright, or threatening of their Masters, to hang themselves."[16] A planter acquaintance of Ligon's, Colonel Walrond, had in a short time lost three or four of his most valuable slaves to suicide. Fearing that they had set a costly example to others, Walrond ordered that one of their heads should be chopped off and fixed to a pole a dozen feet high. He marched all his slaves around the icon, commanding them to gaze at the severed head, and he asked them to acknowledge that this was indeed the head of one of the self-murderers. As they did, Walrond told them that "they were in a main errour, in thinking they went into their own Countreys, after they were dead; for, this man's head was here, as they all were witnesses of; and how was it possible, the body could go without a head." As Ligon remembered it, the Africans were convinced by the "sad, yet lively spectacle." They apparently changed their convictions, and no more hanged themselves.[17]

Walrond may have been spared similar losses, but Africans continued to kill themselves with distressing frequency in the Caribbean, and slaveholders kept resorting to grisly techniques of deterrence. In the late-eighteenth-century Danish West Indies, C. G. A. Oldendorp reported that "the head and hands of such suicides have been put in a cage on public display—a measure not without effective results."[18] In prerevolutionary Saint Domingue, French slavers mutilated the body of the first Ibo slave to die in a given shipment: they beheaded the corpse or sliced off its nose and pried out its eyes to prevent losses among other captives from the Bight of Biafra, who were widely reputed to be prone to suicide.[19] Cuban merchants and masters in the early nineteenth century incinerated corpses to achieve similar objectives with other groups of Africans.[20]

In Jamaica, such practices were widespread throughout the eighteenth century. Just before midcentury, an anonymous Jamaican planter wrote that to prevent Africans from believing that they could escape the island in death, their bodies were "often hanged up" by their masters to show the living that the dead remained in Jamaica.[21] Around midcentury, masters began to apply the punishments for outright rebellion—burning the body down to ash—to suicide as well. And to dramatize the impossibility of repatriation in death, masters threatened to deny suicidal slaves their final rite of passage. In 1751 the Anglican rector of Westmoreland Parish wrote to his bishop that "to deprive them of their funeral Rites by burning their dead Bodies, seems to Negroes a greater Punishment than Death itself. This is done to Self-Murderers."[22] As late as the final decade of slavery, John Stewart remembered a time when newly arriving Africans committed suicide to "return to their native country, and enjoy the society of kindred and friends, from whom they have been torn away in an evil hour." He also remembered the "dismal and disgusting spectacle" of their heads adorning poles along public roads and their bodies "sometimes consumed by fire."[23]

Whether such mutilations in fact constituted an effective deterrent is open to question. Dismemberment certainly represented a compelling metaphysical threat to English Protestants, but there is little or no direct evidence that Africans believed that losing their head or a limb would prevent their return to ancestral lands.[24] Many Africans had surely seen severed heads serving as trophies for warring state authorities in Africa. Indeed, in parts of West Africa, slaves were routinely beheaded after the death of nobles so that they could continue to serve their masters in the spiritual world.[25] Whether or not European masters were aware of African precedents, in Jamaica they beheaded and dismembered their own slaves with a similar desire that the dead continue their service. Through dead bodies they attempted to seize and manipulate African visions of the afterlife in an effort to govern the worldly actions of the living.

Mutilating the bodies of Africans who committed suicide was only part of a broader agenda that used ritual execution to give governing authority a sacred, even supernatural, dimension. As with the punishments for suicide, the punishments for rebellion were meant to inspire in the enslaved terror of their ultimate fate by visiting extraordinary torments on their bodies before and after death.[26] By at least the late seventeenth century the bodies of slave rebels were burned alive. Sir Hans Sloane, who visited Jamaica just before the turn of the eighteenth century, described the grisly tortures meted out to slaves and the meticulous method of executing rebels, "by nailing them down on the ground with crooked Sticks on every Limb, and then applying the Fire by degrees from the Feet and Hands, burning them gradually up to the Head, whereby their pains are extravagant."[27] Only two weeks after Thomas Thistlewood arrived in Savanna la Mar in 1750, he watched his host, William Dorrill, order the body of a dead runaway dug up and beheaded, with the head to be fixed on a pole and the body to be incinerated.[28] Just months later, Thistlewood "saw a Negro fellow nam'd English belonging to Fuller Wood Tried, lost, and hang'd upon ye 1st Tree immediately (for drawing his knife upon a White Man), his head Cutt off, Body left unbury'd."[29] Once he assumed the post of overseer on the Egypt sugar plantation, Thistlewood had the opportunity to use the dead to enhance his authority. In October 1752 he was pleased to receive a letter, two returned fugitives, and "also Robin's head, who was hanged yesterday for running away with those two boys." As a warning to others, he "put it upon a pole and stuck it up just at the angle of the road in the home pasture."[30]

Lady Maria Nugent passed just such a fetish on her way to church one day in 1803. She protested to her diary that if the members of her party had not already promised their attendance to the clergyman in Kingston, "I would not have gone, for we were obliged to pass close by the pole, on which was stuck the head of a black man who was executed a few days ago."[31] Placing the bodies of the condemned along well-traveled paths served to haunt those places with memories and narratives of crime and punishment. Once, while touring western Jamaica in 1816, Matthew Gregory Lewis was inspired to ask "to whom a skull had belonged, which I had observed fixed on a pole by the roadside, when returning last from Montego Bay." As it turned out, the severed head had been there since about 1811, when "a Mr. Dunbar had given some discontent to his negroes in the article of clothing them. . . . [T]his was sufficient to induce his head driver, who had been brought up in his own house from infancy, to form a plot among his slaves to assassinate him."[32] The recycling of these kinds of stories reintroduced past evidence of white power to the present and fastened it to particular places through the bodies of the dead.[33] At times the colonial state even tried to convert the oppositional discourses of the enslaved into such narratives of plantocratic power. Jamaican authorities hanged Eboe Dick in 1816 for "making use of singing, propagating and disseminating seditious and rebellious words, songs, and expressions."[34] Placing his head on "the most public place at Lindhurst" plantation, officials hoped to make him sing a different song.

Such ghoulish displays served clear purposes. They made dead bodies, dismembered and disfigured as they were, into symbols of the power and propriety of slave masters. Severed heads stood sentry over the plantation landscape, watching passersby—white, black, and brown—conveying warnings to potential rebels and assurance to supporters of the social order. Such symbols were thought to be effective because they were affective: they harnessed the otherworldly and the sacred to specific bodies, places, and narratives, which in turn signified the social power of the rulers.[35] Jamaican planters brought most of these conventions from the British theater of social control, but in the Caribbean they had to restage several elements of the exhibition.

Exaggerated tortures and postmortem humiliations were staple punishments in early modern Europe and England. As in Jamaica, they served to graft sacred and social power onto the bodies of condemned criminals.[36] Disfiguration and scorching gave criminals a foretaste of the punishments their souls would receive in hell.[37] Thus man brought the wrath of God to bear on enemies of the state. Dismembering and scattering corpses or exposing them to be "consumed by the air and the birds of the sky" protected living communities from the evil that criminal spirits might continue to work in the world. Incineration of criminals' corpses effected the complete physical and metaphysical eradication of the their presence.[38] Denial of a decent burial arrested the spirit's passage into the otherworld and desecrated the memory of the dead by fixing the attention of the living on the rotting body. Throughout Europe, the public exposure of bodies at places of execution and at well-traveled intersections "formed part of a dual system which maximized display. . . . The executions themselves were primarily meant as an example to the inhabitants. Exposure of corpses along the roads was a special warning directed at non-residents coming in."[39] Indeed, late-seventeenth- and early-eighteenth-century English road books and guides often mentioned gallows and gibbets as road marks.[40]

The fear and submission evoked by such measures depended in part on understandings held in common by both the rulers and the ruled. To a degree, the populace and the people who managed them shared religious idioms for thinking about death and the afterlife, though they surely interpreted them differently, in accordance with their experience of material life and status hierarchies. Also, they shared understandings of the sacred dimensions of courtroom protocol and public execution.

Assize judges, who descended on the eighteenth-century English countryside twice a year, carefully scripted their rhetoric to connote godly paternalism as well as the power and passion of righteous vengeance as a means of legitimating the rule of law.[41] When the time came to pronounce a death sentence, "the powers of light and darkness were summoned into the court with the black cap which was donned to pronounce sentence of death, and the spotless white gloves worn at the end of a 'maiden assize' when no prisoners were left for execution."[42] Most importantly, the rites of legal practice likened judges to God, and they thus derived their authority from the divine.[43] A death sentence, then, represented a supernatural judgment, merely mediated by the state. At the place of execution, dramatic pageants of sin, redemption, and damnation organized scaffold rituals around shared signs. The widespread sale of "last dying speeches and confessions" pamphlets created common idioms and expectations for the drama of the executions.[44] Recurring forms and ceremonies drawn from religious narratives and regional experiences played to "generations highly literate in emblematic meaning."[45] The gallows itself stood as a symbol that a given place was a "city of law" and heralded the majesty of the authorities who enforced it.[46]

Symbolic authority was enhanced by judicial mercy and personal patronage. Judges wielded broad discretion in waiving death sentences. The intervention of well-heeled and influential men often saved the lives of convicted felons. The effect was to force those under threat of execution (disproportionately poor laboring folk) into the keeping of the propertied elite, who generally controlled the legal institutions.[47] In short, to enhance their power, authorities drew on common discourses about legal ritual, symbolic authority, and death produced by local histories of personal and cultural interaction.

Such common discourses were scarcer in Jamaica. Africans and their descendants, schooled to understand very different and disparate emblems of sacred power, replaced the "visually literate audience" educated in the sacred signs of English legal authority.[48] One can only assume that similar rites of terror read quite differently to a Jamaican audience. In Douglas Hay's conception, "Justice, Terror and Mercy," managed with delicacy and circumspection, tutored people to respect the authority of the elite in England.[49] The Jamaican plantocracy, which initially shared few cultural idioms with slaves and perhaps none with Africans, ruled largely through magisterial terror. Despite drawing on cultural resources from England, the planters had to adapt them to the Jamaican situation.

Unlike the English common folk, Africans and their children were cultural outsiders. When Edward Long evaluated Jamaican slave laws in 1774, he opined that the "Africans, first imported, were wild and savage in the extreme." In this he only echoed the language of the 1661 Barbados slave code, which condemned "negroes" as a "heathenish, brutish and an Uncertaine dangerous Kinde of people" who could not be adequately governed by English law.[50] Early in the life of the colony, lawmakers in Jamaica had drawn on the legal experience of both England and Barbados. By the eighteenth century, the legislators had adapted their slave codes to local conditions, chief among them the persistent threat of open rebellion.[51] The legal system was in place, but a belief system was not.

Rapid demographic turnover in the sugar islands meant that the implementers of social order could never count on people knowing or internalizing the rules. Moreover, the meanest enforcers of plantation discipline, the "petty whites," shifted about constantly, from plantation to plantation, from colony to colony, and from life to death.[52] "New-come buckra" regularly confronted "new negroes" of diverse origins. Jamaica was perpetually threatened by a fluctuating and restless enslaved population. As Long put it, expressing the characteristic negrophobia of the planter class, "their intractable and ferocious tempers naturally provoked their masters to rule them with a rod of iron."[53] Their masters also struggled to conjure an effective symbolic discourse to legitimate their rule, a discourse based on quite different principles and practices than those operating in England.

In 1664 the Jamaican Assembly established parallel courts specifically for the trial and sentencing of slaves. In her study of the slave courts in Saint Andrew's Parish (from 1746 to 1782), Diana Paton convincingly argues that judicial practice in Jamaica "emphasized the difference between slave and free, and valorized the slaveholder's private power" rather than "representing the supposed common discipline of all to a single rule of law, as did the contemporary English spectacle of trial and punishment."[54] Throughout most of the century, slave crimes were tried before informal and irregularly scheduled tribunals composed of three freeholders and two magistrates, who were usually prominent planters.[55] Until 1788 there was no jury, and even after the law provided for nine-man juries (paid two pounds each by the parish vestries to attend) and then twelve-man juries in 1816, there was never any opportunity for appeal.[56] At any rate, there was no time because, as planter-author William Beckford remarked, "a negro is often condemned in one hour, and receives execution in the next."[57] Rather than trying to envelop slaves in the idea of a unitary system of justice, slave courts demonstrated to the enslaved that, for most intents and purposes, their masters and the law were one and the same.

It followed that the punishments decreed by the court resembled those routinely meted out by slaveholders. The slave courts ordered corporal punishments much more frequently than did courts in England. The slave courts' punishments featured use of the whip, that enduring symbol of plantation authority. Mutilation for noncapital crimes—the chopping of ears, noses, feet— continued long after European courts had discontinued such punishments. For the capital crime of "assault on a white person" or "rebellious conspiracy," postmortem punishments were common. The frequency of mutilations and aggravated death sentences, reserved for traitors in eighteenth-century England, signaled the expansion and racialization of the concept of treason. Indeed, any "crime committed by slaves might be interpreted broadly as resistance to the social order" and thus defined as betrayal.[58] It was ironic: a population that had fewer reasons to be loyal to the ruling elite than had English common folk was more regularly defined as traitorous. Slave codes and courts in Jamaica operated on behalf of a public that was narrowly viewed in terms of the collective interests of slaveholders. Planters and merchants may have been convinced of the legitimacy of such a system, but they hoped only to terrify the enslaved.

The centerpiece of legal terror was exemplary punishment and execution. Yet unlike the regular, carnivalesque dramas of state authority in England, Jamaican executions consisted of sporadic, localized demonstrations. When groups of rebels were hanged or burned after failed uprisings, crowds certainly gathered, but at most times, in most parts of the island, public executions were used more to dramatize the power of masters than to construct a community governed by recognizably just laws and punishments. After a 1766 uprising in Westmoreland Parish, Thistlewood noted that "2 of the Rebel Negroes were tried yesterday and one of them burnt with a slow fire (alive) near the gallows at Savanna la Mar, yesterday evening; and the other, this morning at Cross-Path, where they killed Gardiner."[59] Killing the second rebel at the same place where the white man had been slain certainly represented an attempt to reclaim the place for white authority. After landing in Saint Ann's Bay, Jamaica, in 1779, Captain Thomas Lloyd of the Royal Navy saw a man and a woman "in irons, bound together, leading to trial, and attended by very few people." He was told that they had been runaway slaves. At the time Lloyd was on his way to dinner at a plantation in the interior, but when he returned in the evening to his ship, the *Hercules Victualler*, he inquired about the couple. An officer from another ship in the harbor who had been ashore described what had transpired: "They were both executed on the wharf, in the sight of the ship's company. . . . [T]he sister of the woman who was executed, bewailing her loss, the owner came to her, and said, Take care of yourself, you B——, you see how your sister is served. Upon enquiring of some of the Planters, the man had been hanged for running away, and the woman for secreting him."[60]

In the late eighteenth century, constables or deputy marshals were paid to attend trials and carry out executions. In 1794, for example, the Saint Thomas in the Vale Parish vestry paid deputy marshal George Coward two pounds for the trial and ten pounds for execution of Frank, a black horse thief. Coward collected one pound, twelve shillings for "the Hire of a Horse and Cart to convey Frank to his gallows at Bog Walk." The vestry also reimbursed him five pounds for providing a party of light dragoons with refreshment. The soldiers had been ordered to attend the execution.[61] The dragoons provided security as well as the imposing presence of the colonial state, but apparently they also comprised most of the audience, as did the sailors in Saint Ann's Bay who watched the execution of the enslaved couple. Perhaps the military officers and the slaveholders conspired not only to keep the enslaved in subjection but also to warn the long-suffering rank and file not to challenge military hierarchy. After all, the West India garrison had an extraordinarily high mortality rate and, according to historian Roger Norman Buckley, the soldiers "were driven to misconduct by the danger of their new lives."[62] To control them, officers were encouraged to "treat them all like slaves."[63] Common soldiers could watch such executions with conflicting feelings of pride and anxiety; they stood with slaves on the gallows but for the grace of colonial power.

The enslaved were often tried, sentenced, and executed in towns, but postmortem punishments usually took place on the plantations where slaves had committed crimes or hatched rebellions. Planters even preferred that the whole demonstration of authority occur locally. In 1731 landowners in the Carpenter's Mountains in Saint Elizabeth Parish sent a petition to the assembly requesting permission to set up a court nearby so that they would not have to travel the "near forty miles to give an account of their white people, slaves, and cattle, in order to be assessed." They also complained that the usual custom of trying slaves in town at Lacovia, at such an inconvenient distance, allowed many of them to escape "just punishment." The planters proposed that they be allowed to try slaves "nearest the place where any facts are committed." "The example of such a trial, and the punishment ordered by the justices and freeholders, in the neighborhood, must strike a greater terror in the other slaves than their bare hearing of its being acted at a distance, although, if condemned to death, the head may be ordered to be put up at the place where the fact was committed."[64] The petitioners hoped to harness the whole ritual of judicial majesty to local authority, thereby making their private land synonymous with public power. Whether they got their way is unknown. A century later, it seems clear that while slave trials took place in towns, the executions had been relocated to countryside crime scenes. In the wake of the 1831 Baptist War, Methodist ministers Thomas Murray and Henry Bleby watched as thirteen convicted rebels were taken from the town of Lucea into the Hanover Parish countryside for execution.[65] In any case, the Carpenter's Mountain planters already possessed the ability to deploy what was perhaps their most fearsome token of authority: the relics that haunted space.

Paton has illuminated the "detailed and finely calibrated language" of the sentences involving mutilation in the Saint Andrew Parish slave court records. Not only was the court specific about which body parts would be removed at what time from each individual criminal, it often ordered that the severed pieces, especially ears, be nailed to significant landmarks. For example, magistrates ordered that ears be nailed to the gallows, to watch hut gates, or, quite often, to great trees.[66] Jamaican authorities employed a "symbolics of mutilation," trying to extend to Afro-Jamaicans the meanings that such punishments had carried in Great Britain a century earlier. They also innovated. The court often ordered lashings to occur beneath large silk cotton trees and body parts to be nailed to the trees. Blacks in Jamaica reportedly believed that the spirits of the dead dwelled in and around such trees, sometimes by choice but more often because they had been caught and trapped by magical means. As Paton notes, "the belief in the symbolic importance of the cotton tree was something that Jamaican whites were aware of, tried to manipulate, [and] to some extent adopted."[67] In effect, they co-opted African understandings of spiritual capture.

The few contemporary descriptions of the African spiritual worlds were recorded by European visitors and missionaries whose biases led them to misrepresent African religious ideas and practices. Nevertheless, they commonly and consistently acknowledged the salience of the spirits of the dead in African social worldviews. In the mid-eighteenth century, the first British missionary to the Gold Coast, Thomas Thompson, noted that Akan-speaking Africans thought "the soul, after death, keeps haunt about the body, and is latent in, or near its repository."[68] Across seventeenth-century West-Central Africa, according to John Thornton, missionaries observed that "those who had died violent deaths, outcasts, or people who were not buried . . . formed a category of ghosts and other wicked spirits. . . . Religious precautions were taken to prevent them from doing harm."[69] But people could also harness and manipulate such spirits. Among Africans shipped to Jamaica from the Loango Coast, who made up the bulk of British captives from West-Central Africa, *minkisi*, or spiritual charms, could be used to effect one's will in the world. According to Robert Farris Thompson, "the *nkisi* [was] believed to live with an inner life of its own. The basis of that life was a captured soul. . . . The owner of the charm could direct the spirit in the object to accomplish mystically certain things for him."[70] By the late eighteenth century, whites certainly knew that such techniques of spiritual capture made strong impressions on slaves. Similarly, whites knew that blacks often feared and shunned the spirits of the dead. Matthew Lewis observed in 1816 that those enslaved on his property held that "the duppies of their adversaries are very alarming beings, equally powerful by day as by night, and who are *spiritually terrific*."[71] Lewis learned that an African man hospitalized with fits had been stricken by the specter of a recently deceased white man whom the African had formerly offended. He had received what Lewis called the "ghostly blow" when passing through a burial ground used exclusively for whites.[72]

Lewis's story highlights a curious congruence between the spiritual beliefs of the enslaved and the disciplinary techniques of the plantocracy. At Half-Way Tree in Saint Andrew, the old cotton tree that gave the spot its name and that commonly bore the bodies and relics of maimed and executed blacks lived next to a well populated (and potentially dangerous) church graveyard for prominent whites. The evidence that the slave courts intended to domesticate the dead in accordance with their understandings of African cosmologies is admittedly as suggestive as it is demonstrative. Yet the rituals of sentencing and punishment, taking place as they did in quick and irregularly scheduled trials before modest audiences, were no doubt less awesome to the enslaved than the lingering presence of body parts and mutilated corpses or, more precisely, the presence of the spirits attached to them. The unfortunate Mr. Dunbar's head driver, Matthew

Lewis learned, had been above suspicion until investigators searched his house. There, they found not only Dunbar's watch "but with it one of his ears, which the villain had carried away, from a negro belief that, as long as the murderer possesses one of the ears of his victim, he will never be haunted by his spectre."[73] The necromancy of the planter class was more impressive than its law.

The way that Africans and their descendants in Jamaica harnessed the dead to political authority was not fully apparent to the plantocracy until after Tacky's Rebellion in 1760. Long before that time, however, Africans brought magical talismans and medicines with them when they crossed the Atlantic and tried to use them against their captors. Cruising off the Windward Coast of Africa in 1751 aboard the *Duke of Argyle*, Captain John Newton discovered that nearly twenty of the captured Africans below decks had broken their chains.[74] The slavers barely averted a rebellion, but days later the Africans tried another tactic: "In the afternoon we were alarmed with a report that some of the men slaves had found means to poyson the water in the scuttle casks upon deck," Newton recorded in his journal, "but upon enquiry found they had only conveyed some of their country fetishes, as they call them, or talismans into one of them, which they had the credulity to suppose must inevitably kill all who drank of it." Relieved, Newton nervously congratulated himself on his own "superior" spirituality: "if it please God thay make no worse attempts than to charm us to death, they will not much harm us, but it shews their intentions are not wanting."[75] Earlier in the century, some Englishmen showed a greater concern about the efficacy of African spiritual power. Thomas Walduck, an army officer stationed at Barbados in the early 1700s, wrote that "white men, overseers of plantations and masters have been forced to leave this island by being bewitched by the Negroes."[76] Yet most Jamaican planters seemed as unconcerned as Newton.

When they wrote in diaries or in published accounts, whites in Jamaica often referred casually to the magical practices of the enslaved. Before 1760, whites considered these practices to be a generally harmless and bizarre feature of slave life, not unlike witchcraft and conjuring in Europe. In the spring of 1753, Thistlewood watched as Guy, from the nearby Salt River Plantation, "acted his Obia, &c. with singing, dancing, &c. odd enough"—odd, but not serious.[77] Early the next year, Thistlewood noted with amusement that Jinney Quashe, a well-known obeah man, was "pretending to pull bones, &c. out of several of our Negroes for which they was to give him money." Somehow, Jinney Quashe's clients discovered that he was a fraud, and "they chased him out of the estate, frightened enough." The event reminded Thistlewood of a scene he had witnessed in Yorkshire when a noted conjurer from Wakefield, Black Lambert, was chased out of the town of Acworth.[78] Such innocent and innocuous comparisons ended a few years later when an islandwide slave conspiracy in Jamaica brought the alarming aspects of obeah to the forefront of planter concerns.

Obeah (obia) was the catchall term used to describe a complex of shamanistic practices derived from different parts of Africa and conducted by ritual specialists working largely outside formal institutions.[79] Obeah practitioners operated as herbalists and wise folk, tending to physical, social, and spiritual needs, though whites generally mischaracterized obeah as simple witchcraft, failing to see its larger role in social and spiritual healing and protection.[80] According to the most recent research on the provenance of obeah, the term probably originated among Ibo-speaking peoples transported from the Bight of Biafra to the West Indies as slaves.[81] There, obeah's closest semantic and phonological analogue, *dbia*, refers to an adept, or master of knowledge and wisdom. Thus, the anglophone Caribbean term *obeah man* probably referred in a similar way to a "master of knowledge and wisdom" in the sacred arts.[82] Through most of the eighteenth century, obeah was mastered almost exclusively by Africans. Nevertheless, one of the earliest reports on Jamaican obeah to the House of Commons claimed that the "Negroes in general, whether Africans or Creoles, revere, consult, and abhor them; to these Oracles they resort, and with the most implicit Faith, upon all Occasions, whether for the cure of Disorders, the obtaining of Revenge for Injuries or Insults, the conciliating of Favour, the Discovery and Punishment of the Thief or the Adulterer, and the Prediction of Future Events."[83]

While the term may have come from the Ibo language, the practice of obeah combined elements from the sacred traditions and medical knowledge of Africans seized from several areas of the continent. For example, many obeah men in Jamaica were Africans from the Gold Coast. Moreover, the term *obeah* also referred to the charms that carried spiritual power and could be placed strategically around the individual who was to be cursed or protected. These were made up of a variety of materials thought to have sacred significance, including blood, feathers, parrot's beaks, animal teeth, broken glass, eggshells, and grave dirt.[84] The materials used in obeah evoke Robert Farris Thompson's description of the Kongo *minkisi* in West-Central Africa. Believers held that *minkisi* worked through "two basic classes of medicine within the charm, *spirit-embedding medicine* (earths, often from a grave site, for cemetery earth is considered at one with the spirit of the dead), and *spirit-admonishing objects* (seeds, claws, miniature knives, stones, crystals, and so forth)."[85]

Capturing souls, or "shadow catching," was one skill that obeah practitioners were thought to possess long after enslaved Africans stopped arriving in Jamaica. In 1826 Alexander Barclay claimed to have been present at the trial of a "notorious obeah-man, driver on an estate in the parish of St. David." One of the witnesses against the driver was another man enslaved on the same plantation. When asked if he knew the accused to be an obeah man, the witness replied, "Ees, massa, shadow-catcher, true. . . . Him ha coffin, (a little coffin produced) him set for catch dem shadow." The court asked for further clarification and the witness complied: "When him set obeah for [somebody], him catch dem shadow and dem go dead."[86]

The similarities between the shadow-catching obeah man and the practices described by Thompson are striking but do not point to the conclusion that obeah was a "Kongo" rather than "Ibo" practice. Indeed, C. G. A Oldendorp recorded in the 1770s that "the Amina," from the Gold Coast, used the same term for "soul" as for "shadow."[87] The practices described by the term *obeah* clearly changed with the arrival of new groups of Africans. Early commentators maintained that only Africans practiced obeah, but by the time the transatlantic slave trade was abolished in 1807, enslaved persons of creole birth had taken up the practice.[88] Sources may never permit us to track all the ways in which the Afro-Jamaican magical practices described by the term *obeah* responded to changes in immigration patterns and political-economic developments. However, it is probably safe to agree with Nigel Bolland that obeah took on a "whole new meaning in the societies of the Caribbean, a meaning derived from the power structures, the social oppositions, in these societies."[89]

In Jamaica, obeah was centrally concerned with spirits, with haunting and spiritual cure.[90] For example, in 1799 one Mr. Graham, a free black man and a Christian, reportedly sought out an obeah man because "his first Wife, who was dead, came into his ground and troubled him." The obeah man prepared "Guinea Pepper and red head Roots," which Graham was to put above his door to drive away the spirit of his former wife. Graham paid the obeah man a rooster and a dollar for his services.[91] If obeah also often acted broadly as a counterhegemonic practice and ideology, as anthropologist Mindie Lazarus-Black maintains, it was most authoritative when dealing with the dead.[92] Rampant death made such a technology of the spirit critical at all times, but as masters recruited dead bodies and parts of bodies to announce their power, the political significance of obeah for the enslaved became most pronounced.

The enslaved used obeah to treat disease, to manipulate human behavior and the spirits of the dead, and to enhance the political authority of ritual specialists and their patrons. During the 1770s, Edward Long described obeah as "a sort of witchcraft of most extensive influence. . . . [T]he authority which such of their old men as had the reputation of wizards, or Obeah-men, possessed over [slaves], was sometimes very successfully employed in keeping them in subordination to their chiefs."[93] In fact, Long was looking back to 1760, trying to explain the role of such "wizards" in the most extensive slave revolt in the eighteenth-century British Caribbean.

Tacky's Revolt, as it was later called, threatened British control of Jamaica for the first time since the Maroon Wars of the 1730s.[94] Taking advantage of Britain's Seven Years' War against France and Spain, more than a thousand enslaved blacks revolted in the first phase of the uprising, which began on Easter, April 7, 1760, and continued until October of the next year. Over that time, rebels killed sixty whites and destroyed thousands of pounds worth of property. Some estimates put the number of blacks involved at 30,000 out of a total enslaved population of less than 150,000.[95] During the revolt and the repression that followed, more than 500 black men and women were killed in battle, executed, or committed suicide, and another 500 were transported from the island for life. "Whether we consider the extent and secrecy of its plan, the multitude of the conspirators, and the difficulty of opposing its eruptions in such a variety of places at once," wrote Long in his 1774 *History of Jamaica*, Tacky's Revolt was "more formidable than any hitherto known in the West Indies." Tacky, an enslaved African from the Gold Coast, had planned and instigated the uprising with obeah practitioners as his closest counselors. He and his coconspirators called on the shamans to use their charms to protect the rebels from bullets and to administer binding loyalty oaths. The oaths required the plotters to consume a concoction made up of blood, rum, and grave dirt, which they believed to have sacred significance.[96] The rebellion ultimately failed, but its aftermath showed direct competition between different forms of sacred authority in stark relief.

In the wave of executions that followed the rebellion, none were more impressive than those of the obeah men. Revealingly, colonial authorities felt that they needed to resort to more awesome displays than they normally projected. In a report to the House of Commons, one witness described the scene: "At the place of execution he bid defiance to the Executioner, telling him that it was not in the Power of the White People to kill him; and the Negro Spectators were astonished when they saw him expire. On the other Obeah-men, various Experiments were made with Electrical Machines and Magic Lanthorns, which produced very little Effect; except on one who, after receiving many severe Shocks, acknowledged his Master's Obeah exceeded his own."[97] The government of Jamaica hoped to overawe the shamans and their adherents with the latest technologies, but most of the displays were less impressive than desired. Perhaps some slaves had witnessed them before as entertainments. In Antigua, experimenters put on exhibitions of "the newly-discovered electric fire" as early as 1753. In one of them, a "Flash of Lightning [was] made to strike a small House, and dart towards a little Lady sitting on a Chair, who will, notwithstanding, be preserved from being hurt; whilst the Image of a Negro standing by, and seeming to be further out of Danger, will be remarkably affected by it."[98] There is every reason to believe that the more wealthy and worldly masters of Jamaica were treated to similar displays of scientific wizardry.[99] In any case, the amusing sight of lightning striking the "image of a Negro" had progressed by 1760 to the "severe" and no doubt excruciating electric shocks given to Tacky's obeah men.[100] Jamaican masters could not abide sources of authority they did not wholly control. After Tacky's Revolt, Jamaican law punished by death, imprisonment, or exile "any Negro who shall pretend to any Supernatural Power."[101] The aggressive prosecution of obeah practitioners remained a preeminent concern in the slave court trials of the late eighteenth and early nineteenth centuries.

Whites both believed and doubted the efficacy of obeah. They continued to regard it as superstition, but of a peculiarly threatening kind. Because black men and women in Jamaica believed in the power of obeah, they could fall into despair and die if they thought they had been bewitched. Obeah practitioners were also expert poisoners and could, when they chose, settle disputes by murder. More importantly from the standpoint of the Jamaican plantocracy, obeah could motivate the enslaved to direct political action. In 1784 Judge John Grant rejected a master's appeal to stop the transportation of a convicted obeah man. "If granted in this instance," warned the judge, "application with equal reason might be made, while a rebellion might be raging throughout the country." The judge clearly worried about obeah's political potential, but in his notes on the case he defined obeah as the "pretended exercise of witchcraft or sorcery, a crime which the new negroes bring with them from Africa, and which does infinite mischief among their fellow slaves."[102] Such ambivalence toward obeah characterized the colonial state's persecution of its practitioners right through to the end of slavery and beyond. As long as people believed in its power, governing authorities would have to punish its practice. The consolidated Jamaica slave act passed in 1823 clarified the real issue at stake: "Obeah practised with intention to excite rebellion, or endangering the life or health of a slave, shall be punished at the discretion of the court."[103] Thus, the ban on obeah was a ban on alternative authority and social power.

The operation of obeah in Jamaican society is difficult to glean. As a highly illicit activity, obeah was almost always practiced in secret, and the whites who left written descriptions probably knew very little about it.[104] The surviving records of obeah trials, however, provide opportunities to ask fundamental questions about obeah's place in the social relations of slavery.[105] The Public Record Office in London possesses a nearly complete record of Jamaica slave trial returns for the period 1814–18. In these years, the colonial government prosecuted eighty-five obeah cases, fifty-one of which resulted in convictions. R. R. Madden claimed that by the 1830s, obeah practitioners were generally old women. Yet less than two decades before Madden's sojourn on the island, only ten of the eighty-three defendants for whom gender can be determined were women.[106] Moreover, women were acquitted of obeah charges in six of the ten cases. For men, the trend was reversed: they were found guilty 62 percent of the time. Unlike earlier witch trials in Europe and North America, neither women's autonomy nor the intersection between the supernatural and the sexual seem to have been a significant concern, at least not for the colonial government.[107]

The most interesting question and puzzling problem presented by the returns concerns the ages of the accused and convicted. Contemporary reports and subsequent scholarship have stressed that persons most commonly accused of practicing obeah were aged Africans. "The oldest and most crafty are those who usually attract the greatest Devotion and Confidence," Jamaica agent Stephen Fuller reported to the House of Commons during the 1770s, "those whose hoary heads" and a "peculiarly harsh and diabolic" appearance "qualified them for successful Imposition upon the weak and credulous."[108] Following Fuller, sociologist Orlando Patterson maintains that "people accused of obeah were in the great majority of cases poor, abused, uncared for, often sick with yaws, and isolated from other slaves. They were also usually old people or Africans."[109] Similarly, Robert Dirks notes "the tendency for witch hunters to persecute only outcasts or anyone alienated from the mainstream" for the whole of the late-eighteenth- and early-nineteenth-century British West Indies.[110] Yet the obeah trial returns hint at other interpretations.

When the Jamaica slave courts condemned the guilty to death or transportation, the courts were required to pay compensation to owners.[111] Specific values were partly determined by the loss of productive labor masters would suffer and so corresponded to age, health, and ability to work. The trial returns for 1814–18 record the appraised value for thirteen convicted obeah practitioners, eleven men and two women.[112] Unfortunately, the returns did not always record the amounts paid out, so the sample is too small to permit the drawing of firm conclusions.[113] Nevertheless, the appraised values challenge the assumption that old and outcast slaves were the primary targets of the witch hunts. The compensation scale progressed from fifteen to one hundred Jamaican pounds. The average value for the condemned men and women was seventy-one pounds but was seventy-five pounds for the two women alone. At the upper limit, four men were valued at one hundred pounds, while only one clearly "superannuated" man was valued at the minimum of fifteen pounds. Three people were valued between seventy-five and eighty pounds, while only one was valued at forty pounds, the second-smallest value. Rather than most zealously pursuing the old and afflicted, the slave regime seems to have had the most success prosecuting vigorous men and women—also the most likely to wield material and social power.

Of course, these findings only raise further questions about the witch hunts. Do the compensations only reflect the influence of planters trying to get maximum value for their confiscated property? Did the highest values go to the most influential planters? Perhaps older obeah practitioners were craftier and harder

TABLE 1

Obeah Cases by Gender (Jamaica, 1814–1818)

	Total Cases	Acquittals	Convictions	% of Total
All Cases	85	34	51	
Men	73	28	45	85.9
Women	10	4	6	11.8
Gender Unknown	2	—	2	2.4

Source: Public Record Office, Colonial Office 137/147.

TABLE 2

Obeah Cases by Sentence (Jamaica, 1814–1818)

	Men	Women	Gender Unknown	Total	% of Total
All Cases	73	10	2	85	
Acquittals	28	6	—	34	40
Convictions	45	4	2	51	60
					% of Convictions
Executions	8	1	—	9	18
Transportations	33	3	2	38	75
Workhouse	4	0	—	4	8

Source: Public Record Office, Colonial Office 137/147

to convict. Maybe the younger practitioners were more prominent among the enslaved (and therefore more threatening), more public, and so more urgently prosecuted. After all, it should not be a surprise to discover that the plantocracy went after potential rebels who combined social and spiritual power more aggressively than it pursued social outcasts. If slaves identified such outcasts as the cause of misfortune, slaveholders blamed their troubles on enslaved men and women of influence.

Most of these queries and possibilities highlight the connection between obeah and other forms of social power in slave society. For example, slave drivers were also at times shamans, witches, and adjudicators. Plantation attorneys and overseers commanded the right to appoint drivers and headmen to subdue the enslaved. Nearly always men, these drivers acted as plantation foremen, enforcing labor discipline and implementing the work regime. As such, they received special privileges and comforts from their masters. They had more freedom of movement around and between the plantations; they lived in larger houses or cabins; they were allotted more land for cultivating provisions and more food from plantation stores; some were even allowed to carry guns for hunting and policing, a clear violation of Jamaican slave codes.[114] Though the drivers ultimately served at their masters' pleasure, they also had to find convincing ways to exert their authority over their fellow slaves. As historian Robert Paquette has observed, drivers "often wore several hats, whether as religious authorities or artisans," and they held a preeminent status as communicators of useful knowledge across distance and social class.[115]

To enhance their eminence, drivers presided over unsanctioned judiciaries. John Stewart was one of the few whites in Jamaica to witness an independent court set up and maintained by and for the enslaved. "On many estates," he observed, "the headmen erect themselves into a sort of bench of justice, which sits and decides, privately, and without the knowledge of whites, on all disputes and complaints of their fellow slaves. The sentences of this court are frequently severe. . . . [T]hey consist in pecuniary fines, which often exceed the means of the party." Quite often, the means of determining guilt or innocence involved trial by ordeal, or spiritual divination via the techniques of obeah.[116] But illicit court was just one space where obeah united sacred and social power. In the first decades of the nineteenth century, drivers also recommended itinerant Christian ministers to white authority. Testifying before the House of Lords in 1832, planter William Shand recollected "a chief man upon an estate coming to me (on Norris Estate, in the parish of St. David's); he applied for permission [to preach] for a man who was a stranger to me, and I was not inclined to think favourably of his being allowed to come there and read prayers to the negroes." As it turned out, one shaman was vouching for another. Three months later, "the negroes charged this Driver with practising obeah." Shand recalled that his slaves claimed to have suffered great injuries by the driver's sorcery "and that he had been the occasion of the loss of many children on the estate." The driver apparently had also bragged that he had caused "the death of the former manager of that estate, Mr. Grant." On the evidence of the slaves, the man was tried, convicted, and executed.[117]

Inevitably, many enslaved headmen in Jamaica used their authority for personal and antisocial ends. At least many slaves assumed they did. On Trouthall Estate in 1809, Johana, an enslaved woman who had lost three children to "putrid sore throats" in quick succession, accused the second driver, Napier, with practicing obeah. Napier had been pursuing Johana's attention. She spurned him, and now she knew Napier was conjuring his revenge.[118] Without proof that could lead to a conviction in court, the plantation managers decided only to confine Napier for several months and then send him back to work.[119] Perhaps Johana suspected Napier had achieved his station as driver through occult means. Such a belief would be consistent with the conclusions of leading anthropologists and historians of African witchcraft. As historian Ralph Austen has noted, "The African conception of the witch is tied to various forms of belief in a world where the apparent production of new wealth depends upon appropriating the scarce reproductive resources of others while collaborating with an arbitrary and destructive external power."[120] Witchcraft accusations have also functioned as a leveling discourse that protected community harmony from prolific accumulators of wealth.[121] As Orlando Patterson has found, "Obeah accusations were also made against people who either threatened to be too successful or were the source of much anxiety."[122]

People who used obeah for selfish ends, especially drivers who collaborated with arbitrary and destructive white power, probably drew more frequent witchcraft accusations from the enslaved than did common folk. As a potential threat to enslaved communal equilibrium, on the one hand, and as a subversive and potentially insurrectionary force, on the other, Jamaican obeah exemplifies Peter Geschiere's supple description of witchcraft as both "a resource for the powerful and also a weapon for weak against new inequalities."[123] For obeah certainly emboldened the enslaved to resist the supremacy of their masters and allowed blacks more generally to believe that they could challenge whites.[124]

Describing the case of Plato, a notorious outlaw in Westmoreland Parish, Matthew Lewis remarked in his typically droll manner that "besides his acknowledged courage, he was a professor of Obi, and had threatened that whoever dared to lay a finger upon him should suffer spiritual torments, as well as be physically shot through the head."[125] In this case, the spiritual threat was perhaps more effective than the material. Plato was captured, tried, and executed, but he

> died most heroically; kept up the terrors of his imposture to his last moment; told the magistrates, who condemned him, that his death should be revenged by a storm, which would lay waste the whole island, that year; and, when his negro gaoler was binding him to the stake at which he was destined to suffer, he assured him that he should not live long to triumph in his death, for that he had taken good care to Obeah him before quitting the prison. It certainly did happen, strangely enough, that, before the year was over, the most violent storm took place ever known in Jamaica; and as to the gaoler, his imagination was so forcibly struck by the threats of the dying man, that, although every care was taken of him, the power of medicine exhausted, and even a voyage to America undertaken, in hopes that a change of scene might change the course of his ideas, still, from the moment of Plato's death, he gradually pined and withered away, and finally expired before the completion of the twelvemonth.[126]

In a world where violent storms were always on their way and where mortal sickness was always on the hunt for a weakened immune system, events often confirmed the awe of sacred authority.

As long as the spiritual power of obeah was credible, black men and women, free and enslaved, wielded it to combat the worldly power of whites. In a report to his cadre back home, John Shipman, the Kingston district chairman for the Wesleyan Methodist Missionary Society, described a fascinating encounter between an overseer and a free black man armed with an obeah charm.[127] One night about midnight, the overseer heard someone digging not far from his house. When he looked out the window, he saw a man, whom he recognized, digging a hole and "depositing something which he knew to be an Obiah-Spell."[128] The overseer said nothing at the time, but the next morning "he sent for the person who had done it and opened the hole and took out the deposit (intimating that something extraordinary had informed him of it) and found it to consist of a Bottle filled, I believe, with rain water, and some feathers and cat's teeth."[129] As Shipman put it, "This Gentleman got to understand that it was intended to remove him from office, by death of course."[130] The overseer harangued the man, "informing him that he could *Hang* him for what he had done," but then let him go, "charging him to escape to America or some other place."[131]

Though the missionaries who arrived in Jamaica in the latter decades of the eighteenth century emphasized the spiritual harm caused by "communication with evil spirits" and with "the Devil" (similar to the concerns of prosecutors in seventeenth-century European and American witchcraft trials), Jamaica's colonial government worried more about the supernatural practices that undercut the plantocracy's ability to harness the dead to its own authority. Because obeah drew its gravest authority from its relationship to spirits and death, the prohibition amounted to a strategy to limit the sacred authority the enslaved derived from the spirits of the dead while maximizing the power of the colonial government to use the dead as an element of social control. In this sense, power in Jamaican slave society operated through various species of necromancy that would influence the course of social events by invoking, animating, or placating the dead.

Various forms of sacred authority were put to different and often opposing purposes even as considerable cultural borrowing and appropriation occurred between slaveholders and the enslaved. Each appropriated from the other symbolic resources that carried social and spiritual power. The use of powerful objects, cultural categories, and symbols did not necessarily correspond to their distinct and original uses in Africa or Europe, even when they were put to distinct and irreconcilable purposes by blacks and whites. Slaves and their overlords wielded intersecting and competing forms of authority that revolved around relations with the dead.

Authority nearly always has a transcendent—that is, sacred—dimension.[132]

The politics of slavery in Jamaica provides an exemplary case in point. The Jamaican plantocracy tried to place its authority above human contestation by alternately appropriating and censuring the spiritual authority of the enslaved. Indeed, masters put what they considered to be distinctly "African" divining techniques into practice for their own benefit. In the first published description of a grave-dirt oath-taking ceremony in 1740, Charles Leslie claimed that Africans in Jamaica administered such oaths at the behest of their masters.

> When any Thing about a Plantation is missing, they have a solemn Kind of Oath which the oldest Negroe always administers, and which by them is accounted so sacred, that except [when] they have the express Command of their Master or Overseer, they never go about it, and then they go very solemnly to Work. They range themselves in that Spot of Ground which is appropriate for the Negroe's Burying-place, and one of them opens a Grave. He who acts the Priest take a little of the Earth, and puts into every one of their Mouths; they tell, that if any has been guilty, their Belly swells and occasions their Death.[133]

Whites in other Caribbean slave societies also held African supernatural power in high regard. Sometimes they tried to employ it for their personal benefit, and sometimes they attempted to co-opt it to extend authority over the enslaved.[134] In Jamaican slave society, the cultural forms that sacred authority took underwent a continual process of convergence and redefinition as they resonated with the practical demands of domination on the one side and of survival struggles within slavery on the other. Colonial masters engaged African spirituality, while black shamans wielded power over material circumstances. In effect, African tradition and European modernity, supernatural beliefs and the mechanisms of the colonial state, became inextricably intertwined.[135] In practice, neither masters nor the enslaved maintained a distinction between material and spiritual power. As a political phenomenon, colonial necromancy thus forces our attention to strategies for manipulating cultural practices in a world where the dead constituted an active social presence and where domination, dissent, and the threat of incredible violence plagued every interaction.

Everyone dies. Consequently, the dead have the ability to hold everyone's attention, acting as a significant fulcrum for political activity in the process. By yoking the dead to their claims to authority, contenders for power in Jamaican slave society could fasten their efforts to powerfully affecting spiritual idioms. Relations with death and the dead made the transcendent available for use in worldly conflicts, wrestling awesome questions of spiritual existence into temporal, place-bound social struggles. The supernatural imagination was the wellspring of a spiritual authority that drew its economic, social, and political efficacy from the haunted and terrifying landscape of Jamaican slavery. Perhaps the most important aspect of the Jamaican social context was the awareness that the dead populated the world and could be conscripted for political use.

NOTES

A version of this article first appeared in *Slavery and Abolition* 24, no. 1 (2003): 24–53 and is reproduced with the permission of Taylor and Francis Group Ltd. (http://www .tandf.co.uk).

The author wishes to thank Edward E. Baptist, Herman L. Bennett, Stephanie Camp, and the participants in the 2003 conference on New Directions in the Study of the Atlantic: Slavery, Continuing Conversations, held at Rutgers University, for lively and engaged discussion about the past, present, and future of our field. The author is also grateful to David Barry Gaspar, Jerome S. Handler, Walter Johnson, Roderick McDonald, Joseph C. Miller, Richard Price, Subir Sinha, Ajantha Subramanian, Mark L. Thompson, the fellows and participants of the 2001–2 McNeil Center for Early American Studies Seminar, the members and attendees of the panel on Political Histories of Death in the Black Diaspora at the 2002 Organization of American Historians conference, the participants in the 2003 Black Atlantic workshop of the Charles Warren Center Atlantic History Seminar, the Department of African and Afro-American Studies and the Program in Latin American Studies at Brandeis University, and the Departments of History at Washington University, Northwestern University, Florida International University, and Harvard University, as well as an anonymous reviewer for *Slavery and Abolition* for questions, comments, and suggestions regarding earlier drafts of this article.

1. Bryan Edwards, *The History, Civil and Commercial, of the British Colonies in the West Indies* (London, 1801), 3:36.

2. As contemporary Philadelphia reformer Benjamin Rush knew, "The punishments of wicked men, in the world of spirits, are invisible; we have no knowledge of their reality, nature, degrees, or duration, but what was revealed to us near eighteen hundred years ago; and yet governments owe their stability, chiefly, to that morality, which the terror of these invisible, remote, and indefinite punishments, excites in the human mind" ("An Enquiry into the Effects of Public Punishments upon Criminals and upon Society," in *A Plan for the Punishment of Crime: Two Essays* [1787; Philadelphia, 1954], 16).

3. Katherine Verdery, *The Political Lives of Dead Bodies: Reburial and Postsocialist Change* (New York, 1999), 27.

4. Ibid., 27–28.

5. For a provocative theorization of such practices, see Achille Mbembe, "Necropolitics," *Public Culture* 15 (Winter 2003): 11–40.

6. As surrealist ethnographer Michael Taussig has explained in another colonial context, "The colonized space of death has a colonizing function, maintaining the hegemony or cultural stability of norms and desires that facilitate the way the rulers ruled in the land of the living. Yet the space of death is notoriously conflict-ridden and contradictory; a privileged domain of metamorphosis, the space par excellence for uncertainty and terror to stun permanently, yet also revive and empower with new life" (*Colonialism, Shamanism, and the Wild Man: A Study in Terror and Healing* [Chicago, 1987], 374). To explore similar themes in another Caribbean context, see Joan Dayan, *Haiti, History, and the Gods* (Berkeley, 1995); see also Douglas R. Egerton, "A Peculiar Mark of Infamy: Dismemberment, Burial, and Rebelliousness in Slave Societies," in *Mortal Remains: Death in Early America*, ed. Nancy Isenberg and Andrew Burstein (Philadelphia, 2003), 149–60;

Kathryn Joy McKnight, "Confronted Rituals: Spanish Colonial and Angolan 'Maroon' Executions in Cartagena de Indias (1634)," *Journal of Colonialism and Colonial History* 5 (Winter 2004): n.p.; Kenneth S. Greenberg, "Name, Face, Body," in *Nat Turner: A Slave Rebellion in History and Memory*, ed. Kenneth S. Greenberg (New York, 2003), 3–23.

7. Testimony of Henry Coor, February 16, 1791, in *House of Commons Sessional Papers of the Eighteenth Century*, ed. Sheila Lambert (Wilmington, 1975), 82:74.

8. Testimony of Dr. Harrison, February 12, 1791, in *House of Commons Sessional Papers*, ed. Lambert, 82:50.

9. Ibid.

10. Testimony of William Fitzmaurice, March 9, 1791, in ibid., 231: "From the observation I have made, three men die to one woman; this I know from experience; the Negro men take everything unpleasant to heart, and often have recourse to different species of suicide; the women have many protections which the men have not."

11. Ibid., 230.

12. Testimony of Thomas Clappeson, March 8, 1791, in ibid., 213; see also other examples in Lorna McDaniel, "The Flying Africans," *New West Indian Guide* 64, nos. 1–2 (1990): esp. 32–33; William D. Piersen, "White Cannibals, Black Martyrs: Fear, Depression, and Religious Faith as Causes of Suicide among New Slaves," *Journal of Negro History* 62 (April 1977): 151, 154–55; Michael Gomez, *Exchanging Our Country Marks: The Transformation of African Identities in the Colonial and Antebellum South* (Chapel Hill, 1998), 114–34; Philip Morgan, *Slave Counterpoint: Black Culture in the Eighteenth-Century Chesapeake and Lowcountry* (Chapel Hill, 1998), 641–42.

13. Testimony of Mark Cook, March 5, 1791, in *House of Commons Sessional Papers*, ed. Lambert, 82:197.

14. The query may seem ridiculous in hindsight, but the committee asked this question while proslavery ideologues and apologists were commonly arguing that black slaves preferred living under the English "rule of law" to living under the "arbitrary and absolute" authority of African rulers; see, for example, the testimony of John Wedderburn, twenty-seven years a planter in Jamaica: "In their own country the stronger party, who are the party of most consequence, often do as they think proper to the weaker party, whether it is attended by justice or not" (March 19, 1790, in *House of Commons Sessional Papers*, ed. Lambert, 72:79; see also Bryan Edwards, *History of the British West Indies* [London, 1819], 2:81–83).

15. Testimony of Baker Davidson, February 25, 1791, in *House of Commons Sessional Papers*, ed. Lambert, 82:185.

16. Richard Ligon, *A True and Exact History of the Island of Barbadoes, 1647–1650* (1657; London, 1976), 17.

17. Ibid.

18. C. G. A. Oldendorp, *History of the Mission of the Evangelical Brethren on the Caribbean Islands of St. Thomas, St. Croix, and St. John*, ed. Johann Jakob Bossard, English edition and translation by Arnold R. Highfield and Vladimir Barac (1770; Ann Arbor, 1987), 246.

19. Moreau de St. Mery cited in Piersen, "White Cannibals, Black Martyrs," 154; see also Dayan, *Haiti, History, and the Gods*, 247–48.

20. Piersen, "White Cannibals, Black Martyrs," 154; Gwendolyn Midlo Hall, *Social Control in Slave Plantation Societies: A Comparison of St. Domingue and Cuba* (Baton Rouge, 1971), 21.

21. Anonymous, *The Importance of Jamaica to Great Britain Consider'd* (London, 1740), cited in Orlando Patterson, *Sociology of Slavery: An Analysis of the Origins, Development, and Structure of Negro Slave Society in Jamaica* (Rutherford, 1969), 196.

22. John Venn to Bishop Sherlock, June 15, 1751, Fulham Papers, Lambeth Palace Library, vol. 18, Jamaica, 1740–undated, p. 47.

23. John Stewart, *A View of the Past and Present State of the Island of Jamaica, with Remarks on the Moral and Physical Condition of the Slaves, and on the Abolition of Slavery in the Colonies* (Edinburgh, 1823), 281. Following the abolition of Britain's transatlantic slave trade in 1807 and the consequent growth of the creole population, the belief of a return to Africa had diminished currency.

24. Fear of postmortem mutilation terrorized common Londoners as much or more than the gallows itself; see Peter Linebaugh, *The London Hanged: Crime and Civil Society in the Eighteenth Century* (London, 2003); Peter Linebaugh, "The Tyburn Riots against the Surgeons," in *Albion's Fatal Tree: Crime and Society in Eighteenth-Century England*, ed. Douglas Hay, Peter Linebaugh, John G. Rule, E. P. Thompson, and Cal Winslow (New York, 1975); Frank McLynn, *Crime and Punishment in Eighteenth-Century England* (New York, 1989), 229. In England, before the eighteenth century, suicide was widely thought to be caused by diabolic possession directly attributed to Satan and his demons. This immediate concern with evil forces yielded to anxieties about the preservation of secular and divine authority. By the eighteenth century, according to McLynn, the self-murderer was abominable because "he offended against the king, whose interests dictated the preservation of his own subjects," and because "he blasphemed against the law of God," usurping the Lord's authority over life and death. "The reign of George III saw the decisive abandonment of the belief that suicide was diabolically inspired. Put simply, the eighteenth century saw the secularization of the crime of suicide" (*Crime and Punishment*, 50, 54). For Anglo-Atlantic slaveholders, however, it seems clear that suicide was conceived very early as a secular crime that ought to be deterred with spiritual punishments.

25. Piersen, "White Cannibals, Black Martyrs," 154–55; see also Robin Law, " 'My Head Belongs to the King': On the Political and Ritual Significance of Decapitation in Precolonial Dahomey," *Journal of African History* 30 (1989): 399–415; Margaret Priestly, "Letters of Philip Quaque," in *Africa Remembered: Narratives by West Africans from the Era of the Slave Trade*, ed. Philip D. Curtin (Madison, 1967), 128–29; diary of Antera Duke, a slave-trading chief in the eighteenth-century Bight of Biafra, in *Efik Traders of Old Calabar*, ed. Daryll C. Forde (New York, 1956), 27–65.

26. For the impact of spectacular punishment on performances of self in antebellum North American slavery, see Saidiya Hartman, *Scenes of Subjection: Terror, Slavery, and Self-Making in Nineteenth-Century America* (New York, 1997).

27. Hans Sloane, *A Voyage to the Islands Madera, Barbados, Nieves, S. Christophers, and Jamaica* (London, 1707–25), 1:lvii.

28. Thomas Thistlewood diary, May 18, 1750, quoted in Michael Craton, *Testing the Chains: Resistance to Slavery in the British West Indies* (Ithaca, 1982), 39.

29. Thistlewood diary, October 2, 1750, quoted in ibid., 39.

30. Thistlewood diary, October 9, 1752, quoted in Douglas Hall, *In Miserable Slavery: Thomas Thistlewood in Jamaica, 1750–86* (London, 1989), 30.

31. Maria Nugent, *Lady Nugent's Journal of Her Residence in Jamaica from 1801 to 1805*, ed. Philip Wright (Kingston, 1966), 165. The man was one of two executed for "rebellious conspiracy."

32. Matthew Gregory Lewis, *Journal of a West India Proprietor Kept during a Residence in the Island of Jamaica* (London, 1834), 181–82. Before the plantocracy made terrifying examples of Dunbar's driver and his conspirators, the murder reverberated among the enslaved in ominous ways. "The stranger-youths, two of Dunbar's negroes, and the driver, were tried, confessed the crime, and were all executed; the head of the latter being fixed upon a pole *in terrorem*. But while the offenders were still in prison, the overseer upon a neighboring property had occasion to find fault in the field with a woman belonging to a gang hired to perform some particular work; upon which she flew upon him with the greatest fury, grasped him by the throat, cried to her fellow—'Come here! Come here! Let's Dunbar him!' and through their strength and the suddenness of her attack had nearly accomplished her purpose before his own slaves could come to his assistance. This woman was also executed" (182–83).

33. As Katherine Verdery has noted, "A body's materiality can be critical to its symbolic efficacy: unlike notions such as 'patriotism' or 'civil society,' for instance, a corpse can be moved around, displayed, and strategically located in specific places. Bodies have the advantage of concreteness that nonetheless transcends time, making past immediately present" (*Political Lives of Dead Bodies*, 27).

34. "Returns of Slave Trials," Saint Elizabeth, March 16, 1816, Public Record Office, Colonial Office 137/147, p. 55.

35. It would certainly be fair to ask, as did contemporary reformers in Europe, if such displays did not lose their evocative power over time. In 1791, Henry Coor testified before the House of Commons that "at my first coming to the island, a common flogging of a Negro would have put me in a tremble, and disordered me so that I did not feel myself right again generally the remaining part of the day, but by degrees and custom it became so habitual, that I thought no more of seeing a Black man's head cut off, than I should now think of a butcher cutting off the head of his calf" (*House of Commons Sessional Papers*, ed. Lambert, 82:99).

36. Folke Strom, *On the Sacral Origins of the Germanic Death Penalties* (Lund, 1942); Michel Foucault, *Discipline and Punish: The Birth of the Prison*, trans. Alan Sheridan (New York, 1979), 32–69; Graeme Newman, *The Punishment Response* (Philadelphia, 1978), 27–51; Mitchell B. Merback, *The Thief, the Cross, and the Wheel: Pain and the Spectacle of Punishment in Medieval and Renaissance Europe* (Chicago, 1999).

37. Newman, *Punishment Response*, 46.

38. Ibid., 44.

39. Pieter Spierenburg, *The Spectacle of Suffering* (New York, 1984), 57.

40. Leon Radzinowicz, *A History of English Criminal Law and Its Administration from 1750*, vol. 1, *The Movement for Reform, 1750–1833* (New York, 1948), 213–14.

41. Douglas Hay, "Property, Authority and the Criminal Law," in *Albion's Fatal Tree: Crime and Society in Eighteenth-Century England*, ed. Hay et al., 28–29.

42. Ibid., 27.

43. According to Hay, it is possible that by the eighteenth century, "the secular sermons of the criminal law had become more important than those of the church" (ibid., 29).

44. Radzinowicz, *History of English Criminal Law*, 178–81.

45. V. A. C. Gatrell, *The Hanging Tree: Execution and the English People, 1770–1868* (New York, 1994), 80.

46. Spierenburg, *Spectacle of Suffering*, 57.

47. Hay, "Property, Authority and the Criminal Law," 40–49.

48. Gatrell, *Hanging Tree*, 83.

49. Hay, "Property, Authority and the Criminal Law," 63.

50. Cited in David Barry Gaspar, "With a Rod of Iron: Barbados Slave Laws as a Model for Jamaica, South Carolina, and Antigua, 1661–1697," in *Crossing Boundaries: Comparative History of Black People in Diaspora*, ed. Darlene Clark Hine and Jacqueline McLeod (Bloomington, 2001), 346.

51. David Barry Gaspar, " 'Rigid and Inclement': Origins of the Jamaica Slave Laws of the Seventeenth Century," in *The Many Legalities of Early America*, ed. Christopher L. Tomlins and Bruce H. Mann (Chapel Hill, 2001), 78–96. In the code of 1696, passed during a particularly unstable period, Jamaica diluted provisions for the protection of slaves included in the 1664 code (copied from the 1661 Barbadian code) and increased the severity of the police regulations, "even to a degree of inhumanity," as Long admitted (Gaspar, "Rigid and Inclement," 95; for the classic analysis of Caribbean slave law, see Elsa V. Goveia, "The West Indian Slave Laws of the Eighteenth Century," in *Caribbean Slave Society and Economy*, ed. Hilary McD. Beckles and Verene A. Shepherd [New York, 1991], 346–62).

52. On the social impact of demographic conditions in Jamaica, see Trevor Burnard, *Mastery, Tyranny, and Desire: Thomas Thistlewood and His Slaves in the Anglo-Jamaican World* (Chapel Hill, 2004), 15–18; Trevor Burnard, "European Migration to Jamaica, 1655–1780," *William and Mary Quarterly*, 3rd ser., 53 (October 1996): 769–96.

53. Long quoted in Gaspar, "Rigid and Inclement," 95.

54. Diana Paton, "Punishment, Crime, and the Bodies of Slaves in Eighteenth-Century Jamaica," *Journal of Social History* 34 (Summer 2001): 923.

55. The first tribunals established in 1664 consisted of one justice of the peace and two "sufficient Neighbors" who adjudicated capital cases and passed sentences to be carried out by slaveholders (Gaspar, "Rigid and Inclement," 83). The number of judges was increased in 1696.

56. Paton, "Punishment, Crime, and the Bodies of Slaves," 927, 950n; St. Thomas in the Vale, Vestry Minutes, 1789–1802, Archives of Jamaica, Local Government 2/1, 1.

57. William Beckford, *Remarks upon the Situation of the Negroes in Jamaica* (London, 1788), 93.

58. Paton, "Punishment, Crime, and the Bodies of Slaves," 939–40. Paton argues convincingly that the extreme punishments meted out for committing violence against

whites expanded on the English legal principle of "petit treason." "Under this theory, murder by a subordinate—a wife, child servant, or apprentice—of the person who had legitimate authority over him or her—husband, father, or master—was considered treasonous within the household, a crime analogous to treason against the state. Jamaican lawmakers expanded this idea so that all white people had legitimate authority over all slaves. A violent act by a slave against a white person could never be just that; it always carried with it the implicit threat of slave rebellion and the overthrow of white power" (931). On punishments for petty treason in England, see McLynn, *Crime and Punishment*, 121–24.

59. Thistlewood diary, October 10, 1766, quoted in Douglas Hall, *In Miserable Slavery*, 142.

60. Testimony of Thomas Lloyd, February 25, 1791, in *House of Commons Sessional Papers*, ed. Lambert, 82:147.

61. St. Thomas in the Vale, Vestry Minutes, 1789–1802, Archives of Jamaica, Local Government 2/1, 1, p. 168.

62. Roger Norman Buckley, *The British Army in the West Indies: Society and the Military in the Revolutionary Age* (Gainesville, 1998), 203–47.

63. Ibid.

64. "Petition from the Carpenter's Mountains, 14 May 1731," *Journals of the Jamaican Assembly* (Kingston, 1826), 3:8.

65. Thomas Murray to Wesleyan Methodist Missionary Society, Montego Bay, April 3, 1832, Wesleyan Methodist Missionary Society, West Indies General Correspondence, box 131, fiche box 9, no. 446.

66. Paton, "Punishment, Crime, and the Bodies of Slaves," 940.

67. Ibid., 942.

68. Thomas Thompson, *An Account of Two Missionary Voyages* (1758; London, 1937), 44–45.

69. John K. Thornton, "Religious and Ceremonial Life in the Kongo and Mbundu Areas, 1500–1700," in *Central Africans and Cultural Transformation in the American Diaspora*, ed. Linda M. Heywood (Cambridge, 2002), 80–81.

70. Robert Farris Thompson and Joseph Cornet, *The Four Moments of the Sun: Kongo Art in Two Worlds* (Washington, 1981), 37.

71. Lewis, *Journal of a West India Planter*, 98.

72. Ibid., 99.

73. Ibid., 182.

74. John Newton, *The Journal of a Slave Trader, 1750–1754, with Newton's Thoughts upon the African Slave Trade*, ed. Bernard Martin and Mark Spurrell (London, 1962), 55.

75. Ibid., 56.

76. Quoted in Jerome S. Handler, "Slave Medicine and Obeah in Barbados, circa 1650 to 1834," *New West Indian Guide* 74, nos. 1–2 (2000): 59.

77. Thistlewood diary, April 25, 1753, quoted in Douglas Hall, *In Miserable Slavery*, 56.

78. Thistlewood diary, January 6, 1754, quoted in ibid., 61.

79. See Jerome S. Handler and Kenneth M. Bilby, "On the Early Use and Origin of the Term 'Obeah' in Barbados and the Anglophone Caribbean," *Slavery and Abolition*

22 (August 2001): 87–100; see also Kenneth M. Bilby and Jerome S. Handler, "Obeah: Healing and Protection in West Indian Slave Life," *Journal of Caribbean History* 38, nos. 1–2 (2004): 153–83.

80. Handler and Bilby, "On the Early Use," 93–94.

81. Ibid., 90–92; see also Douglas Chambers, " 'My Own Nation': Igbo Exiles in the Diaspora," *Slavery and Abolition* 18 (April 1997): 72–97, though Chambers overstates the degree to which obeah can be described as an Ibo practice.

82. Handler and Bilby, "On the Early Use," 92.

83. Lambert, ed., *House of Commons Sessional Papers*, 69:216.

84. Ibid., 217; R. R. Madden, *A Twelvemonth's Residence in the West Indies* (Philadelphia, 1835), 2:69.

85. Robert Farris Thompson and Cornet, *Four Moments of the Sun*, 37. On *minkisi* and their role in manifesting sacred authority in African and American contexts, see also Wyatt MacGaffey, *Religion and Society in Central Africa* (Chicago, 1986); Stephan Palmié, *Wizards and Scientists: Explorations in Afro-Cuban Modernity and Tradition* (Durham, 2002), 159–200.

86. Alexander Barclay, *A Practical View of the Present State of Slavery in the West Indies . . . Containing More Particularly an Account of the Actual Condition of the Negroes in Jamaica* (London, 1826), 190–91.

87. Oldendorp, *History of the Mission*, 198.

88. The open question of how obeah practitioners trained apprentices in their arts remains crucial to a full understanding of how shamanism developed in the West Indies (Jerome Handler, personal communication).

89. O. Nigel Bolland, "Creolisation and Creole Societies: A Cultural Nationalist View of Caribbean Social History," *Caribbean Quarterly* 44, nos. 1–2 (1998): 22, reprinted from Alistair Hennessy, ed., *Intellectuals in the Twentieth-Century Caribbean* (London, 1992), 1:50–79.

90. See Robert Dirks, *The Black Saturnalia: Conflict and its Ritual Expression on British West Indian Slave Plantations* (Gainesville, 1987), 152–53.

91. "St. Ann Slave Court, 1787–1814," March 3, 1794, May 5, 1799, Institute of Jamaica, MS 273.

92. Mindie Lazarus-Black, *Legitimate Acts and Illegal Encounters: Law and Society in Antigua and Barbuda* (Washington, 1994).

93. Long quoted in *The Proceedings of the Governor and Assembly of Jamaica, in Regard to the Maroon Negroes* (London, 1796), xxvii.

94. For descriptions of the war and its aftermath, see Edward Long, *History of Jamaica* (1774; London, 1970), 2:447–72; Edwards, *History of the British West Indies*, 2:75–79; see also Craton, *Testing the Chains*, 125–39; Monica Schuler, "Akan Slave Rebellions in the British Caribbean," in *Caribbean Slave Society and Economy*, ed. Beckles and Shepherd, 373–86.

95. Mary Turner, "The Colonial State, Religion, and the Control of Labour: Jamaica, 1760–1834," in *The Colonial Caribbean in Transition: Essays on Postemancipation Social and Cultural History*, ed. Bridget Brereton and Kevin A. Yelvington (Gainesville, 1999), 26–42.

96. For more on grave dirt and oath taking among Africans and their descendants, see Charles Leslie, *A New and Exact Account of Jamaica* (Edinburgh, 1740), 324; Long, *History of Jamaica*, 2:422–23; Kenneth Bilby, "Swearing by the Past, Swearing to the Future: Sacred Oaths, Alliances, and Treaties among the Guianese and Jamaican Maroons," *Ethnohistory* 44 (Fall 1997): 655–89; see also Dirks, *Black Saturnalia*, 158. For a comparative example, see Gaspar's analysis of the 1736 conspiracy in Antigua, in which he surmises that the Coromantee conspirators might have interpreted the drought, depression, epidemics, and crushing labor requirements of the 1730s "in terms of their ancestors' displeasure with them." Then, "through a solemn damnation oath they appealed for the ancestors' help to change things, to bring back good fortune, and also to destroy slavery" (*Bondmen and Rebels: A Study of Master-Slave Relations in Antigua* [Durham, 1985], 245).

97. Lambert, ed., *House of Commons Sessional Papers*, 69:219.

98. "For the Entertainment of the Curious, There Is Now to Be Exhibited at the House of Messrs. Alleyn & Williams, in Newgate Street, and to Be Continued for a Few Weeks; A Course of Experiments on the Newly-Discovered Electric Fire . . . ," Saint John's, April 25, 1753, in Douglas C. McMurtrie, *Early Printing on the Island of Antigua* (Evanston, 1943). I thank James Delbourgo for bringing this reference to my attention.

99. As early as 1767, Thistlewood began to show his magic lantern (an early type of slide projector) to favored slaves (Thistlewood diary, September 14, 1767, quoted in Douglas Hall, *In Miserable Slavery*, 160). Also, the books Thistlewood received in a 1771 shipment included Benjamin Franklin's *Experiments and Observations on Electricity* (Douglas Hall, *In Miserable Slavery*, 225). Though interest in electricity among planters may have begun with the torture of Tacky's obeah men, it is more likely that interest was early and ongoing.

100. This is potentially the first reference to the use of electricity for purposes of torture. A recent general history of torture maintains that the "use of electricity is the signal contribution of the twentieth century to torture" (Brian Innes, *The History of Torture* [New York, 1998], 144). The authoritative text on early science in the Caribbean also makes no mention of electricity's utility in the torture of slaves; see James E. McClellan III, *Colonialism and Science: Saint Domingue in the Old Regime* (Baltimore, 1992). If indeed the history of punitive electrocution begins in the slave societies of the Caribbean long before electricity's use for the "betterment of mankind," it would seem to support the contention of Paul Gilroy, among others who reject the "mesmeric idea of history as progress," that slavery and terror constituted integral aspects of modernity rather than its opposites; see Gilroy, *The Black Atlantic: Modernity and Double Consciousness* (Cambridge, 1993), esp. 53–54.

101. "Copies of the Several Acts for the Regulation of Slaves, Passed in the West India Islands," in *House of Commons Sessional Papers*, ed. Lambert, 67:111.

102. Helen Tunnicliff Catterall, ed., *Judicial Cases Concerning American Slavery and the Negro*, vol. 5, *Cases from the Courts of States North of the Ohio and West of the Mississippi Rivers, Canada, and Jamaica* (Washington, 1937), 356.

103. The law is quoted in "First Report of the Commissioners of Enquiry into the Administration of Criminal and Civil Justice in the West Indies, dated 29th June 1827," in

Irish University Press Series of British Parliamentary Papers: Colonies, West Indies (Shannon, 1968), 3:381.

104. One plantation manager complained that obeah practitioners were extremely difficult to catch—that masters succeeded only one in ten times (William Anderson to James Chisholme, Trouthall Estate, February 5, 1810, MS 5466–112, Papers of William and James Chisholme, MS 5466–76, National Library of Scotland). I thank Roderick McDonald for providing me with his notes on this source. For historical accounts of obeah drawn from textual and oral sources in another context, see Richard Price, *First-Time: The Historical Vision of an African American People*, 2nd ed. (Chicago, 2002); Richard Price, *Alabi's World* (Baltimore, 1990).

105. "Returns of Slave Trials," Public Record Office, Colonial Office 137/147.

106. Madden, *Twelvemonth's Residence*, 2:74.

107. Carol F. Karlsen, *The Devil in the Shape of a Woman: Witchcraft in Colonial New England* (New York, 1989); Ralph A. Austen, "The Moral Economy of Witchcraft: An Essay in Comparative History," in *Modernity and Its Malcontents: Ritual and Power in Postcolonial Africa*, ed. Jean Comaroff and John Comaroff (Chicago, 1999), 99–103.

108. Lambert, ed., *House of Commons Sessional Papers*, 69:216.

109. Patterson, *Sociology of Slavery*, 193.

110. Dirks, *Black Saturnalia*, 156.

111. For a thorough analysis of compensation claims in another West Indian slave society, see David Barry Gaspar, " 'To Bring Their Offending Slaves to Justice': Compensation and Slave Resistance in Antigua, 1669–1763," *Caribbean Quarterly* 30, nos. 3–4 (1984): 45–59.

112. Public Record Office, Colonial Office 137/147 records 13 compensation values for convicted obeah practitioners: £100 = 4; £80 = 2; £75 = 1; £70 = 1; £67 = 1; £50 = 2; £40 = 1; £15 = 1 (eleven male, 2 female [£70 and £80]); average value = £71.

113. When no value was recorded, it did not mean that no money was paid out. Most parishes simply did not list the compensation values in the general returns ("Returns of Slave Trials," Public Record Office, Colonial Office 137/147).

114. Robert L. Paquette, "The Drivers Shall Lead Them: Image and Reality in Slave Resistance," in *Slavery, Secession, and Southern History*, ed. Robert Louis Paquette and Louis A. Ferleger (Charlottesville, 2000), 32–33.

115. Ibid., 53.

116. Stewart, *View of the Past and Present State*, 262–63. For a broader discussion of such courts in the context of social hierarchies among the enslaved, see Dirks, *Black Saturnalia*, 140–44; see also Mindie Lazarus-Black, "Slaves, Masters, and Magistrates: Law and the Politics of Resistance in the British Caribbean, 1736–1834," in *Contested States: Law, Hegemony, and Resistance*, ed. Mindie Lazarus-Black and Susan F. Hirsh (New York, 1994), 252–81.

117. "Minutes of Evidence Taken before the Select Committee of the House of Lords Appointed to Inquire into the Laws and Usages of the Several West India Colonies in Relation to the Slave Population, &c. &c. &c.," 1831–32, House of Lords Record Office, 220.

118. William Anderson to James Chisholme, Trouthall Estate, April 13, 1809, Chisholme Papers, MS 5466–76. I thank Roderick McDonald for providing me with his notes on this source.

119. William Anderson to James Chisholme, Trouthall Estate, February 5, 1810, Chisholme Papers, MS 5466–112.

120. Austen, "Moral Economy of Witchcraft," 104.

121. The literature on witchcraft as social sanction in Africa is too voluminous to recount here. For a recent comparative article, see Austen, "Moral Economy of Witchcraft." For the classic discussion of witchcraft and wizardry as "behaviour in a social field," see Victor W. Turner, "Witchcraft and Sorcery: Taxonomy versus Dynamics," *Africa* 34, nos. 3–4 (1964): 314–24.

122. Patterson, *Sociology of Slavery*, 194.

123. Peter Geschiere, *The Modernity of Witchcraft: Politics and the Occult in Postcolonial Africa*, trans. Peter Geschiere and Janet Roitman (Charlottesville, 1997), 16. "Healers are always highly ambivalent figures," notes Geschiere, "they can only heal because they have killed" (196). For a more narrowly pessimistic view, see Austen, "Moral Economy of Witchcraft," 105: "It is difficult to depict African witchcraft idioms as a weapon of African resistance. Their immediate moral targets are other Africans while they leave the European bases of power mystified to a point where they can only be avoided."

124. For insightful discussions of African/American spiritual warfare in slavery, see James H. Sweet, *Recreating Africa: Culture, Kinship, and Religion in the African-Portuguese World, 1441–1770* (Chapel Hill, 2004); Palmié, *Wizards and Scientists*, 176–81; MacGaffey, *Religion and Society*, esp. 156–64.

125. Lewis, *Journal of a West India Proprietor*, 91.

126. Ibid., 94.

127. John Shipman, "Thoughts upon the Present State of Religion among the Negroes of Jamaica," 1820, Wesleyan Methodist Missionary Society Archive Special Series, Biographical, West Indies, box 588, fiche box 2, nos. 27–31, pp. 12–13.

128. Ibid., 13.

129. Ibid.

130. Ibid.

131. Ibid.

132. Verdery, *Political Lives of Dead Bodies*, 37.

133. Leslie, *New and Exact Account*, 324.

134. See Vincent Brown, "Spiritual Terror and Sacred Authority in Jamaican Slave Society," *Slavery and Abolition* 24 (April 2003): 45–46.

135. For a sophisticated study of modernity and tradition in the Caribbean, see Stephan Palmié, *Wizards and Scientists: Explorations in Afro-Cuban Modernity and Tradition* (Durham, 2002).

Correspondences in Black and White

Sentiment and the

Slave Market Revolution

PHILLIP TROUTMAN

*I*n 1859, at Harper's Ferry, Virginia, Dangerfield Newby went into battle against slavery armed with more than steel and zeal. He carried in his pocket a small collection of letters written by his wife, Harriet Newby. Living in slavery in Brentville, she had recently urged him to come and buy her, fearing impending doom at her master's hands. "He may sell me," she wrote, "an then all my bright hop[e]s of the futer are blasted." She had but "one bright hope to cheer me in all my troubles," she confided, and "that is to be with you." "If I thought I shoul never see you," she assured him, "this earth would have no charms for me." She signed all her letters, "your affectionate wife, Harriet Newby." Their specific sentimental acts were intended—each in a different way—to unite them: she wrote the letters to plead for a physical reunion; he treasured them as keepsakes to hold her close to his heart as he risked all against slavery. Her bright hopes were indeed blasted, as Dangerfield Newby was killed in John Brown's conflagration at Harper's Ferry. When authorities found her letters on his broken body, she was promptly identified and sold south. These tokens of sentiment, aimed at reuniting them, effected her separation even from his corpse.[1]

In 1861, the letters of another enslaved woman, Emily Plummer, indicated what Harriet's letters might have meant to Dangerfield Newby. Emily and her husband, Adam Plummer, had lived largely apart since 1855. "My heart aches at the thought of this long and painful separation," she wrote to him. Fantasies of Adam's presence taunted her. "I dream of you and think you are once more with me," she wrote, "but wake to find myself alone and so wretchedly unhappy." She urged him "under any circumstances," whether or not he could visit, to "write very frequently." "It is our next great pleasure to seeing your kind face," Emily insisted, "and hearing your voice of affection."[2]

Sentimental language, with its openness about loss, its dwelling on the sorrow of separation, and its attempts to connect people emotionally across long distances, seemed especially suitable to the family correspondence of those very few enslaved African Americans who gained literacy. In the idiom of sentiment, they found concrete images to convey their loss. In the tropes of letter writing, they found words to encapsulate their most heartfelt feelings, perhaps even those they could not express in person.[3] That literate African Americans would do so when writing to their families is not surprising. But some also directed these terms of affection toward certain people who held them in slavery—the same people who had sold these slaves away from their families. Slaves writing home sent their regards to members of the slaveholding family as well: some sent their "warmest love" or signed their letters with "affection." These people had learned to frame letters in the same sentimental language their white masters and mistresses employed. Like the white families—in both the North and the South—who had come to cast family in terms of affection rather than economy, literate African Americans in slavery asserted their family ties and even their ties to white "family" members in exactly that same domestic language.

Understanding what sentimental language meant to the people who used it is a difficult task. Historians and literary scholars have read it as stemming from an eighteenth-century shift in values (in France, England, and in Anglo America) toward "sensibility," both in notions of the family and in one's relationship to other human beings elsewhere in the world.[4] Literary scholars and historians of the United States have tended to associate sentiment with the North and with the ideology of domesticity. But historians of slaveholding gentry in the colonial Chesapeake have identified the beginning of a shift within such families toward sentiment as part of a "softening" of patriarchy (authority relying on crass economic force and violence) to paternalism (where authority was inscribed through more openly affectionate means). By the nineteenth century, white families more broadly employed sentimental language and its tropes, articulating and working to act on "companionate" ideals of marriage. Slaveholders in the nineteenth century also employed this same "domestic" rhetoric to assert mutual affections and obligations between members of their "black and white families."[5]

These correspondences, evidencing the continuity of African American family ties and sometimes the sentimental rhetoric of paternalism, also provided evidence of slaveholders' violation of paternalistic ideals by separating African American family members. The letters were in fact made necessary by the physical distance slaveholders imposed, and African Americans used sentimental language in an effort to close that gap, emotionally if not physically. When directed toward family members, sentimental language stood in for the person missing, the letter a token of that person's emotional presence across such distance. But when aimed a white "family" members, the sentimental language of slaves served a more complicated set of purposes, belying the slaveholders' overtly paternalistic rhetoric. African Americans sought to implicate slaveholders in getting word home, in conveying sentiments to families left behind. African Americans' sentimental ties to their family members thus led them to include certain slaveholders in the larger sentimental community.

The relationship between language and experience in enslaved writers' letters was complex, even paradoxical, and far from hegemonic. Far from representing a relationship bound by common paternalistic values, sentimental language exposed the contingency, the tentativeness, or the downright absence of any such relationship. It asserted rather than assumed values shared between African Americans and "their" white folks and did so explicitly in the face of slaveholders' violation of any values that may in fact have been shared. Instead of rendering paternalist rhetoric inoperable, the omnipresent slave market made sentimental, paternalistic language useful—at least in certain circumstances. Forced mobility and family separation in the market ironically gave rise to both the opportunity and the felt need for language that sought to override the market with sentimental values.[6] Yet just as the reformist ideals of northern domesticity did not permeate all or even most northern households, southern paternalism also met with resistance. Sentimental language appealed to emotional bonds of family (including the paternalistic "family, black and white") but could not eclipse the economic coercion of the slave market.[7]

Why, then, would enslaved African Americans use the language of sentiment? Their experiences surely could not conform to the domestic norm. Perhaps masters' power to intervene in and destroy family life created pressures on African American men and women that could result in family violence.[8] And perhaps African American women who worked closely with whites "mimicked" certain cultural norms or "accepted the ideology of domesticity." But this begs the question. It seems more fruitful to see African Americans appropriating Euro-American norms not because they were the norms but because they meant something to African Americans—that is, they spoke to the experience of the enslaved. Black women sometimes played on notions of a common experience, aspects of life they might share in some way with slaveholding women, especially around issues of rape, childbirth, and the death of children.[9] And we might see sentimental ideology itself arising not solely out of white or middle-class or northern experiences but also out of articulations of African American experience.[10]

We must consider, then, how the expression related to the experiences. Enslaved African Americans had long endured forced mobility, but this process accelerated after the 1820s with the expulsion of native nations from fertile lands in the southern Mississippi Valley, long-distance planter-directed migrations, and the rise of the domestic slave trade. The numbers tell one story: Slave-holding planters and slave traders forced the migration of 1.1 million enslaved African Americans from Eastern Seaboard and Upper South states to trans-Allegheny and Deep South states. The process dissolved up to a third of enslaved African Americans' marriages in the Upper South. An enslaved child living in the Upper South in 1820 stood a 30 percent chance of being sold south by 1860.[11] But these figures provide only the first clue to the trade's impact on life in southern slave society.

The rise of the domestic slave trade in the nineteenth century comprised a key engine of the market revolution, undergirding the massive expansion of cotton and sugar production. That economic transformation itself was insepa-rable from mechanization and dramatically altered middle-class consumption patterns in the northern United States and in Great Britain. The market revo-lution entailed geographic, social, and ideological dislocations throughout the country. But market-driven migration threatened southern black families far more broadly and profoundly than did the industrializing forces feared by do-mestic reformers in the North.[12]

Historians have tended to cast their analyses of these turbulent times in terms of ideology. But the ideology of domesticity was about nothing if not emotions. And perhaps ideology alone is not the best mode for thinking about emotions. Sentiment was no doubt a manipulative language—sentimental novels played on the emotions and manipulated readers' notions of love, romance, family, and discipline.[13] We can see these acts as ideological (not hegemonic), as working to effect some mode of thinking in contention with others rather than as conform-ing to values assumed to be shared in an uncontested way.[14] But it is difficult to distinguish between reflexive and instrumental uses of sentimental language. Cognitive psychologists have had great difficulty finding the line between au-tomatic and learned behavior. We tend to frame our discussion of emotions in terms that imply that they are not cognitive at all but bodily only—liquid, in Victorian theories of emotions (emotions "well up" inside us or we "express" them). We could see all verbal and textual description of emotion as an act of translation. The teller must navigate between feelings themselves (which, even if we acknowledge as existing objectively in a biological sense, we might assume to be beyond the historian's scope) and the cultural signs that signify them. The signs of the writer or speaker are in turn different from the signs and feelings of the listener or reader. The speaker and listener might share something like the same notion of the emotion named, though this is not usually the case. One person's notion of grief may be associated with, for example, a mother while another's with a brother. We all have different expectations and experiences. This is all the more true when we are reading expressions of emotion from the past. Then we must translate from our notions to theirs, which will not always be retrievable.[15]

Despite all the difficulties, as the linguistic analogy implies, translation is possible and is in fact ubiquitous. Articulations of emotion have identifiable relationships to experiences and can to some extent be conveyed to other people, who then draw on their experiences to try to understand. In fact, sentiment itself comprised a kind of lingua franca, a second language people learned so they could communicate. In the antebellum U.S. slave market, the barriers were not linguistic but rather of gender, race, class, and region. Sentiment worked as a medium of conveying emotion (sometimes across these barriers) through the assumption that as humans, everyone had loved and had experienced the pain of loss.[16] Sentiment constituted a language of grief, of parting, of embarkation that made sense in mobile America, including in the forced mobility of the enslaved South.[17] In letters, sentimental language gave people a means of communicating those emotions across the same distances that had engendered them. Slaveholders and enslaved African Americans also used sentimental language in an attempt to communicate across the gulf of social and racial distinctions that divided them. The language of their correspondences contributed to the appearance of a paternalistic norm that the fact of their letters—representing the separation of enslaved family members—in fact called into question.

A slaveholder's individual mix of relative sensibility or market shrewdness in regard to slaves appears clearly in his or her choices about writing. For many slaveholders, the proper role of slaves in family correspondence was absence. Explanations of decisions to buy or sell particular slaves rarely appear in slave owners' private writings. African Americans appeared far more often in planters' ledgers and farm account books.[18] The correspondence of the relatively few slaveholders who did write about slaves is therefore illuminating. These slaveholders were prone to acknowledging the sentimental attachments they were in the process of breaking in the slave market. Their inclusion of enslaved household members within the realm of their personal correspondence, in fact, might be taken as one of the signs of their participation in sentimental notions of the black and white family. Only those sensitive on the matter would bother to contemplate the ramifications of sale. Moreover, those enslaved women, men, and children about whom slaveholders wrote tended to be those more closely associated with running the household, although these people frequently worked in the fields as well. Thus, the African Americans who appeared in slaveholder correspondence—and the ones who wrote back after having been sold—were those most likely to have been included in the fold of paternalism. Slaveholders' musings on these sales rendered paternalistic ideology problematic but at the same time emphasized the affectionate bonds that were supposed to sustain that ideology.[19]

Surviving letters written by enslaved African Americans are equally exceptional and equally illuminating. They are historical gems, their value inherent in both their content and their rarity. Literacy held powerful significance to African Americans, in part for its sentimental implications. First, literacy had long been associated with evangelical purpose. Christians promoted reading among free and slave alike so that all might read the Word and thus be open to salvation. The evangelical implications of reading drew African Americans into a humanity recognized at least by God if not by humans. Second, and more pragmatically, reading—especially when accompanied by writing skills—allowed bondpersons to communicate across the space of slavery, helping them to mitigate the social death that the slave market and long-distance forced migration threatened to impose. William Hayden made clear literacy's dual purpose in his 1846 autobiography. Through a combination of stealth, duplicity, and favoritism among whites, he had learned to write "a tolerably legible hand" and regarded himself privileged. "Yonder is a WHITE man—he has . . . never been able to learn to read the word of God, or transmit by writing one solitary thought to his distant relatives and friends; whilst I, a poor, friendless colored boy,—a slave—can read the consolations held forth in the Scriptures, and inform my distant friends of my progress through life. O, the difference! I would not part with my little knowledge, for all the wealth of your illiterate dealer in flesh and blood!"[20] Hayden explicitly contrasted the spiritual and sentimental fortunes he gained through literacy with the material fortunes gained by slaveholders and slave traders. Literacy made him a fully sentient human, capable of spiritual "progress" and able to conquer the space slavery had imposed between himself and family members. By contrast, slaveholders and slave traders—those who contravened sentiment by dealing "in flesh and blood"—sought by the chattel principle to deny him that sentimental power.

The act of sending such letters also spoke to the nature of slavery and the limits slaveholders placed on that kind of communication. To send letters home after having been sold away, enslaved people had not only to evade the many pitfalls of gaining literacy but also to negotiate the obstacles in the way of corresponding with loved ones they had left. Relatively few slaves gained access to the implements and skills of reading (probably less than a quarter overall) and fewer still (certainly no more than 5 percent) to those of writing.[21] Literacy involved stealth, an evangelical mistress, a tolerant master, or all three. Among this tiny literate minority, few found much time to write. Fewer still succeeded in getting their letters past white censors. When slaves managed to write under such circumstances, they clearly had something important to say. Letters that found their way to loved ones were treasured, kept as tokens of sentimental affection, unfolded and refolded, read over and again until they were worn past preservation.

Passing letters in slavery required a certain degree of geographic and social literacy. It took the skills of reading the social landscape, understanding the connections between and among certain people—slave and free, black and white—and the ability to tap into those connections to transfer information and emotional content from one place to another. The letters that made it through still bear the marks of their sentimental journeys. The fact of their preservation in slaveholders' family papers itself indicates something of the relationship some slaves sustained with white people.[22] Passing letters required one to say the right things in the right ways to the right people, to implicate them in the act of passing a letter that was at once the vehicle of sentimental language and a sentimental object in itself. Thus, the fact of the letters themselves testifies to some slaves' assertion of sentimental bonds, both with their own family members and with some slaveholders.

From the beginning of the slave market revolution during the 1790s and early 1800s, slaveholders understood something of the sentimental bonds being broken. For one thing, they were breaking sentimental bonds of their own, leaving family members behind as they trekked across the Alleghenies into Kentucky and Tennessee. Women especially expressed their grief at abandoning Virginia for the new plantation frontiers. In their correspondence, they expressed their longing for family members and homeplaces they would never see again.[23] Thus, slaveholders could sometimes comprehend the loss enslaved African Americans felt at the prospect of these same removals. One member of the Cabell-Breckinridge family commented on her family's partial removal to Kentucky in 1804, indicating the uncertainty involved in the serial migration in which they were partaking: "Tomorrow the negroes are to get off and I expect there will be great crying and morning, children Leaving there mothers, mothers there children, and women there husbands." This particular separation was to be temporary, yet uncertainty prevailed. As this white family member explained, the "ensuing Faul [Fall] I suppose whoever Lives to see it both black & white will Leave this State." No one, black or white, knew whether they would see their loved ones again.[24]

For slave families, separations usually brought not that uncertainty but the grim certainty of loss. Still, some few slaves were able at least to seek out and to convey information about their families across the mountains. In 1807 a woman named Gooley wrote from Port Royal, Virginia, to her white former mistress in Kentucky. In her letter, Gooley sought information about her family, expressed concern and conveyed affection for them, and offered veiled criticism of slaveholders' actions. She also deftly employed sentimental language to solicit the desired response from the white woman. While Gooley had been left in Virginia, several of her children and her sister, Clary, had been taken to Kentucky. Apparently through the family grapevine, Gooley had somehow heard the terrible news that the migrants had "lost some of your Small Negroes by death," and she sought to affirm or assuage her worst fears by learning who had been lost. Proceeding on the hopeful assumption that none of her children had died, she went on to send word to Clary "not to let my poor children Suffer." Finally, she inquired more specifically about Clary and about "how my little daughter Judith is."[25]

Gooley's careful language permitted her to skirt any direct associations of her family's welfare and treatment with the actions or responsibility of her "Dear Mistress" in Kentucky. The white woman might have blanched at the suggestion that Clary would have to make sure Gooley's children did not suffer, but for the most part Gooley spoke of her family's lives as if detached from that of their white mistress. She asked "what sort of a life Clary leads," for example, or, whether Judith "is now injoying health"—as if they led lives independent from that of the white mistress. Gooley's concern with the number of childhood deaths certainly might imply a criticism of the Kentucky mistress's management, but if so, it remained obscured in the slave's sentimental language toward the mistress. She closed the letter by pledging her "Warmest Love & friendship," and signing it "your Most Affectionate Servant."[26]

Gooley also criticized slave sales and separations but again deflected it through generalization and a deft assertion that the white mistress was in sympathy with her enslaved correspondent. Gooley sent the upsetting news that her Virginia master was "on the brink of death." He "has been very good to me," she insisted, but now he was "about to Sell 40 of his Negroes," Joshua, her husband, probably among them. She told her Kentucky mistress that she wanted to stay with Joshua. "As you must know," Gooley ventured, "its very bad to part man & wife." She thus conveyed the standard by which she expected to be treated and implicated the white mistress in an understanding of that standard. The Kentucky woman was perhaps also to infer that she must act to preserve the marriage of Gooley and Joshua by interceding with the Virginia slaveholders. Gooley used the mistress's presumed sentimental connection with her former slave and her known family or personal connection with the Virginia slaveholders to try to prevent the couple's impending separation.[27]

The difficulties of separation and the entanglement of slaves' lives in their masters' family lives led to troubles within black families, as Elizabeth Keckley's letters testified. She had seen her father, George Pleasant Hobbs, only twice a year, and never again after he moved with his master to Tennessee. But Keckley's parents, she remembered, "kept up a regular correspondence for years." George wrote to his wife, Agnes, in 1833 that he was working to secure his freedom so that they might meet again not only in heaven but also first "on the earth." To young Elizabeth, he conveyed a sense of hope and a reminder of his and of God's ever-watchful parental eyes. He told her "to be a good girl and not to thinke that because I am bound so fare that gods not abble to open the way."[28] As Keckley realized, however, slaves at times had to try to open their own ways back home. Sent to North Carolina as a young woman to live with some of her master's relatives, Keckley wrote a critical letter to her mother in April 1838. "I thought very hard of you for not writing to me," she said. Lonely and isolated from her kin as well as from the white people she had known in Virginia, Elizabeth expressed her fear that "you and all the family have forgotten me." She longed to see any written communication from them, even "if it was only a line."[29]

Similarly, in October 1840, Sargry Brown of Richmond was exasperated by the failure of her husband, Morris, to respond to her missives. "This is the third letter I have written to you, and have not received any from you," she wrote. She took his silence as negligence. "I think very hard of it," she said, warning him, "If you don't come down here this Sunday, perhaps you wont see me any more." A trader had already visited three times, she said. She held out little hope for Morris's ability to find a buyer for her and had given up. She instructed him to give her love to "them all," including her mother, his mother, aunt Betsey, Jane, and "all the children." She closed in sentimental resignation, writing, "I wish to see you all, but I expect I never shall—never no more." It is likely that Sargry Brown's husband never even saw her first two letters. Indeed, this last one wound up in the dead letter office in Washington, D.C., as she had not been able to pinpoint his address more precisely than "goughland county"— Goochland County, just west of Brown's location in Richmond. Her attempts to relay critical information along the best established network of communication available—the U.S. Post Office—had failed her miserably.[30]

Maria Perkins of Charlottesville perhaps found more success at reaching her husband when the slave market threatened, but in the end she may have suffered the same fate as Sargry Brown. On October 8, 1852, Perkins wrote in similar panic to her husband, Richard, who lived in Staunton, forty miles to the west, over the Blue Ridge. Her master had unexpectedly put her and her two children up for sale. A trader had already bought her son, Albert, who was now "gone I don't know where." She had heard, however, that the trader's name was Brady and that he was from Scottsville, twenty miles to the south, on the James River. She had maintained a keener sense of geography and had not quite given up on the resourcefulness of her husband and his potential white benefactors. Her own time was short, however, and Richard would have to act quickly. "I don't want a trader to get me," she insisted. She wanted to hear from her husband immediately, before the next court day, when a sale might take place. Her sellers had left her one hope. She said they had "asked me if I had got any person to buy me" and were open to her finding a local buyer. If either Richard's master or, she suggested, "Dr. Hamilton" would step in as purchaser, she could forestall the separation.[31]

Other details of Perkins's letter gave clues to how she had stayed connected to her husband. She had not had time to gather her possessions, which she said she had kept "in several places," including in Staunton, where he lived. She apparently had experienced relative freedom, perhaps hiring out her own labor at different times in those "several places." At any rate, she had taken advantage of her freedom to travel and had perhaps visited him. He apparently had visiting rights as well, though at the time of her letter, in October, his next trip to see her was not scheduled until Christmas. While this relatively short distance had undoubtedly imposed strains on their marriage, being sold away would mean the end of it. She contained her fears only barely, and, like Sargry Brown, turned to sentiment to convey the grief she already felt. "I am quite heartsick nothing more," she closed, "I am and ever will be your kind wife."[32]

Having failed to stop a separation through sale or migration, enslaved African Americans occasionally wrote letters trying to effect reunion. Pleading their case before slaveholders, these literate slaves sometimes employed sentimental language similar to that which Brown and Perkins had reserved for their own husbands. Vilet Lester, sold in 1852 from North Carolina to Georgia via the Richmond slave markets, wrote in 1857 to Patsey Padison [Patterson], her former mistress and childhood playmate. Lester anxiously opened her letter by "unfolding my Seans [seeings] and fealings," the experiences that had washed over her since her forced departure, which she presumed might influence her former masters to act on her behalf. She sketched briefly the geography of her journey through the slave markets: first to Rockingham, North Carolina, where she remained for five weeks; then to Richmond for three days; then carried to Georgia by trader named Groover, who took nine months to sell her again; bought by a man named Rimes, who sold her again to James B. Lester of Bullock County, Georgia, with whom she had remained the past four years.[33]

She asked about other family members and then moved on to her reason for writing. She asked about her "Presus little girl," whom she had had to leave in Goldsboro in the hands of a man named Walker. She wanted specifically to know whether Walker would sell, for Vilet had convinced Lester—perhaps it had taken four years to do so—to purchase the girl. Vilet pointed out that Lester was "a man of Reason and fealing" who wanted to "grant my trubled breast that mutch gratification." Thus she implicitly challenged Walker to prove himself an equally sentimental slaveholder, to grant Vilet's heart its desire to be with her child.[34]

Vilet was careful not to provoke the North Carolina slaveholders. She had described in only vague terms the details of her forced journey, casting herself as the actor and subject rather than as the object of their severing actions. Instead of stating openly that they had sold her and that traders had carried and confined her, she said she had "left there" and "went to" Richmond "to be Sold"; she "Stade there three days." She did note her deep regret at having been "constrained to leav my Long Loved home and friends," but she veiled her criticism of the family's decision to sell her. Her choice of words instead played on what she presumed was the family members' sense of nostalgia and understanding of homesickness. And here she again restated the point of her letter, offering another solution to her family separation. James Lester planned to keep her in Georgia unless, she hinted hopefully, "Some of my old north Caroliner friends wants to buy me again."[35]

To gain a sympathetic audience and perhaps an advocate, Vilet Lester emphasized her sentimental attachment for Padison and the rest of the white family, ranking it on par with that toward her own family. Sending greetings to her "old Boss," to "Miss Rahol," and to her mother, Vilet exclaimed that she could not decide "which I want to See the worst." She settled on her mother, explaining, "Never befour did I no [know] what it was to want to See a parent and could not." Again, she left Padison to make the sentimental connection, the inference about Vilet's longing to see not only her mother but also her daughter and for her daughter to see her mother again. She closed the letter with a bid for Padison's nostalgia for their mutual childhood, "Enscribing my Self you[r] long loved and well wishing play mate as a Servant until death."[36]

Although sentiment served as a lingua franca—a language all were presumed to understand—it was not the only vocabulary out there. Rather, it worked alongside and in contest with other competing rhetorics. In playing to slaveholders' other values and interests, enslaved correspondents employed the languages of honor, of business, and of family politics. At times these other languages served as implicit critique in ways not always as obvious as sentiment. Slave women working to preserve their families did not always play solely on paternalistic sentiment, instead taking advantage of their knowledge that slaveholders held diverse values and standards of behavior and esteemed themselves differently from their bondpersons.

Virginia Boyd knew Rice Ballard's ways well.[37] In the 1830s and 1840s, Ballard had profited greatly from his partnership with the slave-trading firm Franklin and Armfield. Basing his operations in Richmond, Ballard and his Fredericksburg partner had worked the coastal trade to New Orleans and Natchez. By the late 1840s, he had married and established a residence in Louisville, Kentucky, but he ran several large plantations in Mississippi, Louisiana, and Arkansas. On May 6, 1853, Virginia Boyd wrote to Ballard from still further away, in Houston, Texas. "I am at present," she informed him flatly, "in a negro traders yard, for sale, by your orders." Her humiliation and isolation there were almost complete.

She had been "humbled," left, as she was, pregnant and "a mong strangers with-out one living being to whom I have the least shadow of claim upon." Her down-fall carried great emotional weight. "My heart feels like it would burst asunder," she wrote. But she was also angry and wanted justice. As she wrote, she revealed the cause of her distress: "Do you think . . . that its treating me well to send me off among strangers in my situation to be sold without even my having an opportunity of choosing for my self. its hard in deed and what is still harder [is] for the father of my children to sell his own offspring yes his own flesh & blood." [38]

The enslaved woman was not referring to Ballard but rather to "the old man (I don't call names)" who had asked Ballard to send her down. Given her sur-name and her situation, the "old man" in question was likely Judge Samuel S. Boyd, who had served as legal counsel to Ballard's firm and remained his busi-ness partner, sharing in Ballard's investment and management of the Missis-sippi Valley plantations. [39] Samuel Boyd was already known to have inflicted sexual abuse on at least one enslaved female, and Ballard had expressed to a friend, J. M. Duffield, "horror" at Boyd's predatory actions. In 1848, Duffield reported back that the judge had continued to make this woman a "sufferer of great agony mentally and bodily." "All these cruelties," he wrote, "have been inflicted upon the feeble frame of that girl—and are frequently inflicted." Her health was "sinking," and he feared she would die. He asked Ballard to let him purchase her so he could free her, appealing to Ballard's "humane heart." "Only listen to the dictates of your own kindly nature," Duffield pleaded, "and you will grant the request." [40]

Virginia Boyd played on other aspects of character, both Ballard's and of that of her children's father. Her words expressed simultaneously (and perhaps at cross-purposes) her rage and her attempt to reason with Ballard. "My god," she exclaimed, "is it possible that any free born American would hand his chareter with such a stigma as that"—"to sell his child that is his image." She still held out hope, however, asserting "that [Samuel Boyd] is possest of more honer than that." As for Ballard, she knew he might use his "influence" with the old man, and she both flattered and indirectly threatened him. "I wish you to reflect over the subject," she asked, and called on his sense of honor, fairness, sentiment, and Christianity. She knew he was an "honerable high minded man" and "would wish justice to be done to all." Just as important, he was a husband and father: "You have a family of children," she reminded him, "& no how to simpathize with others in distress." This in fact was the key to sentimental language—the assertion that humans from vastly different social stations in life could learn to "sympathize" with one another. But Boyd also held out an indirect but perhaps stinging threat. Any "mercy & pity you show to me," she assured him, "god certainly will show you. what can I say more." [41]

Finally, Virginia Boyd offered Ballard a viable way out by calling on his self-interest. "All I reques or ask," she said, was for Ballard to appoint an agent in Texas to oversee her while she worked off the cost of her freedom and that of her children. For her part, she would "work my finger ends off" and would "earn . . . evry dime." Furthermore, she would leave the old man alone. "I dont wish to return to harras or molest his peace of mind," she promised, "& shall never try get back if I am dealt with fairly." Her sincerity was backed up by the secrecy she had kept so far in the matter as well as by another, more temporal threat. "I use my precaution to prevent others from knowing or suspecting any thing," she assured Ballard. "I shall not seek ever to let anything be exposed," she promised, "unless I am forced from bad treatment &c."[42]

Ballard was not predisposed to help Virginia Boyd out of her bind, however. He was "prejudist" against her, she knew. She felt she had been the victim of malicious gossip, especially from the lips of a "rascal" woman named Pussel, and Virginia felt she had to discredit this attacker. If only Ballard knew "all that she [Pussel] has said relative to you & matters concerning your family," Virginia scolded, then he would "not have so great a confidence in all the tales she fabricates." To be on the safe side, Virginia repeatedly offered her own apologies for ever having "spoken hastly that which I should not" to or about Ballard. "I hope you will forgive me," she stressed, "for I hope god has."[43]

In the end, all her efforts—the supplication and assertion, pleas and threats, calls to Ballard's honor, piety, generosity, sentimentality, and self-interest—were in vain. By August, Virginia Boyd and her younger child were sold, separated from her older child, while Ballard stood by, doing nothing; however, Ballard may have stepped in to stop the sale of Virginia's older child. Through Louisville trader C. M. Rutherford, Ballard had informed his agent in Houston to refrain from selling her, and as of August 8, she remained unsold. The reasons for Ballard's interest in the older daughter are unclear. At one thousand dollars, her price indicates that she was not a young child. Rutherford may have had his own designs on her: he told Ballard he needed "fancy" girls to sell.[44] Despite his retirement from the slave trade in the 1840s, Ballard apparently still acted periodically as a supplier, perhaps from his own plantations. Whether he had Virginia's older daughter in mind for such a speculation, however, and whether he ever removed her from the Houston trader's jail remain unknown.

While Ballard remained impervious to Virginia Boyd's supplications, other slaveholders were more open to expressions of sentimental attachment, at least to themselves if not between black family members. Perhaps no other slaveholders expressed these sentiments more openly than the members of the Austin and Twyman family of Virginia's southern piedmont. The Austins and Twymans found letter writing a particularly important means both of conducting business and of sharing family news. In its heyday, the Archibald Austin estate, in

Buckingham County, had held more than fifty enslaved workers. But as a result of the patriarch's death in 1837 and that year's economic panic, his heirs had to liquidate much of his slaveholding capital. As John Austin wrote to his sister, Frances, in 1848 or 1849, the family had "spent forty-three negroes" and should avoid selling any more.[45] By 1850, the Austins and Twymans debated the various ways to render the estate financially sound.

When selling off the enslaved people of their father's estate, the family seems to have made some efforts to keep certain people together. But the pressure was on. Debt was literally at the Twymans' door in the form of a slave trader sent by one of the Austins' creditors. Of the forty-eight people sold in the estate division or soon thereafter, thirty-nine left in groups of two or more, twenty-two of those clearly in mother-child pairs or trios. In other cases, the names and ages of the slaves sold clearly indicate that kin were separated.[46]

While "spending" these slaves like money, the Austins still operated under sentimental notions of the black and white family—at least those family names remaining in the 1850s—perhaps in part because of the previous decade's disruptions and losses. The slaves who remained with the family received wide freedom of movement. Enslaved couriers delivered private letters between the Austin plantation in Buckingham County and the home of Dr. Iverson L. Twyman and his wife, Martha E. Austin Twyman, across the James River in Amherst County. These unaccompanied runners also delivered horses, clothing, produce, and even jewelry (sewn into the courier's pockets) back and forth between the white family members. In one case, Twyman considered letting an enslaved man pick up a gun that had been repaired in Lynchburg but decided against it because "some trifling white man" would probably take it regardless of any note or pass Twyman might write.[47] Enslaved members of the Austin household held relative autonomy in their religious participation, and a few gained considerable influence in choosing their employers. Several could read and write and did so with the open acknowledgment of the white Austins. The white Austin women in particular involved themselves in the lives of the enslaved men and women, keeping close tabs on the tasks of household sustenance, such as spinning, looming, and clothes making and occasionally closing letters with the clichéd but significant words, "give my love to the whole family—black and white."

Martha Twyman showed tremendous capacity to express highly emotional sentiments toward some of the slaves. Learning in 1849 that a favored slave family was to be sold, she wrote to her sister, Grace Austin, "I feel very sorry for the poor negroes. Tell Burwell and Linda farewell for me. Tell them that they must be sure to write to us and let us hear from them." She clearly acknowledged the slaves' literacy and understood what use Burwell and Linda were supposed to make of it—that is, the maintenance of the emotional bond that Martha felt she shared with them across the distance that her family was imposing on them. But Martha's sentimentalism reached even greater heights. She went on in the letter to describe the bundle of clothes she and Frances, another sister, had put together for the family. "You will find in it a pair of pantaloons for Burwell, a pair of shoes and stockings for Linda, and a little Sack for Linda['s daughter] little Lizzie. Frances sends Linda a cape and neck ribbon."[48]

It had long been common practice to give slaves new clothes when they were being sold at auction. This practice itself represented something of a bid for domestic respectability even in the slave market, as an indication that the slaves had come from "good homes."[49] Martha often worked to get enslaved men and women ready for market, fitting them with new clothes, shoes, and stockings and even making sure they brushed their teeth. She took pride in her feminine contribution to the marketing of these people, bragging to Iverson that the slave traders, being men of business, "would most probably dress them fine, but not in taste."[50] But Burwell and Linda's case was different. Here Martha's sentimental language was overwhelming. When Grace gave Burwell's family the clothes she was to "tell them that they must think of us when they put them on."[51] These articles were to be tangible reminders, embodiments of the sentimental bond between Martha and Frances on the one hand and Burwell, Linda, and Lizzie on the other. The clothes were meant, like the letters she wanted them to write, to serve as a tokens of sentiment, an emotional bridge spanning the distance that the market imposed.

Burwell and Linda probably understood well what these tokens of affection were meant to do. Another enslaved Austin woman, Mary, writing from South Carolina to her mother, had sent home a letter with a present in it. She talked about sending a little present for her sister and asked her father and uncle to send her something as well. Passing along mementos folded in letters amplified familial letters' role in bringing writer and recipient together in a common psychological space that was emotional and tangible.[52] This was certainly the effect Martha Twyman sought.

Emotions drove Martha Twyman's interactions with enslaved African Americans in other directions as well. Three months after the sad departure of Burwell and Linda, Martha learned that her brother, John, was taking another slave, "Old Mary," to a trader in Richmond. She felt quite differently about the sale of Mary, as she wrote to Frances. "I understand," she said, "that the old hag says that she intends to come back here to live. But I hope that her home is in the 'Sunny South' far away from me." Furthermore, when Martha learned that the traders had not allowed Alfred, another Austin slave, to see Mary before they took her away, Martha said that she was "very glad they did not."[53] Here the slave market proved a tool in the service of Martha's vindictive wishes, erecting an insurmountable geographic barrier not only between Old Mary and herself but between Mary and Alfred (whose relationship remains unknown). Sale constituted an expression not only of an utter lack of sympathy between Martha Twyman and Mary but also of the effective denial of Mary's sentimental bond with Alfred.

Martha's emotions thus ran hot and cold with regard to these enslaved people. The intensity of these sentiments, as she expressed them in this time of family crisis, spoke to the importance she invested in those relations. Her sentiments had been shaped by daily interactions with the bondpeople. Those relations had helped her define situationally who she was as a slaveholder and prevented her from understanding merely as depersonalized commodities the people her family thrust onto the slave market. With Burwell and Linda's family, she felt strong affection, and she assumed—or hoped—it was mutual. Mary, however, Martha believed to be a "hag," and she probably thought Mary felt likewise about her white mistress.

While Martha Twyman focused on the domestic aspect of the family's participation in the slave market, delving into the emotional implications of sale, she also participated in less sentimental conversations about the family's finances. But her husband, Iverson, and her brother, John, took care of most business when the time came. Iverson corresponded regularly with commercial slave traders in Richmond and Lynchburg, asking for the latest price quotes. Whatever reservations he may have had about splitting up slave families, he never recorded any remorse. His correspondence indicates that he may have even sold two teenagers whom traders thought sounded like potential "fancy girls."[54]

On one occasion, however, Iverson Twyman expressed his more sentimental side. Even then, his emotions were laced with hard-nosed calculation. In 1848, an enslaved man named Bob was killed in a work accident while hired out to work on the canal. "This is sad news," Iverson wrote to Martha. "I am sorry for the loss of the poor negro, as property, & I am sorry on account of the loss of a member of our family." Iverson saw perfect symmetry in expressing his sympathy and his pecuniary interest. Ultimately, however, Bob served Twyman's ends, even in death. Bob's demise spurred Iverson to reflect on his philosophy and life and to share those thoughts with his wife. "I look upon my negroes and myself as belonging to the same family," he told her, "and when one is snatched off by the hand of death, it not only leaves us one less but it is eminently calculated to remind us that 'in the midst of life, we are in death.'" Even sentimental Providence, it seemed, had a calculating mind, serving up Bob as an object lesson just for Twyman. Twyman went on to note that Bob's accident had killed him instantly. Rather than sympathizing with Bob or expressing thanks for a quick demise, Iverson again used Bob's death as a point of departure for personal reflection, writing that he agreed with "the great doctor Adam Clark," who preferred "to have a long warning to enable him to buckle on his armor before he went into the presence of God."[55]

Iverson and Martha Twyman may well have needed that armor in facing their God, but they did not indicate that it had anything to do with their participation in the slave market, which they saw simply as part of the slaveholding world. On the one hand, some of its effects were deemed regrettable, mainly for denying the Twymans the privilege of maintaining the sentimental slaveholders' domestic ideal. On the other hand, the owners embraced the convenience with which the commercial slave market allowed them to liquidate their capital investments to pay down estate debts. They saw no contradiction in their behavior, but they did employ sentimental language to channel their mixed feelings about their actions. Martha could lament the sale of one but revel in the sale of another. Sentiment could help soothe her sense of losing the favored Linda and Burwell, just as vindictive language helped her celebrate her triumph over Old Mary. For Iverson, sentimental language about death and the loss of the enslaved Bob helped to channel feelings about the uncertainties not only of death but of his life as a slaveholder.

The white Austins and Twymans were not alone in conveying their sentiments. At least three enslaved Austin women forced to migrate away wrote letters that provided a crucial link both to their families and to their former masters and mistresses. The few surviving letters provide a look at what effect sales and migrations forced by masters had on enslaved families, even when those African Americans had gained relatively privileged access to writing.

The dictates of the various Austin family members scattered enslaved family members across a relatively local sphere but one across which separations were acutely felt nonetheless. An elderly man named London wrote to "Master James" Austin in July 1854 that he was "very sick, sicker than I have been for some time." He asked Austin to allow Sally—perhaps his wife or a daughter—to come live with him, citing two reasons he hoped James would find persuasive: "I am unable to do anything for myself": he thought he would soon die and needed Sally's help. Second, he was concerned for Sally's possessions in his care. "If I do die," he worried, "Sally will loose all of her things that are at my house as there is no one there to take care of them." In a bid for friendly masculine banter, London added the news that "your colt is the likeliest colt you ever saw in your life," counseling James to keep what would be a valuable stallion. London also added that the field hands were "done cutting oats to day," and closed by encouraging Master James to come visit soon.[56] In May 1852, Lucy Patterson, who was at Howardsville with Iverson Twyman, sent a note by him to her son, Beverly, who then lived at the Austin estate in Buckingham County, informing him that the funeral for his sister, Frances, would be preached sometime in the next month and she wanted him to be there. She signed the brief note, "your affectionate Mother until death."[57]

Three enslaved mothers were fortunate enough to hear from their daughters in the 1850s. Mary wrote from Laurenceville, South Carolina; Anika Blew from

Warren County, Tennessee; and Susan Austin from Emanuel County, Georgia.[58] Like Gooley and Lucy Tucker, these women did not have to hide their literacy; in fact, Susan Austin engaged white Austin family members both lovingly and critically in her letter. Their correspondence is instructive because it shows some of the ways enslaved families accommodated themselves to the permanence of their separation and how that permanence helped shape the way they communicated with one another through and with the white family.

The letters, though never intended for publication, often represented a curiously semipublic performance of private sentiment. Even slaves who could write did not often have the luxury of sending private letters directly to their relatives. Many would have to forward them through the hands of white masters and mistresses. In fact, as the Austin letters suggest, the writers often explicitly addressed their letters to a variety of people, black and white. And since they carried news, the letters were passed around and, one hopes, delivered to or read to their intended recipients.

Despite the openness of the enslaved Austin families' writing, however, these women did not always have an easy time passing letters back and forth. Each approached her letter knowing that it passed through the hands and under the observation of new masters as well as the white Austins and Twymans back in Virginia. When Anika Blew wrote in 1857, she said that she had received no reply to her previous letter. Worrying that her message might not reach her mother, on the reverse she inscribed a note to Iverson Twyman: "Mr Twimon Sir, I will be very glad if you would take this to mother a[nd] oblige me being that I am black." Her note to Twyman was as much assertion as plea, his act of passing the letter more duty than favor.[59]

The other two women sent their letters through women of the white Austin family, who were perhaps more sympathetic or attentive than Twyman. Mary addressed her mother in care of Frances Austin. Mary had sent two previous letters and had received two letters in return (though she thought she should have received more). Other than in the address, Mary did not acknowledge the white Austins at all. By contrast, Susan Austin's letter, apparently the first she had written since her fairly recent sale south, interspersed references to both the black and white Austins. She wrote to her mother in care of Grace Austin— Frances and Martha's widowed mother—and informed those back in Virginia of her new address. "When you write," she instructed both black and white, "direct your letters to Swainsboro PO, Emanuel County, Georgia, Directed to Master Richard Edenfield."[60]

Anika Blew's letter and Mary's both focused almost exclusively on their enslaved families. They made no mention at all of the means of their separation from Virginia, seeking only to overcome that distance with their correspondence. Blew began her 1857 letter in typical contemporary fashion: "I take the pleasure of riting you a few lines to let you know that I am still in the land of the living yet." Because Blew had received no answer to her previous letter, she could not know whether her mother knew that Anika was alive and had given birth to her second son, Alex: "I dont now whether you know anny thing about it, and I thought maby that I would rite a gain" to make sure. In any case, Alex was a "fine large boy" and "gron very fast." Andrew, her older son, was also "well and grows finely." She wanted desperately to hear from her mother, to receive news of her life and "all of the rest of the connection." She passed individual messages along to two members in particular. "Father," she wrote, "I want to see you very bad and you to rite to me." And she assured her Aunt Judy that she had not forgotten her advice and that "I intend to do what you told me to do." Repeating the sentiments of many others, she insisted to her mother, "I want you to not greave after me," reassuring her that she was "going well a beter satis fied than I every were."[61]

Blew's letter resonated clearly with the one Mary had written in 1851 to her own mother. Like Blew, Mary wrote of her two children, neither of whom her mother apparently knew about yet. The younger one, Luviania Josy, was only eight months old, and while Mary said she was not married to Luviania's father, he was "very good" to the infant. Like Blew, Mary also reassured her mother she was "well satisfide as I ever was"; she had not yet been put to fieldwork. Mary looked for news of her family, hoping that her sister, Frances, was married and sending her love especially to Aunt Lucy and Clary. In an appended note to her father, Mary asked after him and her grandmother, "Little wathmore," uncles, aunts, and cousins.[62]

Perhaps Anika had seen Mary's 1851 letter, since at the time Anika wrote she had apparently had only recently left the Austin estate. Both women would most likely have learned to write and the proper way to frame a letter from the same teachers. Perhaps Grace Austin or one of her daughters taught the slaves. Or perhaps they learned from one of several other literate enslaved residents of the Austin estate.[63]

By holding to the forms and content of familial letters, these women sought to seize on the conventional vehicle of conveying news and sentiment across the country. By asking after each family member individually, if only briefly, they called up specific memories of these individuals and conveyed that they remembered those people despite the intervening space and time. Thus they let family members know that whatever the physical separation, they remained in the same emotional and spiritual world, represented by the tangible token, the letter.

Moreover, the use of the tropes of familiar letters connected those who had left to the meanings still encapsulated in those tropes. By starting her letter with "I take the pleasure of riting you a few lines to let you know that I am still in the land of the living yet," Anika Blew combined two common tropes that together spoke to the uncertainties of her life and the unlikelihood of her correspondence.[64] "I take the pleasure of riting" echoed the more common "I take this opportunity to write," which itself indicated that such opportunities seldom presented themselves. Blew likely had little time for such pleasures, and letter writers in areas not served by regular mails often had to seize on any possible chance to get a letter out. Her assertion that she was "still in the land of the living" was a common one among white correspondents at the time as well. Written by a slave woman, the trite phrase held deeper meaning still. Without the luxury of regular correspondence, her loved ones could not assume that Blew was still alive.[65]

Mary sought to exchange other tokens of familial sentiment in addition to the letter itself. She hoped to have something to send to little Maria in Virginia next time she wrote home. In turn, she added, "I hope that father will send me somthing and ouncle Wilson also." Other letter writers had similarly asked for and sent such tokens, sometimes even a photograph or a lock of hair.[66]

Mary did offer her mother one disturbing observation on the goings-on in Laurence County, South Carolina. She had "seen a grate many droves of black wones" passing through, headed apparently either to market or west with their masters. With one exception, however, she had "not seen none of my adquatenes" among them.

Remarkable as Mary's and Anika's letters might seem, Susan Austin's letter was even more impressive. She managed simultaneously to ingratiate herself to the white Austins and to criticize their actions in selling her south, to triumph over that forced distance by communicating across it—both to her own family and to the white Austins—a sense of domestic security she had not experienced in her old Virginia home. Susan wrote for many of the same reasons as Anika and Mary. Like the others, Susan employed certain tropes of sentimental letter writing, but perhaps with more skill. She began more elaborately, "Dear mother after my respects and goods wishes I take this opertunity to write you a few lines which will inform you that I am well hoping that these lines will find you and all the rest enjoying the same blessing." She asked after her Virginia family: her father; her aunt, Jane; and her younger brothers, James and Phil. She pleaded also with her mother to "take care of little Dallas and Joe for my sake," perhaps a reference to own young sons she had been forced to abandon. Like the other writers, Susan also sent news of the infant son she had with her in Georgia. "Little James Washington is well," she told her mother, "and can most walk and has four teeth."[67]

Like Anika Blew and Mary, Susan assured her mother that she had a "good home" and was "well satisfied" in Georgia. She sought particularly to assuage her Virginia friends' fears about being sold to the Lower South. "Do tell mary and sam not to be so much alarmed about the south," she insisted, "for it is as good living here as it is there." She knew the rumors, spread by slaveholders to compound the threat that separation already posed. "I have often heard it said that b[l]acks have nothing to eat at the south but cotton seed," she acknowledged, "but I am b[l]essed with a plenty that is good." She was worried about other pending sales on the Austin estate, asking where Henry was "gone" to and whether he "has left his family or not."[68]

Susan Austin reinforced her sentimental ties to the white Austin women as well. Almost as recitation, she went through the names of her former mistresses, qualifying each individual with some special remembrance: "remember my best love to old Mrs Auston, for she has been a kind mistress to me. remember my best love to Francis Auston; how bad I want to see her. remember my best love to Carline; she has been kind and well disposed to me."[69] Near the closing of her letter, she sought out from the white Austin women sentimental tokens of their bond and of their continued correspondence across the distance between them. She asked the widow Grace Austin to write and requested that Frances "write me a letter and send me some flower seed in it." She had now "got to a place where I need them." She recognized the letters as bonds keeping open communications between herself and her family, and she sought out some living sentimental token of Virginia, some tangible tie to her home. Flower seeds would provide a renewable resource, a vehicle of sentimental memory.[70]

Suddenly, in the middle of her letter, Austin found a surprisingly vindictive and mocking voice. Turning to yet another Austin woman, she lashed out:

Rebecca Auston you sent me to the cotton country to make me miserable but . . . I would not swapp homes and go back and live with you for the whole world. . . . [R]ecollect Rebecca Auston when I was confined you would not allow me any thing to eat for four days but I now have a good home and plenty to eat and no fuss about what I have to do. I am so glad that I have got away from the [Horsleys] that they were so mean that I was ashamed to go in the neighborhood.

my good respects to Master George for I was sarrow to leave him but he had such a cruel wife that I am glad that I have left.[71]

In addition to these charges that Rebecca Horsley Austin had treated her with cruelty during her recent pregnancy, Susan alleged that the untoward actions of some unnamed member of Rebecca's family had left Susan feeling "ashamed" to be seen in public.[72]

Susan's unrestrained condemnation of these slaveholders' actions and character demands an explanation, especially since she bracketed her criticism with affectionate expressions of her continued bond to the other white Austin women. She obviously thought she could get away with her attack on Rebecca without risking any retribution toward her family still held by the Austins and without compromising the emotional exchange with her mother and other family members, which her letter also sought. And she may well have succeeded. The explanation for Susan's brazenness, it seems, lay in Austin family politics.

The Austin family had generally disapproved of Rebecca Horsley's marriage to George Austin, son of the widowed Grace Austin and brother to John Austin, Frances Austin, Grace Austin, and Martha Austin Twyman. Frances and Martha Twyman saw Rebecca as an upstart and a gold digger, a woman out to satisfy her desires to the intentional detriment of both white and black members of the Austin household. In 1848, before the marriage took place, Martha saw what was to come, writing to Frances that Rebecca "may *pretend that she loves* [George] as long as he has anything" to spend, "but you know when that is gone she will treat him *like a dog*." Rebecca was already putting her hands on George's assets: slaves he had received in the estate division. "You mind what I say," Martha predicted, "that if Geo[rge] sells Sukey," Rebecca "will take a $100 or more and go to Lynchburg or Richmond and spend it on fine dressing and come back and *splurge* about thinking she will triumph over us greatly." Martha could only pray that by "a merciful Providence" the family might "be delivered from her evil designs."[73] They were not spared and still less were the Twymans' African American "family" members, as Susan Austin well testified from her new home in Georgia.

Susan Austin's letter was no lament, however. She both condemned Rebecca Austin's actions and provided evidence for her triumph over the capricious woman. Susan's assurances to her mother that she now had a good home also taunted Rebecca. Here, Susan's dual agendas in writing came together and became clear. The most significant emblem of her newfound domestic freedom was her son, "Little James Washington," who, despite Rebecca's cruelty during the pregnancy, was thriving. By bragging about the boy to her mother, Susan also drove home the point that she and her son were now free from Rebecca Austin's grasp.[74]

Through a highly selective use of language, Susan Austin carefully included white family members she counted among her sentimental circle. The sentimental lines for her family were intended to bring her into their emotional presence despite the distance the Austins had forced her to cross. It sought to remind them that she was in the same world they inhabited, though they could not see her. By maintaining only the slimmest of connections to her old home and own family, the letter kept Susan Austin from social death. At the same time, her sentimental entreaties to Grace, Frances, and their mother were intended to implicate them in the successful passage of this letter to her mother. By asserting her inclusion in their sentimental world, she maintained a connection to the rest of her own world as well. And as for Rebecca Horsley Austin, Susan's caustic statements were equally well placed. They directed all the anger she felt at her treatment in Virginia and her removal from Virginia at this unbeloved in-law, doubly emphasizing Susan's alliance with Frances and Grace, who also despised Rebecca.

This series of letters among black and white Austin families might be seen as the peak of paternalism in the face of the slave market. These slaveholding women and men expressed in sentimental language their emotions regarding the men and women they cast onto the slave market. Along with death, instances of sale represented the key opportunities for such expression, marking the moment in which slaveholders had proven incapable of or unwilling to live up to their own standard, the moment at which that standard itself was proven an illusion.

While slaveholders may have read African Americans' sentiments as confirmation of paternalistic bonds, the letters also represented the language of sentiment some enslaved African Americans adopted as their own. African Americans used this language to convey to each other the emotional urgency of the crises in which the slave market placed them.

Seizing on the rare opportunities to write letters to family members, enslaved women and (even less often) men sought in some way to overcome the vast space the slave market had opened up between themselves and their loved ones. In sentimental language, they found the motifs of grief that helped them articulate their feelings to each other. By focusing on those feelings of loss, they hoped to bring about a sense of presence, creating an emotional link between writer and recipient. This link might even be embodied in the letter itself, where physical manifestations of the emotional world often served as touchstones of sentiment.

Literate slaves sometimes used these letters explicitly to create mementos of loss, artifacts of emotional strain. In doing so, they turned sentiment inside out, openly exposing rather than veiling their sense of grief at spoiled relations. Emily Plummer's husband, Adam, had at first given up on their marriage, to Emily's shock. "I want you to let me know why you wrote me so troubled a letter," she demanded in 1856, adding, "I was very sorry to hear that you should say you and I are parted for life." Adam continued to struggle with his doubts as the two communicated news of their scattered children. When he wrote to Emily in January 1858, he managed to articulate an expressiveness he may not have possessed in person. Even prose, in fact, seemed inadequate to convey his longing for Emily, so he drafted a few lines of verse, revising them in a March 8 letter and appending a dedication, "This is for Emily Plummer." He wanted to send her a token of his heartfelt affection, something she could read and enjoy over and again, linking her emotionally to him in the act of holding the letter and reading the poem. His verse communicated more effectively than prose his boundless isolation and the only limited relief to be gained through prayer. It closed with his vision of Emily thinking of him and of their mutual despair.

> While sorrows encampass me Round
> and Endless Distresses I see
> astonished I cry can a mortal be found
> thats surrounded with troubles like me
>
> few Hours of peace I enjoy
> and they are succeeded by pain.
> if a moment of praising my God I enjoy
> I have Hours again to complain
>
> this of him you offen Speak of
> and consolation given
> and of Him you sweetly said
> that our Hearts are broken.[75]

In 1861, when their daughter, Sarah Maranda Plummer, was sold, jailed in Alexandria, and shipped to New Orleans, she too gave up on seeing her parents again. In fact, she was angry that no one had visited her during her two months' in jail. She knew her mother had been too far away, but she did "think it very hard that father did not come to see me as he was nearer." Regardless, she sent her love to all and reminded her brother to write to her "as he promised to do." Sarah knew her mother would be "sorry to hear I am so far," but in closing, she indicated what the letter would mean to her mother, writing, "I hope you will have a pleasant time over my letter." Like her father's verse, her letter was a mixed blessing, a bittersweet memento.[76]

Some African American families seized on sentimentalism, the lingua franca among northern and southern white family members in the nineteenth century, precisely because it seemed so well suited to convey the sense of loss imposed by forced migrations across the country. Sentimental language not only provided an emotional link to family members but also helped to mediate between black family members and the white family through whom most letters would have to pass. This process implicated slaveholders in the emotional exchange, helping to ensure their approval of the letters and the conveyance of them to their intended recipients. Enslaved correspondents sought to minimize the effects of the slave market by communicating emotional as well as factual information, to send something of themselves in the language of their letters. Letter writers sought to deny their masters' market decisions full force by conversing in sentimental, human form back across the space over which they had been moved as chattel.

Such letters were always fraught with the tense feelings brought on by the imposed distance. Yet these relatively fortunate few African Americans treasured these rare pieces of evidence of their loved ones' continued affection. In a touching testimony to the power of sentimental literacy in the face of the slave market, Agnes Hobbes kept for decades the "old faded letters" her husband wrote from Tennessee. She passed them on to her daughter, Elizabeth Keckley, who preserved them into the 1860s as "the most precious mementoes of my existence."[77]

NOTES

My sincere thanks go to Ed Baptist and Stephanie Camp and to the other readers who commented on earlier versions of this essay, including Edward Ayers, Reginald Butler, Elizabeth Fenn, Joseph Miller, Sydney Nathans, Franny Nudelman, William Reddy, Brenda Stevenson, Peter Wood, and all the participants in the workshop on New Directions in the Study of the Americas: Slavery, A Continuing Conversation held at Rutgers on May 16–17, 2003. Thanks also go to Jennifer Monaghan for early encouragement in pursuing enslaved correspondence. Their advice, heeded and unheeded, is much appreciated.

1. Harriet Newby to Dangerfield Newby, August 16, 1859, in *Calendar of Virginia State Papers* (Richmond, 1875–93), 11:310–11, reprinted in *Slave Testimony: Two Centuries of Letters, Speeches, Interviews, and Autobiographies*, ed. John Blassingame (Baton Rouge, 1977), 118–19.

2. Emily Plummer to Adam Plummer, August 19, 1861, in Nellie Plummer, *Out of the Depths* (Washington, 1972), reprinted in Dorothy Sterling, *We Are Your Sisters: Black Women in the Nineteenth Century* (1984; New York, 1997), 47.

3. An excellent study of such tropes and their meanings in nineteenth-century American letter writing is William Merrill Decker, *Epistolary Practices: Letter Writing in America before Telecommunications* (Chapel Hill, 1998).

4. Bruce Redford, *The Converse of the Pen: Acts of Intimacy in the Eighteenth-Century Familiar Letter* (Chicago, 1986); Andrew Burstein, *The Inner Jefferson: Portrait of a Grieving Optimist* (Charlottesville, 1995), chaps. 2, 4; Thomas L. Haskell, "Capitalism and the Origins of the Humanitarian Sensibility," in *The Antislavery Debate: Capitalism and Abolitionism as a Problem in Historical Interpretation*, ed. Thomas Bender (Berkeley, 1992), chaps. 4, 5.

5. Willie Lee Rose, "The Domestication of Domestic Slavery" (1973), in *Slavery and Freedom*, ed. William W. Freehling (New York, 1982), 18–36; Eugene Genovese, *Roll, Jordan, Roll: The World the Slaves Made* (New York, 1974). See also Kathleen Brown, *Good Wives, Nasty Wenches, and Anxious Patriarchs: Gender, Race, and Power in Colonial Virginia* (Chapel Hill); Rhys Isaac, *Transformation of Virginia, 1740–1790* (New York, 1988); Jan Lewis, *The Pursuit of Happiness: Family and Values in Jefferson's Virginia* (New York, 1983); Peter Bardaglio, *Reconstructing the Household: Families, Sex, and the Law in the Nineteenth-Century South* (Chapel Hill, 1995). Daniel Blake Smith disagrees on an early-eighteenth-century shift; see *Inside the Great House: Planter Family Life in Eighteenth-Century Chesapeake Society* (Ithaca, 1980).

6. Genovese, *Roll, Jordan, Roll*; Michael Tadman, *Speculators and Slaves: Masters, Traders, and Slaves in the Old South* (Madison, 1989).

7. Amy Dru Stanley, "Home Life and the Morality of the Market," in *The Market Revolution in America: Social, Political, and Religious Expressions, 1800–1880*, ed. Melvin Stokes and Stephen Conway (Charlottesville, 1996), 74–96. If homes in the northern hotbed of reform did not conform to domestic ideals, how much less so did slaveholding households, where violence was openly acknowledged and implemented? This was in fact key to abolitionist critique of slavery; see Gillian Brown, *Domestic Individualism: Imagining Self in Nineteenth-Century America* (Berkeley, 1990), chap. 1. Still, Bardaglio, Weiner, and others affirm ideology's importance in shaping action.

8. See esp. Brenda E. Stevenson, "Distress and Discord in Virginia Slave Families, 1830–1860," in *In Joy and in Sorrow: Women, Family, and Marriage in the Victorian South*, ed. Carol Bleser (New York, 1992), 103–24; Brenda E. Stevenson, *Life in Black and White: Family and Community in the Slave South* (New York, 1996), chaps. 7, 8; Norrece T. Jones Jr., *Born a Child of Freedom, Yet a Slave: Mechanisms of Control and Strategies of Resistance in Antebellum South Carolina* (Middletown, 1990). Others emphasize the relative prevalence of two-parent households and the strength of marriages, even in cross-plantation unions; see Herbert G. Gutman, *The Black Family in Slavery and Freedom, 1750–1925* (New York, 1976); Ann Patton Malone, *Sweet Chariot: Slave Family and Household Structure in Nineteenth-Century Louisiana* (Chapel Hill, 1992); Cheryll Ann Cody, "Naming, Kinship, and Estate Dispersal: Notes on Slave Family Life on a South Carolina Plantation, 1786 to 1833," *William and Mary Quarterly*, 3rd ser., 39 (January 1982): 192–211; Cheryll Ann Cody, "Sale and Separation: Four Crises for Enslaved Women on the Ball Plantations 1764–1854," in *Working toward Freedom: Slave Society and Domestic Economy in the American South*, ed. Larry E. Hudson Jr. (Rochester, 1994), 119–42; Emily West, "Surviving Separation: Cross-Plantation Marriages and the Slave Trade in Antebellum South Carolina," *Journal of Family History* 24 (April 1999): 212–31; Emily West, "The Debate on the Strength of Slave Families: South Carolina and the Importance of Cross-Plantation Marriages," *Journal of American Studies* 33 (August 1999): 221–41.

9. Marli Weiner, *Mistresses and Slaves: Plantation Women in South Carolina, 1830–1880* (Urbana, 1998), 114, 123, 121.

10. Dickson Bruce, *Origins of African American Literature, 1680–1865* (Charlottesville, 2001).

11. Tadman, *Speculators and Slaves*, 12 (table 2.1), 45, 147, 170–71, 296–302.

12. Charles Sellers, *The Market Revolution: Jacksonian America, 1815–1846* (New York, 1992). Harry L. Watson is one of the few to explicitly acknowledge the slave trade as a key component of the American market revolution; see "Slavery and Development in a Dual Economy: The South and the Market Revolution," in *Market Revolution in America*, ed. Stokes and Conway, 43–73. By contrast, see Douglas R. Egerton, "Markets without a Market Revolution: Southern Planters and Capitalism," *Journal of the Early Republic* 16 (Summer 1996): 207–21. For the often violent nature of this upheaval, see Edward Baptist, *Creating an Old South: Middle Florida's Plantation Frontier before the Civil War* (Chapel Hill, 2002). White southern families also felt the stresses of market expansion and migration to the southwest; see Joan E. Cashin, *A Family Venture: Men*

and Women on the Southern Frontier (Baltimore, 1994). Walter Johnson's *Soul by Soul: Life in the Antebellum Slave Market* (Cambridge, 1999) is the first book to assess the cultural implications of the slave market in southern life (black and white) in general, although it remains tightly focused on the sites of sale and inspection in New Orleans. Johnson shows how the market pervaded notions of self, of honor, and of paternalism and that slaves too calculated their narrow range of motion in the market, sizing up buyers and acting accordingly; we might retitle his book "Speculators All!"

13. Richard Brodhead, "Sparing the Rod: Discipline and Fiction in Antebellum America," *Representations* 21 (Winter 1988): 67–96, reprinted in *Culture of Letters: Scenes of Reading and Writing in Nineteenth-Century America* (Chicago, 1993), 13–47.

14. John Comaroff and Jean Comaroff, *Ethnography and the Historical Imagination* (Boulder, 1992), esp. 28–30. Their definition of ideology is that which is contested; hegemony is that which is (largely) not contested. In that framework, then, sentiment (both in domesticity and paternalism) was ideological and not hegemonic, although it sought to be hegemonic with its language of universality.

15. William Reddy, *Navigation of Feeling: A Framework for the History of Emotions* (New York, 2001).

16. Jennifer Fleischner, *Mastering Slavery: Memory, Family, and Identity in Women's Slave Narratives* (New York, 1998); Shirley Samuels, ed., *The Culture of Sentiment: Race, Gender, and Sentimentality in Nineteenth-Century America* (New York, 1992). Thanks to Joe Miller for the concept of a lingua franca.

17. This was made most clear to me in African Americans' nineteenth-century autobiographies about their lives in slavery; see Phillip Troutman, *Sentiment in the Slave Market Revolution: New Perspectives on the History of the South* (Gainesville, forthcoming).

18. In his study, Stephen Stowe found so little discussion of enslaved African Americans—"even familiar, personal servants"—in the planters' papers he examined that he mentions slaves only half a dozen times (*Intimacy and Power in the Old South: Ritual in the Lives of the Planters* [Baltimore, 1987], xvi–xvii). Walter Johnson, by contrast, found slaveholders' letters "full of talk about slaves" (*Soul by Soul*, 13).

19. Tadman calls these people "key" slaves, those on whom slaveholders focused their paternalism while they ignored the mass of field workers (*Speculators and Slaves*, xix).

20. Hayden had gained his literacy (alphabetic and numerical) in part through the teaching of white mistresses, in part on his own. He claimed to have run a school for black children in the area of Lexington, Kentucky, with full permission of local planters and town leaders (William Hayden, *Narrative of William Hayden, Containing a Faithful Account of His Travels for a Number of Years, whilst a Slave in the South; Written by Himself* [Cincinnati, 1846], 32).

21. Jennifer Monaghan points out the crucial difference in the difficulty of attaining reading skills versus writing skills, especially among slaves. Reading was associated with evangelical ends, while writing was considered a skill of commerce, travel, and politics, leading slaveholders to be far less likely to counsel writing than reading. Moreover, learning to read required access only to written materials, while writing required specialized tools. Writing also required time, a commodity slaves found especially scarce ("Reading for the Enslaved, Writing for the Free," Wiggins lecture, American Antiquarian Society,

Worcester, Mass., November 5, 1998, in *Proceedings of the American Antiquarian Society* 108, no. 2 [1999]: 309–41). A unique source indicates what literacy rates enslaved African Americans might achieve under the most favorable conditions Virginia slaveholders had to offer. In a September 1853 petition to the American Colonization Society, slave John Scott indicated that of the 118 slaves on John Enders's plantation, "some 45 or 50" knew how to read and "some 6. or 7." could also write. On Enders's plantation, then, about 40 percent could read only, while 5 percent could both read and write. These represented the maximum respective rates of literacy likely for enslaved African Americans, since Enders's strategy of manumission and colonization had probably encouraged literacy (John Scott to American Colonization Society, September 19, 1853, American Colonization Society Papers, Library of Congress, in *Blacks in Bondage: Letters of American Slaves*, ed. Robert Starobin [New York, 1974], 108–10). Other historians have made estimates and ventured guesses of 5–10 percent literacy among slaves—sometimes higher—but have done so without making Monaghan's (and Scott's) key distinction between rates of reading and rates of writing. See Carter G. Woodson, *The Education of the Negro Prior to 1861* (1919; Salem, 1986), 85, 227–28; Janet Duitsman Cornelius, "We Slipped and Learned to Read: Slave Accounts of the Literacy Process, 1830–1865," *Phylon* 44 (September 1983): 186; Janet Duitsman Cornelius, *"When I Can Read My Title Clear": Literacy, Slavery, and Religion in the Antebellum South* (Columbia, 1991), 8–9, 62–64; W. E. B. Du Bois, *Black Reconstruction in America: An Essay toward a History of the Part Which Black Folk Played in the Attempt to Reconstruct Democracy in America, 1860–1880* (1935; New York, 1964), 638; Sterling, *We Are Your Sisters*, 44n. On evangelical efforts to encourage literacy among slaves, see Cornelius, *"When I Can Read"*; Janet Duitsman Cornelius, *Slave Missions and the Black Church in the Antebellum South* (Columbia, 1999); see also James Bruce Fort, "The Politics and Culture of Literacy in Georgia, 1800–1920" (Ph.D. diss., University of Virginia, 1999).

22. Of course, we often have no way of knowing whether these letters made it to their intended parties. A slaveholder might give the letter to its enslaved recipient or censor, paraphrase, or misrepresent the contents. The slaveholder might keep it or destroy it. The fact that some of these missives remain in slaveholders' family papers might indicate that the recipients never saw the letters. Nevertheless, the retention of any such letters is significant.

23. Cashin, *Family Venture*.

24. Unidentified member of Cabell-Harrison-Breckinridge family, quoted in Gail S. Terry, "Sustaining the Bonds of Kinship in a Trans-Appalachian Migration, 1790–1811: The Cabell-Breckinridge Slaves Move West," *Virginia Magazine of History and Biography* 102 (October 1994): 464. Terry tracks the cycle of hope and despair this enslaved community endured in these serial migrations.

25. Gooley to "Dear Mistress," November 30, 1807, Duke Marion Godbey Papers, University of Kentucky, in *We Are Your Sisters*, ed. Sterling, 51.

26. Ibid.

27. Ibid.

28. Elizabeth Hobbs [Keckley] to Agnes Hobbs, April 10, 1838, in Elizabeth Keckley,

Behind the Scenes; or, Thirty Years a Slave, and Four Years in the White House (1868; New York, 1988), 39–42, reprinted in *Slave Testimony*, ed. Blassingame, 20–21.

29. Applying psychoanalytic theory, Fleischner exposes the domestic rift Keckley was attempting to cover up by inserting the letters in her autobiography (*Mastering Slavery*, 119–20; see also George Pleasant Hobbes to Agnes Hobbs, September 6, 1833, in Keckley, *Behind the Scenes*, 39–42, reprinted in *Slave Testimony*, ed. Blassingame, 19.

30. Sargry Brown to Mores Brown, October 27, 1840, in *National Anti-slavery Standard*, September 16, 1841, reprinted in *Slave Testimony*, ed. Blassingame, 46–47, and in *We Are Your Sisters*, ed. Sterling, 45.

31. Maria Perkins to Richard Perkins, October 8[?], 1852, Ulrich B. Phillips Papers, Yale University Library, New Haven, Conn. This document has been frequently reproduced. I am quoting from the verbatim transcription in *A Documentary History of Slavery in North America*, ed. Willie Lee Rose (New York, 1976), 151; also appears in *Life and Labor in the Old South*, ed. Ulrich B. Phillips (Boston, 1929), 212; and *Slave Testimony*, ed. Blassingame, 96–97. A digitized image of the letter appears in *Valley of the Shadow: Two Communities in the American Civil War*, online at http://valley.vcdh.virginia.edu/ personalpapers/images/augusta/perkins.jpg (accessed April 18, 2005). Perkins's information was correct. James Brady was a saddler and slave trader in Scottsville from the late 1840s through at least 1856, forwarding his purchases to Richmond auctioneers for resale. Some of his accounts, bills of sale, and correspondence are in the Harris-Brady Papers, Alderman Library Special Collections, University of Virginia, Charlottesville.

32. Ibid.

33. Vilet Lester to Patsey Padison [Patterson], August 29, 1857, Joseph Allred Papers, Special Collections Library, Duke University, Durham, N.C.; available at http://scripto rium.lib.duke.edu/collections/african-american-women.html (accessed April 18, 2005).

34. Ibid.

35. Ibid.

36. Ibid.

37. Ed Baptist has read this letter as evidence of African Americans using slaveholders' ideology against them. While I believe this is certainly true, especially in the case of Boyd's letter, I read it somewhat differently. Sentiment was certainly a calculated and manipulative language, but because it sought to convey transparently one's emotions and shaped those emotions as they appeared in prose, other cognitive forces are at work along with conscious ideology. To be taken seriously, Boyd had to be read as sincere. See Edward E. Baptist, " 'Better Than My Present Situation': A Slave Woman Commands Planter Ideology," paper presented at the annual conference of the Organization of American Historians, Washington, D.C., April 12, 2002.

38. Virginia Boyd to Rice C. Ballard, May 6, 1853, Rice C. Ballard Papers, Southern Historical Collection, University of North Carolina, Chapel Hill.

39. The other likely culprit was James Boyd, Samuel's brother, who worked for Judge Boyd and Ballard.

40. J. M. Duffield to R. C. Ballard, May 29, 1848, as quoted in "Africans in America: America's Journey through Slavery," http://www.pbs.org/wgbh/aia/.

41. Virginia Boyd to Rice C. Ballard, May 6, 1853, Ballard Papers.

42. Ibid.

43. Ibid.

44. C. M. Rutherford to R. C. Ballard, August 6, 8, 1853, Ballard Papers.

45. [John Austin?] to Frances Austin, [1848 or 1849], Austin-Twyman Papers, College of William and Mary, Williamsburg, Va..

46. Information gathered from three separate lists of Austin slave sales, in Archibald Austin estate legal file, Austin-Twyman Papers. On African American naming patterns, see Gutman, *Black Family in Slavery and Freedom*, 178–80 (table 25), and more generally 185–201.

47. Iverson L. Twyman to Frances Austin, 1849, Austin-Twyman Papers.

48. Martha E. Twyman to Grace Austin, September 1849, Austin-Twyman Papers.

49. Steven Deyle, paper presented at the annual conference of the American Historical Association, Washington, D.C., January 10, 1999.

50. Martha E. Twyman to Iverson L. Twyman, February 27, 1855; Martha E. Twyman to Frances Austin, October 7[?], 1848; Martha E. Twyman to John Austin, October 14, 1848; Iverson L. Twyman to John Austin, October 14 [n.d.], Austin-Twyman Papers. Martha also knew more hard-nosed market ways, counseling Iverson on one occasion to wait for Richmond prices to rise before sending off the two women she was fixing up for sale (February 27, 1855).

51. Martha E. Twyman to Grace Austin, September 1849, Austin-Twyman Papers.

52. Mary to mother, June 22, 1851, Austin-Twyman Papers. Other enslaved and recently freed African Americans used such sentimental tokens—for example, an ambrotype or a string of beads—to connect to their loved ones; see Sterling, *We Are Your Sisters*, 50; Ira Berlin and Leslie S. Rowland, eds., *Families and Freedom: Documentary History of African-American Kinship in the Civil War Era* (New York, 1997), 98.

53. Martha E. Twyman to Frances Austin, December 1949, December 18, 1849, Austin-Twyman Papers.

54. Seth Woodruff to Iverson L. Twyman, March 5, 1854; R. H. Dickinson and brother to Iverson L. Twyman, November 20, 1854, Austin-Twyman Papers. Whether or not Twyman intended to sell these young women into sexual slavery, traders might do so after the teenagers left Twyman's hands. Twyman corresponded fairly frequently with these and other traders from the 1850s through 1864.

55. Iverson L. Twyman to Martha E. Twyman, September 7, 8, 1848, Austin-Twyman Papers.

56. London to James M. Austin, July 13, 1854, Austin-Twyman Papers.

57. Lucy Patterson to Beverly, May 31, 1852, Austin-Twyman Papers.

58. Mary, c/o Col. F. H. Grby[?], to her mother, c/o Frances Austin, June 22, 1851; Anika Blew to her mother, c/o Iverson L. Twyman, July 26, 1857; Susan Austin to her mother, c/o Mrs. Grace Austin, July 18, 1851, Austin-Twyman Papers. Susan Austin used the spelling *Auston* for both black and white Austins.

59. Anika Blew to her mother, c/o Iverson L. Twyman, July 26, 1857, Austin-Twyman Papers.

60. Susan Austin to her mother, c/o Mrs. Grace Austin, July 18, 1851, Austin-Twyman Papers.

61. Anika Blew to her mother, c/o Iverson L. Twyman, July 26, 1857, Austin-Twyman Papers.

62. Mary, c/o Col. F. H. Grby[?], to her mother, c/o Frances Austin, June 22, 1851, Austin-Twyman Papers.

63. For example, other enslaved letter writers whose documents survive in the Austin-Twyman Papers include Lucy Patterson to Beverly, May 31, 1852; Chambree [Cambridge?] Austin to "Doctor Twyman", n.d.; Absalom to Dr. I. L. Twyman, March 1, 1859; London to James M. Austin, July 13, 1854, Austin-Twyman Papers.

64. Anika Blew to her mother, c/o Iverson L. Twyman, July 26, 1857, Austin-Twyman Papers.

65. For explanations of these tropes and their deeper meanings, including and especially for slaves, see Decker, *Epistolary Practices*, 58, 87–88, 95–96. Another common trope was the assertion that all would meet in heaven if not on this earth. Decker again is lucid on the point: "Unity in God [was] very commonly cited as a consolation for what correspondents knew to be the uncertainty of earthly convergences" (76).

66. Enslaved servants understood the networks along which white people passed similar sentimental tokens. As Phill Anthony dictated in the postscript of a letter to his master, "Miss Bowdoin sent a handkerchief by Miss C. Balfour to be forwarded from Richmond to Mrs Coalter" (September 14, 1807, in *Slave Testimony*, ed. Blassingame, 8–9). Self-emancipated Union soldier Aaron Oats, serving in Virginia in 1864, sent his wife back in Kentucky a portrait he had had made, though she never received it (Lucretia Oats to Aaron Oats, December 22, 1864, in *Families and Freedom*, ed. Berlin and Rowland [New York, 1997], 160–61; Ira Berlin, Steven F. Miller, and Leslie S. Rowland, "Afro-American Families in the Transition from Slavery to Freedom," *Radical History Review* 42 [Fall 1988]: 89–121).

67. Susan Austin to her mother, c/o Mrs. Grace Austin, July 18, 1851, Austin-Twyman Papers.

68. Ibid. Henry could conceivably have run away rather than been sold, but her question about him was immediately followed by the advice to Mary and Sam about their forced exile to the South, so it seems likely Henry was also to be sold.

69. Ibid. I have added punctuation to this quotation to clarify the parallel language of her remembrances.

70. Ibid. She also wrote, "Remember my best love to Agnes Auston and tell her to send me some of her flower seed that bloom all the winter," but it remains unclear who Agnes was. She was most likely a member of the white Austin family, given her placement in the letter. But Susan did mix her references to white and black family members throughout the letter, so Agnes may have been African American kin.

71. Ibid.

72. Ibid. Susan Austin also leveled criticism at the DeWitt family, most likely Bennet M. Dewitt and Julia Horsley DeWitt of Lynchburg. Susan's reasons remain unclear, but Bennet DeWitt had married into the Horsley family, and he occasionally brokered slave

sales from Twyman to traders in Lynchburg and Richmond. See B. M. DeWitt to Iverson Twyman, March 26, December 31, 1846, March 27, 1847; memorandum, November 28, 1863, Austin-Twyman Papers.

73. Martha E. Austin Twyman to Frances Austin, December 29, 1848, Austin-Twyman Papers.

74. Susan Austin to her mother, Austin-Twyman Papers.

75. Adam F. Plummer to Emily Plummer, January 3, March 8, 1858, in *The Mind of the Negro as Reflected in Letters Written During the Crisis, 1800–1860*, ed. Carter G. Woodson (1926; New York, 1969), 524–25. I have added line breaks to Plummer's verse, following his meter.

76. Sarah Maranda Plummer to Emily Plummer, May 24, 1861, in ibid., 527–28. Emily and Adam were reunited in 1863, and in 1866, Sarah's brother traveled to New Orleans and brought Sarah back home (Sterling, *We Are Your Sisters*, 47–48).

77. Keckley, *Behind the Scenes*, 26–27.

"Stol' and Fetched Here"

Enslaved Migration, Ex-slave Narratives,

and Vernacular History

EDWARD E. BAPTIST

*M*y mother and uncle Robert and Joe," said ninety-year-old Margaret Nickerson, seventy-two years after slavery ended in her native state of Florida, "was stol' from Virginia and fetched here." Mary Brown's grandmother, born in Virginia, was sold into Arkansas, but not before one of her children had been "stole," as she remembered it—sold off into the slave trade and never seen again by his family. Cora Gillam's family was "stolen from their home in North Carolina" and taken southwest. Ex-slave Adaline Montgomery said that by selling slaves into the interstate trade in human beings, planters "stole" the enslaved. Lewis Brown explained his genealogy in this way: "My mother was stole. The speculators stole her and they brought her to Kemper County, Mississippi, and sold her."[1] With their words, the formerly enslaved traced the events and persons that formed the roots of their family trees from the southwestern plantation frontier back to the older African American plantation communities of the South Atlantic states. In forms of the verb *to steal*, they made an argument about the nature of slavery and about white folks' relations with blacks in general. They left for us, if we pick up the threads of what they said, a string of clues. The trail leads back in time through a century-long development of genres of thought and speech, at once popular and sub rosa, influential and secret. They spoke a history that marked the move from the Upper to the Lower South as the truest measure of what slavery meant, a process that belied any myths about paternalistic planters and kindly masters, a history both stolen and of being stole.

The experience of theft was not unusual or uncommon, although the academic historiography of slavery in the United States has too often ignored, marginalized, or sanitized it.[2] Between 1790 and 1860, slave traders and planters managed the transportation of more than one million enslaved Africans and

African Americans from the older South Atlantic states to the U.S. South's plantation frontier. States and territories such as Alabama, Arkansas, Florida, Louisiana, Mississippi, and Texas became new homes for those either sold into the domestic slave trade or marched west and south by migrant planters intent on re-creating themselves as cotton or sugar magnates. Millions more spouses, children, parents, and siblings remained behind, in most cases separated forever. For those driven south by owners and traders, the journey was difficult, and what followed arrival was perhaps even harder: new, even harsher labor requirements; unfamiliar disease environments; still more sexual and physical abuse.[3] But worst of all from the perspective of the enslaved, the trade in human beings routinely divided parents, children, siblings, and spouses: planters sold human beings to dealers, who in turn carried the slaves to auction blocks like those of the notorious New Orleans slave market. Those taken by the slave trade would rarely reunite with those left behind. Traders and owners even stole the ability to communicate with those from whom slaves were taken. "Them was terrible times," remembered Ishmael Moore of Virginia in the 1930s. "I had two brothers sold away and ain't never seen 'em no more 'til this day!"[4]

Traders had no monopoly on inflicting division by long distance, of course. Slave owners who moved to Mississippi, Alabama, or elsewhere did not let the off-plantation family ties that many slaves had created hinder the process of uprooting the plantation community. Lorenzo Ivy remembered that when "cotton fever" struck his owner, "Old Tunstall separated families right and lef'," dividing seven sets of husbands and wives whose marriage vows crossed property lines.[5] Even family ties on a single plantation were not safe, for planters left children and the elderly on homeplaces maintained in the old states while dragging adults at the peak of productivity to the frontier, where their labor could be most profitable. "My boss man," recalled Ross Simmons, "carried all the best hands to Texas and carried the scrub hands across Cypress Creek here in Arkansas, and that's where I came." Harve Osborne's North Carolina owner handed control of his plantation to his brother and moved many of his youngest slaves, including Osborne, to a new operation in Arkansas. Osborne's parents remained on the North Carolina plantation. One Louisiana planter owned both Henry Lewis's mother and his father, but after adding a Texas plantation to his holdings, he separated the spouses. Lewis's father stayed in Louisiana, while Lewis's mother, pregnant with Henry, was moved to Texas. And the distributions of estates could split up black families, scattering them southwestward as property divisible and fungible even without the action of the slave trade per se. Reeves Tucker's Alabama owner died, and the man's son, who inherited Tucker's father, decided to move to Texas. But Reeves, his siblings, and his mother went to legatees who were staying put. Faced with separation from his whole family, Reeves remembered, "Pappy begged so hard for some of the children that finally they let me go with him. I never seed Mammy or any of my relatives after that."[6]

Few historians have written about enslaved people forced to move with their owners and about the separations and other difficulties that such persons had to endure. And while some historians have written about the slave trade, few have analyzed the way in which those who suffered from it remembered it. Yet the experience of devastating separation was common during the years of enslavement, especially after the invention of the cotton gin, the growth of world markets, and the territorial expansion of the United States opened an entire subcontinent in which slaveholders could make real their new dreams. Historians who try to measure such things have argued that during the era of peak southwestward expansion, the domestic slave trade destroyed up to one-third of all marriages between enslaved people. Such estimates do not take into account owners' migrations and the disruptions that they engendered.[7] Beyond the impact on spouses divorced against their will were the disruptions inflicted on other sets of relationships. In a half century that saw the forced movement of one million or more African Americans, very few did not lose a spouse, sibling, son or daughter, parent, friend, grandchild, or other loved one. For many enslaved people, like Helen Odom's grandmother, taken from the southeast to Arkansas to be sold after her owner died, forced migration was "the [most significant] event in her life." Indeed, Odom recalled, "I heard [the story of the move and sale] over again so many, many times before grandmother died."[8]

Both during and after slavery, people such as Odom's grandmother made forced migration to the Old Southwest a central part of their collectively created vernacular history of enslavement. By *vernacular history*, I mean a narrative about the past constructed by laypeople in their everyday tongue. A vernacular history can contain the essential elements of a collective past, showing who a people thought they were and how they got to be that way. They compose it of their own rough earth and crooked timbers, their own everyday metaphors and experiences. Of course, by the process of making and telling a story about ourselves, we plane our own identities and even our memories to its curves. In the eighteenth and nineteenth centuries, nations were emerging as the collective identities of peoples who identified themselves as having in common the histories that they believed they shared. The United States was one such example, and politicians, preachers, and intellectuals all struggled to impose their ideas of what America was and what Americans had in common. Yet no metal press stamped the vernacular history held in common by many of the enslaved on a nationalist newspaper. The pericopes—the recited stories that communicated vernacular memory—did not tumble from the mouths of nation-making intellectuals or politicians in a lecture hall, to be taken down and distributed in pamphlet form. This process was different, took a different form, and left behind different traces than did the stories told by nationalist Americans to each other. Instead, this way of understanding experience became a commonly held set of beliefs only because field hands, over many decades, made their metaphors and the images of their personal histories into a collectively held conversation, with quiet words passed to each other through the night air.[9]

Despite the lack of formal education shared by most of its creators, the vernacular history of stolen people emerged as a narrative that was in three important ways profoundly historical. First, survivors of forced migration did not remember or recount their experiences as personal testimony alone. Instead, they shaped their accounts into a collective story that may have been metaphorical but was not mythical, for it took place in historical, chronological time. Next, their narrative was also historical because it revealed the meaning that, for them, bound together all the events of forced migration. Survivors and descendants shaped by this process spoke in many ways about what they endured, but none perhaps reveals more than that strange verb, *stole.* When one begins to look, one finds that African American narrators consistently presented evidence in the forms of several common genres or motifs of personal, family, and apocryphal narratives that characterized forced migration through language and images of theft. To construct their narrative, vernacular historians used methods that might not pass the muster of naive standards of professional-historical truth. Yet the metaphor of theft still managed to fulfill a third major characteristic of historical narrative. It recorded removal to the plantation frontier as a revelation of slavery's deepest, most immoral cruelties. Enslaved African Americans and later free people evaluated the context in which they lived—the institution of slavery and the white power that undergirded it—in light of memories and lessons drawn from being stolen, fetched, kidnapped. Vernacular history thus communicated a moral lesson that evaluated the past and then brought it into contact with present and future.[10]

The oft-criticized interviews of ex-slaves conducted by employees of the federal Works Progress Administration (WPA) during the 1930s are the most important sources for this interpretation. Scholars of slavery have often emphasized the limitations of the WPA interviews, complaining that their situations were not calculated to inspire black informants to speak harshly of slavery or of white people. The majority of interviewers were white, and many were local whites. Some were the children or grandchildren of the people who had owned the interviewees, who may have feared retribution if they expressed sentiments too critical of white slaveholders. Statistical surveys of the interviews have shown that the race of the interviewer apparently influenced the way in which ex-slaves depicted their former owners. Many of the ex-slaves were also very old and presumably forgetful. All of the factors have led some scholars to conclude that we should take the recorded responses of the interviewed ex-slaves with at least a grain of salt.[11]

Indeed, the situations were not conducive to speaking truth to power. Yet many black interviewees told stories that could hardly have sounded complimentary to white people in general and sometimes especially not to the specific whites conducting the interviews. Some ex-slaves were directly confrontational. In an era in which both white social memory and academic consensus insisted on depicting a comforting (to whites) vision of paternalist, stable slave plantations, Laura Stewart of Georgia told her white interviewer, "In spite of what white ladies say in the papers, I can remember slaves being sold at markets, outside," in Augusta, where she and the interviewer still lived. And while these interviewees were near the end of their days, for some human beings those years become the peak of moral courage. Time grows short, there is little left to lose, and the costs of being silent become clearer. As Jack Maddox explains, "I'd say these things now. I'd say them anywhere—in the courthouse—before the judges, before God. 'Cause they done all they could do to me."[12]

If we keep in mind the known irregularities of the WPA interviews, something else interesting emerges from a survey of all of them. Oddly enough, many of the stories told in Virginia, where most interviewers were African American, resembled those told in Texas, where most were not, and so on across the South. Identical elements, tropes, figures of speech, embedded interpretations, and anecdotes appeared in interviews conducted in both the most unpromising and promising of conditions. The constant repetition of some phrases suggests that they occurred often enough—and that interviewees spoke them with enough emphasis—for interviewers to recall and write them down, even when their note-taking habits were poor. The repeated use of particular narrative elements also suggests that the stories had been shaped and spread around the South long before the 1930s and had been etched into the circuits of individual storytellers' minds long before elderly ex-slaves' powers of recollection started to fade. Early, painful memories are not easy to forget, insisted Susan Merritt, an ex-slave from Texas: "I couldn't tell how old I is, but do you think I'd ever forget them slavery days?"[13]

Nor had all survivors of enslavement forgotten early-learned histories that told truths opposed to the lies of enslavers. All across the South, survivors of slavery found that these rhetorical weapons still had some use in the battles hidden—or not so hidden—in the interviews of the 1930s. So while white, often racist interviewers conducted most of these interviews, they did not always control the words and stories that came out of those encounters. In the vernacular histories reported in these interviews, elderly, often illiterate, and always formerly enslaved people encoded a critique of slavery, whiteness, power, and white history that contradicts academic historians' assessment of these interviews as inherently limited. Furthermore, the ex-slaves' critique of enslavement is also foreign to the preferred categories of the debates in which academic scholars engaged the issue of American slavery during the twentieth century. The common elements found in the WPA interviews may represent a fair approximation of what enslaved African Americans were saying and thinking about slavery before it ended, especially in the midst of the plantation system's explosive expansion from the early 1800s to the 1860s.[14]

African American people began to create their vernacular history of being stolen even as they were being "stole." From the beginning, the enslaved understood slave trades and planters' moves as central, shaping moments in individual and collective histories, and the former slaves' stories open a window on the divided and the separated as they were marched away from the families and communities that had given them life and meaning. Yet understanding and shaping the trauma endured is difficult. These moments of separation were so disruptive that many who survived them report that at first they could not find on their own the words to express what was happening to them. Relationships were, of course severed. Hopes shaped in one place died, and so words failed at first. Tongues were stilled in shock, mouths moaned incoherently. Delia Garlic, born in Virginia and taken to Georgia and then Louisiana, saw and felt this trauma: "Course they cry, you think they not cry when they was sold like cattle?" William Grose, enslaved in Virginia, went to the mill one day. While he was there, slave traders, acting with his owner's knowledge, seized and bound him, strapped him on a horse, and rode toward town with him in tow. Four miles down the road, they met Grose's wife, bringing his clean clothes to the farm where he suddenly no longer lived. The two stared at each other in shock. The traders let her turn and walk with him a few miles and took him down from the horse and let him stumble along in his chains while the couple spoke. But the occasion overwhelmed him. Grose's mouth moved and sounds came to his ears, but his dazed, detached consciousness watched the whole thing: "I was so crazy, I don't know what my wife said. I was beside myself to think of going south." People reacted in different ways to all kinds of separations, of course, but Grose's emblematic incoherence suggests the point. An old life was ending in a kind of death, and the person who would emerge—or not—from the tomb would forever define him- or herself by what had happened.[15]

Lazarus, raised, came home to a prodigal feast. William Grose—put on a slave ship for New Orleans, packed in with seventy others—survived his quasi death, but he and others like him had no such celebration to introduce them to the new lives that they unwillingly entered. Like a stumbling resurrect, however, whose jaw did not work properly after the women removed its binding, forced migrants also had to learn to speak again. Said William Holland of being sold by his owner, "It took me most a year to get over it, but there I was, belongin' to another man." If anyone raised them up, helped them to get over the experience, to speak again, it was their new peers. These were other people carried south-westward with them on the flood of planter expansion or other people already living on the new plantations—other people also separated and cast into the vortices of the market. Around the fires built by coffles as they paused at night from their marches, in the holds of ships headed around Florida, in traders' jails, and in the cabins of new plantations, enslaved people told each other who they were and from where and whom they hailed. [16]

Some folks, taken from the people and places that had made them who they had once been, marked the passage by changing their names, a decision that told its own story. According to Aaron Jones, his grandmother, a woman brought from Virginia to Mississippi, called herself "Remember Me"—whether a plea before she left or a message to her Mississippi-born kinfolk, he did not say. After being sent away from her owners and her peers, another woman from Mississippi wrote back angrily to the owners that she now called herself "Sophia Nobody," since she was no longer around anyone to whom she could be "Sophia Somebody." Other adopted names included Mourning and Silence. [17] But most people concentrated on where they came from, whom they had left behind, and how to explain how they had been transformed. Thus they formed their own rough autobiographies and genealogies. The narratives of fugitive slaves Charles Ball and Solomon Northup, published in the nineteenth century, each contained a woman's life story that she had passed on to the narrator. Eliza had told Northup her life history as they rested in a Washington slave pen, while Lydia first whispered to Ball her tale between the cotton rows of a frontier plan-tation. Each had been used and discarded by southeastern white men, and each was then sold into the slave trade to frontier plantations. There they told their tales to Ball and Northup, future sources of fugitive slave narratives, who re-membered these women and gave them to history. [18]

Eliza and Lydia had given their histories to their peers first, and that process, repeated millions of times by forced migrants, created a collectively owned set of oral documents held in the mind of the quarters. "We could collect up at times in the evening, even if we was tired," remembered Foster Weathersby of a new plantation in Mississippi. There the slaves would sit, "tellin' tales." Here, African American culture collectively re-created itself, as migrants shared themselves and what they knew. While "the white folks didn't want them to get 'tached to each other," Toby James recalled, the enslaved people on his Texas planta-tion got to know each other better "on Saturday night when massa 'lowed us to dance. There was lots of tin pan beatin' and dancin'." "After work," remembered Smith Wilson, "they would sit around and talk and go to bed." Wilson, also of Texas, recalled that the slaves passed to each other stories, secrets, powers—whatever they had to give and were willing to share. People from particular subregions within the South sometimes identified the distinctive contributions of other subregions. According to Lorenza Ezell, some forced migrants thought of those brought from South Carolina as born and bred experts on roots, herbs, and conjuring. Meanwhile, people with distinctive individual experiences also shared their lessons. On the Mississippi plantation where Mark Oliver found himself, recently acquired fellow slaves taught him how to read: "They passed on to us what they knew."[19]

As the "old heads," in the words of Mississippi's Will Adams, had their say, the young and even the middle-aged used these occasions to build ties that would blossom into new families, the foundation on which society could survive. This creation began with people sharing where they came from and how they got to where they now were: "My father and mother both came from Virginia," reported James Johnson. "Colonel Terry had bought them at separate times from a slave trader who brought them from Virginia to Mississippi. They had a [liking] for each other when they learned they both came from Virginia." On the Mississippi plantation where Rachel Reed lived, enslaved people from South Carolina, Virginia, and Tennessee, all of whom had "left families back there in the mountains," eventually "had another family on our plantation."[20]

Alliances, new bonds, community, and new families were not the only story. No doubt the quarters of southwestern plantations also abounded with conflict, argument, misunderstandings, and hostility in addition to characteristics more cherished in memory. And while one historian has argued that migration "spread a uniform Afro-American slave culture across the entire South," the result could never be that simple. Elisha Garey remembered "my Grandma Rachel. The Traders fotched her here from Virginny, and she never did learn to talk plain"—never was her speech uniform with that of the new people among whom she found herself or with that of later generations.[21] But later generations did come from her. In the 1930s, formerly enslaved people characterized the plantation frontier as a place of misery and depersonalization as well as a place where black folks built new communities and families by sharing personal histories and distributing knowledge. Not only might the latter picture be "true" as an account of what some experienced, but it also shows what some formerly enslaved people wanted to emphasize as most important in retrospect.

Preemancipation discussions and evaluations of what had happened and what had survived despite the stealing of one's self shaped both the history told and the understanding of history expressed by the 1930s interviewees. Repeated tellings of stories shaped them into scripts, learned, checked against those of others, and passed on to peers and the next generation. Both a standard question asked by WPA interviewers about where one's parents came from and a question about slave trade "speculators" unleashed long—and similar— responses from many ex-slaves. Many described the coffle chains: "I've seen droves of 'em, all chained together"; slavers "led [their captives] off like convicts"; "They was chained together, a chain bein' run 'tween 'em somehow, and they was all men and women, no children." "And when they start the chains a-clankin' and step off down the line, they all just sing and shout and make all the noise they can to hide the sorrow in their hearts and cover up the cries and moaning of them they'd be leaving behind."[22]

In the WPA interviews, stories about the slave trade and the forced separation of families repeatedly take similar forms, and those similarities are meaningful. The commercially organized movements that storytellers had experienced repeatedly divided and chained people in ways that became long practiced. Yet the objects of these techniques chose what to retell, what to emphasize, and whom to tell. Even those who had not seen the chains had heard of them, because earlier storytellers had chosen to emphasize their significance: "I heard my mother tell many times about the slave dealers. She said they would take the slaves from place to place all chained together. They would make them sing to attract attention." Out of the many phenomena associated with the trade, ex-slave narrators focused on a few: the forced singing and dancing; the chains; the crying of mothers and babies as they were separated; the traders' yard, always packed with a hundred people; and similar tropes.[23]

As enslaved and formerly enslaved people spoke to friends, spouses, and children, particular phenomena within personal memories became the most emphasized pieces of the wider social memory of forced migration in slavery. This vernacular view of history hammered home over and over the point that the divisions inflicted by slave owners and traders had made people who they were as individuals, as parts of a family, as a people. For some, the shaping effects of forced migration came from the fact that early separation ensured that they could not know much about what had come before. Those sold as children often did not know much about whom they were or where they came from before they reached the block. Lewis Chase did not "know where I come from," because his owner "kept my hat pulled down over my face so I couldn't see the way to go back." "I don't remember much about my Mammy and Pappy 'cause I was took away from them by the speculators when I was thirteen years old," said John Smith, born in North Carolina and transported to Alabama. Clara Young remembered not her date of birth but her age at sale—seventeen.[24]

Other formerly enslaved people talked about what they knew they had lost. Separation shaped all kinship, and kinship shaped the memory of sales and movements. Forced migration intruded on most stories about relations: "Where did my Pappy and Mammy come from? Mammy was born a slave of the Furman family in Charleston, and Pappy was bought out of a drove that a Baltimore speculator fetched from Maryland long before the war." Whenever the slave trade came up, they mentioned separations: "I seen 'em sell people . . .

just like cattle. They would be chained together. They took mothers from children even just a week old and sold 'em." In the process, the former slaves unrolled for interviewers genealogical tales instilled by parents and others. Some, like Minerva Davis of Arkansas, who had not even been in slavery could recount entire genealogies of trades and divisions and origins. Davis knew that her father had been sold from Virginia to Tennessee when he was eighteen and that her maternal grandmother had also been bought by slave traders who took her to Tennessee. Davis knew that her mother was born there, "heired" to an owner's daughter, and then met her father about the time that the Civil War began. Davis thus knew the places to which the lines led back, even if they were broken there.[25]

African Americans had remembered, shaped, retold and passed down such tales before slavery ended as well as long after emancipation. Survivors of forced migration explained to the next generation how both the teller and the told came to be who they were. "My Mother," recalled Laura Shelton, "used to sit down and talk to us and tell us about slavery." Stories were all around one in the black communities of the Southwest. Elmo Steele, born free in Ohio, moved south after the Civil War and married a formerly enslaved woman, and he could tell the story in the same language as ex-slaves. And stories mattered deeply to those who told them: Louisiana-born Melinda remembered the urgency of her grandmother's deathbed words: "You got to remember all this, you hear me? . . . [F]irst thing I can remember is that I was standin' on a slave block in New Orleans alongside my ma." She hoped to fix herself in the memories of her descendants, ensuring that as they remembered her, they would also remember that the slave trade and its threat of loss was the beginning of her knowing herself and thus of them as well in a way. These tales were always a struggle against chaos, knowledge against not knowing: traders "always stopped at all the trading places to buy, sell, and trade slaves. In this way many of them was liable to be sold any where along the way," said Minerva Wells, whose mother was taken by a trader from South Carolina to Texas. "This is why so many colored folks don't know nothing about their folks and forefathers."[26]

Struggling against the chaos of not knowing, parents in both the Southwest and Southeast told their children what they knew, in the process demonstrating why they did not know more. Telling the tale of forced migration explained to young people who they were—and who they could no longer be. "They sold my sister Lucy and my brother Fred in slavery time, and I have never seen 'em in all my life," recalled Lizzie Baker. "Mother would cry when she was telling me 'bout it," and then, in the middle of the interview, so did Lizzie, even though she had never met her sister and brother. As Tom Morris told his interviewer, he must have also have told his children that "Mammy cried when they took my pappy to New Orleans; she cried at nights." Milton Ritchie recalled that his mother had told him that she and her brother were sold on the block in Virginia when she was twelve. They had been sleeping under the same blanket the night before, and when they were sold to different owners, the brother and sister cut the blanket in two. Each took half, and putting hers around her shoulders, she left for Georgia. There she would grow up, get married, and give birth to Milton. But "she never heard nor seen none of her folks no more, she told me," said Milton as he wept, mourning the rending of a blanket ninety years earlier.[27]

Countless enslaved parents in the older states told children of relatives shipped south and west, and countless mothers and fathers in the frontier states told their offspring of those left behind. Geneva Tonsill's owner sold her father to a slave trader when she was three: "I don't remember it, but Ma told us children about it when we grew up." The loss marked both the moved and the left behind, and its sorrow shaped them even in later generations. Carey Allen Patten, born in Arkansas, buried her Virginia-born mother with a treasured pair of gloves in the coffin. Carey's mother's grandmother had made those gloves in Virginia, and they were all that Carey's mother had been able to keep when she was taken west.[28] People had survived, but the cost was high. Many who survived would always mourn the shearing off of part of the self through the rending of kinship.

Voices spoke for more than a century, talking through nights in half-lit cabins of the stealing of one million, until the last person who had lived through it fell silent. People moved south, told their stories, often shaping the ways in which they told their autobiographies along the lines of others they heard as they recognized the key and common elements. Then they shaped the lines a little themselves and eventually told stories to their children. People still in the old states also told their tales of the lost and sometimes were taken south to follow those who had gone before.[29] The vernacular history of slavery bubbled in all these tellings, just as it did in the 1930s WPA narratives. It breathed and grew under the surface of a society that strove to repress from its social and academic memories the instability, the division, the torture, the murder, the rape, and the trade in human beings at the heart of slavery in the United States.[30] "A white man can't give a history of the Negro," said one interviewee. Whites, such survivors argued, could not because they would not. They could not bear to tell or hear the truths about the past that African American vernacular history was willing to tell: "White folks here don't like to hear about how they fathers and mothers done these colored folks."[31]

So when speaking of forced migration in the 1930s, survivor Lorenzo Ivy told his interviewer, "Truly, son, the half has never been tol'."[32] His half was untold by those publicly authorized to certify the past, but his half was also not mere raw material ready for historians to gather, compile, and shape. His contained and was shaped by its own questions and interpretations. Yet like all powerful historical topics, the half untold returned obsessively to questions deep and perhaps unanswerable, to a problem forever insoluble. "I could tell you 'bout it all day but even then you couldn't guess the awfulness of it," said Delia Garlic.[33] Perhaps Garlic did not mean so much that the essence of what happened, the experience, was ultimately untellable. Such a statement might be true of all experience. The trauma she described was so intense that making sense of its moral awfulness was a difficult and troubling proposition. The central question of this untold half of history nagged at the back of every speaker's consciousness. What can it mean, they wondered, that this has happened to us? This uncertainty was even implicit in the way that genres of stories enabled survivors to talk in coherent ways about slave trading, slave transporting, family separation. In each case, the recounting of experience was at least as likely to emphasize loss as success, incompleteness as completion. In each case, the critique also admitted that the theft of person could potentially dehumanize those subject to it. While many longed for pain to end in affirmation, there was no certainty of such an outcome. Theirs was a difficult problem that no one could talk away. Yet just as the key questions that shape historical interpretations are broad, striking, unnerving, and untamable, so too did African Americans produce as a partial answer a metaphor that was deep, rich, and subtle, with all the strengths and weaknesses that can come from ambiguity and complexity.

The central pillar of the unauthorized story told by slaves and ex-slaves was the image of theft—of being stolen. This supple word invoked a crime and in so doing crystallized from the process of forced migration the essence of enslavement. Describing her grandmother's account of being sold into the interstate slave trade, Jane Sutton said, "They stole her back in Virginny and brung her to Mississippi, and sold her to Marse Berry." Many ex-slaves who seemed to have been sold and transported described what had happened to them as being "stolen." Like those cited at the beginning of this chapter, these narrators suggested that forced migration was a much more lawless process than the neat commercial transactions that appear in white ledgers, bills of sale, and receipts might indicate. The verb *stole* covered a broad, uncertain area of experience. Lee Pierce, sold to Texas from Mississippi, said that his new owner "didn't have too much regard for the black folks. Two families of them was stolen niggers. A speculator drove stole them in Arkansas and fetch them to Texas." Perhaps he meant that these families told him that they had been kidnapped by passing slave traders. Or perhaps Pierce, who referred to his own experience on the block as being "sold just like a cow or horse," was commenting on the immorality of selling human beings, yanking them out of their communities and families. Betty Simmons's owner, in debt up to his neck, needed some cash. He sent Simmons, who was mortgaged to a creditor and probably scheduled to be attached for his debts, to his brother's farm. There, as arranged, slave traders came and looked her over. They purchased her, paying cash that at auction would have gone directly to his creditors. Simmons viewed herself as having been "stolen," although she did not say whether she saw the process this way because the sale was illegal or because she had been shipped away from all her family by slave traders.[34]

Stole could become shorthand for an entire process, as in George Ward's words: "My mother . . . was stolen from Winchester, Tennessee and brought to the Cotton Belt" of Mississippi. So she had described it to him, in part because in forced migration, black people could not be sure what white people were planning to do with them or who held final legal title to them. White folks' machinations and maneuvers with enslaved property on the cotton and sugar frontiers led them to deceive each other as well as enslaved people. Parents did not know where traders had taken their children, the children never got to say good-bye. So, like Harry Johnson, many said, "I was stole from my mammy when I's about 10 or 12 and she never did know what became of me." Hettie Marshall's mother said that she had been "stole when a child [in South Carolina] and brought to Tennessee in a covered wagon" like that used by many slave traders and migrant planters. Marshall's mother later heard that her mother had died from the grief of losing her daughter. Indeed, the whole process blended together crime and commerce in the practical legal senses of the time as well as in more philosophical senses. "My Pa named Bill. He was stole from Virginia," said George Fleming, and "I don't know how Marse got him. Sometimes they would buy them and sometimes they would steal 'em, sort of like stealing a dog. They bought Negroes, stole 'em from Virginia and places and drove them through the country like a bunch of hogs." Comparing slave sales to the sale of livestock signaled humiliation, the theft of dignity that for some left a lingering sense of shame, and the theft of rights.[35]

Single words can be endlessly rich in possibility, as none know better than those whose only legal use of language is oral. But perhaps three crucial motifs found in the stories of ex-slaves best illuminate what forced migrants meant when they ruefully played upon the phonetic line between *sold* and *stole*. These three motifs cut facets in the rock of experience, revealing new elements of the problems posed by forced migration that lasted for generations after the experience itself. First, African Americans often connected southwestward removal to earlier, similar events, describing African-born parents who told them of being "stolen" into the Middle Passage across the Atlantic: Carlyle Stewart remembered that "they brought my granpa from Africa. . . . They stole him from there."[36] In fact, argued Shang Harris, the Middle Passage was the beginning of an entire history of theft far more criminal than the petty larcenies of black folks looking to survive: "They talks a heap 'bout the niggers stealin'. Well, you know what was the first stealin' done? It was in Afriky, when the white folks stole the niggers." "They always done tell it am wrong to lie and steal," said Josephine Hubbard, "so why did the white folks steal my mammy and her mammy" from Africa? So the children and grandchildren told it, and we have evidence that African-born elders had used the same words during slavery. In 1844, asked to give his age, one African-born Florida man replied, "Me no know, massa, Buckra man steal nigger year ago."[37]

Stories about the Middle Passage suggested that it was an act of theft by enticement. Shack Thomas, Toby Brown, and Mariah Calloway reported that slavers used red cloth—a staple trade good on the African coast—to lure victims on board ships.[38] Of course, most of the unfortunates caught up in the slave trade were not initially seized from their villages and homes and battlefields by whites. Yet even as they created a semimythological account of the Middle Passage, ex-slaves never denied that other Africans participated in supplying slaves. "My ma told me how they brought her from Africa," said Susan Snow. "Seems like the chief made some arrangements with some men and he had a big goober grabbin' for the young folks, and they stole my ma and some more and took her to this country." Other kinds of tricks, followed by being "stolen," also paint Africans who sought to gain pay for labor, trade goods, or power only to find themselves locked below the hatches of a slave ship sailing west.[39] All these metaphors of Africans lured and tricked paint whites as the instigators of a relationship that turned on Africans' desires to gain rewards and ended with chains stapled shut around black wrists and ankles. The enslaved knew that whites were the real beneficiaries of the trade. Even Africans who for a time gained tempting rewards often eventually found themselves belowdecks. The parents who survived one passage told their children of theft. The children possessed this term and consequently used it to depict their transport south and west.[40]

In a different but also common story line—sometimes metaphorical, sometimes ambiguous, and sometimes exact—many ex-slave narratives describe forced migration as kidnapping. In a sort of mythic symbolism, forced migration seemed to recapitulate the originating theft on the Atlantic's eastern shores and to reveal the theft of a person that constituted the heart of slavery. In fact, whites sometimes did kidnap free African Americans from their homes and sell them as slaves. Solomon Northup, a free New Yorker kidnapped in Washington and shipped to Louisiana, was but one of the authenticated cases.[41] In Florida, Ambrose Douglass claimed that his parents were free people in Detroit who returned south to visit relatives still in slavery and were themselves reenslaved. Samuel Smalls recalled that his father, Cato Smith, born free in Connecticut, came south to work as a carpenter and voluntarily indentured himself for seven years to the Florida owner of the woman he loved; the seven years eventually became indefinite. Similar stories came from all corners of the South, especially from those areas where the slave trade had been most active in delivering forced migrants. Mary Reynolds's father, a free black piano repairman from New York, fell in love with a field slave on a Louisiana plantation and agreed to work in the fields alongside her. Julia Blanks said that her grandmother was freeborn, but "they stole her." "They" were white people who lured Julia and her grandmother into a coach in Washington, D.C., drove them to the White House, and presented them as a gift to a "Miss Donaldson."[42]

Many of those allegedly kidnapped were not from the North. And like Julia Blanks, many had been children, either free or supposedly promised freedom, when slave dealers or others seized and sold them. By the Red River in the Indian Territory (later Oklahoma), three-year-old Spence Johnson followed the lure of candy into the wagons of the slave traders, whom he described as "nigger-stealers." Clayton Holbrooke said that the Tennessee owner of his mother and grandmother had willed the two women their freedom. "But what they called 'nigger traders' captured them and two or three others, and sold them." Carey Davenport's father, promised freedom by his "old, old master" in Richmond, fell after the old man's death to the son, and the "young man steal him into slavery again." Mother Ann Clark reported a confusing story of being free in Memphis but being taken to Louisiana by "my marster," who "made a slave outta me."[43]

The vagueness of these stories often frustrates modern readers. They frustrated the tellers at times, too, because something did not quite seem right no matter how they shaped the story. Evie Herrin of Mississippi grew confused as she repeated what her mother had said: "My mother wasn't born in slavery. I never understood just how that came about. She came from North Carolina, and she told us many times that she was free before she came to Mississippi." Others, including Sim Greeley, claimed that before being kidnapped and sold south, they or their parents were free Indians in a nineteenth-century Virginia nearly denuded of native people. Some of the stories might have been more true in symbolic than in simplistic senses. James Green, who was sold from Virginia for eight hundred dollars in stolen money, claimed that before his sale he had been freed. His father, whom he called "a full-blooded Indian," had "done some big favor for a big man high up in the courts, and he gets me set free." His mother's owner, "Master Williams, laughs and calls me 'free boy.' " But not long thereafter, Williams walked Green down the street to the auction block and sold him out of Petersburg and Virginia. But after Green told the story to an interviewer in the 1930s, his daughter, listening to the interview, "took exception to her father's claim that he was half Indian." Perhaps Green, like some other African Americans, preferred to attribute his lighter skin and ambiguous status ("I never had to do much work [in Virginia] for nobody but my mother") to Indian ancestry than to white. Perhaps Green's daughter saw Williams as both her paternal grandfather and the betrayer of his child.[44]

Accounts of kidnapping and slave stealing might all be "true" in the strictest sense as particular stories. Conversely, some might actually constitute a different sort of evidence. Particular thefts and kidnappings could be parables for the more generalized stealing and robbery of all black people in slavery in general but especially in the traumatic forced migration that destroyed families and kinship networks in the Southeast. Thus, parents who explained to children that bondage was theft perpetrated on those who should be free and should be living elsewhere with long-separated relatives and friends back in their home states might raise children who asserted that their parents had actually been kidnapped from legal freedom. Several aspects of the domestic slave trade also made the term *kidnapping* applicable to even legal sales. The trade's separations were often violent in character, helping to support the understanding of them as felony. Slave traders, having made their bargain with owners in the Chesapeake or Carolinas, resorted to all sorts of trickery and preemptive violence to limit the resistance of the sold. They came in groups to seize strong men by surprise. They took mothers at night, when babies were asleep. They cruelly prevented farewells—"Naw! Hell'" they said, "Get in this buggy! Nigger don' [get to] tell nobody goodbye!" In Samuel Boulware's memory, sobbing children ran down a dirt road after wagons heading south and west, carrying mothers sold out of South Carolina to the Louisiana market while the speculator wielded his whip to drive the children back. Finally, white heirs often curtailed dying owners' verbal and even written promises of freedom. Black people who assumed that they would get their freedom often ended up not only disappointed but sold south. When whites gave their word and then stole it back, the black victims of such lies might never know if they had been legally sold. In a practical sense it might not matter. All that remained was the lesson that enslavers' promises to the enslaved did not hold legal water in a society dedicated to commodifying black bodies.[45]

Ex-slaves also remembered slave traders in particular as "nigger stealers" or kidnappers. Former bondpeople sometimes meant such terms literally. Sometimes, however, they meant to call the whole process of the slave trade—and indeed, all forced migration to the South's plantation frontiers—as a giant act of kidnapping, of theft.[46] Such charges took the uncertainty experienced by enslaved African Americans and pinned its causation where it belonged, on southern white planters and slave traders. By calling whites criminals whose title to human property was always shaky, ex-slaves depicted the entire system as a criminal enterprise, in the process shedding further light on all their uses of the term *stole*.

The claim that one or one's parents had been kidnapped could introduce its own ambiguity, however. Those who claimed to have been kidnapped free people or to come from free parents might have been looking for some sort of individual rescue from the dreadful depersonalization of slavery. Not I, the story might suggest, *I* did not belong in slavery because *I*, as an individual, was kidnapped or tricked out of freedom or came from an Indian mother. Other folks—well, perhaps *they* were legally enslaved. So despite all the ways in which forced migration, with its attendant separation from kin and identity and its rituals of depersonalization, stole identity, the trope of kidnapping might evade a general critique of enslavement's falsehoods in its hope for an individual way out. Only with some uncertainty could people use the language of stealing and theft to probe, to try to understand, the evil they had survived.

Yet a third favorite theme among vernacular historians evoked more clearly than could anything else the criminal assault on family and personal identity by those who stole people. This theme also suggested the magnitude of the disruptions that enslaved people faced and the difficulty of ever coming to any comfortable resolution of what it meant to have been stolen. According to an ex-slave's retelling, Louisiana slave Pierre Aucuin was sold by his mother's owner at the age of two. Years later, Aucuin married a woman named Tamerant and had three children. One day, his regular barber was unavailable, and so she began to cut his hair. "You know, Pierre," she said, as she noticed something she had not seen before, "this scar on the back of your head sets me a-thinkin' way back when I was a gal. . . . I had a little brother then. . . . [T]he master sold my little brother from us, and five years later they sold me from my ma and pa. Since then I ain't seen none of my folks." Tamerant continued, not yet realizing what she was saying: "One day my little brother and me was playin', and he hit me and hurt me. I took an oyster shell and cut him on the back of his head right where you got that scar."[47]

The story of Pierre and Tamerant Aucuin crystallized in horrifying form what enslaved African Americans may have feared most. So brutal a crime was the chaotic, commodified forced migration that shaped the antebellum South that its disruptions threatened to steal the identities most basic to human society: the divisions of kinship that bounded individuals and marked them in relationship to each other as husband, wife; mother, son; sister, brother. These two individuals had lost their personal and family histories. Because of that loss, they unknowingly transgressed one of the most basic rules of their culture, the bar against incest. Yet incest was only the exclamation point to the complete theft of self the storyteller feared. The solvent of the auction block, a commodity trade more caustic than any Karl Marx criticized, had here dissolved social ties, boundaries, and rules and left Pierre and Tamerant formless. Such was the terror of the trade and of the depersonalization and disruption of human relationships inherent in forced migration that variations of the story of brother and sister Aucuin appear several times in the WPA interviews as well as in other sources. In each case, selling and buying stole the capacity of the enslaved and formerly enslaved to recognize even their closest kin.[48]

Such stories revealed the harshest ways in which the enslaved could be "stole." They also suggest that vernacular historians sought, even as they told tales, to prevent the worst possible effects of such thefts. Legal felonies, repeated a million times over until some variation of Shang Harris's "first stealing" was inflicted on virtually every enslaved African American, threatened to snatch out the most basic pillars of personal histories and identities. Yet had Pierre and Tamerant told their stories and grappled with the experiences of forced migration, they could have saved themselves and their children. Almost every version of the incest story pivoted on family members' recognition of a long-remembered scar. Metaphorically, the tracks left by wounds were always the subject of storytelling about forced migration, and their revealing was its process. When one described one's origins, one also showed the scar of separation from that place. One could describe one's parents and how they were separated from oneself or each other. That too was a poorly healed place, a scar from torn flesh and blood. Stories of successful recognition of lost relatives could pivot on scars in a direction opposite from that of tragic incest. After freedom came, one Tennessee woman answered a knock to find at her door a woman and a boy. "The boy said, 'This is your mother, and I'm your brother.' I said 'No, my mother's sold and my brothers are dead. . . . You're none of my mammy; I know my mammy.'" She did not know her mother until she "took off her hat, and I saw that scar on her face."[49]

Displaying scars—in both the literal and actual senses—right from the beginning gave other people a chance to know who one was and what one had survived. Telling one's story certainly cut down the chance for incest. In a broader sense, talking about what had happened attempted to turn back the worst effects of being stolen. The sharing of experiences created common ground and shaped new versions of old selves that could live in a new social context. Still, the narratives developed in this process also underlined the impossibility of assuring tellers and listeners that meaning and order were the structures of their autobiographies. Nothing, it seemed, could have stopped the events of stealing and selling as they were happening. So said Cheney McNair, at any rate: "Did I feel bad when my father was sold? I don't know if I did or not. I had to make the most of it, slaves did. They could come and take you at any time, maybe husband, maybe children." And nothing could remove the scars that knotted where white people had ripped away the limbs of life. Even after the Civil War, when some ex-slaves tracked down and regained lost family members, most could not do so. For decades after emancipation, plaintive advertisements in African American newspapers implored "INFORMATION WANTED"—"Of my father, Jerry Hodges, of Norfolk County, Va. I was sold from him when a small girl, about 30 years ago. My mother's name was Phebe, and she belonged to a man named Ashcroth. . . . Please address Emeline Hodges, Leavenworth Kansas." Most had only scraps of information about where their relatives had gone and very little opportunity to search for them. Slave traders and owners had stolen relatives beyond almost any hope of recovery.[50]

For many, there could be no reunion, and by the time ex-slaves told their stories in the 1930s, they could look back and see that to some extent, they had lived their entire lives with absence, a loss dictated by the criminal acts of white people. Caleb Craig, given to an owner's daughter—"In that way us separated from our mammy"—still felt her absence in journeys of both day and night: "I have visions and dreams of her yet." Edwin Walker "mourned and grieved" for his sister, who had been carried back from Mississippi to South Carolina by a new owner. After the war he and his siblings and her husband "tried to find her but till this day we don't know what became of her." Isaac Johnson, sold away from his North Carolina family as a small boy, could not even tell his daughter his age or the names of his sisters. He could give her only a family history shaped primarily by what the whites had taken from him. Calling the injury that had been inflicted "stealing" put a name on the hurt but did not resolve the problem. Naming and telling revisited and perhaps revived painful injuries. Even the kidnapping motif could provide the occasion for intentionally or unintentionally falsifying one's nativity, leading to further confusion.[51]

The discussion of the ways in which one and one's people had been "stole" was powerful and complex. It allowed enslaved and formerly enslaved people to wrestle with the memories of events that afflicted them while grimly reminding them that they had lost much along the way. But one must pause and consider another issue before one can understand the full implications of vernacular history. The 1930s WPA interviews were far from the first time that anyone had recorded the argument that whites had "stolen" black folks. Indeed, this trope had first appeared in print more than a century earlier. White and black abolitionists had depicted the Atlantic slave trade as a process of theft, based on the stealing of souls, the kidnapping of free people. More immediately, nineteenth-century narratives published by fugitive ex-slaves sometimes had also used the word *stolen*, in these cases as a multifaceted, complex term of interpretation and critique almost identical to the uses of the term by formerly enslaved people interviewed in the 1930s. William Wells Brown wrote in 1849 that his master, who claimed legal ownership of Brown as property, was in fact merely a "man who stole me as soon as I was born." Brown also remembered what captives in a slave trader's coffle sang in the 1830s as they traveled to Mississippi or Louisiana. Their song linked Shang Harris's "first stealing" to their present "theft":

See these poor souls from Africa
Transported to America
We are stolen and sold to Georgia.

Indeed, the song suggests that each generation of the stolen had inherited terms, metaphors, and tunes from another. In the 1790s, many Virginia-born children of Africans were taken to Georgia in the first wave of cotton expansion by traders then known as "Georgia-men," and Georgia was the metaphorical destination that Mississippi and Louisiana were becoming by the time this group of the stolen sang.[52]

Thomas Smallwood, who escaped slavery and ended up in Canada, argued that the guilt of the theft in question derived not only from the initial act but also from its perpetuation: "Those who hold [people] in bondage are either the thieves or receivers, the one class being no better than the other and therefore the both are robbers." Other nineteenth-century authors argued that all forms of separation by forced migration were felonies. Isaac Williams's mother, Williams reported, mourned the three other sons whom the slave trade "stole" from her. Charles Ball said that the slave trader who, having legally bought him from his Maryland owner, grabbed him by the collar and tied his hands behind his back had in fact "kidnapped" him. Moses Roper and others reported kidnappings in which slave traders and migrant planters "stole" enslaved people claimed by other whites, while J. W. Loguen repeated his mother's lesson to her children—that she had been a free woman stolen into slavery.[53]

Perhaps one might assume that white editors and amanuenses injected the language of "stolen" and "kidnapping" into nineteenth-century published accounts. Indeed, Frederick Douglass cited the white man whom he called "the slave's poet," John Greenleaf Whittier:

Gone, gone, sold and gone
To the rice swamp dank and lone,
From Virginia hills and waters—
Woe is me, my *stolen* daughters![54]

One brand of abolitionist critique indicted slavery as the theft of labor. But scholars have shown that many of the great published ex-slave narratives contained their own battles in which African American authors sought to seize control of their language and texts from white abolitionists.[55] Moreover, the uses of *stolen* in published narratives are more complex than simple critiques of a system that stole labor rather than paying for it. So perhaps these uses come from the formerly enslaved themselves. The use of almost identical terminology in the twentieth-century WPA interviews, however, presents a further problem that first complicates and then suggests a resolution to the question of the origin of the metaphor in the published narratives. This language probably did not enter the WPA interviews via white interviewers, since most were southern and hardly neoabolitionist in their tendencies. Chronologically, the interviews come a lifetime later than the classic narratives of the nineteenth century that are considered the beginnings of the African American literary and cultural canon. Perhaps those works of genius, then, were the sources of the critique of slavery in the 1930s interviews.

Yet ex-slaves across the Depression-era South were probably not steeped in the nineteenth-century literature of abolitionism. Most of them were illiterate, too poor to have extensive libraries or time to read much besides the Bible (if that), and scattered far from urban centers of literary production and discussion. The most likely explanation that fits all the available evidence is in fact the reverse: the nineteenth-century narratives are not the sources for the use of *stole* in the WPA ex-slave interviews. Nineteenth-century African American writers such as former bondmen Frederick Douglass and William Wells Brown were in fact steeped in the same oral culture of enslaved people that the interviews, in modified form, reveal. By the time Brown, Douglass, and other writers were growing up, their culture had already produced its vernacular history of slavery and forced migration, which eventually surfaced in the 1930s interviews. After Brown and Douglass gained their freedom, they used their access to the pen to launch into the literate world the vernacular history's criticism of slavery as an institution that "stole" human beings. Therefore, despite the fact that the 1930s interviews come chronologically later, they are our best source for the preemancipation nature and creation of this critique. They provide a window on antebellum ways of remembering as well as a look at the probable roots of much of the literary production by nineteenth-century fugitives who stole themselves.[56]

Enslaved people, the combined evidence of the interviews and the nineteenth-century fugitives' narratives suggests, were criticizing white planters and slave traders for "stealing" human beings at least by the 1830s and probably earlier. And the slaves launched such criticisms from one side of the South to the other. The desire for historical narratives that would shape meaning and order from individual and collective lives was particularly strong and insistent as the expansion of the plantation realm drove individuals apart from families. While no way of thinking about the world could in those circumstances render order from the chaos of the slave market revolution, the understanding of slavery as a process or state of being stolen did give people a language with which to speak and to criticize. It also served as a shield with which to protect oneself and one's spirit.

People who face systems and ideologies of domination often develop historical explanations of present status that support "hidden transcripts" of resistance.[57] Such explanations frequently invert the justifications erected by the ruling class to defend the prevailing order. If the upper class justifies its power by depicting a subject race as savages in need of firm control, the lower class identifies the ways in which the rulers of society are actually brutish, violent, and uncivilized. So slaves and ex-slaves, by talking about forced migration, identified the absurdity of planters' justification of slavery. Ex-slaves were particularly critical of the slave auction, the point in slavery at which the claim of property rights in slaves was most obvious. Amanda Jackson recalled, "Folks used to put 'em on the block an' sell 'em like they would a chicken or something like that."[58] The formerly enslaved firmly criticized those whites who commodified people: Emma Hurley remembered that she belonged to "a family that bought and sold slaves as they did cattle and thought of them only in terms of dollars and cents." No matter how often southern planters tried to defend their system from charges of inhumanity, selling human beings as if they were livestock made the planters liars. Mariah Snyder recalled a woman named Venus who ridiculed the whites eagerly bidding on her, interrupting the auctioneer's patter with her sarcastic shout, "Weigh them cattle!"[59]

Ex-slaves also argued that the stealing of human beings meant that white slave owners, a people who identified themselves as the bringers of the light of Christianity to the heathen African, were in fact destined by rights and by their persistent attempts to defend their indefensible behavior to the interior walls of the pit of hell. "Speculatin' on us humans! God's going to punish they chillun's chillun, yes sir!" proclaimed Ishmael Moore. Another former slave passed on the story that a brutal master had, on his deathbed, asked in delirium for someone to bring the seven thousand dollars he had saved "to pay my way out of Hell." In arguments defined by both direct points and telling anecdotes, ex-slaves criticized not only the more formalized defenses of slavery as paternalist and Christian—ideas that many African Americans had heard from white preachers—but also the practical ideologies that enabled slavery to exist and that its day-to-day patterns and relationships implied. The right to commodify human beings was crucial to the institution, but ex-slaves left little doubt that they believed that the entire concept of human beings as marketable property was absurd. The only way in which the buying and selling and owning of people had anything to do with the language and concepts of property rights was in the sense that to sell someone away from his or her family was to "steal" them.[60]

Yet the vernacular history of forced migration did more, in the end, than invert white ideas about property and slavery. True to their roles as interpreters and synthesizers of individual and collective pasts, those who survived to pass on experiences outlined a wider lesson about the relationship between the plantation world and its most profitable frontiers. Survivors of enslavement identified the plantation frontier as home to a deeper, more complete form of the institution of slavery. "The biggest punishment," said a man once enslaved in Virginia, "was to tell you 'I'll sell you down south.'" When African Americans said that "all them old white folks [further] down South was mean to slaves," they did not mean that Virginia whites were any better than those in Mississippi.[61] They readily identified Virginians as being just as committed to second-hand frontier exploitation as Alabamians were to firsthand exploitation. Frank Bell, who grew up in Virginia, remembered "Old Joe Bruins—slave trader of the District—shook hands with [my] brother—wished him well—sold him to Memphis."[62]

Instead, those who made the passage south and west—or saw those close to them taken—emplotted their experience as a revelation about slavery's true form, a move from childhood into the full knowledge of slavery's evil, from shadows into deeper, terrifying night. For Ceceil George, South Carolina—"the old country"—was not good, but the Louisiana where she slaved in the sugar fields was "the most wicked country . . . heathen . . . wicked, wicked, wicked!"[63] The experience of being "stole" became the most symptomatic and instructive element of enslavement, taking one to a place that revealed the truth about whites' desires, blacks' past, and what might be expected in the future. With both personal experience and vernacular-historical knowledge of this geographical shift came a parallel shift in one's understanding of human bondage.

Ultimately, the homemade historiography of the stolen competed, both before and after emancipation, against a rival: southern whites' increasingly frequent claims in the latter years of slavery that their peculiar institution rested on a paternalistic bargain between generous masters and protected, grateful slaves.[64] Paternalist defenders of slavery then and now naturally wished to underestimate the disruptions inflicted by the slave trade. In private, black folks had a rejoinder, a different history first constructed around fires and on porches of cabins, whether on raw new frontier plantations or on old plantations among those left behind. This narrative inverted white claims and offered a completely different explanation of the past. Ex-slave Charles Grandy offered a powerful example of this reading of southwestward migration—as expansion of the scope and authority of the institution and as perfect revelation of its true nature. In 1937 he spoke of a statue memorializing the Old South: a Confederate soldier standing by Norfolk Harbor and facing South, into the heart of the planters' realm. "Know what it mean?" Grandy asked. Did the soldier look away toward Dixie land, gazing at the traditions and history of an old paternalist society? No, Grandy said. In the statue, which stood on a spot that he had passed once long ago in the hold of a slave ship bound for New Orleans, another meaning of old times was not forgotten. From the figure facing south, the direction of planters' dreams and blacks' forced migrations, Grandy derived the lesson that forced migration taught the true history of slavery: "Carry the nigger down south if you wanna rule him."[65]

Grandy spoke in context and concert with two thousand other ex-slave narrators, encapsulating a whole vernacular history. They spoke in turn for hundreds of thousands more who no longer lived but whose stories had helped to shape that of their descendants. The interviewees retold a history of uncounted cost in which the chains clanked and the stolen sang to cover up moans and wails—in their ears, in their throats. The auctioneer hummed, and the crickets chirped in the night around the lonely hut on the new plantation, down in the South that was the end of you. Yet this was not the end. The remembering of this history raked harrows across whole ridges of scars, but it was better to speak than to hide one's misery. So they did. In their remembering, in their interpretation of movement as a theft of historical dimensions, the enslaved ensured that instead of paternalist froth, they and their descendants would remember a different, bitter, truer history: stolen, stole, stol'.

NOTES

Thanks for comments on earlier versions (but no blame for any weaknesses of this essay) go to Alexander Byrd, Stephanie Camp, Russ Castronovo, Ann Fabian, Priscilla Wald, an anonymous reviewer for the University of Georgia Press, and Stephanie Baptist and David Feinberg.

1. George P. Rawick, *The American Slave: A Composite Autobiography* (Westport, 1972–79), 17:251 (Margaret Nickerson); Moses Grandy, *Life of Moses Grandy, Late a Slave in the United States of America* (Boston, 1844), 10–11; Rawick, *American Slave*, vol. 8, pt. 1, p. 299 (Mary Brown); vol. 7, pt. 2, 152 (Jane Sutton); supp. ser. 2, vol. 1, pt. 3, 68 (Cora Gillam); supp. ser. 1, vol. 9, pt. 4, 1514 (Adaline Montgomery); vol. 8, pt. 1, 292 (Lewis Brown).

2. On slave migration and movement to the south and west in general, the grand tradition of American slavery studies is oddly quiet. A recently published synthetic history of enslaved African Americans may reverse this trend (Ira Berlin, *Generations of Captivity: A History of African-American Slaves* [Cambridge, 2003]), but older works on slavery, including the sequence of synthetic books published in the 1950s, 1960s, and 1970s, do not make forced migration a central part of their argument. Such works include Eugene Genovese, *Roll, Jordan, Roll: The World the Slaves Made* (New York, 1974), which says little on the subject (the domestic slave trade is mentioned on pp. 419, 453, 625, and masters' migrations are not discussed); Kenneth Stampp, *The Peculiar Institution* (New York, 1956), 239–78, discusses the slave trade but not masters' migrations; Stanley Elkins, *Slavery: A Problem in American Intellectual and Institutional Life* (Chicago, 1959), mentions the domestic slave trade twice (53, 211); both Leslie Howard Owens, *This Species of Property* (New York, 1976), 173–91, and John Blassingame, *The Slave Community*, 2nd ed. (New York, 1979), 173–76, discuss the interstate slave trade and family separations, as does as Herbert Gutman, *The Black Family in Slavery and Freedom, 1750–1925* (New York, 1976). Gutman's is the only synthetic work on American slavery to discuss extensively the outcomes of slave migration, as he does with his work on plantation communities in transition (144–84). Much early debate, following the pattern of abolitionist critique, centered on the issue of family separations in the domestic slave trade: see Frederic Bancroft, *Slave Trading in the Old South*, (Baltimore, 1931); Winfield Collins, *The Domestic Slave Trade of the Southern States* (New York, 1904); Robert Fogel and Stanley Enger-

man, *Time on the Cross: The Economics of American Negro Slavery* (Boston, 1974), 42–58; Herbert Gutman and Richard Sutch, "The Slave Family: Protected Agent of Capitalist Masters or Victim of the Slave Trade?" in *Reckoning with Slavery: A Critical Study in the Quantitative History of American Negro Slavery*, ed. Paul David et al. (New York, 1976), 94–133; Herbert Gutman, *Slavery and the Numbers Game: A Critique of* Time on the Cross (Urbana, 1975), 106–7. More recent works have expanded discussion on the slave trade: see Michael Tadman, *Speculators and Slaves: Masters, Traders, and Slaves in the Old South* (Madison, 1989); Walter Johnson, *Soul by Soul: Life in the Antebellum Slave Market* (Cambridge, 1999); Phillip D. Troutman, "Slave Trade and Sentiment in Antebellum Virginia" (Ph.D. diss., University of Virginia, 2000); Robert Gudmestad, *A Troublesome Commerce: The Transformation of the Interstate Slave Trade* (Baton Rouge, 2003).

3. A few works have examined the scope and effects of forced migration, often in a local context; see Ann Patton Malone, *Sweet Chariot: Slave Family and Household Structure in Nineteenth-Century Louisiana* (Chapel Hill, 1992); Allan Kulikoff, "Uprooted Peoples: Black Migrants in the Age of the American Revolution, 1790–1820," in *Slavery and Freedom in the Age of the American Revolution*, ed. Ira Berlin and Ronald Hoffman (Charlottesville, 1983), 143–71; Steven Miller, "Plantation Labor Organization and Slave Life on the Cotton Frontier: The Alabama-Mississippi Black Belt, 1815–1840," in *Cultivation and Culture: Labor and the Shaping of Slave Life in the Americas*, ed. Ira Berlin and Philip D. Morgan (Charlottesville, 1993), 155–69; Allan Kulikoff, *The Agrarian Origins of American Capitalism* (Charlottesville, 1992), 226–63; Joan Cashin, *A Family Venture: Men and Women on the Southern Frontier* (Baltimore, 1989), 49–51; Gail S. Terry, "Sustaining the Bonds of Kinship in a Trans-Appalachian Migration, 1790–1811: The Cabell-Breckenridge Slaves Move West," *Virginia Magazine of History and Biography* 102 (October 1994): 455–76; Brenda Stevenson, *Life in Black and White: Family and Community in the Slave South* (New York, 1996), 218–25; Don H. Doyle, *Faulkner's County: The Historical Roots of Yoknapatawpha* (Chapel Hill, 2001), 128–31, 145–46; Edward E. Baptist, *Creating an Old South: Middle Florida's Plantation Frontier before the Civil War* (Chapel Hill, 2002).

4. Charles L. Perdue Jr., Thomas E. Barden, and Robert K. Phillips, eds., *Weevils in the Wheat: Interviews With Virginia Ex-slaves* (Charlottesville, 1976), 205.

5. Ibid., 151–52.

6. Rawick, *American Slave*, vol. 10, pt. 6, p. 157 (Ross Simmons); supp. ser. 2, 1:115 (Harve Osborne); vol. 5, pt. 3, pp. 8–9 (Henry Lewis); supp. ser. 2, vol. 10, pt. 9, p. 3891 (Reeves Tucker); see also supp. ser. 2, vol. 2, pt. 1, pp. 355–61 (Isabella Boyd); supp. ser. 2, vol. 1, pt. 3, p. 117 (Ollie Frasier); vol. 7, pt. 2, p. 19 (John Cameron); vol. 12, pt. 2, pp. 304–5 (Snovey Jackson); supp. ser. 1, 12:4 (Sam Anderson); supp. ser. 1, 12:99 (Betty Chessier); supp. ser. 1, 12:300–301 (Eva Strayhorn); vol. 10, pt. 5, pp. 150 (Charity Morris), 207 (Lettie Nelson), 107 (Gracie Mitchell), 145 (Olivia Morgan), 41–42 (Perry Madden); vol. 8, pt. 3, p. 1203 (Edward Jones); vol. 9, pt. 4, pp. 1367 (Lucy McBee), 1482–83 (George Washington Miller); vol. 5, pt. 3, pp. 252 (Mariah Robinson), 30 (Giles Smith); supp. ser. 2, vol. 10, pt. 9, pp. 3914 (Adaline Walton), 4058 (Allen Williams), 4078 (Daphne Williams), 4162 (Sampson Willis); supp. ser. 1, vol. 10, pt. 5, pp. 1957 (James Singleton), 2197 (James Washington); vol. 4, pt. 1, p. 295 (Eli Davidson); vol. 4, pt. 2, p. 193 (Nancy Jackson);

Unwritten History of Slavery, in Rawick, *American Slave*, 18:16, 76, 96, 110; *God Struck Me Dead*, in Rawick, *American Slave*, 19:192, 205; plus numerous planters' records. For only two examples of the many I have found, see Sarah Sparkman to brother, November 4, 1835, Brownrigg Papers, folder 3, Southern Historical Collection, University of North Carolina, Chapel Hill; Cameron Family Papers, folder 2044, vols. 120, 124, Southern Historical Collection.

7. Gutman and Sutch, "Slave Family," 129; Paul D. Escott, *Slavery Remembered: A Record of Twentieth-Century Slave Narratives* (Chapel Hill, 1979), 46–48. In *Reckoning with Slavery*, Gutman and Richard Sutch contend that 29 percent of Maryland slave marriages were destroyed by forced separation and that 32.4 percent of Mississippi ex-slaves had experienced such division (129). Escott finds that 21 percent of ex-slave interviewees recalled family separations by owners. And Gutman argues in *Slavery and the Numbers Game* (126–29) that from 1820 to 1860, the breakup of marriages by sale only (excluding the breakup of nonmarital relationships or marriages broken up by owners' migration) directly or indirectly affected (as spouses, siblings, parents, children, and friends) 2,752,000 people, or almost all people enslaved in the U.S. South during this period.

8. Rawick, *American Slave*, vol. 10, pt. 5, pp. 227 (Helen Odom), 209 (Lettie Nelson).

9. The explosion of new interest in nationalism that traces itself in large part back to Benedict Anderson, *Imagined Communities: Reflections on the Origins and Spread of Nationalism* (London, 1991), often though not always identifies the stories told about constructed common identities as histories. True or false, those histories are "made," and on them imagined communities are built. But these histories are almost without exception portrayed as having been told by educated people, usually of the perpetually rising bourgeoisie and usually on the printed page. For the United States, see, among many others, David Waldstreicher, *In the Midst of Perpetual Fetes: The Making of American Nationalism, 1776–1820* (Chapel Hill, 1997); Jill Lepore, *A is for American: Letters and Other Characters in the Newly United States* (New York, 2002); Dana D. Nelson, *National Manhood: Capitalist Citizenship and the Imagined Fraternity of White Men* (Durham, 1998).

10. See Hayden White, "The Value of Narrativity in the Representation of Reality," in his *The Content of the Form: Narrative Discourse and Historical Representation* (Baltimore, 1987), 1–25.

11. Two systematic critics of the use of such interviews are John Blassingame, introduction to *Slave Testimony: Two Centuries of Letters, Speeches, Interviews, and Autobiographies* (Baton Rouge, 1977), xliii–lxii; Donna J. Spindel, "Assessing Memory: Twentieth-Century Slave Narratives Reconsidered," *Journal of Interdisciplinary History* 27 (Autumn 1996): 247–61. Escott, *Slavery Remembered*, provides the major statistical analysis of the narratives.

12. Rawick, *American Slave*, supp. ser. 2, vol. 7, pt. 6, p. 2521 (Jack Maddox); supp. ser. 1, vol. 4, pt. 2, p. 593 (Laura Stewart). David Blight's magisterial analysis of the development of white social memory of race, slavery, and the Civil War is key here: see his *Race and Reunion: The Civil War in American Memory* (Cambridge, 2001).

13. Rawick, *American Slave*, vol. 5, pt. 3, p. 75 (Susan Merritt); see also *Unwritten History*, 1, 45, 141; Rawick, *American Slave*, vol. 6, pt. 1, pp. 60 (Amy Chapman), 157 (Mary

Ella Granberry), 353 (Annie Stanton); vol. 5, pt. 3, p. 67 (William Mathews); vol. 5, pt. 4, pp. 103 (Penny Thompson), 190 (Lulu Wilson); supp. ser. 1, vol. 10, pt. 5, p. 2228 (Foster Weathersby); vol. 4, pt. 1, p. 204 (Cato Carter); vol. 4, pt. 2, pp. 47 (Milly Forward), 180 (Carter Jackson).

14. See the important assessment of these interviews in Mia Bay, *The White Image in the Black Mind: African-American Ideas about White People, 1830–1925* (New York, 2000), esp. 113–16. See also Rawick, general introduction to *American Slave*, supp. ser. 1, 11:ix: "There is no great virtue to, or historical breakthrough in, using the slave narrative only to buttress ancient arguments and preconceived notions. The reading of the narratives ought to lead to fresh questions, new insights, a new historiography of slavery."

15. Benjamin Drew, ed., *A North-Side View of Slavery: The Refugee; or, The Narratives of Fugitive Slaves in Canada* (New York, 1856), 83; Rawick, *American Slave*, vol. 6, pt. 1, p. 129 (Delia Garlic).

16. Rawick, *American Slave*, vol. 4, pt. 2, p. 106 (William Holland). Both Johnson, *Soul by Soul*, and Troutman, "Slave Trade and Sentiment," discuss these conversations in depth.

17. Rawick, *American Slave*, supp. ser. 1, vol. 8, pt. 3, p. 1185 (Aaron Jones); Sophia Nobody to Sallie Amis, June 7, 1858, Elizabeth Blanchard Papers, folder 45, Southern Historical Collection; Thomas Brey to Obadiah Fields, June 10, 1823, Obadiah Fields Papers, Rare Book, Special Collections, and Manuscript Library, Duke University, Durham, N.C.; Joseph Sheppard to James and John Sheppard, September 17, 1843, James Sheppard Papers, Rare Book, Special Collections, and Manuscript Library, Duke University.

18. Charles Ball, *Slavery in the United States* (New York, 1837), 151–60, 194–97, 263–67; Solomon Northup, *Twelve Years a Slave*, ed. Sue Eakin and Joseph Lodgson (1853; Baton Rouge, 1968), 28–32; see also Rawick, *American Slave*, vol. 2, pt. 2, pp. 125 (Pick Gladdney), 112 (Louisa Gause); supp. ser. 1, vol. 4, pt. 2, pp. 478–80 (Anna Peele). No doubt the white interlocutors and editors who wanted to shape Ball and Northup's narratives to their own purposes also tried to do the same to the histories of these women.

19. Rawick, *American Slave*, supp. ser. 1, vol. 10, pt. 5, p. 2228 (Foster Weathersby); vol. 4, pt. 2, pp. 250 (Toby James), 32 (Lorenza Ezell); supp. ser. 1, vol. 9, pt. 4, p. 1664 (Mark Oliver); supp. ser. 2, vol. 10, pt. 9, p. 4239 (Smith Wilson).

20. Ibid., vol. 4, pt. 1, p. 2 (Will Adams); vol. 4, pt. 2, p. 216 (James Johnson); supp. ser. 1, vol. 9, pt. 4, p. 1817 (Rachel Reed).

21. Ibid., vol. 12, pt. 2, p. 2 (Elisha Doc Garey); Gutman, *Black Family in Slavery and Freedom*, 165.

22. *Unwritten History*, 254; Rawick, *American Slave*, vol. 5, pt. 3, pp. 110–11 (Charley Mitchell), 163 (Mary Overton); Perdue, Barden, and Phillips, *Weevils in the Wheat*, 253.

23. Rawick, *American Slave*, supp. ser. 1, vol. 10, pt. 5, p. 2278 (Maria White); see also supp. ser. 2, vol. 10, pt. 9, pp. 4127 (Rose Williams), 4217 (Sarah Wilson); vol. 14, pt. 1, p. 123 (Henry Bobbit).

24. Ibid., vol. 8, pt. 2, p. 50 (Lewis Chase); vol. 6, pt. 1, pp. 349–50 (John Smith); vol. 7, pt. 2, p. 169 (Clara Young); see also vol. 4, pt. 2, p. 106 (William Hamilton); vol. 2, pt. 1, p. 180 (Sylvia Cannon); vol. 5, pt. 4, pp. 37–38 (Jordan Smith); *Unwritten History*, 60.

25. Rawick, *American Slave*, vol. 2, pt. 1, p. 42 (Anderson Bates); supp. ser. 1, 12:192

(Lewis Jenkins); vol. 8, pt. 2, pp., 126–27 (Minerva Davis); see also supp. ser. 1, vol. 4, pt. 2, p. 357 (Robert Kimbrough).

26. Ibid., vol. 10, pt. 6, p. 150 (Laura Shelton); supp. ser. 1, vol. 10, pt. 5, p. 2030 (Elmo Steele); Ronnie W. Clayton, ed., *Mother Wit: The Ex-slave Narratives of the Louisiana Writers' Project* (New York, 1990), 167; Rawick, *American Slave*, supp. ser. 1, vol. 10, pt. 5, pp. 2257–58 (Minerva Wells); see also supp. ser. 2, 1:80 (Cora Gillam); vol. 6, pt. 1, pp. 106 (Carrie Davis), 215 (Emmett Ingram), 58 (Amy Chapman); vol. 10, pt. 5, pp. 227 (Helen Odom), 51 (Avalena McConico), 93 (Nathan Miller); supp. ser. 1, 12:267 (C. G. Samuel); vol. 4, pt. 2, p. 42 (Sara Ford); vol. 9, pt. 4, p. 1751 (Charlie Powers); vol. 5, pt. 3, p. 29 (Lewis Love); vol. 5, pt. 4, p. 70 (Bert Strong); supp. ser. 2, vol. 10, pt. 9, p. 4090 (Julia Williams); vol. 4, pt. 1, p. 125 (Monroe Bradkins); vol. 8, pt. 3, pp. 816 (Henry Gibbs), 952 (Mollie Hatfield), 1215 (Julius Jones), 1292 (Robert Laird); vol. 9, pt. 4, p. 1659 (Mark Oliver); vol. 2, pt. 2, pp. 274 (Zack Herndon), 25 (Roger Emanuel), 125 (Pick Gladdney), 149 (David Goddard); vol. 7, pt. 2, p. 158 (Mollie Williams); vol. 12, pt. 2, pp. 42 (Alice Green), 127 (Tom Hawkins), 328 (Georgia Johnson), 338 (Manuel Johnson); vol. 2, pt. 1, p. 18 (Frances Andrew); vol. 10, pt. 5, p. 123 (Patsey Moore); *Unwritten History*, 309; Clayton, *Mother Wit*, 147.

27. Rawick, *American Slave*, vol. 14, pt. 1, p. 69 (Lizzie Baker); vol. 10, pt. 6, p. 48 (Milton Ritchie); vol. 9, pt. 4, p. 1487 (Tom Morris).

28. Ibid., supp. ser. 1, vol. 4, pt. 2, p. 373 (Geneva Tonsill); vol. 10, pt. 5, p. 298 (Carey Allen Patten); vol. 2, pt. 2, p. 207 (Adeline Gray); Perdue, Barden, and Phillips, *Weevils in the Wheat*, 92. For a few of the numerous parents who told children of separated relatives, see Rawick, *American Slave*, vol. 6, pt. 1, pp. 129 (Delia Garlic), 35 (Ank Bishop); supp. ser. 1, 12:328 (Jim Threat); vol. 10, pt. 6. pp. 73 (WillAnn Rogers), 170 (Arzilla Smallwood), 310 (Ellen Briggs Thompson); vol. 4, pt. 2, p. 209 (Gus Johnson); vol. 10, pt. 5, p. 64 (Nellie Maxwell); vol. 9, pt. 4, p. 1726 (Cora Poche); vol. 5, pt. 4, p. 3 (Clarissa Scales); supp. ser. 2, vol. 10, pt. 9, p. 4200 (Mary Wilson); vol. 4, pt. 1, p. 188 (Jeff Calhoun); vol. 4, pt. 2, p. 21 (John Ellis); vol. 8, pt. 3, pp. 963–64 (Wash Hayes), 1109 (Dora Jackson), 937 (Virginia Harris); vol. 2, pt. 2, pp. 207 (Adeline Grey), 94 (Minnie Folkes); vol. 14, pt. 1, p. 69 (Lizzie Baker); vol. 2, pt. 1, pp. 339 (Silvia Durant), 9 (Emanuel Elmore); vol. 7, pt. 2, p. 119 (Henri Necaise); vol. 12, pt. 2, p. 49 (Isaiah Green); vol. 10, pt. 6, p. 12 (Diana Rankins); Perdue, Barden, and Phillips, *Weevils in the Wheat*, 92.

29. See Charles T. Davis and Henry Louis Gates Jr., eds., *The Slave's Narrative* (New York, 1985), esp. John W. Blassingame, "Using the Testimony of Ex-slaves: Approaches and Problems," 78–98; Paul Escott, "The Art and Science of Reading WPA Slave Narratives," 40–47; and Davis and Gates, "Introduction: The Language of Slavery," xix–xxiv. I have here revised the exaggerated "dialect" spelling of some words imposed by WPA interviewers according to the standards suggested by Sterling Brown, "On Dialect Usage," in *Slave's Narrative*, ed. Davis and Gates, 37–39.

30. Perhaps two of the best sources on the determined attempts to sanitize slavery and erase the memory of southern white brutality are John David Smith, *An Old Creed for the New South: Proslavery Ideology and Historiography, 1865–1918* (Westport, 1985), and Blight, *Race and Reunion*. Numerous other writers have also addressed this subject, from

the works of other historians of slavery commenting on their predecessors to scholarship on Margaret Mitchell and D. W. Griffith to studies of disfranchisement in the New South.

31. *Unwritten History*, 87, 141.

32. Perdue, Barden, and Phillips, *Weevils in the Wheat*, 153; the phrase is repeated in *Unwritten History*, 86

33. Rawick, *American Slave*, vol. 6, pt. 1, p. 129 (Delia Garlic).

34. Ibid., vol. 7, pt. 2, p. 152 (Jane Sutton); see also William Wells Brown, *Narrative of William Wells Brown, a Fugitive Slave* (Boston, 1849), 13; Carol Wilson, *Freedom at Risk: The Kidnapping of Free Blacks in America, 1780–1865* (Lexington, 1994); Rawick, *American Slave*, vol. 5, pt. 3, pp. 186, 183 (Lee Pierce); vol. 5, pt. 4, p. 20 (Betty Simmons); supp. ser. 2, vol. 9, pt. 8, pp. 3533–43 (Betty Simmons); supp. ser. 2, vol. 5, pt. 4, p. 1577 (James Green).

35. Rawick, *American Slave*, supp. ser. 1, vol. 10, pt. 5, pp. 100 (George Ward), 111 (Hettie Mitchell); vol. 4, pt. 2, pp. 212–13 (Harry Johnson); supp. ser. 1, 11:127–33 (George Fleming).

36. Clayton, *Mother Wit*, 206; see also 62; Rawick, *American Slave*, vol. 2, pt. 1, pp. 30–31 (Charley Barber); vol. 7, pt. 2, p. 136 (Susan Snow).

37. Rawick, *American Slave*, vol. 12, pt. 2, p. 119 (Shang Harris); vol. 4, pt. 2, p. 163 (Josephine Hubbard); Henry Benjamin Whipple, *Bishop Whipple's Southern Diary, 1843–1844*, ed. Lester B. Shippee (Minneapolis, 1937), 17. This trope is also common in British- and American-published narratives by ex-slaves who had survived the Middle Passage; see John Jea, *The Life and Unparalleled Sufferings of John Jea, the African Preacher* (Portsea, 1811), 3. Other uses of the trope of being "stole" to describe the Middle Passage include Clayton, *Mother Wit*, 62, 206; Rawick, *American Slave*, vol. 4, pt. 1, p. 307 (Victor Duhon); *Unwritten History*, 152, 198.

38. Rawick, *American Slave*, 17:335–40 (Shack Thomas); vol. 2, pt. 1, p. 122 (Toby Brown); vol. 12, pt. 1, p. 172 (Mariah Calloway); see also vol. 12, pt. 2, p. 119 (Shang Harris); supp. ser. 1, vol. 8, pt. 3, p. 1095 (Joanna Isom); supp. ser. 1, 12:268–69 (Annie Scott); A. M. H. Christensen, *Afro-American Folk Lore: Told Round Cabin Fires on the Sea Islands of South Carolina* (1892; New York, 1969), 4–5, quoted in Lawrence W. Levine, *Black Culture and Black Consciousness: Afro-American Folk Thought from Slavery to Freedom* (New York, 1977), 86. Levine identified and quoted these tales but focused on their importance as symbols of blacks' acknowledgment of their African roots.

39. Rawick, *American Slave*, supp. ser. 1, vol. 10, pt. 5, p. 2004 (Susan Snow); see also vol. 2, pt. 1, p. 316 (Elias Dawkins); for other tricks, see vol. 2, pt. 1, pp. 30–31 (Charley Barber); supp. ser. 1, vol. 9, pt. 4, p. 1416 (Chaney Mack); vol. 4, pt. 1, p. 200 (Richard Caruthers); vol. 4, pt. 2, pp. 163 (Josephine Howard), 201 (Thomas Johns), 290 (Silvia King); supp. ser. 2, 1:378 (Henry Johnson); supp. ser. 1, 11:164 (Charlie Grant). See also the story retold by Joseph Miller, *Way of Death: Merchant Capitalism and the Angolan Slave Trade, 1730–1830* (Madison, 1988), 3–4.

40. Charles Ball, *Fifty Years in Chains; or, The Life of an American Slave* (New York, 1858), 9–15. One of many such examples is the narrative of Luke Dixon (Rawick, *American Slave*, vol. 8, pt. 2, pp. 157–58). Dosia Harris reported that her grandmother, like (no doubt) many others, endured both the international and the domestic slave trades (vol.

12, pt. 2, pp. 108–9); see also vol. 12, pt. 1, p. 2 (Benny Dillard); supp. ser. 1, vol. 10, pt. 5, p. 2004 (Susan Snow); vol. 4, pt. 2, p. 163 (Josephine Howard).

41. Northup, *Twelve Years a Slave*; Wilson, *Freedom at Risk*. Franklin and Schweninger, *Runaway Slaves*, 192–97, identify a number of well-authenticated cases from white southern sources.

42. Rawick, *American Slave*, 17:101 (Ambrose Douglass), 300–301 (Samuel Smalls), 93 (Douglas Dorsey), 62 (Florida Clayton); supp. ser. 2, vol. 8, pt. 7, p. 3284, and vol. 5, pt. 3, p. 236 (Mary Reynolds); vol. 4, pt. 1, p. 93 (Julia Blanks). For other examples, see Rawick, *American Slave*, supp. ser. 1, vol. 6, pt. 1, p. 143; supp. ser. 2, vol. 8, pt. 7, p. 3284 (Mary Reynolds).

43. Rawick, *American Slave*, vol. 4, pt. 2, pp. 228–29 (Spence Johnson); supp. ser. 2, 1:286 (Clayton Holbrooke); vol. 4, pt. 1, pp. 284 (Carey Davenport), 223 (Mother Ann Clark).

44. Ibid., vol. 8, pt. 3, p. 988 (Evie Herrin); vol. 2, pt. 2, p. 190 (Sim Greeley); vol. 4, pt. 2, p. 87, and supp. ser. 2, vol. 5, pt. 4, pp. 1577–83 (James Green).

45. Perdue, Barden, and Phillips, *Weevils in the Wheat*, 319; Rawick, *American Slave*, vol. 2, pt. 1, p. 67 (Samuel Boulware). Other examples of violent separations or separations by subterfuge are rife throughout the WPA narratives: a few particularly chilling ones appear in Perdue, Barden, and Phillips, *Weevils in the Wheat*, 253; Rawick, *American Slave*, vol. 14, pt. 1, p. 59 (Viney Baker); vol. 6, pt. 1, p. 72 (Laura Clark); vol. 12, pt. 2, p. 239 (Bryant Huff); supp. ser. 1, vol. 9, pt. 4, p. 1903 (Rose Russell); *Unwritten History*, 305.

46. See Rawick, *American Slave*, 17:62–63 (Florida Clayton), 92–93 (Douglas Dorsey); vol. 7, pt. 1, pp. 295–97 (Andrew Simms); vol. 5, pt. 3, p. 10 (Henry Lewis). Parents also told such tales to enslaved children to teach them to beware of too-close association with white outlaws. Such men, like the notorious (and mostly mythical) John Murrell, were suspected by whites and blacks alike of stealing, selling, reselling, and restealing blacks. In such stories, the enslaved accomplices of the outlaws usually ended up as corpses floating in swamps. Dead men told no tales. See Rawick, *American Slave*, vol. 4, pt. 2, p. 230 (Spence Johnson); James Lal Penick Jr., *The Great Western Land Pirate: John A. Murrell in Legend and History* (Columbia, 1981); H. R. Howard, *The History of Virgil A. Stewart* (New York, 1836); Baptist, *Creating an Old South*, 207–8. Stories told to slave children sometimes conflated slave-stealing white outlaws like Murrell, slave traders, and the ghostly bogeyman "Raw-Head and Bloody-Bones"; see Rawick, *American Slave*, vol. 12, pt. 1, pp. 6 (Rachel Adams), 312 (Callie Elder); vol. 12, pt. 2 (Ga.), 249 (Easter Huff); vol. 2, pt. 1, pp. 143 (Sara Brown), 311–12 (William Henry Davis); supp. ser. 1, vol. 8, pt. 3, pp. 943 (Virginia Harris), 1200–1201 (Charity Jones); vol. 10, pt. 6, p. 326 (Laura Thornton); supp. ser. 1, 12:193 (Lewis Jenkins), 374 (Mollie Watson); 17:63 (Florida Clayton), 337 (Shack Thomas), 13 (Samuel Simeon Andrews); supp. ser. 1, vol. 9, pt. 4, p. 1487 (George Washington Miller). See also John Brown, *Slave Life in Georgia: A Narrative of the Life, Sufferings, and Escape of John Brown*, ed. L. A. Chamerovzow (London, 1855), 50.

47. Clayton, *Mother Wit*, 21–23.

48. See Gutman's lengthy investigation of cultural barriers against even cousin-cousin intermarriage among enslaved Africans and African Americans in *Black Family in Slavery and Freedom*, 88–93, which also adds several additional examples of incest tales, though

he does not analyze them as symbolic in any way. For other incest tales, see Perdue, Barden, and Phillips, *Weevils in the Wheat*, 89, 105; Rawick, *American Slave*, vol. 2, pt. 1, pp. 124–25 (Henry Brown); vol. 9, pt. 3, pp. 321–24 (Cora Horton), 102–3 (Lizzie Johnson). See also Eliza Suggs, *Shadow and Sunshine* (Omaha, 1906), 75, who retells the same story, though she was born in 1875.

49. *Unwritten History*, 274; William Henry Singleton, *Recollections of My Slavery Days* (n.p., 1922), 4.

50. Rawick, *American Slave*, supp. ser. 1, 12:213 (Cheney McNair); Emeline Hodges in the *Philadelphia Christian Recorder*, August 27, 1870; see also Michael P. Johnson, "Looking for Lost Kin: Efforts to Reunite Lost Kin after Emancipation," in *Southern Families at War: Loyalty and Conflict in the Civil War South*, ed. Catherine Clinton (New York, 2000), 15–34; Leon Litwack, *Been in the Storm So Long: The Aftermath of Slavery* (New York, 1979), esp. 229–47; Ira Berlin and Leslie P. Rowland, eds., *Families and Freedom: A Documentary History of African-American Kinship in the Civil War Era* (New York, 1997).

51. Rawick, *American Slave*, vol. 2, pt. 1, p. 229 (Caleb Craig); supp. ser. 1, vol. 10, pt. 5, p. 2155 (Edwin Walker); vol. 8, pt. 2, p. 131 (Virginia Davis).

52. William Wells Brown, *Narrative*, 13, 51; Richard Hildreth, *The White Slave; or, Memoirs of a Fugitive* (Boston, 1852), 25.

53. Thomas Smallwood, *A Narrative of Thomas Smallwood* (Toronto, 1851), 19; *Aunt Sally; or, The Cross the Way of Freedom* (Cincinnati, 1858), 89; Charles Ball, *Slavery in the United States*, 36; Moses Roper, *A Narrative of the Adventures and Escape of Moses Roper* (Philadelphia, 1838), 62; J. W. Loguen, *The Rev. J. W. Loguen as a Slave and a Freeman* (Syracuse, 1859), 14–15. See also Charles Wheeler, *Chains and Freedom; or, The Life and Adventures of Peter Wheeler, a Colored Man* (New York, 1839), 36–45; William and Ellen Craft, *Running a Thousand Miles for Freedom; or, The Escape of William and Ellen Craft from Slavery* (London, 1860), 3–7; Henry Brown, *Narrative of Henry Box Brown* (Boston, 1849), 15; Kate Pickard, *The Kidnapped and the Ransomed: Being the Personal Recollections of Peter Still and His Wife "Vina" after Forty Years of Slavery* (Syracuse, 1856); Lunsford Lane, *The Narrative of Lunsford Lane* (Boston, 1842), 20. Other narratives that used terms such as "stolen from Africa" to describe parents or grandparents include John Brown, *Slave Life in Georgia* (London, 1855), 1, 64; John Andrew Jackson, *The Experience of a Slave in South Carolina* (London, 1862), 7; Frederick Douglass, *Narrative of the Life of Frederick Douglass* (Boston, 1845), 40; Henry C. Bruce, *The New Man: Twenty-nine Years the Slave, Twenty-nine Years the Free Man* (York, 1895), 129–31; Francis Fedric, *Slave Life in Virginia and Kentucky* (London, 1863), 4.

54. Douglass, *Narrative of the Life*, 48.

55. William S. McFeely, *Frederick Douglass* (New York, 1991); Waldo E. Martin Jr., *The Mind of Frederick Douglass* (Chapel Hill, 1984). See also the synthetic work of Dickson D. Bruce Jr., *The Origins of African American Literature, 1680–1865* (Charlottesville, 2001); Sterling Bland, *Voices of the Fugitives: Runaway Slave Stories and Their Fictions of Self-Creation*, (Westport, 2000).

56. The links between vernacular storytelling by slaves and former slaves, on the one hand, and literary production by African Americans on the other, have been explored by various scholars and authors: see William L. Andrews, *To Tell a Free Story: The First*

Century of Afro-American Autobiography, 1760–1865 (Urbana, 1985), 274; Marion W. Starling, *The Slave Narrative: Its Place in American History* (1946; Boston, 1981); Davis and Gates, *Slave's Narrative*; Henry Louis Gates Jr., *The Signifying Monkey: A Theory of Afro-American Literary Criticism* (New York, 1988).

57. James C. Scott, *Domination and the Arts of Resistance: Hidden Transcripts* (New Haven, 1990).

58. Rawick, *American Slave*, vol. 12, pt. 2, p. 292 (Amanda Jackson). Such references are endless in the WPA interviews; see, for example, Rawick, *American Slave*, vol. 5, pt. 4, pp. 79 (Jake Terriel), 101 (Mary Thompson); vol. 10, pt. 6, pp. 76–77 (William Henry Rooks), 336 (J. T. Travis); supp. ser. 1, 12:29–30 (Mollie Barber); vol. 6, pt. 1, p. 58 (Amy Chapman); vol. 2, pt. 1, p. 173 (Nelson Cameron); vol. 2, pt. 2, p. 280 (Lucretia Heyward); Perdue, Barden, and Phillips, *Weevils in the Wheat*, 161; *Unwritten History*, 31, 81, 105, 204–5, 216, 298–99.

59. Rawick, *American Slave*, vol. 12, pt. 2, p. 274 (Emma Hurley); vol. 5, pt. 4, p. 53 (Mariah Snyder); vol. 7, pt. 2, p. 1 (Jim Allen); vol. 8, pt. 2, p. 15 (Maria Sutton Clemmons); vol. 12, pt. 1, p. 10 (Wash Allen); vol. 2, pt. 2, p. 280 (Lucretia Hayward); Perdue, Barden, and Phillips, *Weevils in the Wheat*, 161, 185, 211, 250, 318; Bay, *White Image in the Black Mind*, 117–49; Edward E. Baptist, " 'Cuffy,' 'Fancy Maids,' and 'One-Eyed Men': Rape, Commodification, and the Domestic Slave Trade in the United States," *American Historical Review* 106 (December 2001): 1619–50.

60. Perdue, Barden, and Phillips, *Weevils in the Wheat*, 21; *Unwritten History*, 118. For white preachers defending slavery to slaves, see Rawick, *American Slave*, vol. 5, pt. 3, p. 213 (Jenny Proctor).

61. Perdue, Barden, and Phillips, *Weevils in the Wheat*, 102, 123.

62. Ibid., 23.

63. Clayton, *Mother Wit*, 84–87. The concept of emplotment is borrowed from Hayden White, *Metahistory: The Historical Imagination in Nineteenth-Century Europe* (Baltimore, 1973).

64. Genovese, *Roll, Jordan, Roll*, is the sine qua non of this historiography in the present and at the same time one of the best evocations of the late-antebellum planter-paternalist (attempts at) hegemony. See also Eugene Genovese, *The World the Slaveholders Made: Two Essays in Interpretation* (New York, 1969); Elizabeth Fox-Genovese, *Within the Plantation Household: Black and White Women of the Old South* (Chapel Hill, 1988); Peter Kolchin, *American Slavery: 1619–1877* (New York, 1993); Jeffrey Young, *Domesticating Slavery: The Master Class in Georgia and South Carolina, 1670–1837* (Chapel Hill, 1999).

65. Perdue, Barden, and Phillips, *Weevils in the Wheat*, 115. He almost certainly refers to a statue of a Confederate soldier erected in 1907 near Norfolk's docks: see Great Elena Couper, *An American Sculptor on the Grand Tour: The Life and Works of William Couper (1853–1942)* (Los Angeles, 1988), 38–39, 45, 85, 109. The assistance of David Feinberg, reference librarian, Virginia State Library, on this point is gratefully acknowledged.

British Slavery and British Politics

A Perspective and a Prospectus

CHRISTOPHER L. BROWN

*T*he past quarter century has brought a burst of new scholarship on slavery in the British American colonies. The historiography displays a depth and sophistication it lacked twenty years ago. Taking note in 1980 of the disproportionate focus on the antebellum era, Ira Berlin concluded that students of American slavery had tended to hold "time constant and ignore the influence of place." Now, a generation later, we have, at the very least, satisfactory studies of slavery in every British colony where it mattered as well as fine studies of slavery in those settlements where it scarcely existed. Historians of the British Caribbean have yet to produce overviews comparable to the massive surveys published recently by Ira Berlin and Philip Morgan on slavery in North America, but thoughtful work has emerged on each of the key sugar islands and for most time periods. At the same time, Robin Blackburn's provocative grand narrative of the rise and fall of New World slavery has clarified the history of British plantation societies by situating it in a wider international context. If the most recent scholarship has not quite rectified the overemphasis on the first half of the nineteenth century, there is now a more proportionate attention to what Berlin has properly called the first two centuries of slavery in British America.[1]

Most of this new work has focused on social, economic, and, to a lesser extent, cultural history. The questions important to researchers concern the work that slaves performed, the commodities that they produced, the lives that they lived, and the worlds that slaveholders and slaves made together as well as apart. The political history of slavery, with a few crucial exceptions, has been served less well.[2] Historians interested in antebellum American history cannot ignore the politics of slavery, since those contests culminated in the 1860s in a bloody civil war. Without a crisis of comparable magnitude to explain, historians of the British empire have treated the political history of slavery during the colonial era in a less sustained, more fragmentary fashion—as isolated episodes detached from the central themes in imperial history. In important respects, the political history of British slavery is in its infancy, though its outlines may be dimly traced and certain elements have been studied in depth. A rich body of work, for example, details slave resistance and transatlantic antislavery movements. But these subjects typically are studied in foreshortened time spans and treated as separate topics.[3] It becomes clear, moreover, that an exclusive focus on resistant slaves and abolitionists underestimates the complexity of the conflicts in question. Recent work on the Spanish frontier, the American Revolution, and the Haitian Revolution have established the pertinence of military history to the study of slavery. At the same time, a renewed attention to imperial contexts has highlighted the importance of contests between colonial slaveholders and the British state, conflicts pregnant with consequence for the institution of slavery throughout British America.[4] The pieces of the puzzle begin to fall into place. But scholars and students do not yet have a connected account of the political history of slavery in the early British empire, from the first years of colonial settlement through the last years of colonial slaveholding.

Even more to the point, few observers have a clear picture of what such a history might look like, the structure it might take, or the themes it could develop. If a political history of slavery must encompass more than the history of slave resistance and the history of abolitionism, what are the proper boundaries of the subject? What historical problems should such work address? Words written nearly sixty years ago by Frank Tannenbaum, a pioneer in the comparative study of slavery, may provide a clue: "Slavery changed the form of the state, the nature of property, the system of law, the organization of labor, the role of the church as well as its character, the notions of justice, ethics, ideas of right and wrong. Slavery influenced the architecture, the cooking, the politics, the literature, the morals of the entire group—white and black, men and women, old and young. . . . Nothing escaped . . . nothing and no one."[5] Tannenbaum knew that understanding the history of slavery meant comprehending its external history as well as its internal dynamics, the difference it made in the broader Atlantic world as well as within specific colonies. Because of the work of Eric Williams and the controversy that his 1944 study, *Capitalism and Slavery*, inspired, scholars have come to appreciate the ways human bondage in the colonies affected economic change in the British Isles.[6] Yet as things stand, it is more difficult than it should be to characterize the impact of colonial slavery on the political life of the British Atlantic world during the early modern era. And this is a shame, because in at least five very basic ways the institution of slavery in the colonies made a profound difference: it produced political power, defined political interests, generated political conflicts, shaped political thought, and, by the late eighteenth century in particular, influenced political culture.

The ownership of slaves gave British men power as well as wealth. Slaveholding figured in the rise of a social group distinctive to the subtropical colonies in the Americas—the planter class. Distinguished by their command of outsize quantities of land and labor, the planters dominated by the early eighteenth century each of the provincial governments in the British Caribbean and the southern mainland.[7] The renowned stability of these colonies in the half century before the American Revolution owed much to the political supremacy of the slaveholding gentry, which managed, with a few important exceptions in these years, to prevent effective challenge to their authority from below. Slaveholding not only empowered men on the peripheries but in some instances gave them influence in the metropole. Given the present state of research, it is not easy to determine the extent to which slave-produced wealth heightened the political standing of merchants in outports such as Glasgow, Liverpool, and Bristol, where trade with West Africa and British America was brisk.[8] Clearer is the success of absentee planters in transforming sugar profits into political power. By the middle decades of the eighteenth century, the West India interest represented the most influential colonial lobby in London, and absentee sugar planters held several dozen seats in the House of Commons.[9] A political history of slavery, then, would need to assess the political power of the planter class and certain overseas merchants, both in the colonies and at home, and to chart the ebb and flow of their influence over time.

A comprehensive account would have to consider as well the role of slavery in state formation during the seventeenth and eighteenth centuries. Slavery produced public as well as private wealth and, as a consequence, figured significantly in the enhancement of national power. Duties collected by the customs service represented between a fifth and a third of the revenues collected by the state between 1690 and 1790, and throughout this era tobacco and sugar remained among the most heavily taxed of commodities.[10] The increased revenue helped Britain finance the wars that opened up foreign markets and expanded imperial possessions. Unfortunately, the history of the British government's relation to the development and evolution of slavery—unlike the U.S. government's[11]—remains unwritten. Nonetheless, the process of empire building during the seventeenth century clearly depended heavily on state investment in the Atlantic slave trade and the control of slave-produced commodities. To win wars in Europe and North America, the British sometimes sacked French and Spanish plantations to deprive those empires of colonial wealth. And the state exhausted enormous resources in money and men during the wars with France in the 1700s to attain supremacy in colonial trade. Slaves served the British army in the Americas during the Seven Years' War, the American Revolution, and the French Revolution. Throughout the early modern era, slavery affected how wars were fought and sometimes where and when. Acquiring and sustaining international power during the eighteenth and early nineteenth centuries meant, in many instances, commanding the territories where the slaves were, even if that required the reduction of commitments elsewhere.[12]

Slavery therefore not only produced political power but also defined political interests for individuals as well as for the state. To some degree, most propertied men in the Americas sought wealth, autonomy, security, and mastery in their households. The institution of slavery gave these more common ambitions a distinctive shape. As the owners of factories in the field, planters favored, as a rule, ready credit, low production costs, protection from foreign competition, high consumer prices for their commodities, and extensive markets in which to sell. They dedicated much of their formal political activity to obtaining economic policies that served these ends. In slave societies, mastery meant ruling a small army of laborers, not merely a household. And so planters throughout the slave societies of British America established elaborate slave codes that, in unprecedented ways, made public authorities the guarantors of quasi-feudal powers. Moreover, the risk of revolt from within made British plantations attractive targets for seizure in time of war. Thus, far more than elsewhere in British America, the colonial elite in slaveholding societies proved consistently reluctant to play a prominent role in Britain's colonial wars. In the Caribbean, furthermore, eighteenth-century planters actively sought a standing army capable of defending the colonies from their own slaves. In other respects, though, slaveholders possessed an unusual preoccupation with securing independence from metropolitan oversight. Not only did they resent impositions of imperial authority, as other British colonists did, but they also tried to prevent Church of England missionaries and sectarian enthusiasts from challenging the customs and values fundamental to the plantation regime. As must be stressed and as the present historiography well reflects, the producers of tobacco, rice, indigo, and sugar had varying experiences and needs. At no time before the American Revolution did they think of themselves as a unitary slaveholding interest. Nonetheless, as owners of colonial plantations and as masters of men, they had common interests and therefore, in ways too frequently neglected, a common history.

The contours of this common history become clearer if we consider the variety of political conflicts that slaveholding inspired. The British Atlantic planter class shared not only interests but also a set of antagonists. Most prominent were the enslaved themselves, who challenged slavery from within from its moment of inception through emancipation in 1834 and the abolition of apprenticeship four years later. In several instances, slave resistance culminated in insurrections or mass desertions. More commonly, it crystallized as local, private struggles for rights, liberty, and autonomy. In either case, slave resistance defined the choices available to slaveholders. In times of peace, planters sustained local militias or soldiers to discourage collective rebellion. In times of war, slaveholders faced the risk of a fight on two fronts—against an internal enemy within the colonies as well as rivals without. Enslaved men and women, moreover, sometimes benefited from the assistance of dissidents in the colonies, free blacks or whites without slaves who resented the political supremacy of the slaveholders and, as a consequence, could prove unreliable allies in the defense of human bondage. Internal opposition coordinated by slaves and other dissidents, of course, created opportunities for hostile outsiders—Native Americans, maroons, the French, and the Spanish—to pose as armed liberators and thus threaten the survival of slavery from without. The slave societies of British America often faced their greatest danger when enemies stood poised to exploit their vulnerability to revolution from below.

Competing economic interests in the metropole or in the northern and middle colonies in North America could also present significant threats to the planters' welfare. Planters often wanted an exclusive right to supply their goods to markets within the empire, but merchants, refiners, and consumers sometimes found it in their interest to obtain tropical commodities elsewhere if they could be had at better prices. A prolonged dispute emerged in the early nineteenth century between the planters of the West Indies and the metropolitan merchants trading to the east who wished to import sugar from India for sale in markets in Britain. Less spectacular conflicts with British creditors occurred with some regularity, since planters in the colonies often purchased land, slaves, equipment, goods, and provisions with the expectation of producing a substantial crop. Now and again, moreover, planters found themselves at odds with both the shipowning interests and the state when they looked to foreign carriers, such as the Dutch in the seventeenth century or Americans after the war for independence, who were willing to carry commodities for sale in foreign markets. In numerous instances indeed, planters found that their interests conflicted with the agendas of Parliament or the Crown. The state raised duties when planters wanted them reduced. Whitehall sometimes chose war when planters would have been happier with peace. Over time, British officials proved less reliable in defending white supremacy than slaveholders would have liked. The government established regiments of enslaved black soldiers to fight in the Americas during the 1790s and in the process ignored the many planters who preferred to keep arms out of the hands of African slaves. These conflicts over economic and strategic policy sometimes merged, especially at the end of the era, with concurrent contests between metropolitan and colonial values. Throughout the early modern era, British critics, often clergy, denounced the way planters treated enslaved men and women and pushed for the conversion of the enslaved to Christianity. These reformers typically wanted to ameliorate slavery, but at the end of the eighteenth century, an antislavery movement emerged to insist that planters should not keep slaves at all.

These threats to British slave societies, from within and from without, gave rise to a distinctive set of political ideas. In general, we currently know far too little about how the defense of colonial slavery affected the development of Anglo-American political thought.[13] Nonetheless, at least five claims originated by the slaveholders and rehearsed frequently in their formal political literature proved especially consequential. One concerned the value of the slaveholding colonies to the empire. The owners of plantations sought favor and favorable legislation by insisting on the economic importance of such endeavors. In the process, they helped to generate a rival set of ideas attractive to those suspicious of the planters' influence on commercial policy, ideas that questioned the benefits of the American colonies and that promoted, as an alternative, an empire based primarily on trade. The rise of free-trade ideology in the late eighteenth and early nineteenth centuries is incomprehensible without reference to the concurrent attack on the privileged position of the West India interest. Planters also affected attitudes toward property in persons by insisting on a right to hold human chattel. Masters of households and employers of labor had long possessed extensive power over their dependents. But the planter class was the first to suggest that with respect to slaves, these powers should be absolute and unqualified, a claim that over time raised more general questions about the appropriate limits of patriarchal authority. Planters buttressed their professed right to slave property by insisting on the inferiority of African peoples. If members of the slaveholding elite did not originate the idea of race, they gave it a salience and currency in Anglo-American political thought it otherwise would have lacked. Proslavery arguments repeatedly had unforeseen consequences. Colonial slaveholders were the first to suggest that the entire nation, not merely the owners of slaves, bore responsibility for the slave system in British America—a claim that ironically proved of great value to abolitionists in the 1780s, who hoped to make antislavery a public concern by describing colonial slavery as a national sin. And the slave owners were the first to suggest that workers in industrializing Britain lived no better and in some respects worse than the enslaved men and women for whom the abolitionists expressed concern. Planters attempted to silence metropolitan critics by calling attention to the prevalence of wage slavery in the British Isles, but in the process—and again inadvertently—they helped pave the way for later nineteenth-century critiques of free labor.

Similarly, the campaigns against colonial slavery touched off broader transformations in British political culture. Abolitionism helped unite a nation recovering from the loss of North America and the political divisions that conflict had caused. Abolitionism allowed members of Parliament to express their commitment to reform while discouraging institutional change at home. At the same time, the antislavery movement initiated significant change in public politics. The campaigns provided an unprecedented opportunity for political participation among disenfranchised groups. It helped the marginalized—particularly Quakers and Anglican evangelicals—achieve social respectability. The movement brought thousands of British women into formal political canvassing, and they in turn expanded the established repertoire of political agitation by organizing consumer boycotts of slave-grown sugar. At times between 1787 and 1838, the issue of slavery dominated national politics. The formal parliamentary debates generated extensive discussion out-of-doors, an astounding number of antislavery petitions, and a substantial corpus of controversial literature. A bibliography published in 1932 identified more than five hundred pamphlets published on slavery in the late eighteenth and early nineteenth centuries. An updated search likely would turn up a good deal more. Most fundamentally, British abolitionism helped establish opposition to slavery as an expression of collective virtue, a tradition that significantly influenced British political life into the early twentieth century and helped it become a fundamental component of national identity as well as the moral basis for the exertion of imperial power.[14]

In all of these ways—by producing power, shaping interests, generating conflicts, inspiring debate, and forming identities—slavery mattered to the political history of the British Atlantic world. A simple enumeration of the key topics, however, can tell us little about the dynamic aspects of this history, the way contests for power within and over slavery changed over time, or how the political history of slavery reflected and figured in the broader political developments of the era. It becomes a relatively simple task to develop a chronology for the half century after the American Revolution, when conflicts between abolitionists and the slaveholding interests took center stage. More difficult is devising a chronology for the first century and a half of colonial slavery, since, at first glance, the political experience of the slaveholding colonies in this period would seem to be defined by their individual histories rather than by a common struggle. Yet as I have suggested, the British Atlantic planter class often had shared interests and a shared set of antagonists. And these commonalities make it possible to treat aspects of the political history of slavery as a single story. The questions helpful for the era after American independence, as it happens, serve equally well for the decades before: in the struggle to establish, profit from, and preserve colonial slavery, what were British planters up against? When and how did those challenges change during the course of the colonial era?

When it was established in the colonies during the early seventeenth century, chattel slavery represented a substantial departure in English social and economic history. The colonists who settled in the Chesapeake and the Caribbean had no experience with the operation of large-scale plantations or the management of slave labor. The settlers had in front of them, it is true, the example of other European colonists—especially the Spanish and the Portuguese—who had begun to use slave labor extensively by the late sixteenth century. And enslaved African men and women were available in the Americas to those who could afford to purchase them from merchants—primarily Dutch in this period—engaged in the Atlantic slave trade. But it took several decades for slavery to emerge in the new English colonies, in part because of the adjustment it required to English customs. The founders did not set out to establish slave societies. The trading companies and individual proprietors thought of the first settlers as employees rather than entrepreneurs and expected them to work for metropolitan investors rather than for themselves. As tenants rather than landowners, the first colonists lacked the incentive to invest in plantation agriculture. It took time for settlers to identify and successfully cultivate viable crops. And in the Chesapeake, in Saint Kitts, and on Providence Island, colonists were vulnerable in the early years to raids by the neighboring Powhatans, Caribs, and Spanish. But in the development of colonial slavery, the first significant political struggle that mattered took place between colonists seeking property rights in land and the metropolitan promoters seeking a return on their investment. The development of slavery in the English colonies depended heavily on the liberation of the English colonists from the control of metropolitan overseers, a process that began for some colonies shortly after their founding and was completed for all during the turmoil of the Civil War and the interregnum that removed the last vestiges of proprietary control over the plantation economies.

If the ownership of land and command of the colonial economy represented the first political victory for the planters, the reduction of labor into a commodity represented the second. Profitably exploiting the land meant intensifying the exploitation of labor. Especially in the Chesapeake and on Barbados, planters abandoned the "pre-capitalistic, moral-paternalistic ideological superstructure of traditional servitude," as historian Hilary McD. Beckles has put it, in favor of a system that transformed indentured servants into "temporary chattels." Servants in seventeenth-century England, it is true, also endured arduous labor, physical punishment, and recapture when they fled from an employer. They too were unfree in critical respects. What made service in the Chesapeake and the West Indies different in the early and mid-seventeenth century for both voluntary and involuntary migrants was their almost complete transformation into private property. In early Barbados, according to Beckles, planters routinely "bought, sold, gambled away, mortgaged, taxed as property, and alienated in their wills their indentured servants." There, as in the other plantation colonies, the institutions that might have protected laborers from maltreatment—the courts in particular—lay under the control of the planters. The English state, moreover, was an unreliable guardian. Acts of Parliament in 1652 and 1654 licensed the shipment of the defenseless poor to the colonies. And combatants during the midcentury wars in the British Isles added to the total by exiling the defeated to the Americas. The independence that allowed the early colonial elite to establish private landownership also allowed them to exploit the human flotsam dispersed by political conflict at home. The supply of servants available to the plantation colonies declined in the late seventeenth century as the number of migrants to the Americas fell, as the indentured looked for opportunities elsewhere, as an intensifying concern with the rights of the freeborn gradually discouraged the reduction of English nationals into near slavery, and as an emerging English trade in the eastern Atlantic made more African slaves available. But when planters in the Caribbean turned decisively to the employment of Africans after the Restoration, they had already established for themselves the apparently unrestricted right to employ and govern human property as they saw fit.[15]

In the first half century of colonial settlement, then, the nascent planter class waged a successful fight to control land and labor. The fifty years that followed, from 1660 to 1713, were characterized by a struggle to persist through a series of setbacks that destabilized the emerging plantation regime. Slavery in English America had first taken root when the overseas settlements lay outside the constant scrutiny of rulers in the metropole. Its future became less certain as the Crown began to recognize the commercial and strategic importance of the colonies. Before the 1650s, the plantation colonists depended heavily on Dutch merchants for manufactured goods and the export of their produce to Europe. Because of the Navigation Acts, English planters lost their short-lived liberty to find the best market for their goods. At the same time, new duties imposed on sugar and tobacco threatened to reduce their profits just as the first boom years for tropical commodities passed. Royal government, moreover, threatened not only a loss of wealth but also a decline in political power. A campaign inaugurated by Charles II and extended during the short reign of James II threatened to reduce the independence of the colonies and the authority of the colonial elite. Royal governors sent to Virginia and the English West Indies during this period tried to stifle the lower houses of assembly and tighten the enforcement of the acts of trade. To make matters worse, the planters stood to lose a great deal from the colonial wars conducted by the state. England spent half of the era between the Restoration and the Treaty of Utrecht at war with the Netherlands or France. In the short run, these conflicts had a disastrous effect on property holdings in the plantation colonies. Enemies wrecked havoc on each of the English Caribbean islands at least once during this period. Saint Kitts alone was sacked seven times. In becoming valuable to the empire, the slave colonies also became a chief prize in the high-stakes contests for local political authority and international supremacy.[16]

The planters were especially vulnerable in such contests. Settlements in South Carolina, Jamaica, and the Leeward Islands would achieve social stability and consistent economic success only after the achievement of lasting peace in Europe. Planters lost white servants by the hundreds to the army and navy. When the French and Dutch invaded, they often carried off slaves by the thousands from the English plantations. Predictably, the frequent unrest endangered landowners' already uncertain authority over their servants. Revolts by Irish laborers in Barbados in the 1630s and 1640s had led several colonies to limit, as they could, subsequent Irish immigration. The Catholic workers, the planters believed, represented not only a disgruntled labor force but also a potential fifth column. Royal governors sent by James II to the British West Indies in the late 1680s turned to Irish servants as well as small landowners and (in Jamaica) buccaneers to humble the English planter class. With the encouragement of Jacobite governor-general Nathaniel Johnson, Irish workers on Saint Kitts destroyed the English plantations in June 1689, clearing the way for a French conquest of the island months later. Seditious behavior, of course, followed as much from the resentments of class as from the fault lines of religion and politics. English servants oppressed by their employers in Saint Kitts welcomed a Spanish invasion force in 1628 with grateful cries for liberty. Nathaniel Bacon famously rallied servants, slaves, and others among the dispossessed in a 1676 rebellion against the Virginia elite. Interracial conspiracies, such as an aborted 1692 plot in Barbados, especially unnerved planters because they threatened to unite the black majority with disgruntled and landless whites unsympathetic to the plantation regime. Enslaved men and women, though, did not need the assistance of white servants to seek their freedom. And the growth of slaveholding throughout the plantation colonies in the late seventeenth century led to repeated attempts among the enslaved to overthrow human bondage.[17]

If slaveholders faced a genuine threat to their social and political position between 1713 and 1763—that is, from the Treaty of Utrecht until the end of the Seven Years' War—it came from the slaves themselves. The demographic imbalances that resulted from the growth of the slave trade helped make slave plots and conspiracies a frequent occurrence. Unconquered maroon communities prevented planters from achieving supremacy in Jamaica and negotiated terms of peace that gave them legal recognition. Although Britain seized Jamaica from Spain in 1655, nearly a century and a half would pass before the British could claim authority over the entire island. In some instances, the enslaved found allies in the enemies of the slaveholders. The Spanish in Florida compromised the security of British low-country settlements by offering liberty to slaves who escaped to Saint Augustine, a policy that precipitated the well-known Stono Rebellion in South Carolina in 1739. For reasons that need more research, the 1730s and 1740s witnessed an unparalleled cycle of plots and conspiracies.[18] Planters in the British colonies escaped a revolution from below in the decades before the American Revolution but did so only by responding with brutal reprisals.

Outside the constant threat of insurrection, the planters faced few serious challenges to their interests during the first six decades of the eighteenth century. In this period, they consolidated their authority in the colonial assemblies and all but silenced local dissent. Greater political security in the colonies led to a more energetic engagement with politics in the metropole. Because of a dependence on the state for military protection as well as a need for protection from competing sugar producers in the French West Indies, planters sought influence within the empire rather than independence from it. Slaveholders won substantial victories over competing economic interests in the first half of the eighteenth century. They assisted the successful campaign that culminated in 1714 against the Royal Africa Company's monopoly on the British slave trade. An increasingly influential West Indian lobby achieved an important victory with the passage of the Excise Tax of 1733, which severely restricted the North American and Irish trade in rum and the French Caribbean colonies' trade in other commodities. In 1739, over the objections of shipowners, refiners, and metropolitan grocers, sugar planters managed to drive up the price of their product in Britain by winning the privilege of selling directly to European purchasers. And in the 1740s, South Carolina slaveholders would figure critically in the successful campaign in colonial Georgia for the introduction of chattel slavery. The half century following the Peace of Utrecht represented the heyday of the planting interest. By the 1760s, there was little reason to think that the planters or the slave system would find their political fortunes reversed.[19]

Those who opposed slavery on moral grounds scarcely looked like a credible threat during these years. From the establishment of the first slaveholding colonies in English America, planters had faced both colonial and metropolitan critics discomfited by the practice of human bondage, including a substantial number of exceptionally pious men and women angered not only by the enslavement of human bodies but also by the neglect of redeemable souls. Slaveholders in the British colonies, almost as a rule, showed no interest in converting enslaved men and women to Christianity or exhibiting the paternal values that, the critics said, would encourage loyal service among the enslaved. As a consequence, the devout, on their own initiative, tried to promote Christianity on the plantations. Quaker settlers in Barbados began this missionary work in the late seventeenth century. The Church of England, through the auspices of the newly founded Society for the Propagation of the Gospel, sponsored a more comprehensive program for all of plantation America in the early eighteenth century. Scholars have tended to dismiss this campaign to Christianize slavery because it failed spectacularly. There were few Protestant Christians among the nearly half million enslaved men and women in the colonies on the eve of the American Revolution. The commitment to missionary work within the Church of England was inconsistent at best. But the Christianization initiatives failed because planters had no desire to reform the ethos of the labor system, raise the expectations of the enslaved, or permit outsiders to patrol the plantations and spread potentially subversive ideas. And in this regard, until the early nineteenth century, when their evident hostility to the clergy began to enrage metropolitan opinion, the planters got their way.[20]

Alongside the effort among some clergy to make slaves Christians, a more secular critique of slavery also took shape during the first three-quarters of the eighteenth century. The literary record of the period is littered with evidence of distaste for human bondage in the Americas. Historians often have focused on the pronouncements of well-known Scottish intellectuals such as Frances Hutcheson, Adam Smith, and John Millar, but as the planters knew, a discomfort with colonial slavery ran widely, if not deeply, through polite society in the British Isles. A pamphlet published in London had challenged the morality of slavery on the grounds of natural rights as early as 1709. And in the 1730s the Reverend Robert Robertson of Nevis was bemoaning the "current and longstanding Humour" in England of judging planters "by the most rigorous severity."[21] The antislavery critiques intensified during the 1760s and 1770s as social and commercial connections with the colonies deepened, as the newspaper and pamphlet literature reported on events in British America with greater frequency, and as poets and novelists increasingly used colonial settings to explore the themes of civility and barbarism, virtue and savagery. The growth of antislavery sentiment in the second half of the eighteenth century followed in large part from the internal logic of cultural change, from the growing value placed on sensibility, charity, and enlightenment. It reflected broader trends in the intellectual culture of Western Europe, trends that had little to do with the specifics of Anglo-American politics. But it was the conflict over the rights of the colonies in the years before the American Revolution that galvanized antislavery sentiment into an organized movement.

If American colonists had presented their case for independence in more parochial terms—perhaps if they had argued only for the customary rights and liberties of Englishmen, as before—few would have thought about the rights of

Africans. However, by invoking purportedly universal principles rather than established law or custom, by describing liberty as a natural right, and by defining their political crusade as a campaign against slavery, the colonists inadvertently drew attention to the dubious justice of holding men, women, girls, and boys in lifelong bondage. Defenders of imperial authority eager to expose the hypocrisy of American planters—Samuel Johnson most famously—condemned colonial slavery in the 1770s to discredit the colonial movement for political liberties. And several of the growing number of commentators on imperial affairs decided that the overgrown authority of slaveholders in the plantation colonies of Virginia and South Carolina had contributed directly to their pursuit of independence. As a consequence, the first emancipation schemes circulated in Britain during the 1770s aimed not only to liberate slaves but also to subject the slaveholding colonies to greater metropolitan control.[22]

As might have been predicted, the rise of antislavery sentiment and the threat of coercion by the imperial state put slaveholders on the defensive.[23] Planters typically reacted by insisting on self-government and property in slaves as fundamental to the rights of Englishmen. Sometimes they held British slave traders responsible for the growth of slavery in the colonies. The possibility that metropolitan intervention might overturn colonial planters' power figured significantly in the provincial elite's calculations in the months before the outbreak of war with Britain in 1775. When royal governors threatened to turn slaves against their owners to restore imperial authority, it helped drive landholding elites in South Carolina and Virginia into revolution. The war for American independence ruined the plantation colonies on the southern mainland in the short term, as thousands of enslaved men and women fled to the British for liberty and protection. In the long run, however, liberation from imperial oversight freed planters in the South to win greater security for slavery under a new federal union. Although the American Revolution spawned antislavery agitation in the northern states as well as in the British Isles, it paved the way for a substantial expansion of the slaveholding empire in the southern territories of the newly independent United States. As before, a weak central government facilitated the extension of private property in slaves.

In the British West Indies, the American Revolution had a very different impact. Instead of strengthening colonial slavery, the war inaugurated a series of conflicts that culminated in the destruction of slavery. Historians for many years understood the declining fortunes of the Caribbean planter class during the early nineteenth century in economic terms. Beneath the complex sequence of events that led to emancipation in 1838 seemed to lie the steady erosion of the planters' economic position, an influential 1928 study contended. In the last half century of British West Indian slavery, Lowell Joseph Ragatz argued, the soil of the old Caribbean colonies had declined in productivity while new lands were opening for sugar cultivation, both in neighboring French colonies and within the British empire after the Seven Years' War. To some extent, the West India lobby in London could discourage the migration of sugar planting to new settlements, but the lobbyists had almost no control over the quantity or quality of sugar produced elsewhere in the Americas. As a consequence, planters in Barbados and the Leeward Islands in particular found themselves increasingly uncompetitive in European markets, a situation made much worse in 1784 by restrictions imperial officials placed on trade with the newly independent United States and in 1807 by the abolition of the British slave trade. By the 1820s, according to Ragatz, the planter class was caught in a death spiral of low profitability and high debt. The campaign to abolish colonial slavery succeeded in 1833, Ragatz intimated, because the plantations were no longer economically viable. Building on this theme sixteen years later, Eric Williams argued that the abolitionists had not only benefited from changing economic conditions but represented economic interests in disguise.[24]

Most scholars now believe that the decline of the West Indian economies was as much a consequence as a cause of the antislavery movements that emerged in the 1780s.[25] The abolitionists have reemerged in recent accounts as a deciding influence in the fall of British slavery. If no doubt now remains about their significance, though, too many continue to overlook the broader political context that allowed the abolitionists to succeed. As the planters knew well, the opponents of the West India interest multiplied in the decades after the American Revolution. What declined steadily and perceptibly after the American war was less the planters' economic position than their political standing. Time and again, in the later eighteenth and early nineteenth centuries, slaveholders found it difficult to get their way on what they regarded as matters of importance. The imperial state emerged after the American Revolution as an almost constant antagonist rather than a reliable ally. Relations between planters and Parliament broke down first over the admission of U.S. ships to West Indian ports. The mercantilists at Whitehall had established doctrine on their side when they banned American carriers from the British Caribbean colonies in the 1780s. But the West Indians experienced the preference given to military and metropolitan commercial interests as a sacrifice of the plantation economy. The restrictions on inter-American trade would remain a lingering grievance among the planters until 1822, when Parliament finally opened Caribbean ports to American ships. But by that time, as far as slaveholders were concerned, the evidence of official betrayal was indisputable. Import duties increased by the state during the American and French revolutions remained high in times of peace. And in several instances, imperial officials displayed a cavalier attitude toward the enforcement of white supremacy. Planters opposed the British army's decision to arm slaves during the French revolutionary and Napoleonic wars. The planters opposed even more ardently British military officials' tendency to put blacks and whites on an equal footing. Just when the slave uprising in Saint Domingue seemed to show the dangers of unsettling racial hierarchies, the state seemed all too willing to blur differences between white and black. For these reasons, the abolition of the slave trade in 1807 looked to planters like only the most concrete proof of their rapid decline in political influence.[26]

The abolitionists represented the best organized of the several metropolitan interest groups that took on the slaving interest after the American Revolution. The origins of the movement lay in the disastrous experience of the American war, which directed new attention to the character of overseas empire and fostered new efforts to bring colonial institutions in line with concepts of national virtue and English liberty. Quakers and Anglican evangelicals, the leaders of the movement, thought of abolitionism as a way to make religion matter in politics and public life. And they succeeded by the early 1790s in making moral opposition to the slave trade an essential aspect of what it meant to be British. The movement achieved noteworthy peaks of influence between 1814 and 1816, during the effort to ban the international slave trade and regulate the inter-colonial slave trade, and after 1823, when British slaveholding itself came under sustained attack. In these campaigns, the abolitionists benefited from the co-operation of a diverse set of economic interests—merchants, shipowners, and grocers particularly—that had grown resentful of the privileged position West India sugar producers held in the imperial economy. A merger of these moral and economic interests took shape during the 1820s in the offices of the Liver-pool East India Association, the leaders of which hoped to substitute cheaper sugar produced by "free labor" in India for the more expensive, slave-grown sugar produced in the West Indies.[27]

If this were not enough, planters also faced new threats to their supremacy from within the colonies. An emerging class of mixed-race freedmen in the early nineteenth century pushed for the political and economic rights of white men and played a critical role in the dissemination of Protestant Christianity through the British West Indies. Moravian and Methodist preachers had established religious meetings on the Caribbean plantations in the last decades of the eighteenth century, and Baptist and Anglican clergy joined them in the decades that followed. But an emerging network of black and mixed-race ministers would prove to be the chief exponents of Christianity in the slave quarters, and their version of Christianity placed far less emphasis on submission to earthly authority than on the promise of divine redemption. Three major slave rebellions occurred in the British West Indies in the early nineteenth century—in Barbados in 1816, in Demerara in 1823, and in Jamaica in 1831 and 1832. In each instance, the enslaved acted after hearing rumors that planters were withholding rights that Parliament had granted to the slaves. In each instance, privileged and Christian slaves provided the leadership for the revolt. In each instance, the planter class responded with savage reprisals designed to restore order to plantation society. And in each instance, the brutal suppression of the rebellions intensified metropolitan distaste for the colonial slaveholding class. Slavery came to an end in the British empire because the reformed Parliament of 1832, itself unusually responsive to the expression of public opinion, abolished slavery in 1834. But emancipation almost certainly would have come much later if the enslaved engaged in freedom struggles in the British West Indies had not eroded the institution of slavery from within.[28] British slavery took shape in an era when planters enjoyed almost complete independence from contending political factions in the metropolis. It collapsed before a bevy of hostile strategic, economic, religious, moral, and revolutionary agendas that, taken together, left British planters by the late 1820s without a significant political ally.

The political history of slavery, then, might be told as the rise and fall of the British Atlantic planter class, as the history of its efforts to establish, command, and sustain the institution of human bondage through a series of internal and external challenges from the reign of James I to the ascension of Victoria 220 years later. The intersection between politics and slavery might be approached in other ways, of course. In his outstanding study of slave revolts in the British West Indies, Michael Craton has shown how the evolving fortunes of British slavery might be explored through patterns of resistance among the enslaved.[29] I have concentrated on the planters because of the broad perspective that their experience provides. The planters were the men in between, at once the elite in the colonies where they lived and the subjects of an imperial state over which they had little control. A focus on the planters makes possible a view of how local conflicts between masters and slaves shaped the broader history of the British empire and of how macropolitical crises in the empire affected the relationship between masters and slaves on the ground. The history of British slavery took place outside the plantation colonies as well as in those territories that had slaves. The task at hand involves relating these realms of experience to each other and tracing them from beginning to end. At that point, the political history of slavery in the British Atlantic world may be written.

NOTES

An earlier version of this chapter was published as "The Politics of Slavery," in *The British Atlantic World, 1500–1800*, ed. David Armitage and Michael Braddick (New York, 2002), 214–32, and is reproduced with permission of Palgrave Macmillan. Research for this essay was facilitated by a senior fellowship at the Gilder Lehrman Center for the Study of Slavery, Resistance, and Abolition at Yale University and a research fellowship at the Huntington Library sponsored by the Omohundro Institute for Early American History and Culture (OIEAHC). Early drafts drew helpful comments from David Armitage, Bernard Bailyn, Kristen Block, Eliga Gould, Simon Newman, Jane Ohlmeyer, Sarah Pearsall, Carla Pestana, and the audience for the panel on Aspiration and Experience in the British Atlantic World at the seventh annual OIEAHC conference in July 2001. I owe special thanks to Kristen Block and Lesley Doig of Rutgers University for assistance in tracking down the pertinent scholarship.

1. Ira Berlin, "Time, Space, and the Evolution of Afro-American Society on British Mainland North America," *American Historical Review* 85 (February 1980): 45; Ira Berlin, *Many Thousands Gone: The First Two Centuries of Slavery in North America* (Cambridge, 1998); Philip D. Morgan, *Slave Counterpoint: Black Culture in the Eighteenth-Century Chesapeake and Lowcountry* (Chapel Hill, 1998); Robin Blackburn, *The Overthrow of Colonial Slavery* (London, 1988); Robin Blackburn, *The Making of New World Slavery: From the Baroque to the Modern* (New York, 1997).

2. James Oakes, "Slaves without Contexts," *Journal of the Early Republic* 19 (Spring 1999): 103–9.

3. Merton Dillon, *Slavery Attacked: Southern Slaves and Their Allies, 1619–1865* (Baton Rouge, 1990), and Peter Linebaugh and Marcus Rediker, *The Many-Headed Hydra: Sailors, Slaves, Commoners, and the History of the Revolutionary Atlantic* (Boston, 2000), represent two notable exceptions.

4. David Geggus, *Slavery, War, and Revolution: The British Occupation of Saint Domingue* (Oxford, 1982); Sylvia Frey, *Water from the Rock: Black Resistance in a Revolutionary Age* (Princeton, 1991); Jane G. Landers, *Black Society in Spanish Florida* (Urbana, 1999); Robert Olwell, *Masters, Slaves, and Subjects: The Culture of Power in the South Carolina Low Country* (Ithaca, 1998); Woody Holton, *Forced Founders: Indians, Debtors, Slaves, and the Making of the American Revolution in Virginia* (Chapel Hill, 1997); Jeffrey Robert Young, *Domesticating Slavery: The Master Class in Georgia and South Carolina, 1607–1837* (Chapel Hill, 1999); Andrew J. O'Shaughnessy, *An Empire Divided: The American Revolution and the British Caribbean* (Philadelphia, 2000); Laurent Dubois, *A Colony of Citizens: Revolution and Slave Emancipation in the French Caribbean, 1787–1804* (Chapel Hill, 2004); Anthony J. Parent, *Foul Means: Reformation of a Slave Society in Virginia, 1660–1740* (Chapel Hill, 2004).

5. Frank Tannenbaum, *Slave and Citizen* (Boston, 1946), 117.

6. Eric Williams, *Capitalism and Slavery* (Chapel Hill, 1944); Stanley L. Engerman and Barbara L. Solow, eds., *British Capitalism and Caribbean Slavery: The Legacy of Eric Williams* (Cambridge, 1987).

7. For the planter class at the apex of its political power in the eighteenth century, see Olwell, *Masters, Slaves, and Subjects*, on South Carolina; O'Shaughnessy, *Empire Divided*, on the British Caribbean; and, for Virginia, Allan Kulikoff, *Tobacco and Slaves: The Development of Southern Cultures in the Chesapeake, 1680–1800* (Chapel Hill, 1986), esp. chap. 7.

8. David Hancock has shown how fortunes earned from trade with the colonies helped several men from modest backgrounds attain seats in the House of Commons during the middle decades of the eighteenth century (*Citizens of the World: London*

Merchants and the Integration of the British Atlantic Community, 1735–1785 [Cambridge, 1995]).

9. Richard B. Sheridan, *Sugar and Slavery: An Economic History of the British West Indies, 1623–1775* (Baltimore, 1974), 60.

10. John Brewer, *The Sinews of Power: War, Money, and the English State, 1688–1783* (New York, 1989), 98.

11. Don E. Fehrenbacher, *The Slaveholding Republic: An Account of the United States Government's Relations to Slavery* (Oxford, 2001).

12. In addition to Geggus, *Slavery, War, and Revolution*, and O'Shaughnessy, *Empire Divided*, see Richard Pares, *War and Trade in the West Indies, 1739–1763* (Oxford, 1936); Michael Duffy, *Soldiers, Sugar, and Seapower: The British Expeditions to the Caribbean and the War against Revolutionary France* (Oxford, 1987); Roger N. Buckley, *Slaves in Red Coats: The British West India Regiments, 1795–1815* (New Haven, 1979).

13. Dale H. Porter, *The Abolition of the Slave Trade in England, 1784–1807* (Hamden, 1974); Joyce E. Chaplin, *An Anxious Pursuit: Agricultural Innovation and Modernity in the Lower South, 1730–1815* (Chapel Hill, 1993); Gordon K. Lewis, *Main Currents in Caribbean Thought: The Historical Evolution of Caribbean Society in Its Ideological Aspects* (Baltimore, 1983); Larry Tise, *Proslavery: A History of the Defense of Slavery in America, 1701–1840* (Athens, 1987).

14. Linda Colley, *Britons: Forging the Nation, 1707–1838* (New Haven, 1992), 350–55; David Brion Davis, *The Problem of Slavery in the Age of Revolution, 1770–1823* (Ithaca, 1975); David Brion Davis, *Slavery and Human Progress* (Oxford, 1984); Clare Midgley, *Women against Slavery in the British Campaigns, 1788–1870* (London, 1992); Seymour Drescher, *Capitalism and Antislavery: British Mobilization in Comparative Perspective* (London, 1987); Lowell Joseph Ragatz, *A Guide to the Study of British Caribbean History, 1763–1834, Including the Abolition and Emancipation Movements* (Washington, 1932).

15. Hilary McD. Beckles, *White Servitude and Black Slavery in Barbados, 1627–1715* (Knoxville, 1975); Hilary McD. Beckles, "The Concept of 'White Slavery' in the English Caribbean during the Early Seventeenth Century," in *Early Modern Conceptions of Property*, ed. John Brewer and Susan Staves (London, 1995), 572–83; Robert J. Steinfeld, *The Invention of Free Labor: The Employment Relation in English and American Law and Culture, 1350–1870* (Chapel Hill, 1991), chaps. 2, 3.

16. Richard S. Dunn, *Sugar and Slaves: The Rise of the Planter Class in the English West Indies, 1624–1713* (Chapel Hill, 1972).

17. Beckles, *White Servitude and Black Slavery*, 38–39; Dunn, *Sugar and Slaves*, 88–100, 133–34, 156–63; Kathleen M. Brown, *Good Wives, Nasty Women, and Anxious Patriarchs: Gender, Race, and Power in Colonial Virginia* (Chapel Hill, 1996), 137–86.

18. For the British Caribbean, see Michael Craton, *Testing the Chains: Resistance to Slavery in the British West Indies* (Ithaca, 1982). On South Carolina, see Peter Wood, *Black Majority: Negroes in Colonial South Carolina* (New York, 1975), 308–26. The cycle of unrest in the 1730s and 1740s is detailed in Linebaugh and Rediker, *Many-Headed Hydra*, 193–98.

19. Frank Wesley Pitman, *The Development of the British West Indies, 1700–1763* (New Haven, 1917); Sheridan, *Sugar and Slavery*, 54–74; Tim Keirn, "Monopoly, Economic

Thought, and the Royal African Company," in *Early Modern Conceptions of Property*, ed. Brewer and Staves, 427–45; K. G. Davies, *The Royal African Company* (London, 1957), 97–152; Rebecca Starr, *A School for Politics: Commercial Lobbying and Political Culture in Early South Carolina* (Baltimore, 1998), 28–29.

20. Jon Butler, *Awash in a Sea of Faith: Christianizing the American People* (Cambridge, 1990), 132–51; Sylvia R. Frey and Betty Wood, *Come Shouting to Zion: African American Protestantism in the American South and British Caribbean to 1830* (Chapel Hill, 1998), 63–79.

21. Jack P. Greene, " 'A Plain and Natural Right to Life and Liberty': An Early Natural Rights Attack on the Excesses of the Slave System in Colonial British America," *William and Mary Quarterly*, 3rd ser., 57 (October 2000): 793–803; *Gentleman's Magazine* 11 (March 1741): 145–47.

22. Christopher L. Brown, "The Ends of Innocence: Slavery, Politics, and the Idea of Moral Responsibility, 1764–1783," paper presented at the International Seminar on the History of the Atlantic World, 1500–1800, Cambridge, Mass., August 17, 2000; Christopher L. Brown, "Empire without Slaves: British Concepts of Emancipation in the Age of the American Revolution," *William and Mary Quarterly*, 3rd ser., 56 (April 1999): 273–306.

23. Jack P. Greene, "Liberty, Slavery, and the Transformation of British Identity in the Eighteenth-Century West Indies," *Slavery and Abolition* 21 (April 2000): 1–31; Michal J. Rozbicki, "The Curse of Provincialism: Negative Perceptions of Colonial American Plantation Gentry," *Journal of Southern History* 63 (November 1997): 727–52.

24. Lowell Joseph Ragatz, *The Fall of the Planter Class in the British Caribbean* (New York, 1928); Williams, *Capitalism and Slavery*, 169–96.

25. Seymour Drescher, *Econocide: British Slavery in the Age of Abolition* (Pittsburgh, 1977); Seymour Drescher, *From Slavery to Freedom: Comparative Studies in the Rise and Fall of Atlantic Slavery* (New York, 1999), 87–115, 379–98; David Eltis, *Economic Growth and the Ending of the Transatlantic Slave Trade* (Oxford, 1987).

26. Ragatz, *Fall of the Planter Class*, 173–285; Buckley, *Slaves in Red Coats*.

27. Roger Anstey, *The Atlantic Slave Trade and British Abolition, 1760–1810* (Atlantic Highlands, 1975) pts. 2, 3, 4; Drescher, *Capitalism and Antislavery*.

28. Frey and Wood, *Come Shouting to Zion*, 129–39; Michael Craton, *Empire, Enslavement, and Freedom in the Caribbean* (Kingston, 1997), 263–305.

29. Craton, *Testing the Chains*.

Recommended Readings

In addition to the books and articles cited in the notes, the authors recommend the following readings to those interested in delving deeper into modern slavery:

SLAVERY IN AFRICA

Barry, Boubacar. *Senegambia and the Atlantic Slave Trade.* Cambridge: Cambridge University Press, 1988.

Berry, Sara. *No Condition Is Permanent: The Social Dynamics of Agrarian Change in Sub-Saharan Africa.* Madison: University of Wisconsin Press, 1993.

Glassman, Jonathon. *Feasts and Riot: Revelry, Rebellion, and Popular Consciousness on the Swahili Coast, 1856–1888.* Portsmouth: Heinemann and James Currey, 1995.

Haenger, Pete. *Slaves and Slave Holders on the Gold Coast: Toward an Understanding of Social Bondage in West Africa.* Basel, Switz.: Schlettwein, 2000.

Klein, Martin. *Slavery and Colonial Rule in French West Africa.* New York: Cambridge University Press, 1998.

Miller, Joseph. *Way of Death: Merchant Capitalism and the Angolan Slave Trade, 1730–1830.* Madison: University of Wisconsin Press, 1988.

Piot, Charles. "Of Slaves and the Gift: Kabre Sale of Kin during the Era of the Slave Trade." *Journal of African History* 37, no. 1 (1996): 31–49.

Thornton, John. *Africa and Africans in the Making of the Atlantic World, 1400–1680.* Cambridge: Cambridge University Press, 1992.

SLAVERY IN THE AMERICAS AND THE ATLANTIC WORLD

Berlin, Ira, and Philip D. Morgan, eds. *Cultivation and Culture: Labor and the Shaping of Slave Life in the Americas.* Charlottesville: University Press of Virginia, 1993.

Burnard, Trevor. *Mastery, Tyranny, and Desire: Thomas Thistlewood and His Slaves in the Anglo-Jamaican World.* Chapel Hill: University of North Carolina Press, 2004.

Costa, Emília Viotti da. *Crowns of Glory, Tears of Blood: The Demerara Slave Rebellion of 1823.* New York: Oxford University Press, 1994.

Drescher, Seymour. *The Mighty Experiment: Free Labor versus Slavery in British Emancipation.* New York: Oxford University Press, 2002.

Dubois, Laurent. *Avengers of the New World: The Story of the Haitian Revolution.* Cambridge: Belknap Press of Harvard University Press, 2004.

Fick, Carolyn. *The Making of Haiti: The St. Domingue Revolution from Below.* Knoxville: University of Tennessee Press, 1990.

Gaspar, David Barry, and Darlene Clark Hine, eds. *More Than Chattel: Black Women and Slavery in the Americas.* Bloomington: Indiana University Press, 1996.

Gould, Philip. *Barbaric Traffic: Commerce and Antislavery in the Eighteenth-Century Atlantic World.* Cambridge: Harvard University Press, 2003.

Mintz, Sidney W. *Caribbean Transformations.* New York: Columbia University Press, 1989.

Paton, Diana. *No Bond but the Law: Punishment, Race, and Gender in Jamaican State Formation, 1780–1870.* Durham: Duke University Press, 2004.

Rediker, Marcus, and Peter Linebaugh. *The Many-Headed Hydra: The Hidden History of the Revolutionary Atlantic.* Boston: Beacon Press, 2000.

Reis, João José. *Slave Rebellion in Brazil: The Muslim Uprising of 1835 in Bahia.* Translated by Arthur Brakel. Baltimore: Johns Hopkins University Press, 1993.

Schwartz, Stuart B. *Slaves, Peasants, and Rebels: Reconsidering Brazilian Slavery.* Urbana: University of Illinois Press, 1992.

————. *Sugar Plantations in the Formation of Brazilian Society: Bahia, 1550–1835.* Cambridge: Cambridge University Press, 1985.

————, ed. *Tropical Babylons: Sugar and the Making of the Atlantic World, 1450–1680.* Chapel Hill: University of North Carolina Press, 2004.

Scott, Rebecca J. "Defining the Boundaries of Freedom in the World of Cane: Cuba, Brazil, and Louisiana after Emancipation." *American Historical Review* 99, no. 1 (1994): 70–102.

Sweet, James. *Recreating Africa: Culture, Kinship, and Religion in the African-Portuguese World, 1441–1770.* Chapel Hill: University of North Carolina Press, 2003.

Thompson, Alvin O. *Unprofitable Servants: Crown Slaves in Berbice, Guyana, 1803–1831.* Barbados: University of the West Indies Press, 2002.

Wood, Marcus. *Blind Memory: Visual Representations of Slavery in England and America, 1780–1865.* New York: Routledge, 2000.

SLAVERY IN THE UNITED STATES

Berlin, Ira. *Generations of Captivity: A History of African-American Slaves.* Cambridge: Belknap Press of Harvard University Press, 2003.

Buchanan, Thomas. *Black Life on the Mississippi: Slaves, Free Blacks, and the Western Steamboat World.* Chapel Hill: University of North Carolina Press, 2004.

Campbell, Edward D. C., Jr. with Kym S. Rice, eds. *Before Freedom Came: African-American Life in the Antebellum South.* Charlottesville: University Press of Virginia, 1991.

Carney, Judith. *Black Rice: The African Origins of Rice Cultivation in the Americas.* Cambridge: Harvard University Press, 2001.

Creel, Margaret Washington. *A Peculiar People: Slave Religion and Community-Culture among the Gullahs.* New York: New York University Press, 1988.

Egerton, Douglas R. *Gabriel's Rebellion: The Virginia Slave Conspiracies of 1800 and 1802.* Chapel Hill: University of North Carolina Press, 1993.

Franklin, John Hope, and Alfred Moss Jr. *From Slavery to Freedom: A History of African Americans.* 8th ed. New York: Knopf, 2000.

French, Scot. *The Rebellious Slave: Nat Turner in American Memory.* New York: Houghton Mifflin, 2003.

Hahn, Steven. *A Nation under Our Feet: Black Political Struggles in the Rural South from Slavery to the Great Migration.* Cambridge: Belknap Press of Harvard University Press, 2003.

Hall, Gwendolyn Midlo. *Africans in Colonial Louisiana: The Development of Afro-Creole Culture in the Eighteenth Century.* Baton Rouge: Louisiana State University Press, 1992.

Harris, Leslie. *In the Shadow of Slavery: African Americans in New York City, 1626–1863.* Chicago: University of Chicago Press, 2003.

Horton, James Oliver. *Free People of Color: Inside the African American Community.* Washington, D.C.: Smithsonian Institution Press, 1993.

Johnson, Walter. *Soul by Soul: Life inside the Antebellum Slave Market.* Cambridge: Harvard University Press, 1999.

Jones, Norrece T. *Born a Child of Freedom and Yet a Slave: Mechanisms of Control and Strategies of Resistance in Antebellum South Carolina.* Hanover, N.H.: University Press of New England and Wesleyan University Press, 1990.

Kolchin, Peter. *Unfree Labor: American Slavery and Russian Serfdom.* Cambridge: Belknap Press of Harvard University Press, 1990.

McLaurin, Melton A.. *Celia, a Slave: A True Story of Violence and Retribution in Antebellum America.* Athens: University of Georgia Press, 1991.

Morgan, Philip D. *Slave Counterpoint: Black Culture in the Eighteenth-Century Chesapeake and Lowcountry.* Chapel Hill: University of North Carolina Press, 1998.

Morton, Patricia, ed. *Discovering the Women in Slavery: Emancipating Perspectives on the American Past.* Athens: University of Georgia Press, 1996.

Painter, Nell Irvin. *Soul Murder and Slavery.* Waco, Tex.: Markham Press Fund, Baylor University Press, 1995.

Parent, Anthony. *Foul Means: The Formation of a Slave Society in Virginia, 1660–1740.* Chapel Hill: University of North Carolina Press, 2003.

Stevenson, Brenda. "Distress and Discord in Virginia Slave Families, 1830–1860." In *In Joy and in Sorrow: Women, Family, and Marriage in the Victorian South, 1830–1900,* edited by Carol Bleser, 103–24. New York: Oxford University Press, 1991.

Stuckey, Sterling. *Slave Culture: Nationalist Theory and the Foundations of Black America.* New York: Oxford University Press, 1987.

Thompson, Robert Farris. *Flash of the Spirit: African and Afro-American Art and Philosophy.* New York: Vintage Books, 1984.

Vlach, John Michael. *The Afro-American Tradition in Decorative Arts.* Athens: University of Georgia Press, 1990.

———. *Back of the Big House: The Architecture of American Slavery.* Chapel Hill: University of North Carolina Press, 1993.

White, Shane, and Graham White. *Stylin': African American Expressive Culture, from Its Beginnings to the Zoot Suit.* Ithaca: Cornell University Press, 1999.

Wood, Peter H. *Strange New Land: Africans in Colonial America.* Oxford: Oxford University Press, 2003.

OTHER

Basker, James G., ed. *Amazing Grace: An Anthology of Poems about Slavery.* New Haven: Yale University Press, 2002.

Horton, James. *Slavery and the Making of America.* New York: Oxford University Press, 2005.

Contributors

Edward E. Baptist teaches history at Cornell University. He is the author of *Creating an Old South: Middle Florida's Plantation Frontier before the Civil War* (Chapel Hill, 2002) and several articles on slavery and the antebellum U.S. South. He is writing a book about the expansion of slavery and the experience of forced migration in the American South from 1789 to 1865.

Herman L. Bennett, a member of Rutgers University's History Department, is the author of *Africans in Colonial Mexico: Absolutism, Christianity, and Afro-Creole Consciousness, 1570–1640* (Bloomington, 2003.) He is currently completing a project on freedom in seventeenth-century Mexico.

Christopher L. Brown teaches history at Rutgers University. He has coedited with Philip D. Morgan *The Arming of Slaves: Classical Times to the Modern Age* (New Haven, 2005). His *Moral Capital: Foundations of British Abolitionism* will be published in 2006.

Vincent Brown teaches history at Harvard University. He is the author of the forthcoming *Specter in the Cane: Death and Power in the World of Atlantic Slavery* as well as several articles on slavery, sugar, and Caribbean history.

Stephanie M. H. Camp teaches African American history at the University of Washington in Seattle and is the author of *Closer to Freedom: Enslaved Women and Everyday Resistance in the Plantation South* (Chapel Hill, 2004). She is currently at work on a book about the interactions between black and white women in the slave societies of the English Americas.

Sharla M. Fett teaches history at Occidental College in Los Angeles. She is the author of *Working Cures: Healing, Health, and Power on Antebellum Slave Plantations* (Chapel Hill, 2002), which won the 2003 Frank L. and Harriet C. Owsley Award, the Julia Cherry Spruill Prize, and the Willie Lee Rose Prize and was the corecipient of the James A. Rawley Prize. She is writing a transatlantic history of U.S. encounters with the illegal slave trade in the 1850s.

Barbara Krauthamer teaches history at New York University. She is revising a manuscript on the transition from slavery to freedom in Texas and the Indian Territory. Her book, which focuses on women, children, and African Americans' family and community life, attempts to understand the meanings of freedom that developed in freedpeople's relationships and conflicts with each other.

Jennifer L. Morgan teaches history and women's and gender studies at Rutgers University, New Brunswick. She is the author of *Laboring Women: Reproduction and Gender in New World Slavery* (Philadelphia, 2004) and is currently working on a new study of demography, numeracy, and slavery in colonial North America.

Dylan C. Penningroth, who teaches history at Northwestern University, is the author of *The Claims of Kinfolk: African American Property and Community in the Nineteenth-Century South* (Chapel Hill, 2003), which won the 2004 Avery O. Craven Award from the Organization of American Historians.

Phillip Troutman teaches writing at George Washington University in Washington, D.C. His essay, "Grapevine in the Slave Market: African American Geopolitical Literacy and the 1841 Creole Revolt," appears in *The Chattel Principle: Internal Slave Trades in the Americas*, edited by Walter Johnson (New Haven, 2005). He is also the author of the forthcoming *Sentiment in the Slave Market Revolution*.

Index